AI
FOR NONPROFITS

DARIAN RODRIGUEZ HEYMAN & CHERYL CONTEE

Foreword by Jonathan Brill
Afterword by Blaise Agüera y Arcas

AI FOR NONPROFITS

Putting Artificial Intelligence to Work for Your Cause

Practical tips and tools for strategic fundraising, marketing, programs, and back-office operations

WILEY

Copyright © 2025 by Darian Rodriguez Heyman and Cheryl Contee. All rights reserved.

Published by John Wiley & Sons, Inc., Hoboken, New Jersey.
Published simultaneously in Canada.

No part of this publication may be reproduced, stored in a retrieval system, or transmitted in any form or by any means, electronic, mechanical, photocopying, recording, scanning, or otherwise, except as permitted under Section 107 or 108 of the 1976 United States Copyright Act, without either the prior written permission of the Publisher, or authorization through payment of the appropriate per-copy fee to the Copyright Clearance Center, Inc., 222 Rosewood Drive, Danvers, MA 01923, (978) 750-8400, fax (978) 750-4470, or on the web at www.copyright.com. Requests to the Publisher for permission should be addressed to the Permissions Department, John Wiley & Sons, Inc., 111 River Street, Hoboken, NJ 07030, (201) 748-6011, fax (201) 748-6008, or online at http://www.wiley.com/go/permission.

The manufacturer's authorized representative according to the EU General Product Safety Regulation is Wiley-VCH GmbH, Boschstr. 12, 69469 Weinheim, Germany, e-mail: Product_Safety@wiley.com.

Trademarks: Wiley and the Wiley logo are trademarks or registered trademarks of John Wiley & Sons, Inc. and/or its affiliates in the United States and other countries and may not be used without written permission. All other trademarks are the property of their respective owners. John Wiley & Sons, Inc. is not associated with any product or vendor mentioned in this book.

Limit of Liability/Disclaimer of Warranty: While the publisher and author have used their best efforts in preparing this book, they make no representations or warranties with respect to the accuracy or completeness of the contents of this book and specifically disclaim any implied warranties of merchantability or fitness for a particular purpose. No warranty may be created or extended by sales representatives or written sales materials. The advice and strategies contained herein may not be suitable for your situation. You should consult with a professional where appropriate. Further, readers should be aware that websites listed in this work may have changed or disappeared between when this work was written and when it is read. Neither the publisher nor authors shall be liable for any loss of profit or any other commercial damages, including but not limited to special, incidental, consequential, or other damages.

For general information on our other products and services or for technical support, please contact our Customer Care Department within the United States at (800) 762-2974, outside the United States at (317) 572-3993 or fax (317) 572-4002.

Wiley also publishes its books in a variety of electronic formats. Some content that appears in print may not be available in electronic formats. For more information about Wiley products, visit our web site at www.wiley.com.

Library of Congress Cataloging-in-Publication Data is Available:

ISBN 9781394298419 (Paperback)
ISBN 9781394298426 (ePub)
ISBN 9781394298433 (ePDF)

Cover Design : Wiley
Cover Image : © d1sk/Shutterstock

SKY10112590_060525

I dedicate this book to my incredible son, Rafael. Rafi, my love for you has served to deepen my commitment to helping usher in the thriving, equitable, and just world I know is possible. You deserve no less and I'm only sorry this book doesn't have more math in it! —DRH

I dedicate this book to my son, Colm Contee. Buddy, you are the future we've all been waiting for. Being your mom has made me a better person and every day I learn something, create something, or imagine something new with you. I hope this book inspires you and your peers to use innovation to build a better world not only for yourselves but also for everyone. Special shoutout to my brother Clarence Contee Jr., who has been my rock through both sunny and rainy days. Honorable mention to Fluffy and his warm companionship while I was writing! —CC

Contents

Foreword: Your Future Is NOW   xiii
Jonathan Brill

About the Book   xvii
Darian Rodriguez Heyman and Cheryl Contee

Acknowledgments   xxiii
Darian Rodriguez Heyman and Cheryl Contee

PART I   INTRODUCTION TO AI: LAYING THE FOUNDATION FOR RESPONSIBLE ADOPTION   1
Darian Rodriguez Heyman and Cheryl Contee

1   The Future Is Now: AI 101, the Basics   5
Jonathan Waddingham

2   Before You Get Started   17
Contributed by Beth Kanter

    Understanding the AI Adoption Life Cycle   28
Kate Gage

3   90-Day Blueprint for AI Success   33
Charlene Li

    Key Ingredients for AI Adoption Success   43
Gary A. Bolles

4   Adapting and Thriving in the Age of AI   47
danah boyd

**Predictive Medical Analytics Case Study: Michael J. Fox Foundation
and Sensoria Health** — 56
Davide Vigano

5 How to Sell AI Upstream and Downstream Within Your Organization — 59
Shawn Olds

AI as Your Institutional Memory — 72
Astrid J. Scholz, PhD

6 AI and Technology Planning: Figuring Out Your Tech — 77
Afua Bruce

Guidelines for AI Vendor Selection — 87
Alfredo Ramirez

7 Prompt Engineering: Asking AI the Right Questions — 91
George Weiner

**Introducing Arnold, the StaffBot: Lung Cancer Foundation
of America Case Study** — 104
Donna Whitney

**PART II FUNDRAISING: STRENGTHENING RELATIONSHIPS,
NOT REPLACING THEM** — 107
Darian Rodriguez Heyman and Cheryl Contee

8 Prompting Next Gen Donors to Give — 111
Josh Hirsch

9 Donor Research — 127
Nathan Chappell

Political Fundraising — 137
Mike Nellis

10 The Future of Philanthropy: AI and Donor Engagement — 141
Allison Fine

CRM 2.0: The Road Map Ahead — 150
Lori Freeman

| 11 | Peer-to-Peer Fundraising and Ambassador Engagement | 155 |

Jennifer Ybarra

| 12 | Foundation Prospecting | 167 |

Ann Mei Chang

| 13 | Grant Writing and Reports | 177 |

Susan Mernit

Securing Funding for Your AI Upgrades — 186

Michael Belinsky

PART III   MARKETING AND COMMUNITY ENGAGEMENT: BUILDING MORE MEANINGFUL RELATIONSHIPS THROUGH AI — 189

Darian Rodriguez Heyman and Cheryl Contee

| 14 | Audiovisual (AV) Content Creation | 191 |

Darian Rodriguez Heyman and Cheryl Contee

Translation — 204

Nicholas Martin

| 15 | Social Listening | 209 |

Julia Campbell

Using Machine Learning to Segment Your Lists — 218

Brian Young

Social Media Analysis — 222

Robin Sukhadia

Volunteer Recruitment and Management — 226

Geng Wang

| 16 | Community Engagement | 231 |

Eli Pariser

| 17 | Lobbying and Advocacy | 239 |

Brian Rubenstein

PART IV PROGRAMS: REDEFINING MISSION DELIVERY WITH AI 249
Darian Rodriguez Heyman and Cheryl Contee

18 Preparing for AI Integration 251
Kim Ghatalia and Noah Halton

Leveraging Emerging Technology: Save the Children Case Study 261
Ettore Rossetti

19 Strategic Planning 265
Sam Azar

20 Dashboarding: Impact Measurement and Data Visualization 279
Rachel Ward and Rajesh Naik

Program Evaluation 289
Chaitra Vedullapalli

Ensuring Data Quality 293
Nick Hamlin

21 Developing Your Own Custom Large Language Model 297
Craig Johnson

22 Public-Facing Chatbots 305
Jim Fruchterman

23 Dealing with Mis/Disinformation 315
Adam Fivenson

PART V THE INVISIBLE BACKBONE: TRANSFORMING BACK-OFFICE OPERATIONS WITH AI 325
Darian Rodriguez Heyman and Cheryl Contee

24 Human Resources 329
Tierney Yates

25 Finance and Bookkeeping 341
Justin Muscolino

26	**Board Recruitment and Engagement** Matt Strain	**349**
	Recruiting Tech Executives to Your Board Aaron Hurst	**361**
27	**IT Infrastructure and Software: The Tech Stack Needed to Support AI Integration** Tim Lockie	**365**

PART VI POLICIES AND PROTECTIONS: SAFEGUARDING THE MISSION AND AVOIDING TROUBLE IN THE AGE OF AI 377
Darian Rodriguez Heyman and Cheryl Contee

28	**Cybersecurity in the Age of AI** Joshua Peskay	**379**
29	**Enhancing Legal Operations and Compliance** Olga V. Mack and Kassi Burns	**397**
30	**Data Privacy and Ethical AI Adoption** Amy Sample Ward	**407**

PART VII AI ACROSS MISSIONS: INNOVATING FOR PHILANTHROPY, SOCIAL ENTERPRISE, AND HIGHER EDUCATION 415
Darian Rodriguez Heyman and Cheryl Contee

31	**Foundations and Philanthropy** Jean Westrick	**417**
	Best Practices in Funding Nonprofit Technology Chantal "Coco" Forster	**428**
32	**Social Enterprises and Mission-Driven Companies** Barbara Clarke	**433**
33	**Higher Education** Darian Rodriguez Heyman and Cheryl Contee	**443**

Closing Thoughts: The Journey Ahead — 453
Darian Rodriguez Heyman and Cheryl Contee

Afterword: The Future of AI in Nonprofits — 455
Blaise Agüera y Arcas

Book Underwriters — 461

AI for Nonprofits Resource Directory — 463
Doug Nelson

About the Editors — 477
Darian Rodriguez Heyman and Cheryl Contee

Glossary of Terms — 479
Craig Johnson

Name Index — 485
Subject Index — 495

Foreword
Your Future Is NOW

The future isn't just something that happens—it's something we create with every action we take. I've spent my career helping leaders anticipate and adapt to the turbulence of exponential change, and there's no question that AI is one of the most significant forces reshaping our world today. ***The remarkable surge of AI capabilities in the last few years is unlocking advancements poised to transform every corner of our society—including the nonprofit sector***. AI for Nonprofits arrives at precisely the moment when nonprofit executives, social entrepreneurs, and philanthropists need actionable guidance on how to harness the power of intelligent systems for social good.

Our world is more interconnected than ever before. The challenges we face—climate change, income inequality, public health crises—are increasingly complex and intertwined, and the need for innovative solutions has never been more urgent. In the technology realm, ***AI stands out as a game changer for two main reasons: its ability to process massive amounts of data in real time and its capacity to transform that data into decisions, predictions, and insights at scale***. From my vantage point as a futurist, I see AI as an extraordinary lever for change. But just as important, I see it as a tool that can liberate our most human qualities of compassion and creativity by reducing the complexity and repetition in our work.

The question I most often hear in my discussions with corporate executives and nonprofit leaders is, "How do we begin?" It's a fair concern, given the pace of transformation. In response, I always share the need to ***break AI adoption into manageable steps: start by clarifying your mission and objectives, then identify specific pain points where AI-driven solutions might be beneficial, and*** *finally, cultivate a culture of experimentation*. This book provides a tactical road map for doing exactly that.

At the heart of this road map is the idea that AI is not an end in itself. Yes, it's a powerful tool—one that can reduce the time staff spend on repetitive tasks, improve donor engagement, identify at-risk communities earlier, and free up valuable resources for the frontline work that truly matters. Yet technology is only as effective as the humans behind it. I often remind organizations that while we use AI to automate, accelerate, and amplify our capabilities, it's our people and our values that give technology its meaning. *AI for Nonprofits shows you not just how to adopt new tools, but how to integrate them holistically into your mission, preserving the best of what makes your organization human and mission-driven*.

One recurring theme from my interviews with social sector executives is the reluctance some leaders feel about AI. They worry about biases in algorithms or fear that advanced technologies might distract from their nonprofit's human-centric mission. These concerns are real and legitimate. The solution is to lean in, not step away: by understanding AI's strengths and limitations, you equip your organization to steer AI in an ethical and inclusive direction. *This book emphasizes best practices for transparency, accountability, and responsible innovation—keys to ensuring AI supports, rather than supplants, the values at your nonprofit's core*.

In my work, I often talk about "futureproofing" organizations—identifying ways to stay resilient and adaptable in times of uncertainty. In the nonprofit world, *futureproofing* means staying relevant and impactful in the face of rapidly changing social and technological realities. *AI might not solve every challenge, but as you'll discover in this book, it can dramatically increase the speed and scale of solutions that do*. With the right guidance and governance, AI becomes a force multiplier for every cause.

As you explore the pages of *AI for Nonprofits*, you'll learn the fundamentals of AI, unpack the jargon that often confuses leaders, and walk through practical case studies of how nonprofits across different sectors are transforming their strategies. You'll see *real-world examples of how AI enhances donor outreach, reduces operational costs, and strengthens program delivery*. You'll discover strategies to unleash the potential of your team: freeing staff from repetitive tasks, tapping into new insights from the wealth of data you already have, and creating more dynamic relationships with the communities you serve.

Above all, my hope for you, as you read this book, is that you'll cultivate an *innovator's mindset*—a willingness to explore, iterate, and learn alongside your colleagues. AI is still evolving. **The ultimate competitive advantage in the social sector will go to those who lean into this new frontier with curiosity, creativity, and courage.** In my experience, the most promising organizations recognize that the best time to prepare for the future is *now*.

In these pages, you will find not only the technical and tactical guidance to make AI a driving force in your nonprofit, but also the inspiration to reimagine what's possible. I'm convinced that AI, when wielded responsibly, will unlock the full potential of your team and significantly amplify your impact—helping humanity take leaps forward in our quest to create a more equitable, thriving world.

So, let's get started on this journey! **The insights and practical tools ahead are designed to fuel your mission, elevate your strategies, and catalyze the next era of nonprofit innovation.** In my conversations with nonprofit leaders, I am often reminded that every bit of technological progress is ultimately about improving lives. AI is the frontier that can propel us to greater collective good, if we embrace its possibilities.

The future is now. Let's shape it together!

Interviewee Bio

Jonathan Brill is a renowned futurist, strategic advisor, and author committed to helping organizations navigate uncertainty and prepare for disruptive change. As the former global futurist at Hewlett Packard and author of *Rogue Waves*, he has guided nonprofits, global brands, and government agencies to anticipate, adapt, and thrive amid emerging challenges. His expertise lies in scenario planning, innovation strategy, and leveraging AI-driven insights to craft resilient road maps for the future. A trusted advisor to Fortune 500 leaders and a sought-after keynote speaker, Jonathan's thought leadership empowers nonprofits to embrace uncertainty as an opportunity to strengthen their strategies and serve their communities more effectively. https://www.linkedin.com/in/jonathanbrill1/

About the Book

"You don't need to know all the answers; you just need to know where to find them."

—Albert Einstein

In November 2022, the launch of ChatGPT 3.5 changed everything. More than just the fastest technology to reach 100 million users, which it did in just two months, it marked a tipping point: a moment when artificial intelligence (AI) became accessible to everyone through simple, conversational interactions. Beyond offering the world's knowledge at your fingertips, AI now acts as a virtual assistant capable of helping you brainstorm, create, predict, and execute with unprecedented ease. It's no exaggeration to say we are all now living on the jagged frontier of this technology with a rapidly evolving future ahead.

For nonprofits—particularly grassroots organizations often stretched thin on time, staff, and resources—AI isn't just another tool. This is an opportunity to rewrite the rules. ***AI is a Swiss Army knife for the social sector, with three primary capabilities:***

- **Streamlining tasks:** From drafting emails and summarizing reports to automating workflows, AI can save countless hours and let you focus on what matters most.
- **Enhancing creativity:** AI can brainstorm with you, offering fresh ideas for outreach, fundraising, campaigns, and strategies you might not have considered.
- **Seeing into the future:** Through predictive analytics, AI can identify patterns and anticipate challenges, giving you insights to make data-driven decisions.

In short, AI can amplify your efforts in ways previously unimaginable. The question is, "Where do you want to point that thing?"

Book Purpose and Flow

This book exists because nonprofits are at a crossroads. With urgent community needs and the ever-present challenge of doing more with less, ***it's critical to harness the tools that can make your work more efficient and effective***. Yet AI—and the technology landscape overall—changes fast. How can we offer guidance that stays relevant in a rapidly evolving field?

The answer is simple: we focus on what's *timeless*. Instead of detailed how-tos on specific platforms, ***this book provides real-world strategies, best practices, and tactical tips and tools that empower you to approach AI adoption with confidence***. Whether you're looking to raise more money, expand awareness, enhance programs, or streamline operations, the chapters ahead will give you the foundation to get started.

This book begins with a foundational section designed to help you set the stage for success. You'll find essential guidance on understanding AI basics, preparing your organization for adoption, crafting a strategic plan, and building the confidence to use AI effectively. Through these, we provide you with the groundwork needed to approach AI as a partner in your work.

The core of the book focuses on four key areas where AI can make the most significant difference:

- **Fundraising:** Discover how AI can help identify prospects, build relationships, and optimize your development efforts with both donors and funders.
- **Marketing and community engagement:** Learn how to connect with your audience more effectively, amplify your message, and foster deeper relationships.
- **Program delivery:** Explore how AI can enhance service design, improve outcomes, and scale your impact.

- **Back-office operations:** Reduce administrative burdens and streamline essential functions like HR, finance, and board engagement.

Beyond these core areas, ***the book also addresses three critical supplemental topics:***

- **Policies and protections:** Guidance on implementing AI responsibly and ethically, with tools to mitigate risks and align your efforts with your mission
- **AI for other mission-led organizations:** Tailored advice for foundations and donors, social enterprises, and higher education institutions, showcasing how they can apply these strategies in their unique contexts
- **Resource directory:** A curated list of tools, platforms, publications, and providers to support your AI journey, helping you stay informed and equipped to adapt as the landscape evolves

Together, these sections form a comprehensive road map for nonprofits seeking to harness the potential of AI. Whether you're just starting out or looking to refine your approach, this book offers the insights and strategies needed to build a brighter future for your organization and the communities you serve.

How to Use This Book

Think of this book as your AI owner's manual. It's not meant to be read cover-to-cover unless that suits your style. Instead, ***approach it as a reference guide: dip into the chapters that address your current challenges, and revisit them as your needs evolve.***

Each chapter is structured consistently to maximize your time and impact:

1. **Introduction:** A quick overview of why the topic matters
2. **Critical skills and competencies:** Tactical tips and tools, plus frameworks to guide your adoption of AI
3. **Pitfalls and solutions:** Common missteps and how to avoid them
4. **Road map to the future:** Emerging trends and how to stay ahead

5. **Dos and don'ts:** Bite-sized, actionable takeaways underscoring key insights from each chapter
6. **Conclusion:** A recap of key points to leave you inspired to action
7. **Resource review:** Publications, platforms, and tools to explore further

Some chapters also feature insets on relevant subtopics and case studies to showcase real-world examples and inspire new ideas.

A Note on Formatting

We know you're busy. To help you get straight to the point:

- ***Bold italics*** highlight actionable tips and key takeaways.
- **Bold** text signals section headers or list introductions.
- *Italics* emphasize suggested AI prompts or specialized terms.

AI Disclosure

In an effort to practice what we preach, ***we used AI extensively when producing this book***. This was in part to walk in the shoes of nonprofit leaders and understand from experience what works, what doesn't, and what's coming soon. Specifically, we used Fireflies.ai to record and automatically transcribe our virtual Zoom interviews with all 57 experts. We then used ChatGPT, Claude, and our publisher Wiley's private large language model Scribble to help draft all book content based on the interviews with author edits, and once again to integrate feedback and proposed edits from our interviewees. Craig Johnson, one of our experts, adapted his software, Change Agent AI, to help analyze our manuscript, facilitating the creation of our glossary of terms. Please note however that ***we remained the humans in the loop (HITL) at all times***. Every single page of this book received human attention in review and editing. AI is inescapable in modern society and functions behind the scenes in more ways than most people may realize in daily life. Yet it's how humans adapt this multipurpose utility knife, especially generative AI, that will determine our future.

On behalf of the 57 expert contributors who helped shape this book, we hope these insights empower you to make a greater impact. ***While no book can answer every question, this one is designed to provide you with a solid foundation for using AI to further your mission***. Together, let's work smarter, dream bigger, and build a better world.

Acknowledgments

It truly takes a village. This book is the result of countless hours of hard work and dedication—not just from the two of us, but from an incredible community of supporters who made this effort possible.

First and foremost, we want to express our deepest gratitude to the 57 extraordinary individuals who shared their hard-won insights, savvy suggestions, and practical wisdom. Your insightful contributions serve as the cornerstone of this work, enabling us to provide actionable tools and strategies for nonprofit leaders. Thank you for your shared dedication to strengthening the social sector and for offering your expertise to support others during this pivotal moment in the adoption of AI.

We also owe a heartfelt thanks to our families, whose support and understanding made it possible for us to devote so many hours to this project—often well beyond the demands of our day jobs. Your grace and encouragement have been invaluable.

Special thanks go to Gabriella (Gabby) De La Cruz, Sonam Tsering, Zach Bell, and Raina Pahade for their indispensable aid coordinating and managing this complex undertaking. Your efforts and ideas helped make this book possible! Much gratitude to the staff and board of The Impact Seat Foundation and Egeria Enterprises for their support during the intensive process of interviewing, writing, and editing for this project. Much appreciation and awe to Craig Johnson of Change Agent AI who applied his team's frontier tech to help us create a glossary of terms to ensure everyone's maximum understanding. We are also deeply grateful to our team at Wiley for their enthusiasm, dedication to nonprofit capacity building, and patience as we brought this community-centered vision to life.

Finally, to all the nonprofits tirelessly working to build a better world: thank you! And to you, our reader: we know the demands on your time are immense as you tackle pressing community needs every day. The fact that you've chosen to invest time in building your capacity and exploring how AI can amplify your impact speaks volumes about your leadership, foresight, and commitment. We hope this book serves you well on that journey.

Together,
Darian and Cheryl

Part I

Introduction to AI: Laying the Foundation for Responsible Adoption

"Knowledge corresponds to the past. It is technology. Wisdom is the future. It is philosophy."

—Herbie Hancock, legendary American jazz artist and UNESCO Goodwill Ambassador

AI is not a distant future—it's here, now, transforming how nonprofits operate. Whether you're drafting grant proposals, engaging donors, managing programs, or streamlining operations, AI has the potential to revolutionize every aspect of your work. But **realizing this potential isn't just about knowing the tools; it's about using them thoughtfully and responsibly**.

This opening section lays the groundwork for your nonprofit's AI journey. It equips you with the knowledge, frameworks, and practical strategies to start strong and avoid common mistakes in AI adoption. Each chapter provides a critical piece of your foundation, ensuring you adopt AI in ways that align with your mission, maximize your resources, and amplify your impact.

Part I begins with "The Future Is Now: AI 101, the Basics," where we break down the basics of AI—what it is, how it works, and why it's an incredible resource for nonprofits. From there, "Before You Get Started" guides you through assessing your organization's readiness for AI adoption, with a practical framework for understanding the chapter inset, "Understanding the AI Adoption Life Cycle," to help you move from experimentation to implementation with clarity and confidence.

The "90-Day Blueprint for AI Success" offers a step-by-step road map for launching your AI journey. The inset "Key Ingredients for AI Adoption Success" introduces the mindset, skill set, and tool set framework that ensures you're setting your nonprofit up for long-term success. "Adapting and Thriving in the Age of AI" explores how nonprofits can foster a culture of experimentation and resilience, staying ahead in a rapidly changing landscape, and it includes a case study showcasing how the Michael J. Fox Foundation leveraged emerging technology to advance its mission.

In "How to Sell AI Upstream and Downstream Within Your Organization," we address the critical challenge of securing buy-in, offering strategies to bring your board, leadership, and staff along on the journey. The inset on "AI as Your Institutional Memory" supports the case for adoption by speaking to the benefits of AI as it relates to helping your nonprofit learn from past efforts to support strategy development and programs.

Once you're ready to select tools, "AI and Technology Planning: Figuring Out Your Tech" provides guidance for choosing platforms that align with your needs, including the inset "Guidelines for AI Vendor Selection" to help you evaluate potential partners. "Prompt Engineering: Asking AI the Right Questions" dives into how to communicate effectively with AI, featuring a case study that speaks to how a small nonprofit built a private large language model (LLM) "staffbot" to streamline their operations, raise awareness, and support fundraising.

These chapters were chosen and crafted consciously, aimed at collectively equipping you with the knowledge, tools, and confidence to embrace AI as a partner in your work. Whether you're taking your first steps or refining your approach, this foundational section ensures your nonprofit is prepared to leverage AI strategically and in support of your ultimate mission and goals.

Darian and Cheryl's Top 10 List: Critical Guidelines for AI Adoption

To help you succeed, **we've distilled the essentials of effective AI use into 10 actionable principles:**

- **Play around:** Experiment with AI across various tasks to uncover its potential, even for tasks where its value isn't immediately clear. Try it on for size and practice a beginner's mindset!

- **Ask for options:** Have AI generate multiple versions of outputs, refreshing as needed to explore a wide range of creative possibilities.
- **Start with teasers:** Begin with short summaries or outlines to ensure AI is aligned with your vision before diving into longer-form outputs.
- **Iterate for excellence:** Use follow-up prompts to refine AI's initial outputs, taking them from good to great before finalizing manually.
- **Be a hero, not a zero:** Guide AI by providing examples of desired outcomes to set clear expectations and achieve better results, also known as "multi-shot prompts."
- **Prompt properly:** To generate the most helpful AI outputs, structure prompts to include your AI tool's role, desired outcome, goal, and format, plus examples for context.
- **Create a culture of experimentation:** Encourage staff to try out AI tools, share successes, and collaborate on challenges through forums, contests, and shared learnings.
- **Produce a policy:** Develop a clear AI policy outlining acceptable use, approved platforms and those to avoid, and alignment with organizational goals and values.
- **Dial in your data:** Keep your data accurate and secure, avoiding public tools for sensitive information and considering private LLMs when appropriate.
- **Human in the loop (HITL):** Always maintain human oversight to verify AI outputs, ensuring quality, accuracy, and appropriateness before taking action or sharing externally.

By following these guidelines and the advice offered in this section, you'll be equipped to embrace AI not as a replacement for human ingenuity but as a tool to amplify your efforts, ensuring your nonprofit thrives in the age of AI.

Chapter 1

The Future Is Now: AI 101, the Basics

Based on insights from an interview with Jonathan Waddingham.

Have you ever said, "Hey Siri" and asked a question, searched or texted something that autofilled after you started typing, enjoyed a Netflix recommendation, or scrolled through your social media feed? All these activities and much, much more are powered by AI. *As AI becomes increasingly integrated into various aspects of our lives, nonprofits must understand how to harness this technology to enhance impact, streamline operations, and make data-driven decisions.*

This chapter covers the basics of AI, providing you with the foundational knowledge needed to confidently begin your AI journey. Whether you're seeking ways to save time, tell better stories, or raise more funds, this chapter represents a helpful starting point. If you're keen to spend more time focusing on your mission and less cycles on administrative tasks, this "primer coat" will demystify AI, offering practical guidance on how to integrate it into your nonprofit's operations.

Critical Skills and Competencies

What Is AI, Anyway?

Artificial intelligence encompasses a range of technologies, including Machine Learning, Deep Learning, and large language models. These, then, encompass natural language processing (NLP), computer vision, and much more. When you put it all together, the future we've dreamed of since *The Jetsons* is suddenly at your nonprofit's fingertips, but it helps to understand the underlying breakthroughs and the role of each. So, let's start from the beginning and break down the cornerstone technologies that underpin all the amazing developments you've seen on ChatGPT and other platforms in recent years:

- **Artificial intelligence** (AI) is the umbrella term for computer programs that have the ability to reason and learn like humans. *Originally, computers were programmed in a very explicit way, with computer scientists working hard to map out a wide range of "if-then" loops,* telling the program how to respond to a range of different, predetermined scenarios. But now, you can ask, "Hey Siri: What's the temperature outside?" and it can figure out your location, find the forecast, and speak it back to you.

- **Machine Learning** (ML) is a field of AI that involves training algorithms to recognize patterns in data and make predictions or decisions based on those patterns. This represented a huge shift in the approach to programming, since *computers can now program themselves based on examples, without clear instructions.* Think Amazon or Netflix recommendations, where people who bought or liked what you did frequently enjoyed something similar.

- **Deep Learning** (DL) is a subset of ML where AI uses neural networks *based on the design of the human brain to ingest and learn from huge datasets.* This makes it especially useful for pattern recognition, in addition to practical applications like understanding and creating human-like text. DL is incredibly versatile and can be used to interpret and produce text, images, video, audio, and more. Think facial recognition in the photos you upload to social media.

- **NLP** is a branch of AI that enables computers to understand, interpret, and respond to human language in a natural way, whether spoken or written. For nonprofits, NLP can be a game changer by powering tools like chatbots for donor engagement, sentiment analysis to understand community needs, and automated report generation for back-office efficiency.

- **Large language models** (LLMs) are Deep Learning algorithms that process and generate human-like text. They share ideas and information, and can help summarize, translate, and predict. This is the core technology underpinning

ChatGPT, Claude, Gemini, Copilot, and the other generative AI (GenAI) platforms. They ***vacuum up tons of information and data sources, then use their powerful algorithms to spot patterns within this mountain of inputs, just like people.*** That makes them incredibly versatile and well suited for interacting with folks in ways that feel surprisingly natural. Current models predict that after 2027 there will be no more publicly available data sources to feed them, which is why we're increasingly seeing data sharing deals with publishers and content-rich platforms like Reddit.

Generative pre-trained transformers (GPTs) are LLMs specifically designed for NLP tasks. **GenAI** simply refers to it generating outputs like text or imagery, and "pre-trained" speaks to how they're fed huge amounts of training data to identify patterns. But ***"transformer" technology is the big breakthrough—ultimately, all these tools use neural networks to predict the next word in a series,*** just like when your texts or Google searches auto-complete based on popular other entries. In short, ChatGPT and all the other tools are simply guessing what next word will make you happiest and using that approach to string together something as long as this book! But, since AI can't currently tell the difference between fact and fiction, this can oftentimes lead to **hallucinations**, false statements your AI will share as confidently as something true. As a result, ***keeping a human in the loop (HITL) is critical at this early stage of AI development; meaning, you always need to double-check AI's work.***

To get started with AI, familiarize yourself with these core concepts and explore how they can be applied to your nonprofit's needs. For example, ***ML can help you identify trends in donor behavior and predict future giving patterns.*** NLP can enhance your communication strategies by analyzing donor feedback and optimizing messaging. Computer vision, a type of AI, can streamline event management by automatically tagging and organizing photos. ***By understanding the basics of AI, you can make informed decisions about which technologies to adopt and how to integrate them into your operations.***

Feed AI the Right Tasks

So, how can it best be leveraged? ***Think of AI as your digital assistant or savvy intern, who can bolster your capacity and team, but not take things completely off anyone's plate.*** As a general enabling technology just like the railroad, printing press, or even the internet itself, AI can be deployed in limitless ways. But ***it helps to start with a simple framework and closely consider the three ways that AI is most likely to support your efforts.***

Unlock Efficiencies: Automating Recurring Functions

Most nonprofits suffer through a wide range of repetitive yet important tasks. While it's critical that we quickly acknowledge donations, send out regular impact updates, and submit grant reports, are those really things that need to be handled manually over and over again? ***Convene your team and create a list of your most common, repetitive tasks, and then consider if and how you can use AI to streamline these.*** Note this will include tactical activities like sending that standard donor recognition email after customizing a few minor elements, but you should also ***think about using AI to support recurring creative tasks like brainstorming*** the subject lines for your email appeals, researching potential funders and identifying why they'd consider supporting your work, and identifying new community engagement strategies. Finally, some of these activities may not be happening at all right now but could expand your work, so consider things like translating materials to reach new audiences, exploring a new voice in your materials, and more.

Data Analysis: Crunch the Numbers and Insights

Most of us have access to huge troves of information, but do you really have the time to pour through that government study, annual report, or check off all the books on your lengthy reading list? Well, fret no more! ***AI is great at summarizing robust content and top-lining what you really need to know,*** whether that's comparing and contrasting different sources, clarifying the relationship between two organizations or resources, and sharing insights on what kinds of (fill in the blank here) are best at generating any desired result. Increasingly, AI tools are getting adept at producing not only text outputs but also helpful imagery, graphs, charts, and other visualizations that can help you powerfully convey your story and ideas. Plus, if you ever need help with finding the right formula to complete your spreadsheet, AI tools can help you write them and save hours of banging your head against unknown cell references.

Predictive Analytics

We all wish we had a crystal ball, especially fundraisers! *AI is well suited to take a dispassionate view of your past efforts and predict what's likely to happen, when, and how.* That means offering educated guesses about which donors are ripe for follow-up this week, which messages and updates would likely be most resonant, how much money to ask for, and much more. Or, applying a programmatic lens, which clients may be struggling and why, who's dropped off your radar and could benefit from a call, and so on.

Shop Around and Sample the Goods

There are a bunch of AI-powered platforms and tools out there, and the list keeps growing. AI is increasingly being integrated into the tools you already use, but *as you're looking at the landscape of dedicated AI tools, there are a few types or classes of resources you should explore, get to know, and consider adopting.*

GenAI Platforms and GPTs

OpenAI's ChatGPT 3.5 (https://chatgpt.com/) took only two months to reach 100 million users after its release in November 2022, making it the fastest-adopted consumer technology in history. That set off a ton of interest in AI across every industry, including nonprofits. Now *there are a wide range of GenAI platforms that can instantly provide you with answers to just about any question or need, and the opportunity to create your own custom chatbot or GPT*, including Anthropic's Claude (https://claude.ai/), Microsoft's Copilot (https://copilot.microsoft.com/), Google's Gemini (https://gemini.google.com/), and Perplexity (https://www.perplexity.ai/).

Writing Assistants

Should that sentence include a comma or a semicolon, and is there a better way to communicate your ideas? Writing tools like Grammarly (https://www.grammarly.com/), Copy.ai (https://www.copy.ai/), and Jasper (https://www.jasper.ai/) are great to help you bang out a first draft or identify helpful edits to your work.

AV (Image, Video, and Audio) Production

There's an entire chapter dedicated to this later in the book, but the key thing to keep in mind as you get started is that you no longer need to hire an expensive designer or agency to translate your idea for that jingle, gala video, or hero image into a reality. ***AI tools, many of which are free or inexpensive, now enable you to instantly whip up helpful AV content.*** For images, OpenAI's Dall-E is now integrated into ChatGPT, and Midjourney (https://www.midjourney.com/) is a popular, versatile dedicated imagery resource, while platforms like Lumen5 (https://lumen5.com/), Google Vids (https://workspace.google.com/products/vids/), and Pictory (https://pictory.ai/) can help you make your video dreams manifest!

Trend Analysis

In an ideal world, we would have infinite interns and data analysts to crunch all the data that our nonprofits generate, enabling easy access to data-informed, actionable insights. Luckily, there are many AI tools that can do some of the heavy lifting here. For example, Crayon (https://www.crayon.co) will analyze other organizations' digital footprints to help you benchmark your performance. Tools like Hubspot (https://www.hubspot.com), Dataro (https://dataro.io), and Beacon (https://www.beaconcrm.org/feature/ai) provide AI-powered insights into your CRM data, turning data into knowledge; the latter two are designed specifically with nonprofits in mind.

Dive in, the water's fine! Don't be afraid to play around with a range of tools and try them on for size. See what best fits into your existing workflows and produces the best results. But the landscape is constantly shifting, so ***don't be fooled into thinking one-time research is all that's needed: plan for quarterly reviews to check out new platforms and functionality and ensure you're using the right AI tools.***

Master Prompting

AI is getting exponentially better at speaking "human," but it's not quite there yet. So, instead of just thinking out loud, take the time to learn how to "speak computer." This is the increasingly popular field of prompt engineering, to which we've dedicated an entire chapter in this first section. Although this skill may prove less critical over time, ***taking the time to learn how to interact with AI and optimize outputs is one of the most critical investments of time as you get started.***

Pitfalls and Solutions

Ignoring Ethics

AI systems perpetuate biases present in their training data, leading to unfair or discriminatory outcomes. To address these ethical issues up front, ***ensure your AI policy includes guidelines for fairness and bias mitigation.*** For example, how will you test the AI outputs for inclusivity? Ask yourself, "How will we ensure AI is fair and doesn't cause harm?" And if the AI is involved in any decision-making processes, can you verify this by conducting regular audits of your inputs and its outputs to identify and address any biases? Involve diverse stakeholders in the development and review of AI applications to ensure a broad perspective on ethical considerations. By proactively addressing ethical concerns, you can build trust with your supporters and ensure that your AI initiatives align with your organization's values.

Overreliance on AI

As mentioned, AI systems produce inaccurate results if the underlying data is flawed, and currently, these platforms can't tell the difference. That means while their outputs can be incredibly helpful, ***you always have to verify AI's work by keeping a HITL, prioritizing data quality, and implementing a robust data governance framework*** that includes data accuracy checks, validation processes, and ongoing monitoring. Engage domain experts to review AI outputs and provide feedback. By ensuring the accuracy of your data and AI models, you can make more reliable decisions and avoid undermining your credibility.

This is particularly important in areas such as donor communications and sentiment analysis, where understanding subtle cues and nuance is essential. Once again, this is best addressed by complementing AI tools with human oversight. ***Use AI to identify patterns and trends, but involve human experts in interpreting the results, sending the final version of any communications, and making final decisions.*** Invest in training your staff to work effectively with AI tools and ensure a more nuanced and accurate understanding of your data. By blending AI with human creativity and empathy, you can create authentic and engaging content that resonates with your supporters.

Data Privacy

Data privacy is a critical concern when implementing AI in your nonprofit, especially if sensitive information is involved. ***Ensure your AI policy includes strict data privacy guidelines and complies with relevant regulations such as General Data Protection Regulation (GDPR) or the California Consumer Privacy Act.*** Implement robust data security measures to protect against breaches and unauthorized access. Be transparent with your supporters about how their data is used and give them control over their information. By prioritizing data privacy, you can build trust with your supporters and avoid potential legal and reputational risks.

Road Map to the Future

It is often said in the world of AI that the AI you are using today is the worst version you'll ever use, because ***the only thing we can be sure of is that every model will improve:*** they will get faster, be able to do more and more things, and cost less. So, expect everything to change again, and again, and again. At the very least, you should understand that making the most of AI is an ongoing process and is not a one-and-done situation. Plan for having to make changes as this technology inevitably and inexorably develops.

Sticking your head in the sand to avoid the rise of AI is not a realistic option, as it will increasingly become a key part of more and more technologies that we use at work and in our daily lives. The operating systems on our laptops and phones, and the applications we use to do our jobs, are only going to have *more* AI in them in the coming years. In fact, ***it will be surprising if any of the digital tools we use every day do NOT incorporate some form of AI in the next two to three years.*** Get your guidance and policies drafted *now* to prepare and plan, because AI is going to be involved in every part and process of your organization, whether you like it or not.

Dos and Don'ts

Do

- Take the time to learn the basics of AI and to play around with a wide range of platforms to identify your favorites
- Map out the most common, recurring tasks you plan to use AI to support, identifying not only tactical, rote activities but creative brainstorming as well
- Use AI to automate simple, recurring tasks, analyze data, and predict the future
- Establish a clear and comprehensive AI policy, including your approach to data security, privacy, and bias
- Invest in staff training on data literacy and AI fundamentals
- Regularly clean and update your data for accuracy and reliability

Don't

- Underestimate the importance of prompt engineering and learning how to ask AI platforms for what you need and generate the best results
- Cut corners on AI implementation and resources; invest now for best results over time
- Forget to involve various stakeholders in drafting your AI policy, ensuring a diversity of viewpoints
- Outsource anything completely to AI: always keep a HITL to ensure you don't spread misinformation and always keep that human touch

Conclusion

AI holds immense potential for transforming the nonprofit sector. By understanding the basics of AI and implementing best practices, your nonprofit will harness this technology and enhance your impact, streamline operations, and unlock powerful, data-driven decision-making. Remember to **get your digital house in order, establish a clear and ethical AI policy, prioritize data privacy and security, and invest in staff training.** Embrace a proactive approach to AI adoption and encourage a culture of experimentation and innovation within your organization.

As you embark on your AI journey, keep in mind that the goal is not to replace the human touch but to augment your capabilities and amplify your impact. **By leveraging AI effectively, you can spend more time focusing on your mission and less time on administrative tasks.** The future is now, and with the right approach, AI can help you achieve your nonprofit's goals and create a lasting positive change in the world!

Interviewee Bio

Jonathan Waddingham is a nonprofit technology leader with two decades of experience helping charities embrace digital tools to increase their impact. As Chief Product Officer at Lightful, he oversees the design, development, and delivery of AI-powered solutions and applied learning programs that help nonprofits build digital skills and confidence in strategy, storytelling, and fundraising. Previously, Jonathan spent 12 years at JustGiving, where he helped scale its Crowdfunding product to become the UK's leading donation-based platform, raising over £100 million in five years. https://www.linkedin.com/in/jonathanwaddingham/

Resource Review

- NTEN's Nonprofit Technology Readiness Assessment: https://www.nten.org/learn/nonprofit-tech-readiness—A free tool to evaluate your nonprofit's tech capacity, including AI readiness.

- AI for Social Good by Google: https://ai.google/social-good/—A great resource to help you understand how AI can be used for social impact projects.
- Microsoft AI for Good: https://www.microsoft.com/en-us/ai/ai-for-good—A platform offering tools and resources to help nonprofits leverage AI for social good.
- Salesforce.org's AI for Nonprofits: https://www.salesforce.org/solutions/nonprofit/ai/—Provides AI solutions tailored for nonprofit organizations to drive impact.
- *Nonprofit Tech for Good*: https://www.nptechforgood.com/—A blog providing news and resources on AI and technology for nonprofits.
- AI Ethics Lab: https://aiethicslab.com—A resource offering guidance on ethical AI practices, relevant for nonprofits implementing AI solutions.
- Lightful: https://lightful.com/—Helps nonprofits embrace AI responsibly and effectively by providing tools, training, and support that empower organizations to enhance their digital engagement, storytelling, and fundraising while prioritizing ethical practices and social impact.

Chapter 2

Before You Get Started

Based on contributions from Beth Kanter.

In the whirlwind of emerging technologies, AI stands out as an enabling force that stands to transform all aspects of your nonprofit's operations, fundraising, marketing, and programs. The opportunities are truly limitless, as detailed throughout the various chapters that follow, each of which is complete with the tactical, practical tips and tools needed to ensure success. But before diving in headfirst, it's crucial to pause, learn, and strategize. **This chapter will guide you through the essential considerations and steps to take** before *integrating AI into your nonprofit's work.* And it can also help you take a step back if your nonprofit jumped into AI adoption but are somehow stuck, likely as a result of skipping the following steps, which ensure your organization leverages AI effectively, efficiently, and ethically, enhancing impact without compromising your core values.

Critical Skills and Competencies

Slow Down

The rapid development of AI and surrounding hype can create a sense of urgency or fear of being "left behind," but ***it's important to take a measured, methodical, and modular approach to the adoption of new technology.*** So, take your time and be thoughtful, as this leads to better return on investment and a more sustainable approach. First and foremost, reflect on how AI can best serve your mission and optimize your workflow: ***planning for success means clarifying exactly how you intend to use AI and to what end.*** That means considering how your team can leverage AI to address pain points, save time, or improve the quality of your work. Taking the time to understand the technology and its potential benefits enables you to make informed decisions.

Take this a step further by not only looking at your plans with AI but also how to best leverage your newly expanded capacity. ***Consider the time saved by AI tools and how you will leverage these hours to improve your processes and overall impact.*** This might mean streamlining administrative tasks, enhancing program delivery, or dedicating more time to relationship building. By slowing down and being deliberate, you can ensure that AI integration aligns with your organization's goals and values.

Understand Co-Intelligence

Many organizations initially approach AI adoption as if it were a genie in a bottle that will grant all your wishes instantly. You ask it to draft a grant proposal and out pops a perfectly formulated proposal. As much as we wish it did, AI doesn't work like that! ***Working with AI to help with staff tasks like writing or editing requires understanding "co-intelligence."*** This concept is refers to when humans work alongside the technology and are always in charge of the final output, and was popularized by Ethan Mollick, who wrote a great book on the topic (*Co-Intelligence: Living and Working with AI*, Portfolio, 2024).

Understanding this concept helps set the stage for a new collaboration between staff and our new digital assistants. We, as humans, need to guide this partnership in a direction that is always *human-centered*. Humans need to consider how AI fits into our workflow and tasks. ***Encourage critical thinking about tasks: which can benefit from AI assistance, and which require irreplaceable human insight?***

Develop Your AI Strategy and Ethics Policy

Because there isn't just one monolithic type of AI, there isn't just one AI strategy. ***There are three strategic approaches you can take:***

- **AI skilling:** Use of generative AI (GenAI) to help staff save time or improve task workflows

- **AI for organizational efficiency:** Integrated AI features into technology stacks such as your customer relationship management (CRM), human resources system, productivity suite, and so on
- **AI for program delivery:** Using AI to deliver programs and services that directly interact with your stakeholders

Your mission and values should guide your AI adoption, but understand that *each of these strategies has a continuum of ethical risks that require having norms and guardrails in place.* As detailed in the dedicated chapter on the topic, an AI ethics policy is not about saying no to the technology but channeling the enthusiasm for AI into safe, effective, and human-centered practices for completing job tasks. Your policy sets the ethical boundaries while enabling safe experimentation, support, and training.

Different strategies require different policies, and it's often best to build out your AI policy in a modular way, as the landscape is sure to change over time and with use. *Treat your policy as a living document, updating regularly as technology evolves and new use cases emerge.* For example, if you are focusing on an AI skilling strategy, you'll need an acceptable use policy that spells out ways to use GenAI that reduce bias, ensure accuracy, and protect privacy of stakeholder data. It should also spell out how you will disclose the use of AI on externally facing content. If you are developing an AI for organizational efficiency strategy, you will need to have a robust AI and data ethical governance policy. And, if you're building or deploying AI apps to deliver programs and services, you will need a process for testing and monitoring, called an "ethical pipeline." You'll also need to have formal ethical practices about the use of chatbots including, for example, disclosure when someone is interacting with a bot versus a human or when to route someone to a human.

Don't let this overwhelm you or stop you. Again, you're best off thinking about AI ethical policy development in a modular fashion. *Many nonprofits begin with an acceptable use policy focused on AI skilling because it is at the lower end of the risk continuum and a lighter operational lift.*

Your nonprofit's AI policy should typically include four sections:

- **Ethical guidelines:** Value statements that align the use of the technology with your organization's values

- **Norms:** What use cases are permitted and which aren't? What tools can be used or not? What tools will be provisioned by the organization?
- **Guardrails:** What are the specific practices you will follow up to uphold your ethical values?
- **Implementation:** How often will the policy be updated and reviewed for compliance? What training and support will your organization provide?

Values Come First

Develop your AI policy so that it ensures AI remains a tool to enhance human oversight, not replace it. Again, aside from ensuring a human-centered approach, your policy also needs to address the ethical implications of AI. *Assess the ethical implications and potential impact on your stakeholders, asking not only if you can do something but also if you should.* Engage in ethical deliberations with your team and stakeholders to evaluate the potential benefits and risks of AI projects. As nonprofits, we understand what ethical behavior is; we just need to connect it to the use of AI technology.

As you reach consensus, *take the time to properly document your shared organizational principles about AI utilization.* Your AI policy must include these stated values to guide decisions and norms when using AI. These statements should closely align with your nonprofit's mission, core beliefs, norms, culture, and interactions with stakeholders. *You can find many examples of ethical frameworks for nonprofits developed by Nonprofit Technology Enterprise Network (NTEN)* (https://www.nten.org/), *TAG* (https://www.tagtech.org/), *Fundraising.AI, and others.*

Human-Centered Norms and Values-Aligned Tool Selection

Ultimately, your policy should define norms for how people and AI will collaborate to practice co-intelligence, unlocking new ways to work together to more effectively and efficiently achieve your goals. In it, be clear the intent is not only on efficiency or doing more work faster. Include your thoughts and speak to time dividends in your policy. Ultimately, *you need a policy that speaks to how you'll leverage any newly available hours to advance your mission.* By prioritizing what's important, you can harness AI in a way that truly benefits your organization and stakeholders.

Identify specific tools, use cases, and clarify how the tools will be provisioned. When developing your policy, **start by being clear about how your nonprofit will handle AI tool access: whether you'll provide them as a benefit, reimburse employees for personal subscriptions, or take a hybrid approach.** It's important to spell out which tools are recommended or required, especially because there are differences between free and paid versions. Your policy should also clearly identify any tools that should be avoided and establish a clear approval process for new AI tool adoption.

Your policy also needs to explicitly outline approved use cases, covering everything from content creation and editing to translation, summarization, and analysis. Consider how these tools can enhance different aspects of work, from streamlining meeting notes to boosting research capabilities and creative brainstorming. Don't forget to address who needs to follow these guidelines—whether it's just employees or extends to contractors and volunteers. By clearly stating recommended tools and provisioning as well as use cases in your acceptable use policy, everyone is on the same page.

Define Guardrails and Responsible Use

Guardrails are the specific rules and practices that bring your ethical AI principles to life. ***Think of guardrails as safety features that keep your nonprofit on track, empowering your team to use AI tools responsibly.*** For example, if your organization is implementing an AI skilling strategy for GenAI, ensure your policy and training includes specific guardrails and responsible practices for privacy and confidentiality, bias, IP, accuracy, and disclosure, as covered next.

Let's take privacy as an example. In the nonprofit world, we often handle sensitive information about donors, beneficiaries, and our work. A privacy guardrail might look something like this, especially if using a free or non-enterprise version of GenAI tools: "Never share personally identifiable information (PII) in your prompts when using generative AI tools. PII includes names, email addresses, phone numbers, and any sensitive data connected to an individual."

This guardrail creates a clear boundary—PII is off-limits for AI tools—while still encouraging the use of AI for tasks that don't involve sensitive data. You might **complement this with a traffic light system: green data is safe to use with AI, yellow requires caution and possibly redaction, and red is never to be used with AI.** By setting up such guardrails, you're not just protecting sensitive information. You're also giving your staff the confidence to explore GenAI's potential without fear of inadvertently causing harm. They know where the boundaries are, which allows them to work freely within them.

Remember, **guardrails aren't about saying no to AI use. They're about saying yes, and here's how to do it safely and ethically.** By clearly communicating these guidelines and incorporating them into your AI training and onboarding processes, you're setting the stage for responsible AI adoption that amplifies your nonprofit's impact while staying true to your values.

Beware Bias

AI systems perpetuate biases present in their training data, and using GenAI tools for staff tasks is no exception. When working with tech tools, it's essential to **have a diverse team carefully review AI outputs through an equity lens, paying special attention to how different groups are represented and whether responses show unintended skews, hidden biases, or one-sidedness.** Take the time to learn how different AI models are fine-tuned for fairness, which you can check through resources like Decoding Trust (https://decodingtrust.github.io/). Use this insight to help you make informed choices about which tools best align with your commitment to mitigating bias. Remember, it's all about continuous improvement—regularly refining your prompts based on what you learn and staying mindful of how biases might creep into the output help create more inclusive and fair results.

Check for Accuracy

AI systems, especially large language models (LLMs) like those used to power ChatGPT, Claude, Gemini, and other GenAI platforms, sometimes generate incorrect or misleading information, known as "hallucinations." As such, **you cannot rely on AI-produced output without first verifying its accuracy,** especially if you're counting on it to generate externally facing content. Implement checks and balances to identify and critically review outputs and correct hallucinations, and always, always double-check AI's work!

Train your team to recognize and address hallucinations promptly. **_Develop protocols for cross-checking AI-generated information with reliable sources_** and ensure these are integrated into your nonprofit's AI policy. By mitigating the impact of hallucinations, you can prevent the spread of misinformation and ensure the reliability of your AI tools.

Navigate Intellectual Property

Managing intellectual property (IP) considerations with AI tools doesn't have to be overwhelming or require legal counsel on retainer. The key is taking a thoughtful approach to how you use these tools. **_When working with AI, it's best to avoid sharing copyrighted materials or requesting outputs that mimic specific artists' styles._** Instead, focus on paraphrasing concepts and adding your own creative touch to AI-generated content. For sensitive projects, consider using open-source models or those with IP-cleared datasets to stay on the safe side. Since this is such a dynamic field, it's worth keeping an eye on the latest legal developments and best practices as they emerge. Think of it like being a good digital citizen—respecting creators' rights while still harnessing AI's potential to enhance your work.

Trust Through Transparency

Being transparent about AI's role in externally facing content builds trust and shows respect for our audience and donors. **_When sharing AI-assisted content on your website, be clear about how technology was used in the process._** This could be as simple as noting that an article was cowritten with an AI platform while highlighting the human touch in its creation and editing, or sharing the prompt used to generate an image. Using platforms that include watermarks for AI-generated images adds another layer of transparency. **_Honesty about AI collaboration with our staff isn't just about disclosure—it's about celebrating the innovative ways we're combining human creativity with new technology_** while maintaining our human authenticity and expression.

Pitfalls and Solutions
Believing the Hype

Many nonprofits are excited about the quantum leap represented by AI since the launch of ChatGPT, but don't expect AI to be a quick fix. As with any technology, it takes time and a measured approach to responsibly, effectively integrate this tool into your efforts, and you want to avoid disappointment and wasted resources if the technology doesn't deliver immediate, spectacular results. Instead, ***approach AI with a balanced perspective, taking the time to understand both its capabilities and limitations, and to integrate it into your operations gradually and thoughtfully.***

Waiting

Waiting for the "perfect" version of AI means missing out on the benefits it can offer now. The technology will continue to evolve, as will your understanding and proficiency with it. The tech is always improving, but ***the sooner you get started putting this powerful tool to work for your cause, the more fluency you'll develop, the faster you'll enjoy its many benefits, and the more you can do over time.***

Move past your fears and *learn by doing*. ***Start small with controlled pilot projects to test AI's effectiveness, enabling you to iterate and improve while gaining valuable insights.*** As you become more comfortable and proficient with AI, you can expand its use and unlock more significant benefits for your nonprofit.

Road Map to the Future

As technology advances, AI tools will become more accessible and sophisticated, enabling nonprofits to achieve greater impact. The tech will be increasingly at your fingertips, and integrated into the tools you already use daily. Prepare for a future when AI is deeply integrated into all aspects of nonprofit operations—one in which you can expect to see AI agents assisting us to automate many aspects of our work, saving time while eliminating errors. ***To gear up and make the most of what's ahead, invest in AI training for staff, develop robust ethical guidelines, and foster a culture of innovation.*** By staying ahead of the curve, your nonprofit will harness the full potential of AI to drive positive change and fulfill your mission.

Dos and Don'ts

Do

- Develop your AI strategy and policy in a thoughtful way without succumbing to the urgency of AI hype
- Implement AI in a modular way, starting with AI skilling and then moving on to organizational systems and program delivery
- Develop a policy that speaks to your goals with approved AI tools, how to responsibly use them, how you protect sensitive data, how to leverage newly available capacity, and how you ensure human oversight
- Scrutinize outputs for biases and ensure diverse perspectives in AI training
- Evaluate different AI tools and conduct pilot tests to find the best fit
- Be transparent about your AI practices, clarifying how you use AI and the associated benefits
- Verify all AI-generated outputs to prevent misinformation and mitigate hallucinations
- Provide team orientation on your AI policy and tools, and encourage a culture of innovation by hosting regular team meetings to share success stories and workshop shared challenges
- Train your staff in using AI tools well and responsibly by creating an environment for online learning and experimentation
- Stay informed of new tech features, changes in privacy policies, and the evolving IP environment, adjusting your policy accordingly

Don't

- Assume information entered in AI prompts or uploaded into free GenAI platforms is private and secure; unless you use a paid platform that automatically opts you out of training its algorithm or you uncheck that feature, be careful of what private data, confidential information, or copyright materials you are sharing in your prompts

- Wait for the "perfect" version of AI; start small and learn by doing
- Cut and paste another organization's AI acceptable use policy and skip the conversation about ethics contextualized to your organization
- Roll out AI tools without having training and ongoing support in place

Conclusion

Taking the time to thoughtfully consider AI before diving in is crucial for nonprofits. ***By slowing down, aligning AI use with your goals and values, strategizing how to best collaborate with AI and leverage any capacity unlocked, and addressing ethical and practical concerns, you set the stage for successful AI integration.*** This approach not only enhances your impact but also ensures your organization remains true to its mission and values. Embrace AI with a strategic mindset and unlock new possibilities for your nonprofit. Start small, learn as you go, and continually refine your approach to ensure AI serves your mission effectively and ethically.

Contributor Bio

Beth Kanter is a recognized thought leader in the nonprofit sector, with over three decades of experience helping organizations build capacity and embrace innovation. As a sought-after speaker, trainer, and author, Beth has championed the responsible use of technology to advance social impact. She coauthored *The Smart Nonprofit: Staying Human-Centered in an Automated World* and has been at the forefront of educating nonprofits on how to adopt AI responsibly while safeguarding ethics, equity, and mission alignment. https://www.linkedin.com/in/bethkanter/

Resource Review

- BethKanter.org https://www.bethkanter.org—Our interviewee for this chapter helps you stay updated with practical insights on AI and nonprofit technology, all available through her website, training resources (https://bit.ly/Beth-Kanter-AI-Resources), speaking and training engagements, and books.
- *The Smart Nonprofit: Staying Human Centered in an Automated World*—This helpful book, coauthored by our interviewee, is designed to help you learn how

to embrace AI responsibly by focusing on human-centered strategies that enhance donor relationships and ensure technology aligns with your nonprofit's mission (Beth Kanter and Allison Fine, Wiley, 2022).

- Every.org: https://www.every.org—Follow our interviewee's co-author, Allison Fine, for her thought leadership on AI and its ethical use in nonprofits.

- *Co-Intelligence: Living and Working with AI*—Research-backed book that explores how AI can be harmonized with human values, including practical insights into integrating AI into social good initiatives while ensuring fairness, inclusivity, and transparency (Ethan Mollick, Portfolio, 2024).

- NTEN's Nonprofit Technology Readiness Assessment: https://www.nten.org/learn/nonprofit-tech-readiness—A free tool to evaluate your organization's tech capacity, including AI readiness.

- TAG (Technology Affinity Group): https://www.tagtech.org—Offers valuable summaries and resources for nonprofits and funders on the latest technology trends, including AI.

- Fundraising.AI: https://fundraising.ai—A dedicated platform for advancing the use of AI in nonprofit fundraising, offering tools, insights, and case studies to help you optimize donor engagement and streamline operations.

- Decoding Trust: https://decodingtrust.github.io/—Explore this valuable resource for evaluating AI tools through an equity lens, helping your nonprofit make informed decisions about adopting fair and inclusive technology solutions.

- GivingTuesday Best Practices Library: https://data.givingtuesday.org—A comprehensive library of best practices for using AI and LLMs in nonprofits, including a prompt library.

- Microsoft Nonprofits: https://www.microsoft.com/nonprofits—Provides a wealth of resources and tools to help nonprofits integrate technology and AI into their operations.

- AI for Nonprofit Organizations LinkedIn Group: https://www.linkedin.com/groups/14431695/—Join this group for great posts and discussions on AI in the nonprofit sector, as shared by the good folks at Nonprofit Tech for Good.

Chapter 2.1

Understanding the AI Adoption Life Cycle

Based on insights from an interview with Kate Gage.

If you're serious about leveraging AI to advance your nonprofit's mission, it's incredibly helpful to have a road map before you dive in. What should you expect, in terms of the phases of AI-powered development and impact that lie ahead, how do you know which stage you're in, and most important, how can you advance from one to the next? Understanding this will help you identify the right strategies to move forward and maximize the value AI can offer your organization.

By comprehending the AI adoption life cycle, you'll be able to meet your team where they are and guide your organization through each stage of AI integration. So, let's dive in and see how you can take your nonprofit from curious to AI-savvy.

The Four Stages of AI Adoption
Individual Use

This is where the magic begins, and where roughly 95% of nonprofits currently live. ***Before nonprofits even dip their organizational toes in the AI waters, adoption is driven by individuals who are curious and eager to experiment.*** These are your in-house champions, the ones who fiddle with ChatGPT to draft emails or use AI tools for brainstorming sessions. They typically don't have an official policy or guidelines to guide their efforts, but they're discovering AI's potential on their own and learning by doing.

Keys to Progress

- **Encourage experimentation:** Make time for your team to play around with AI tools, inviting them to use them for work tasks.
- **Share insights:** Set up regular team meetings where individuals discuss their AI use, what worked, what didn't, and what they learned.
- **Identify champions:** Keep an eye out for those particularly enthusiastic about AI. They will be instrumental in driving adoption forward.
- **Craft a policy:** *The key action needed to move you to step 2 is creating an acceptable use policy for AI* throughout your organization, as detailed in Chapter 30. Your champions and executives are typically the ones best suited to draft this for the group's review.

Important Considerations

- **Data security:** Even in the absence of an official policy, *take steps to ensure that no nonpublic or personally identifiable information is used in AI prompts.* This is crucial to prevent potential data breaches.

Organizational Adoption

Only about 3% of nonprofits are currently at this stage, where *your organization starts to see the value in AI and formalize its use.* Often, this takes the form of you adopting enterprise-level AI tools or implementing specific applications like note-taking apps or chatbots.

Keys to Progress

- **Training and access:** Provide orientation and ongoing training for both staff and board members to ensure everyone understands how to use AI effectively and responsibly.
- **Ethics and guardrails:** Discuss and establish the values, ethics, and risks associated with AI use in your organization.

- **Update your policy:** Update your initial policy with these insights and any other useful refinements now that you're trying AI on for size as an institution.
- **Detail goals and needs:** *To advance to step 3, document both recurring tasks and strategic goals that are ripe to be supported by AI tools.* Clarifying your needs and objectives will guide your efforts to ensure AI is deployed in a way that advances your work and objectives, instead of distracting your team with a shiny new object. These insights can serve as the basis for updates to your policy or a request for proposal (RFP), as detailed in the inset on guidelines for AI vendor selection in Chapter 6.

Important Considerations

- **Focus on specific use cases:** Start with clear, beneficial applications of AI to demonstrate value and build confidence.

Strategic Implementation

Now that your nonprofit is comfortable with AI, it's time to think strategically. This means entering the top 1.5% of nonprofits today, putting you near the head of the pack. *This stage involves leveraging AI to advance your strategic goals,* whether it's expanding your client base by offering programs in new languages or using AI to enhance community engagement. Having documented the recurring tasks and strategic goals you hope to support with AI tools, now it's time to dive in and put them to work.

Keys to Progress

- **Create work plans:** Map out a plan for any of the goals and tasks you aim to leverage AI to advance, including roles and responsibilities, timelines and milestones, budget and other resource allocations, and key performance metrics against which you can evaluate your efforts.
- **Enhance programs:** Use AI to improve program delivery, from personalized services to data-driven decision-making.

- **Engage the community:** Develop AI-driven initiatives that enhance your connection and communication with your community.
- **Think bigger:** Now that you've internalized AI strategically, odds are you will bump up against the boundaries of what's possible. Pushing beyond may be expensive and time-consuming, but *if you identify any clear needs for AI that aren't addressable by standard tools, create an RFP or work plan* providing the same details as the work plan mentioned, noting that in many cases, you'll need to look externally to find someone who can build it for you. It's also helpful to split your budget into what you can afford to pay a third party and what you can allot for staff time and other internal support resources, both initially and ongoing.

Important Considerations

- **Continuous improvement:** Regularly revisit and refine your AI strategies to ensure they remain aligned with your goals and the evolving landscape.

Proprietary Solutions

The final stage of the AI adoption life cycle is all about innovation. No more than 0.5% of nonprofits have made it to this advanced step, where *your nonprofit isn't just using AI tools developed by others; you're creating your own.* That means developing custom AI solutions tailored to your unique needs and goals, whether through internal efforts or, more likely, a professional third party with relevant experience.

Keys to Progress

- **Build and iterate:** What's that they say about the best-laid plans? Once you achieve step 4, *your first step is to actually design and create the tools you've dreamt up, and then to put them to work.* Be sure to review the inset on guidelines for AI vendor selection in Chapter 6 if you look externally for support. Either way, don't expect the first version of your tool to be perfect; instead, plan for ongoing refinements and allocate the staff and resources needed to support this until you get what you need.

- **Invest in research and development:** Allocate resources for research and development to stay ahead of the curve and continuously innovate.
- **Foster a culture of innovation:** Encourage your team to think creatively about how else AI can be used to achieve your mission. And even once your AI tools are exactly what you need, make sure you audit them at least a couple times a year to ensure there's no room for improvement, evolution of needs, or new, better applications in the marketplace.

Important Considerations

- **Stay mission-focused:** Ensure that any proprietary AI developments are firmly aligned with your nonprofit's mission and values.

Interviewee Bio

Kate Gage is a seasoned leader in innovation and technology for social impact, bringing extensive experience in leveraging emerging tools like AI to transform nonprofit operations and outcomes. As a senior advisor at USAID's Global Development Lab, Kate spearheaded initiatives that harnessed technology to solve complex global challenges, setting a precedent for innovation in the nonprofit sector. She also cofounded Open Gov Hub, a coworking community for nonprofits focused on transparency and accountability, which exemplifies her dedication to empowering mission-driven organizations with cutting-edge solutions. Her work at the intersection of public service and technology has been featured in top-tier outlets like *The Washington Post* and *Stanford Social Innovation Review*. https://www.linkedin.com/in/katebgage/

Chapter 3

90-Day Blueprint for AI Success

Based on insights from an interview with Charlene Li.

If you're one of the many busy nonprofit leaders who have heard the buzz about AI but haven't yet taken the plunge, you're probably worried about the unknown. You may be asking, "What kind of commitment are we talking about here, anyway, and do I have the bandwidth to move forward responsibly?" While new technology adoption is often daunting, the good news about AI is that it doesn't need to be that complicated. And we're here to help!

So, let's break it down. ***This chapter will provide you with a quick guide to navigating the crucial first 90 days of responsibly adopting AI in your nonprofit.*** This blueprint shared below is based on the book *Winning with Generative AI: The 90-Day Blueprint for Success* by Charlene Li and Katia Walsh (Amplify Publishing, 2025). Think of it as your road map to ensuring AI helps you achieve your mission faster, better, and with greater impact, all while adhering to any guardrails needed to protect your organization and those you serve.

Critical Skills and Competencies

Week 1: Establish Your Minimum Viable Team

Your first step is to create your minimum viable team, or MVT. ***This team of at least two leaders will draft an 18-month plan to be fleshed out by the remainder of your staff.*** Again, your MVT can be limited to as few as a couple of people, but the key is that this group must represent multiple perspectives:

- **Tech-savvy leader:** This person is comfortable with AI and innovation, who is a strategic thinker.
- **CEO or head of strategy:** This person ensures the AI implementation aligns with your core mission.
- **Client representative:** This person understands the needs and perspectives of the people you serve.
- **Human resources representative:** This person considers the impact on your staff and organizational culture.
- **Fundraising expert:** This person understands how AI can enhance your fundraising efforts.

Once your MVT is in place, get them trained up and personally comfortable using AI technology. *Allocate at least one hour a day for MVT members to access AI resources and advance their professional development, plus experiment with AI tools.* They need to understand how AI works firsthand by using it to complete various tasks. Hands-on experience is crucial for everyone on the team to appreciate AI's capabilities and limitations.

Week 2: Develop Goldilocks Governance

Now that you've selected your inner circle and leveled up their capacity, it's time to *develop a governance framework to guide your nonprofit's AI adoption* in a way that feels "just right"—not too restrictive, but not too loose. This entails the MVT drafting AI governance policies for these issues:

- **Security and privacy:** Articulates the protections and protocols needed to ensure no one uploads sensitive information into public AI platforms. As detailed in Chapter 30, this should include what sensitive data you manage and how it must be handled.
- **Accountability:** Who is responsible for what, and what do you do if something goes wrong?

- **Transparency:** How transparent will you be about using AI, both internally and externally?

Use existing policies as your starting point, adapt them to fit your AI strategy, and use AI tools to draft and refine these policies. This framework will set the foundation for responsible and ethical AI use within your organization.

Week 3: Define AI Value Creation

Now that you have a sandbox within which it's safe to ideate and experiment, it's time to consider how AI will create value for your nonprofit. To accomplish this, *your MVT creates a simple document that details three dimensions of utility and applications of AI technology:*

- **Efficiency:** Identify repetitive tasks that AI can automate or streamline.
- **Engagement:** Look at how AI can support more creative and judgment-based tasks, like brainstorming and campaign planning.
- **Transformation:** Consider how AI can help you reach more people and have a greater impact.

By the end of week 3, you should have a clear understanding of the processes and tasks where AI can make the most difference. This helps you begin with the end in mind. Now that your MVT has clarified where AI can contribute to your work, it's time to consider what you have to work with to employ the technology, and then we get to try it on for size!

Week 4: Conduct a Capabilities Audit

Now that you know where you want to go with AI, it's time to *inventory the expertise, information, and other resources you have available to achieve your goals.* Conduct an audit to evaluate these issues:

- **Skills and workforce:** What skills and capacity do your team members have, and what will you need to add?
- **Leadership and culture:** Is your leadership team ready to support AI adoption? What cultural shifts might be necessary?
- **Data readiness:** Is your data accurate, organized, and clean enough for AI to use effectively?
- **Tech stack:** Can your current technology infrastructure support AI integration? Can it support the tasks and goals outlined in week three, and are there any limitations to consider?

This audit will highlight any assets you'll want to leverage as your nonprofit adopts AI, and perhaps even more important, will bring to light any gaps and help you plan for the resources you need.

Weeks 5–6: Pilot Projects

Start small with pilot projects. *Choose initiatives that align with your mission and have clear, measurable goals against predefined targets.* Perhaps you want to shave a few hours off on the time needed to produce grant reports or applications, craft email subject lines that deliver improved open rates, or increase board engagement in meetings by automating note-taking. Whatever trials you envision, take into account these projects must be designed to help you:

- Test and refine the governance policies you drafted in week 2. Week 6 is typically a good time to *layer in acceptable use guidelines, where you detail which AI tools are approved for which applications,* along with tips to maximize outcomes.
- Measure the impact of AI on efficiency and engagement.
- Gather feedback from your team and stakeholders.

These early wins will build confidence and provide valuable insights for scaling AI across your nonprofit. With this, you can expand the scaffolding needed to support larger projects and even greater wins.

Weeks 7–8: Produce Your Plan

Take time to evaluate the results of your pilot projects. *Gather data, analyze outcomes, and identify what worked and what didn't, and consider why.* Use this information to do the following:

- **Refine your AI strategy:** What new kinds of value can AI add to your efforts, and which tools can best support your work?
- **Update your governance framework:** Now that it's been field-tested, integrate any changes to ensure its guidelines are as useful and realistic as possible.
- **Plan for broader implementation:** Building on the lessons learned from your pilot projects, what are the next applications you're excited to explore?

Once you've done all this, *integrate your AI strategy, governance framework, and value creation goals into your nonprofit's AI plan, including concrete quarter-by-quarter goals over 18 months and individual roles and responsibilities.* Provide an opportunity for everyone on staff and on the board to review and comment on this key document, as a shared sense of ownership is crucial to your nonprofit's success.

Once your AI plan is finalized, everyone in the organization should know the following:

- What's the future we're trying to build toward?
- What's our strategy to get there?
- What's my role in making that a success?

Remember, this is a learning process. Iteration is key to long-term success, and *the cycle of strategize-experiment-reflect is one that you should repeat over and over again as you employ AI to support an ever-widening list of tasks and priorities.*

Weeks 9–10: Scale Up

With the lessons learned from your pilot projects, producing your plan, and with new applications in your sights, ***start standardizing the use of proven applications and scaling AI across more areas of your organization.*** Focus on these tasks:

- **Training more team members:** Embrace a culture of innovation and experimentation, and strive to build a nonprofit where every staffer has a voice and agency, whether that's helping with new experiments or adopting proven techniques after they've passed your tests.
- **Integrating AI into more processes:** Use the efficiency, engagement, and transformation framework to consider an unlimited number of options but be sure to update your AI plan accordingly.
- **Continuously monitoring and refining your approach:** *Your ongoing AI experiments should always consider what success looks like in advance and set targets against which to assess results.*

By the end of this period, AI should be an integral part of your daily operations, and not just for some of your team, but for everyone.

Weeks 11–12: Iterate and Celebrate

Life happens, and there will be some left turns as you begin implementing your nonprofit's AI plan. That's OK, and in fact, inevitable! ***Plan a quarterly meeting to revisit your plan, reflect on successes and obstacles, and add another quarter*** so that it always covers a rolling 18-month period. As you reach the furthest levels of AI maturity, you can consciously opt out of this practice and mindfully let your plan wind down.

Now that you've made it to the other side of the rainbow, it's important to ***share your successes with your team, stakeholders, and community.*** Highlight how AI has helped you achieve your mission more effectively. This not only boosts morale but also reinforces the value of AI to your organization. Celebrate your efforts and showcase your openness to innovation, especially when it enables you to advance your mission.

Pitfalls and Solutions

Starting Too Big

Starting with large, complex AI projects might feel exciting, but it can quickly lead to frustration, wasted resources, and even failure. ***When you dive into a big initiative, you're likely to encounter unexpected challenges—for example, data quality issues, unclear workflows, or gaps in team knowledge—that can derail progress.*** Plus, the larger the project, the harder it is to measure success or pinpoint what's working and what's not.

To avoid this pitfall, focus on starting small. ***Identify specific, manageable problems that AI can solve with measurable outcomes against clear objectives,*** such as drafting email campaigns, segmenting donor lists, or automating routine data entry. Set measurable goals so you can track progress and evaluate the project's impact. Once your pilot is under way, involve your team. Encourage staff to share feedback, document what's working, and learn together. Use these insights to refine your approach and build momentum for larger initiatives. By starting small and scaling up gradually, you'll reduce risk, boost team confidence, and set your nonprofit up for long-term success with AI.

Failing to Iterate

AI is evolving at a breakneck pace, and it seems likely to continue to do so for years to come. That means ***the speed of change will only increase and no matter how much hard work you invest into your nonprofit's AI plan, some of your assumptions will prove false.*** Avoid stagnation by continuously evaluating the results of your AI initiatives and making necessary adjustments. This will keep you nimble and alert, enabling you to capitalize on new technologies or opportunities, while mitigating against inefficient use of resources. And if the landscape changes in any way, you'll be able to pivot and make the most of any shifts, instead of getting caught in the past.

Road Map to the Future

AI will continue to evolve and offer new opportunities for nonprofits. As AI technology advances, it will become even more accessible and capable of transforming nonprofit operations, and will increasingly, seamlessly be integrated into our everyday interactions with technology. Nonprofits that embrace AI and integrate it into their mission-driven work will be better positioned to achieve their goals and make a greater impact. ***By diving in and putting AI to work for your cause and then staying informed and proactive about ongoing professional development and refinements to your organization's AI strategy, you can ensure your nonprofit stays ahead of the curve and maximizes the benefits of AI.***

Dos and Don'ts

Do

- Create a diverse MVT to draft and execute your AI strategy, allocating at least an hour a day for 90 days to each member for related duties
- Use AI tools to reference existing policies and establish an AI governance framework to guide AI adoption, including policies for security and privacy, accountability, and transparency
- Take the time to articulate how AI can add value to your work, detailing goals for efficiency, engagement, and transformation
- Conduct a capabilities audit to inventory the expertise, information, and other resources you have available to achieve your goals with AI, including exploring your team's skills and capacity, culture about innovation, data readiness, and tech stack
- Create an AI plan for your nonprofit, including concrete quarter-by-quarter goals over 18 months and individual roles and responsibilities
- Update your nonprofit's AI plan quarterly, taking into account successes and obstacles, and adding another quarter to your rolling plan
- Train your entire team on AI, enlisting their help with new experiments and ensuring they're clear on how to use proven techniques and applications

Don't

- Dive headfirst into big AI projects, instead of starting small with pilot projects with clear, measurable goals against predefined targets
- Forget to leverage your pilot projects to update your AI plan with guidelines for acceptable use, including detailing which AI tools are approved for which applications
- Ever stop experimenting with potential applications of AI, as long as at each pass you update your nonprofit's AI plan and use the efficiency, engagement, and transformation framework to ensure an intentional approach
- Consider your road to responsible AI adoption complete until every person in the organization is clear about three things:
  - What's the future we're trying to build toward?
  - What's our strategy to get there?
  - What's my role in making that a success?
- Neglect to communicate your AI successes and learnings to your team and stakeholders

Conclusion

By following the 90-Day blueprint for AI success, you will set a strong foundation for AI adoption in your nonprofit. Remember, ***the goal is not just to implement AI but to use it as a tool to advance your mission.*** Start with a clear plan, involve the right people, and continuously evaluate and iterate. With this approach, you'll be well on your way to leveraging AI for greater impact.

Interviewee Bio

Charlene Li is a pioneering thought leader in digital transformation and disruptive innovation, bringing deep expertise to help organizations thrive in a rapidly evolving tech landscape. As the founder of Altimeter and a *New York Times* bestselling author, her research and frameworks have guided Fortune 500 companies and mission-driven organizations toward embracing new opportunities. Charlene's work focuses on the leadership required to navigate emerging technologies, including AI, helping organizations understand the basics and strategically implement a 90-day blueprint for success. Her insights distill complex concepts into actionable steps, empowering nonprofits to build trust, agility, and resilience as they integrate AI into their operations. In a world where the future is now, Charlene provides a clear road map for leaders to harness AI's potential and drive meaningful impact. https://www.linkedin.com/in/charleneli/

Resource Review

- NTEN (Nonprofit Technology Network): https://www.nten.org—Access courses, research, and a supportive community to build your nonprofit's AI readiness and improve your tech adoption efforts.

- TechSoup: https://www.techsoup.org—Take advantage of discounted software and technology solutions to implement AI tools without exceeding your budget.

- AI for Good Global Summit: https://aiforgood.itu.int—Attend sessions showcasing AI innovations that address social impact challenges, helping you envision how to apply these tools in your nonprofit.

- Beth Kanter's blog: https://bethkanter.org—Learn practical tips for using AI to enhance nonprofit programs and build capacity while avoiding common pitfalls.

- Fast Forward—Tech for Good: https://www.ffwd.org—Discover tools, trends, and case studies from tech-forward nonprofits and learn how to integrate AI into your mission-driven work.

- Microsoft AI for Nonprofits: https://www.microsoft.com/nonprofits—Explore AI solutions and grants tailored for nonprofits to accelerate your digital transformation.

- OpenAI blog: https://openai.com/blog—Stay updated on advancements in AI technology and learn how to implement OpenAI tools to meet your organization's goals.

- AI Ethics Lab: https://aiethicslab.com—Use their frameworks to ensure your nonprofit adopts AI responsibly, prioritizing fairness, transparency, and accountability.

Chapter 3.1

Key Ingredients for AI Adoption Success

Based on insights from an interview with Gary A. Bolles.

Preparing your nonprofit to leverage the advantages of AI adoption requires more than just purchasing the latest technologies. To maximize the benefits of AI and ensure it aligns with your mission, you need a balanced approach that incorporates three critical elements: mindset, skill set, and tool set. ***These elements provide a simple yet powerful framework to help your nonprofit develop the flexibility, capabilities, and technologies necessary to thrive in the AI era.*** By focusing on these ingredients, you'll create a foundation that enables your team to adopt AI thoughtfully and effectively, ensuring long-term success and mission alignment.

Mindset, Skill Set, and Tool Set

Mindset

Mindset includes the attitudes and perspectives your team adopts when approaching challenges, opportunities, and change. For nonprofits adopting AI, mindsets like flexibility and adaptability are essential. With the exponential pace of technological innovation, a *fixed* mindset can slow your ability to innovate and respond to emerging challenges. By embracing a *flexible* mindset, organizations can continuously learn and adapt as new tools and techniques emerge.

To cultivate a flexible mindset, create an environment where experimentation is encouraged, and failure is simply seen as an opportunity for learning. As you experiment with the various AI applications outlined in this book, be sure to choose one or two specific uses where you can pilot one or two AI tools, gather feedback from your team, and keep tweaking your approach before rolling that solution out to the full organization. Encourage constant communication between teams to ensure everyone understands the potential benefits and risks of AI adoption. And hold regular brainstorming sessions to explore creative ways AI can enhance your work. Challenge your team to think beyond existing processes—and to practice a flexible mindset.

Skill Set

Skill set refers to *the human abilities and knowledge necessary to thrive in an AI-powered world.* **The most important knowledge to power your team's use of AI tools will be an understanding of the best ways to use the software, so that's the first skill set to develop.**

When it comes to abilities, though nonprofit catalysts need a range of skills, there are four capacities that are most crucial to help you navigate the PACE of change: acting as a **p**roblem-solver, being **a**daptive, using **c**reativity, and demonstrating **e**mpathy.

- **Problem-solver:** It's your team's ability to define problems clearly and develop potential solutions that can drive the most meaningful actions with AI tools. Ask "What's the root cause of this issue we're facing?" and "How can AI help solve this in a way that aligns with our mission?" Teach your team structured problem-solving *techniques* such as design thinking and rapid prototyping to make the most of AI-driven insights.

- **Adaptive:** An adaptable team will embrace the rapid and inevitable evolution of AI tools, viewing changes in technologies, workflows, and roles as opportunities. **To build adaptive skills, prioritize cross-functional teams and cross-training,** giving team members continuous opportunities to step into new roles and solve new problems—and to teach each other.

- **Creativity:** GenAI tools generate the best results with creative input. Think of this as **"AI-deation"—challenging your team to leverage GenAI to brainstorm completely new ways to solve problems,** such as alternative approaches to providing services, or breakthrough ideas to suggest to funders.

- **Empathy:** It's your team's ability to empathize with your nonprofit's mission, empowering stakeholders to solve problems, that defines your organization's unique value. ***AI tools can turn empathy into a superpower,*** such as using chatbot tools to identify and promote your stakeholders' interests, creating customized responses to stakeholder requests, and articulating solutions in language that best resonates with stakeholders. Your team's ability to maintain personal connections in an increasingly wired world will help build trust and alignment with your mission.

Tool Set

Your tool set includes the technologies and techniques your nonprofit uses to enhance operations and achieve its mission. While AI tools such as predictive analytics, GenAI, and natural language processing (NLP) stand to revolutionize how nonprofits operate, the effectiveness of those tools depends on how they are selected and implemented. ***A poorly chosen or misaligned tool can drain resources and fail to deliver results,*** so it's critical to choose and use your tool set with intentionality.

Start by conducting a technology audit to assess your current systems and identify gaps that AI could address. When evaluating new tools, prioritize those that align with your strategic goals and can integrate effectively with your existing systems. ***Ensure your team receives proper training on these tools and establish clear metrics to measure their impact.***

Your best deliverable: ***create a process through which your team can continually evaluate, experiment with, and implement new tools as they arise.*** GenAI and related tools will continue to change at a rapid rate, and so must you and your team.

Interviewee Bio

Gary A. Bolles is a globally recognized expert in the future of work, AI, and social impact, serving as the Global Fellow for Transformation with Singularity University. Gary helps organizations and leaders navigate the transformative impact of AI and other exponential technologies to build more inclusive, adaptive, and innovative systems. As the author of *The Next Rules of Work: The Mindset, Skillset and Toolset to Lead Your Organization Through Uncertainty* (Kogan Page, 2021) and as a cofounder of key initiatives like SoCap, he has championed strategies to empower underserved populations and foster equitable access to opportunity. https://www.linkedin.com/in/gbolles/

Chapter 4

Adapting and Thriving in the Age of AI

Based on insights from an interview with danah boyd.

As a nonprofit leader, you are constantly striving to serve your community more effectively and efficiently, stretching resources to the limit for the benefit of those you serve. In an era when technology is rapidly evolving, it is crucial to stay ahead of the curve, especially when it comes to AI. ***Understanding and anticipating the trends in AI over the coming years is not just about keeping up with the latest technological advancements; it's about leveraging these tools to enhance your organization's operations, amplify your mission, and create a more significant impact.***

In this chapter, our focus is on speaking to how you can catch and then ride the wave of innovation that kicked into high gear with the release of ChatGPT 3.5 in November 2022. Our goal is not just to prepare you for today or tomorrow but also for the years ahead. While a range of perspectives, skills, and tools will undoubtedly play critical roles in helping you blaze the path forward, ***there are a handful of crucial ways of thinking and acting that will play the largest role in determining your success and impact with putting AI and other emerging tech tools to use in your nonprofit.*** And just like the five fingers of your hand can be combined to make a much more powerful fist, it's when you employ all five of these together that you can unlock the full benefits of AI and ensure your place at the head of the pack as we move into this bold future.

Critical Skills and Competencies

Separate Reality from Rhetoric

First, it is essential to recognize that the rhetoric of AI often outpaces reality. While there is much hype about AI's transformative potential, the actual implementation and utility of these tools is just getting started. AI is a tool, and its effectiveness depends on how it is integrated into your nonprofit's programs and processes. **Rather than getting caught up in the excitement of adopting new technology, focus on how AI can serve your specific needs and enhance existing workflows.**

Too many of us get caught up chasing the next shiny object. To combat this natural tendency, **as you deploy AI and other emerging technologies, always be sure to map to mission.** That means taking the time to contemplate how and why any given tool makes sense for you and the community your nonprofit serves. Consider it an exercise in intentionality, which is best supported by introspection, conversation, and action. That means visualizing possibilities and ensuring they're aligned with your strategic goals and reason for being, and then engaging your team and stakeholders in conversations to explore pros and cons. The latter is key to ensuring your internal needs do not take precedence over those of your clients. Any tech tools need to be in service to them, as well as you. Once you've completed these internal and external processes, you're ready to take the time to **write down your thoughts, goals, resources, potential challenges, intended use cases, and the metrics you'll use to gauge performance down the road.**

Augmentation, Not Automation

AI can help you and your team be more productive and efficient by handling mundane and repetitive tasks, allowing you to focus on higher-level strategic work. It can assist in grant writing by analyzing past successful grants and providing insights into what works, with budgeting by identifying patterns and trends in your financial data and helping you plan and allocate resources more effectively, and much, much more. AI-powered chatbots can manage routine inquiries from donors and beneficiaries, offering instant responses and freeing up your staff to handle more complex issues. AI can enhance your decision-making processes by providing data-driven insights and predictive analytics, helping you identify potential opportunities and risks more accurately. There's not much it can't do, so like we said in the book's Introduction, where do you want to point that thing?

Just make sure as you're contemplating how to leverage AI, that you remember ***AI should be seen as a complementary tool that augments human capabilities rather than replacing them.*** As one of the myriad examples detailed in this book, AI-driven analytics can help you understand patterns in donor behavior, enabling you to tailor your fundraising strategies more effectively. However, ***the human touch in relationship-building and storytelling remains irreplaceable.*** By balancing AI's capabilities with human insights, you can create a more robust and effective approach to achieving your mission.

Cultivate Your Inner Circle

To successfully integrate AI into your nonprofit, it is essential to have passionate champions who can lead by example and help demystify the technology for others. These ***AI ambassadors play a crucial role in ensuring that AI tools are effectively adopted and used across your organization.*** Leveraging these superstars to provide training, share best practices, and connect with peers so everyone on your team can learn from their experiences and overcome their fears and reservations.

A strong inner circle doesn't just focus on training and adoption—it also fosters a culture of curiosity and experimentation. ***Encourage your AI ambassadors to regularly explore new tools and applications, pilot innovative projects, and share lessons learned with the broader team.*** Give them paid time every week to play with new tools and try them on for size, enabling them to identify new resources and bring them back to the team. This approach not only builds confidence and promotes leadership but also keeps your nonprofit on the cutting edge of technology. Finally, make it a priority to ***empower these champions by providing them with opportunities for professional development, such as attending AI-focused conferences or participating in specialized training programs.*** By investing in their growth, you ensure that your ambassadors remain motivated and well informed, ready to help your organization stay ahead in the ever-evolving tech landscape. When your inner circle thrives, so does your ability to adapt, innovate, and lead.

Maintain Fluency in Speaking AI

The art of **prompt engineering—the ability to communicate effectively with AI systems—is a foundational skill in the age of AI.** Crafting clear, concise, and contextually rich prompts significantly affects the quality and relevance of AI outputs, whether you're generating donor outreach messages, analyzing program data, or brainstorming new campaign ideas. **This competency isn't just about knowing how to phrase requests; it's about understanding the nuances of how AI interprets language and how to fine-tune your inputs to get optimal results.**

Chapter 7 spells out a range of best practices in detail. But for starters, **hone your prompt engineering skills by practicing with accessible AI tools like ChatGPT or Jasper, experimenting with different ways of framing your questions or requests.** Pay attention to how small tweaks in wording or additional context can lead to vastly different responses. And be sure to **gain some firsthand practice with the impressive power of few-shot prompts, meaning those where you give your AI tool a sample of what you're looking for.** Encourage your team to document effective prompts as they're discovered, creating a shared library of best practices for your organization. But keep in mind this technology is constantly evolving, so the science of prompt engineering is sure to as well. Regularly revisiting and refining your prompts will ensure you stay fluent in "speaking AI" and unlock the full potential of these tools.

Never Stop Experimenting

Innovation thrives on experimentation, and the same is true when it comes to technology adoption. **You may be tempted to dive in the deep end with AI, but piloting new tools and iterating based on real-world results is almost always the way to go.** Start by selecting small, manageable projects where AI can make a tangible difference, such as automating donor acknowledgment letters or analyzing event feedback surveys. Set clear goals and metrics for success, and ensure you have a process in place to gather feedback and evaluate results.

Once you've completed a pilot, take the time to assess what worked and what didn't. Use those insights to refine your approach and expand AI adoption in other areas of your organization. **Maintain a culture of experimentation by encouraging your team to continuously explore and test emerging tools.** Consider setting up an innovation fund to support these efforts or designating a portion of your team's time to explore and experiment with AI applications. By fostering an experimental mindset, your nonprofit will remain adaptable, innovative, and primed to harness the full power of AI.

Pitfalls and Solutions

Overlooking Ongoing Professional Development

Failing to provide continuous training for your entire team—not just your AI ambassadors—limits your nonprofit's ability to fully leverage AI and adapt to technological advancements. ***Without professional development, your team will likely struggle to use AI tools effectively, leading to missed opportunities and inefficiencies.*** So, be sure to offer training and support across your organization. Develop structured AI training programs tailored to various roles, from frontline staff to executives, ensuring everyone understands how to apply AI tools in their work. Take advantage of on-demand learning, AI-focused workshops, conferences, and webinars produced by the nonprofits and publishers highlighted throughout this book, including the "Resource Review" at the end of this chapter. Schedule regular AI learning days to keep your team updated on advancements and include AI literacy as a key component in onboarding processes for new hires.

Undervaluing Clean, Private, and Accurate Data

Using outdated or inaccurate data undermines the effectiveness of AI, while poor data security practices expose your organization to breaches and reputational risks. ***Without clean, up-to-date, and secure data, your AI systems will produce unreliable insights and erode stakeholder trust.*** There are many tactics and practices spelled out throughout this book, but at a high level, be sure to conduct regular audits of your data to ensure accuracy, completeness, and relevance. Implement strict data security protocols, such as encryption and access controls, and comply with privacy regulations like General Data Protection Regulation (GDPR) or the Health Insurance Portability and Accountability Act (HIPAA). That may entail developing a custom large language model or generative pre-trained transformer (GPT) so anything you share in your prompts isn't integrating into public leaning sets, as detailed in Chapter 7.

Failure to Reflect and Assess

Failing to track the return on investment of AI initiatives and neglecting feedback loops will leave your nonprofit blind to what's working, resulting in wasted resources and missed opportunities. After all, how can you achieve a goal if you don't know what success looks like, and if you don't take stock of your progress and experience? ***Without clear metrics and regular evaluations, you risk continuing ineffective practices and failing to refine your strategy to maximize impact.***

To avoid this, ***establish clear key performance indicators (KPIs) at the outset of every AI project,*** such as time saved, funds raised, or engagement rates improved, and ensure these are tied to your organization's strategic goals. ***Pair this with structured feedback mechanisms, such as quarterly reviews, staff surveys, and stakeholder focus groups,*** to gather insights on AI performance and impact. Regularly review and refine your approach based on both quantitative and qualitative data, ensuring your AI initiatives remain effective, adaptive, and aligned with your mission.

Lack of Clear Ownership

When no one is explicitly responsible for overseeing AI initiatives, projects often stall or become directionless, leading to inefficiencies and wasted resources. ***Without a clear breakdown of responsibilities, critical opportunities may be missed and your team may struggle to leverage these powerful tools.***

This doesn't have to be complicated. Simply ***assign a dedicated AI lead or team to oversee implementation, training, and ongoing optimization of any AI tools.*** Clearly define roles and responsibilities within your organization, ensuring accountability and alignment with your strategic goals. Once everyone is clear on their role and how everything ties together, the potential of AI is at your fingertips.

Ignoring Ethical Considerations

Without clear ethical guidelines, your AI tools can unintentionally reinforce inequities or compromise your organization's values, as well as yield discriminatory outcomes and a loss of stakeholder trust. That's the last thing you want as you're adopting new tools to better serve your community!

To ensure you don't fall into this trap, ***develop an ethical AI framework that emphasizes transparency, fairness, and accountability.*** Regularly audit your data and algorithms for biases and establish protocols to ensure that AI outputs are reviewed by human decision-makers. Clearly communicate your ethical approach to your team, stakeholders, and beneficiaries to build trust and demonstrate your commitment to responsible AI use.

Dos and Don'ts

Do

- Create a clear, mission-driven road map for AI adoption to ensure alignment with your nonprofit's strategic goals and the needs of your community
- Encourage collaboration and a culture of innovation by empowering internal AI ambassadors to lead training, share best practices, and demystify the technology for others.
- Invest in continuous professional development for your entire team to build AI literacy and ensure effective adoption across all roles
- Establish an ethical AI framework that emphasizes transparency, fairness, and accountability, safeguarding your organization's values
- Maintain clean, private, and accurate data through regular audits and robust security measures, ensuring AI outputs are reliable and trustworthy

Don't

- Dive into large-scale AI projects without piloting smaller initiatives, as this can lead to inefficiencies and missed opportunities for learning
- Overlook the importance of clear ownership for AI initiatives, which can result in stalled progress and lack of accountability
- Ignore feedback loops and ROI tracking, leaving your nonprofit without the insights needed to refine and maximize the impact of AI tools

- Rely solely on automation without human oversight, risking errors and the loss of nuanced, mission-critical decision-making
- Neglect to communicate the value and purpose of AI tools to stakeholders, potentially undermining trust and buy-in for your initiatives

Conclusion

By staying informed about the latest trends in AI and thoughtfully integrating these tools into your nonprofit's operations, you can enhance your efficiency, improve your program delivery, and create a more significant impact in your community. As a nonprofit leader, *it is essential to focus on how AI can support and augment your mission, rather than getting distracted by the latest technological advancements.* By responsibly deploying AI tools within your organization to gain practical experience, combined with continuing to sharpen your saw with ongoing professional development, you can stay ahead of the pack and ensure your organization remains at the forefront of innovation in the nonprofit sector.

By carefully considering how AI can enhance your operations, engaging AI ambassadors within your organization, and maintaining a focus on ethical and responsible use, you can leverage AI to drive positive change and outperform your peers. Stay curious, keep learning, and remain adaptable as you navigate the ever-evolving landscape of AI in the nonprofit sector.

Interviewee Bio

danah boyd is a distinguished scholar and thought leader whose work explores the intersection of technology, society, and ethics. As the founder and president of Data & Society, a research institute dedicated to studying the social implications of data-centric technologies, danah has been at the forefront of examining how AI, big data, and Machine Learning shape societal norms and institutions. She is also a professor of communication at Cornell University, contributing to the discourse on technology's role in governance, equity, and privacy. Recognized as one of the leading voices in tech ethics, danah's research on online communities and algorithmic accountability has influenced policy and practice globally. Her insights underscore the critical need for nonprofits and other organizations to navigate AI adoption responsibly, ensuring it serves the public good. https://www.linkedin.com/in/danahboyd/

Resource Review

- Nonprofit Technology Network (NTEN): https://www.nten.org—Join a community of nonprofit tech leaders and explore training opportunities to build your organization's AI capacity.

- TechSoup: https://www.techsoup.org—Access affordable software and tools, plus webinars and guides on implementing AI and other tech solutions tailored for nonprofits.

- Beth Kanter's blog: https://bethkanter.org—Dive into Beth's insights on technology and social impact, including practical advice on using AI to enhance nonprofit effectiveness and innovation.

- Nonprofit Tech for Good: https://www.nptechforgood.com—Stay informed with articles, a newsletter, active social media presences, webinars, and resources on the latest technology trends, including AI, to help your nonprofit enhance digital strategies and maximize impact.

- Nonprofit Learning Lab: https://www.nonprofitlearninglab.org—Attend webinars and workshops to gain practical skills for AI adoption, data privacy, and fostering a culture of innovation in your nonprofit.

- AI for Good Foundation: https://ai4good.org—Access initiatives, events, and tools designed to promote the ethical and effective use of AI for social impact, including nonprofit-specific applications.

- Fundraising.AI: https://fundraising.ai—Explore this hub of AI-focused resources, tools, and best practices designed to help nonprofits integrate AI into their fundraising strategies and operations.

- Candid.org: https://learning.candid.org—Learn from courses, webinars, and articles on how AI is revolutionizing grantmaking and program evaluation.

- GrantStation: https://grantstation.com—Use AI-supported tools to find funding opportunities that align with your mission and streamline grant application processes.

- *MIT Technology Review*: https://www.technologyreview.com—Read expert analysis on AI trends and emerging technologies that can help you remain at the cutting edge of nonprofit innovation.

Chapter 4.1

Predictive Medical Analytics Case Study: Michael J. Fox Foundation and Sensoria Health

Based on insights from an interview with Davide Vigano.

Background and Problem Statement

The Michael J. Fox Foundation (MJFF) has long been at the forefront of Parkinson's disease research, with a mission to find a cure and improve the quality of life for those affected by the disease. Despite significant advancements, **one of the persistent challenges has been the ability to diagnose, and then monitor and eventually predict, the progression of Parkinson's disease in individual patients.** Accurate and early detection and prediction is crucial for tailoring personalized and timely treatments, improving patient outcomes, and accelerating research efforts.

Sensoria Health (Sensoria), a company specializing in truly wearable technologies, remote patient monitoring, and data analytics, recognized the potential of AI in addressing this challenge. The goal was to collect accurate human locomotion data and then **leverage Machine Learning (ML) and AI-driven predictive analytics to provide accurate and individualized insights into disease diagnosis and progression, ultimately enhancing patient care and research precision.**

AI-Driven Solution

In collaboration with MJFF, Sensoria developed an innovative ML/AI-driven solution that integrated wearable technology with advanced predictive analytics. They **equipped patients with "smart socks" embedded with textile pressure sensors** *and microelectronics to monitor gait, balance, and other movement-related metrics in real time.* These wearables collected meaningful data, which was then analyzed using ML algorithms to detect subtle patterns and may eventually help predict disease progression.

Their AI model is being trained on a dataset comprising historical patient data, clinical findings, and sensor-derived metrics, with AI identifying patterns people may have missed. By continuously learning from this data, the AI system will improve its predictive accuracy over time. The system then uses this data and its sense of the associated patterns to identify early warning signs of disease progression, enabling proactive interventions and personalized treatment plans.

Results and Impact

The implementation of predictive medical analytics through AI provided significant results for both MJFF and the patients involved. Key outcomes included the following:

- **Increased predictive accuracy:** The AI-driven solution demonstrated a remarkable improvement in predicting disease progression compared to traditional methods. This allowed for better-informed clinical decisions and more timely interventions. It also directly benefitted patients, since *the sensors in the smart socks may help accurately predict risk of falls* before *they happen, thereby mitigating a key health risk for those with Parkinson's.*

- **Personalized treatment plans:** With more precise predictions, researchers and health care providers may be able to tailor treatment plans to individual patients, enhancing the effectiveness of therapies and improving patient outcomes.

- **Enhanced research capabilities:** The rich dataset generated by the wearables provided researchers with invaluable insights into the disease's progression, facilitating the development of new therapeutic approaches and accelerating the search for a cure.

- **Patient empowerment:** Patients benefited from real-time feedback on their condition, enabling them to be more proactive in managing their health and participating actively in their treatment plans.

Lessons Learned

The collaboration between MJFF and Sensoria highlighted several critical lessons for nonprofits considering AI-driven solutions:

- **Data is key:** The success of AI-driven predictive analytics hinges on the availability of high-quality, comprehensive data. Investing in robust data collection and management processes is essential.
- **Embrace collaboration:** The partnership between a nonprofit and a technology company proved to be highly effective. *Combining domain expertise with technical prowess can drive innovation and achieve impactful results.*
- **Continuous learning:** AI systems improve over time as they learn from new data. It's important to *establish mechanisms for continuous data collection and model refinement to maintain and enhance predictive accuracy.*
- **Client-centric approach:** Engaging end users and beneficiaries—patients in this case—and incorporating their feedback ensures any technology you deploy is user-friendly and provides tangible benefits to those you serve, driving both adoption and impact.

Interviewee Bio

Davide Vigano is the cofounder and CEO of Sensoria, a leading developer of smart garments and wearable fitness technology. With over 25 years of experience in engineering, marketing, and product management, he has been instrumental in integrating AI and proprietary textile sensors into wearable devices, transforming health and fitness monitoring. Under his leadership, Sensoria has developed the Human Augmentation Platform, which combines microelectronics and AI algorithms to convert data into actionable information for patients and clinicians in real time. Prior to founding Sensoria, Davide had a distinguished career at Microsoft, where he served as general manager of the Health Solutions Group and vice president of the Worldwide Small and Midmarket Solutions & Partners Medium Business division.

Chapter 5

How to Sell AI Upstream and Downstream Within Your Organization

Based on insights from an interview with Shawn Olds.

Interest in AI has surged since the launch of ChatGPT, which helped GenAI enter the mainstream of both society and the nonprofit sector. It's also disrupted traditional models of technology adoption. Gone are the days of enterprise technology licenses approved by the board and CEO. Now, anyone on your team can log in to GenAI platforms like Claude, Gemini, or ChatGPT and access them for free. But the data is clear: *organizational adoption in the nonprofit sector is lagging behind individual use.*

That means it's up to passionate evangelists like you to introduce the potential of AI to your organization. This is a bottom-up movement, and trailblazers not afraid to try the tech on for size are the ones driving progress. But many falling behind are scared, resistant to change. Guardrails are needed to protect sensitive data and client information, but somehow this must align with and even bolster a culture of innovation and experimentation. So, how do you walk all these lines and encourage the responsible adoption of AI and other technologies, while safeguarding your nonprofit and the community it serves? *How do you build excitement within your organization and support a graceful, intentional transition to embracing a more tech-forward philosophy?*

Critical Skills and Competencies
Lead with Impact and Application

The first thing to realize if you're passionate about introducing the wondrous possibilities of AI to a resistant organization or leader is that ***it's critical to avoid technology for tech's sake or lead off with** how the tech works; instead, step 1 is to clearly articulate **WHY it stands to benefit a teammate and the organization.*** This book covers a huge range of use cases and applications to help your nonprofit and your team raise more money more easily, expand your audience and impact, run a tighter ship with less time, and conceive and execute new and better programs. *That* is why AI is most likely to excite your colleagues. Meet them where they are, taking the time to identify challenges, obstacles, or opportunities for efficiencies, and then explaining in simple terms how AI can address those needs. Or better yet, *show them*. ***Consider busting out your laptop when meeting with a resistant colleague and prompting AI to complete an actual task in real time, showcasing the technology's power and quickness.***

Sample Dialogue

Colleague: "I don't have time to learn AI—my plate is full!"

You: "I totally get that! In fact, AI is meant to *save* you time. Let's take something you already do, like drafting an email. Watch this—I'll ask ChatGPT to write a donor thank-you email in 10 seconds. Now, instead of spending 20 minutes drafting one from scratch, you can edit and personalize it. ***Think of AI as your personal assistant rather than extra work.***"

Once you've helped folks understand why they stand to benefit by adopting the technology, then you can move into how it works, sharing elementary concepts and definitions like those covered in Chapter 1. Most likely, though, you'll also have to overcome a few concerns and objections about the technology itself.

Navigate Resistance

As a nonprofit leader advocating for the adoption of AI, you'll likely encounter resistance from colleagues who feel wary of this new technology. ***Concerns about a Terminator future, job loss, or the potential for unethical use of AI are common and valid.***

Acknowledging these fears is not just about diffusing tension—it's about building trust and creating an open environment where colleagues feel heard. These conversations are critical because they lay the foundation for thoughtful and strategic AI implementation that aligns with your mission and values. ***The more you can address concerns head-on, the easier it will be to move forward as a unified team,*** leveraging AI to advance your organization's goals in fundraising, program delivery, and beyond.

Sample Dialogue

Colleague: "AI is going to take over jobs. I don't want to be replaced."

You: ***"AI is a tool to help us work smarter, not replace us.*** Think of it like Excel—spreadsheets didn't replace accountants, they just made them more efficient. AI can automate repetitive tasks so you can focus on high-impact work that requires creativity, relationship-building, and strategic thinking."

When these topics come up, ***focus on transparency and empathy, followed by education and examples, and end on the big picture by once again reinforcing how AI is a tool to advance your mission.*** Start by validating their concerns with statements such as "I completely understand why AI might feel intimidating—it's a big shift." Then pivot to education by sharing how your nonprofit can use AI responsibly, such as automating repetitive tasks so staff can focus on deeper, mission-driven work. Use real-world examples—like how chatbots have helped other nonprofits enhance donor engagement without replacing human connection. Finally, ***frame AI adoption as a tool to amplify your impact, not replace people.*** To prepare for these conversations, consider reading *Co-Intelligence: Living and Working with AI* by Ethan Mollick (Portfolio, 2024), attending webinars from the Nonprofit Technology Network (https://www.nten.org/), or leveraging any of the resources featured at the end of this chapter to create talking points tailored to your organization's mission. With preparation and compassion, you can turn AI skepticism into meaningful dialogue that drives progress.

Address Job Security

One of the most common and pressing concerns with AI is job security. The best way to address this is to ***help your team understand that bots aren't coming for their*** *jobs; people who know how to use them are.* Embracing the wave is the only way to stay relevant. Stress from day one that *the most powerful AI team is the human-machine team.* There are tasks AI can accomplish in minutes that would take a human weeks or months, but there are also things that only humans can do.

For instance, consider the process of writing grant applications. AI can quickly analyze past successful proposals, identify recurring themes, and even draft initial templates. However, the nuance of aligning a grant proposal with your nonprofit's mission, values, and the unique priorities of the funder requires the expertise of your development staff. Not to mention, *it's imperative to double-check AI's work as it regularly includes "hallucinations" in its outputs,* and false citations or factually incorrect statements in a grant application will almost always sink your battleship. AI can save hours of administrative work, but it's your team's insight, creativity, and relationship-building skills that will ultimately win the funding.

By clearly delineating the roles AI can play versus the irreplaceable contributions of your staff, you can alleviate concerns about job displacement and instead inspire excitement about the potential for greater impact. Equip your team with training to use AI as a collaborator, not a competitor, and emphasize how it can make their work more fulfilling by freeing them to focus on the aspects of their jobs they value most.

Encourage Experimentation

AI is still in its early stages, and although it's growing fast, many people haven't used it. Unlike you, your colleagues don't yet think of AI as a key tool when they face challenges, and they may even be a bit scared by it. Now that you've assuaged these concerns and connected the dots between the technology and your mission, the next step is to invite your colleagues to give AI a test drive. *Encourage everyone in the organization to spend 10–15 minutes a day on AI for any tasks they'd like.* Keeping your proposal to embrace AI bite-sized helps mitigate the fear of integrating new technology. Break down the implementation process into manageable steps to ensure smooth adoption. Maintain open communication and provide support to address any concerns or challenges that arise.

When you begin this experiment, some may draft emails or reports, while others create images or even short videos, but either way, they'll get used to leveraging AI as a tool to support their work. Initially, this may not yield significant results, but after a couple of weeks, you'll start seeing six-hour projects completed in an hour with a high level of excellence. These tipping points spark excitement and quickly lead to AI being integrated into daily workflows. Your approach will likely differ if you're not a senior executive who can institute a staff-wide policy like this. For example, *if you're a frontline staffer, request a month to experiment and prove the value, and track return on investment (ROI) meticulously.*

Promote At-Home Use

One reason AI is more "sticky" than other workplace technologies is that people can use AI in their personal lives, making it easier for them to get comfortable with AI before bringing it into their jobs. *Expand your efforts to encourage experimentation by inviting colleagues to try AI in everyday life,* whether that's planning a trip and using AI tools to generate itineraries, thinking up recipes based on whatever's in the fridge, drafting emails and social media posts, and supporting just about any form of education, from learning new languages to coding. *By getting people comfortable using AI outside of work, you reduce their resistance and make workplace adoption much easier.*

Cultivate Community

As your nonprofit begins to take baby steps toward AI adoption, it's important to create a sense of shared purpose and camaraderie. Laggards who feel uneasy about the transition are more likely to feel isolated, which can deepen their insecurities. Meanwhile, others on the team may be thriving, and their enthusiasm can serve as powerful encouragement for peers. To bridge this gap, *host a weekly full-team meeting during the first month or two of your AI experimentation to celebrate small wins, address challenges, and create a space where everyone—regardless of their comfort level—can learn together.* Encourage team members to share their experiences, such as how AI has saved them time or helped solve a problem, and make sure to validate concerns or roadblocks as part of the learning process.

One of the most powerful aspects of generative AI (GenAI) is its ability to benefit the entire organization—not just a single department. While predictive AI might focus solely on fundraising or program delivery, as a general enabling technology, GenAI can empower *every* team, from finance and marketing to development and operations. For example, one team's success in using AI to streamline donor communications might inspire another to explore how it can improve budget forecasting. ***Use these weekly meetings to showcase cross-functional wins, emphasizing the broad impact of AI across the organization.*** Document these early successes and share them widely—through internal case studies, presentations to your board, or even external communications with donors and stakeholders. By cultivating a sense of community and celebrating progress together, you'll create a culture of innovation and learning that builds momentum for AI adoption.

Technical Integration

Now that you've successfully learned to crawl and walk, it's time to run! This book contains a wide range of practical tips and tools for applying AI in myriad ways throughout your nonprofit. Just remember that ***as you prepare to graduate to more advanced use cases, as your efforts mature, taking an intentional, methodical approach to leveraging AI is critical to your success.*** That means taking the time to clearly articulate your goals, needs, and expectations before you dive in the deep end of any AI applications, especially when it involves integrating AI into your nonprofit's existing systems and processes. And ***any plans to use AI should begin with mini experiments to assess value and confirm assumptions: start small and scale up.***

Begin by identifying specific tasks where AI can make an immediate impact, such as data entry, content creation, or social media management. Use AI tools to automate these tasks and free up your team's time for more strategic activities. Establish a clear plan for integrating AI tools into your workflows, ensuring that they align with your organization's goals and objectives. Ensure that everyone on the team is on board with the new technology. ***Even after you've wrapped up the weekly all-hands meetings, continue to offer training sessions and create opportunities for team members to learn from each other.*** During team meetings, have members share how they've used AI to solve problems or complete tasks more efficiently, and invite them to share any challenges or obstacles in hopes that someone else may offer solutions. This peer learning approach helps demystify AI and encourages its adoption across the organization. Continuously evaluate the effectiveness of AI integration and make necessary adjustments to optimize performance and achieve desired outcomes.

Track AI's ROI

One of the biggest challenges in selling AI internally is demonstrating its ROI. Many nonprofits are hesitant to adopt new technology without concrete evidence of its benefits. ***To build confidence in AI, track key metrics that showcase its impact,*** such as the following:

- **Time savings:** Measure how much time AI saves by streamlining or automating common tasks (e.g., AI-generated emails versus manual writing time).
- **Cost reduction:** Track decreases in outsourcing or administrative expenses.
- **Donor engagement:** Compare email open rates, donation conversion rates, and engagement metrics before and after AI-assisted campaigns; it's often also helpful to quantify responsiveness in terms of turnaround time when news breaks or a window of opportunity opens.
- **Increased program reach and impact:** Use AI to analyze trends and identify new opportunities for program expansion, and track how this translates to more clients served or services provided.

To measure these effectively, ***set up before-and-after comparisons, track outcomes using analytics tools, and collect feedback from staff about how AI has affected their workload.***

Pitfalls and Solutions

Ignoring Data Privacy and Security

Nonprofits often handle sensitive donor, beneficiary, and program data, making data privacy and security a critical consideration when adopting AI tools. Any breach of this information could not only harm the people you serve but also damage your organization's reputation and erode trust with stakeholders. *As AI tools process and analyze data, it's critical you ensure compliance with data protection regulations like General Data Protection Regulation (GDPR), the California Consumer Privacy Act (CCPA), or other local privacy laws.* Overlooking this aspect could lead to compliance issues, financial penalties, or even loss of donor confidence.

To address this pitfall, *start by conducting a data audit to identify the types of sensitive information your organization handles and assess your current security measures.* Choose AI tools with a proven track record of strong encryption, secure storage, and compliance with relevant data protection regulations. Consider creating your own custom large language models or generative pre-trained transformer (GPT), as detailed Chapter 21, so that none of the information you share in prompts is integrated into public AI training data. *Create a clear data privacy policy that outlines who can access sensitive data and how it will be used.* Establish a data governance team or point person to oversee security protocols and respond to potential threats. Finally, make it a habit to regularly review and update your data security measures, especially as new threats and technologies emerge. By embedding privacy and security into your AI strategy, you can protect your data while building confidence in AI adoption across your organization.

Relying on AI Champions

In these early days, too many nonprofits assume that because one or two staff members are successfully using AI tools, the organization has "checked the box" on AI adoption. *While having enthusiastic early adopters is a great start, treating AI as the responsibility of just a few individuals limits its potential impact and creates bottlenecks.* AI's true power lies in its ability to enhance operations across departments—from fundraising and program delivery to marketing and operations.

Failing to embed AI across the organization risks leaving valuable opportunities on the table and reinforces silos that can stifle innovation.

To avoid this, take a strategic approach to AI adoption by ensuring it becomes part of the organizational culture, not just the responsibility of a few champions. ***Start by identifying areas across all teams where AI can streamline workflows or solve recurring challenges, such as drafting or editing communications and reports, automating meeting transcription, analyzing large datasets, creating presentations, or managing routine scheduling and follow-ups.*** Again, organization-wide training sessions help to demystify AI tools, showcase success stories, and address obstacles impeding adoption. Finally, ***set clear goals and metrics for AI adoption that align with your nonprofit's mission,*** and hold leaders accountable for encouraging their teams to explore and use AI tools. By positioning AI as an organization-wide asset rather than an individual effort, you can unlock its full potential and amplify your impact.

Failure to Align AI to Strategic Objectives

One of the most significant strategic pitfalls nonprofits face when adopting technology is failing to align AI initiatives with your nonprofit's overarching goals. ***Without a clear strategy, AI efforts can become fragmented, focusing on isolated projects rather than driving meaningful impact across the organization.*** This can lead to wasted resources, missed opportunities, and frustration among staff. For example, implementing an AI tool to analyze social media sentiment might seem innovative, but if your primary focus is improving service delivery or scaling volunteer engagement, this initiative may divert resources from more impactful priorities. To avoid this, ***start by identifying your nonprofit's key objectives and asking how AI can help you achieve them.*** Then, develop a clear plan that outlines specific goals, timelines, and measurable outcomes for AI implementation. Share this plan with your team to ensure everyone understands how AI supports the organization's mission and revisit it regularly to adjust based on feedback and results.

Another strategic misstep is neglecting to track ROI for AI initiatives. ***Without proper measurement, it's difficult to evaluate whether AI tools are delivering value or to make the case for continued investment.*** Build ROI tracking into your strategy from the start by setting metrics tailored to each initiative, such as time saved, funds raised, or improvements in program efficiency. For instance, if you're using AI to optimize donor outreach, track the increase in donor retention or gift size. Regularly share these results with staff, board members, and other stakeholders to build buy-in and enthusiasm for AI. *By treating AI as a strategic asset rather than a one-off experiment, you'll not only maximize its impact but also position your organization for long-term innovation and success.*

Road Map to the Future

As we move forward, no doubt AI technology will become increasingly accessible and tailored to the nonprofit sector. *Tools will evolve to be more user-friendly, cost-effective, and mission-aligned, enabling even small organizations to integrate AI into their daily operations.* Expect to see AI tools that can simplify program evaluation, automate donor stewardship with highly personalized outreach, and even predict community needs to guide program design. However, as the technology becomes more pervasive, the gap between AI adopters and non-adopters will widen. *Organizations that fail to embrace AI risk falling behind, as funders, donors, and other stakeholders start to expect nonprofits to leverage data-driven solutions to demonstrate impact and efficiency.* That means the need for trailblazing champions—those within nonprofits who see the potential of AI and actively advocate for its adoption, just like you—has never been greater. *Now* is your time!

Dos and Don'ts
Do

- Use AI in real time when meeting with resistant colleagues to help them wrap their heads around how the tool can be used to quickly, effectively solve real problems
- Help your team understand that AI isn't coming for their jobs; people who know how to use it are
- Clarify the irreplaceable contributions of your staff as opposed to the roles AI can play or support to address concerns about job displacement

- Start small and encourage your nonprofit to agree to a short trail period where everyone is expected to spend 10–15 minutes a day exploring AI tools and weekly meetings are used to share progress, successes, and challenges
- Request a month to experiment and prove the value of AI, tracking ROI meticulously, if you're a frontline staffer
- Clearly articulate your goals, needs, and expectations before you adopt any advanced AI applications, especially those that require integration with existing systems and processes
- Support data privacy and security by conducting a data audit and creating a clear data privacy policy
- Create a clear AI strategy aligned with your strategic objectives by identifying your nonprofit's key objectives and asking how AI can help you achieve them

Don't

- Dive right into how AI works, instead of leading off with determining why it can help your nonprofit increase impact and save valuable staff time
- Ignore the concerns and reservations of your colleagues—listen to their concerns with empathy, educate them on why AI is a game changer, including illustrative examples, and always connect the tech tools to your strategic objectives and mission
- Try to split tasks into what's best done by people or machines, versus promoting the concept that the most powerful AI team is the human-machine team
- Stop hosting AI-focused team meetings and offering training and support after your initial experimentation; sustained forums are key to long-term success
- Ignore data privacy and securing, including ensuring compliance with regulations like GDPR, CCPA, or other local privacy laws
- Assume that just because you have one or two staffers using AI, that's sufficient, instead of pushing for adoption throughout the organization

Conclusion

AI offers immense potential for nonprofits to enhance efficiency, effectiveness, and overall impact. By strategically implementing AI, you can streamline workflows, empower your team, and improve a wide range of existing systems and processes. But you probably already know that, and the real question addressed in this chapter is how you can bring the rest of your organization along for the ride, build excitement, and overcome resistance to AI adoption. Start small and go from there, tackling concerns head-on and demonstrating AI's value across various departments to foster a culture of innovation and drive positive change. ***Help your team recognize that the jobs of the future will involve working with technology, and if they're concerned about job security, then embracing AI is one of the best things they can do to protect their careers.*** Don't forget to keep a close eye on pitfalls such as data security concerns and the lack of alignment with organizational goals, as these will quickly derail any progress. And as you get traction, ensure your organization cultivates a culture of constant learning by staying informed about the latest developments and continuously exploring new ways to leverage AI. As you do all this, you will help your nonprofit unlock the full potential of this transformative technology and create a lasting impact for your organization and the communities you serve.

Interviewee Bio

Shawn N. Olds is a technology and communications thought leader who is the cofounder and founding CEO of boodleAI. Shawn has found ample success in the private, government, and higher education sectors and continues to dedicate time to supporting nonprofit organizations and their missions. He has served on nonprofit boards primarily focused on youth education and veterans service organizations for 30 years, while continuing to build companies both domestically and internationally. He has taught as an adjunct at the University of Dubai, authored a textbook on entrepreneurship, and in 2024 was inducted into the American Society for Artificial Intelligence. https://www.linkedin.com/in/shawnnolds/

Resource Review

- TechSoup Courses: https://techsoup.course.tc/—A wide range of helpful, low-cost online courses for nonprofit leaders around all aspects of technology, including a series on AI for Nonprofits: How to Get Started, where you can learn how to present AI tools and their value to your stakeholders, while making a compelling case to both executive leadership and team members for adoption.

- AI for Everyone by Andrew Ng: https://www.coursera.org/learn/ai-for-everyone—This course will help you understand AI fundamentals, so you can confidently engage both top executives and your team when selling AI across all levels of your organization.

- NTEN: https://www.nten.org—Find resources on how nonprofits can build a strategic approach to data and AI adoption, including advice on how to communicate AI's value to all levels of your organization.

- *MIT Sloan Management Review*: https://sloanreview.mit.edu/—Their AI Leadership Forum offers access to articles and case studies on how leaders are introducing AI to their organizations, offering tips for how you can engage senior leadership and your team with AI strategies.

- Microsoft AI for Social Good: https://www.microsoft.com/en-us/ai/ai-for-good—Explore how AI can drive social impact and learn strategies to effectively communicate this potential to key stakeholders, helping you sell AI solutions internally.

- ITU AI for Good Global Summit: https://aiforgood.itu.int—Engage with global leaders to explore the opportunities AI offers nonprofits and find best practices for championing AI to different levels within your organization.

- Ethan Mollick on LinkedIn: https://www.linkedin.com/in/emollick/—Prolific, unbiased GenAI influencer from Wharton Business School, offering insights and updates on AI trends.

Chapter 5.1

AI as Your Institutional Memory

Based on insights from an interview with Astrid J. Scholz, PhD.

A lot of the excitement about "AI for good" or "AI for nonprofits" focuses on two major concerns in the social sector: fundraising and program delivery. It is therefore not surprising that significant energy in this book and elsewhere is focused on using AI to parse the interests of funders, use their publicly available documents to write better grant applications, and digest information to craft better communications. On the program delivery side, there are some clever applications of AI, such as using chatbots to connect clients to the content, services, and experiences they need.

All this is important, but it overlooks **a major use case for AI: to leverage the knowledge of what has already been done, and why, to address the wicked problems of the world.** As an industry, the nonprofit world routinely forgets what it already knows. Theories of change and logic models evolve, staff leave, and data about why, what, and how an organization is working is stored in disparate systems and storage media that may lose backward compatibility.

AI enables us to analyze past projects for efficacy more quickly than human effort would allow and suggest optimization iterations for the future. **What if instead of continuing to repeat ineffective approaches due to staff turnover, we were able to learn instantly what has worked within our organization, what hasn't, and get ideas about how to improve our strategies for success?** As the costs of large language models (LLMs)-as-a-service come down, and as it becomes ever easier and cheaper to build new applications, it becomes possible to ingest an organization's data stores, derive insights from across a multitude of sources, and serve them up in ways that integrate into the workflow.

The Price of Data Graves

Take major foundations, for example. Many of them have long supported program areas like sustainable sanitation that requires lots of innovation, years of testing, prototyping, scaling solutions, and involves hundreds, if not thousands, of stakeholders around the world. ***A typical foundation will amass many thousands of internal documents in a variety of formats detailing their research, field analyses, diligence and grantmaking processes, grant agreements, outcome measurements, and staff reports*** assessing the efficacy of their programs. The vast majority of that information never sees the light of day and languishes in internal systems.

Similarly, ***the typical nonprofit or social enterprise generates a lot of research, analysis, insights, strategies, and program designs—again, across a multitude of media and formats—that all remain largely internal.*** The exceptions are the targeted communications designed for your funders and general audiences. The bulk of the information about what you do, how, and why it works remains in your internal systems. Typically this is poorly organized and does not lend itself to institutional memory and sensemaking. All this is completely understandable: the curation and organization of all the things that program staff are learning while developing and implementing programs are typically not included in the already scarce funding that many organizations work with, and ***it's hard to set aside the time and resources to capture the collective wisdom of an organization and its people.***

This is what we think of as "data graves," and they're the places where experiences, insights, and learnings from doing the work of social change go to die. ***Data graves occur when you fail to take a systematic approach to storing, documenting, and making sense of your accumulated data and the knowledge and wisdom contained therein.*** Too often, this internal data is stored in haphazard collections of digital, analog, writings, recordings, databases, and multimedia files.

I saw the impact of this up close and personally. Some eight years after I left a good-sized nongovernmental organization, I still regularly received phone calls and emails from current staff, asking for context and clarification for some work I had done more than a decade prior. I spent hours reiterating information that was shared when I first presented the report, and aside from wasting my time, no doubt the information I shared was a bit foggy after so many years, which is a breeding ground for human error. ***Sticking with manual systems to archive programs, best practices, and organizational intelligence simply won't cut it anymore.***

Using AI to Create Data Lakes

A better way is possible, and surprisingly, it's not going to break your bank. In an example from India, SELCO Foundation (https://selcofoundation.org/), a 30-year-old nonprofit focused on community-centered design of clean energy solutions, ***trained an AI platform (Apurva.Ai) on several years of internal data from reports, case studies, stakeholder interviews, documentation, contemporaneous notes, voice and video recordings,*** and so on. As a result, the AI can now seamlessly insert insights from this collective knowledge system into meetings, or new documents being created, in a variety of languages. They have turned what might have been a "data grave" into a "data lake" that can enhance and refresh the organization's impact.

It's hard to convey how impressive this application is: ***SELCO's AI does not just sit in a Zoom meeting like so many transcription bots but actively participates with references to internal documents.*** The LLM serves up pertinent information as you are writing, say, a program plan—drawing on the organization's specific trove of past insights, foundational documents, and learnings. And in my favorite use case, it ***helps new staff get up to speed on the historical work of the organization as part of their onboarding process,*** supporting their learning about the organization's history, programs, and foundational beliefs and narratives.

SELCO's AI ***makes the rich, deep institutional knowledge and insights that the organization has amassed from staff and stakeholders over the years easily accessible,*** not just the shallow information that is typical of grant reports and customer relationship management (CRM) records. The mind boggles with the possibilities if more organizations systematically mined their data graves and turned them into data lakes that can inform sector-specific AI models and tools to help the social change industry do its work better, cheaper, and more effectively.

Interviewee Bio

Astrid J. Scholz, PhD, is a polypreneur with a purpose: she is the cofounder and CFO/COO of Armillaria, a tech-for-good company that creates digital infrastructure that more effectively and equitably mobilizes data, people, and capital toward addressing the most urgent challenges of our time. She is also a cofounder and game master at Game The System, a company that is creating serious games about stupid systems, using the power of empathy to change real-world outcomes. Previously, Astrid cofounded Zebras Unite, a global movement for and by founders and investors who are building the businesses that are better for the world. https://www.linkedin.com/in/ajscholz/

Chapter 6

AI and Technology Planning: Figuring Out Your Tech

Based on insights from an interview with Afua Bruce.

In this chapter, you will uncover the essential steps to effectively plan and integrate AI and technology within your organization. Many nonprofits are eager to dive into AI tools for fundraising, marketing, or program delivery, but ***without a solid technology plan, you risk ending up with unused solutions that don't align with your mission.*** Proper technology planning ensures that your tools fit seamlessly into your workflow, maximizing impact and utility.

Technology doesn't implement itself; it requires dedicated capacity, including both people and money. By thinking ahead, you can leverage AI to enhance your operations and better serve your community. Just don't forget that ***data is the currency of today's information economy, so your nonprofit must thoughtfully manage both its internal and external data.*** So, let's look at the key steps necessary for successful technology planning.

Critical Skills and Competencies
Answer the Big Questions

Begin your technology planning by answering foundational questions: What is your organization here to do? Whom do you serve? And who is delivering that work? Specificity is key. Review your mission, vision, values, and strategic plans. ***Engage all levels of employees—from executive management to entry-level staff—to understand their goals and any key obstacles impeding impact, taking the time to ensure*** *that addressing those challenges aligns with your organizational objectives.* Consolidate these insights into a brief document, no more than a page, to highlight what truly matters, and make sure to circulate that document internally to confirm a shared understanding. By having clarity and consensus on these foundational aspects, you create a solid groundwork for your technology planning process.

Look Inside

Next, examine how your nonprofit accomplishes its mission. What does service delivery look like? *Identify internal data, processes, systems, and workflows; mapping these will help you understand how to best support your staff and volunteers with technology.* Often, initial conversations about activities provide insights into decision-making processes and internal workflows. Use follow-up questions to pull on these insightful threads and provide a more comprehensive understanding of how work is done.

Consider how your daily operations align with your stated strategic goals. Ensure that your time and resources are directed toward activities that support your goals. Understanding these internal dynamics is crucial for identifying where technology can enhance efficiency and effectiveness. *By thoroughly examining your internal data and processes, you can pinpoint specific areas where technology can streamline operations, reduce redundancies, and improve overall productivity.* Add these key use cases and applications to the draft of your technology plan, likely adding another couple of pages to detail how AI can serve as a *tool* to advance your efforts.

Assess Existing Tech Tools

Review your current tech stack. *What tools are you already using, and how well do they serve your needs?* Slack, Salesforce, Google Docs—it all counts. Are there any that should be retired to streamline operations? Document your findings in a way that your team can easily understand, adding this to your tech plan. For more tech-savvy organizations, you can also include technical specifications, required capacity, available APIs, and how datasets are maintained. *By conducting a thorough technology assessment, you can identify gaps, redundancies, and opportunities for improvement within your current tech stack, setting the stage for informed decision-making about future technology investments.*

Envision Possibilities

Once you have a clear understanding of your current situation, it's time to envision the future, tech-empowered version of your organization. Explore how AI and other advanced technologies can enhance your mission and operations. Engaging stakeholders in brainstorming sessions can be particularly valuable during this phase. By fostering a collaborative environment, you can gather diverse perspectives and innovative ideas that may not have been considered otherwise. Add this critical information to your technology plan, since *envisioning possibilities enables you to think beyond immediate needs and consider long-term impacts, ensuring that your technology investments are forward-thinking and capable of driving sustained growth and success.*

Resource Planning

The final step before you start identifying potential solutions and providers is to invite intentionality into resource allocation, enabling you to successfully implement and sustain new technology initiatives. *Identify the human, financial, and technical resources needed to implement and maintain your chosen technology solutions.* Develop a detailed resource plan that outlines the required investments in staff training, software, hardware, and ongoing support.

Consider potential funding sources, such as grants, donations, or partnerships, to support your technology investments. *Without careful, proactive resource planning, your AI adoption efforts will likely be undermined by unforeseen budget constraints and staffing limitations.* Finally, supplement these resource allocations with the goals and objectives they're intended to support. *Setting realistic timelines and milestones to track progress and ensure that your technology projects stay on track and within budget is the final component of your technology plan.* Once this is integrated, you're all set to go shopping!

Identify Potential Providers

Now that you've assessed your current tech stack, envisioned future possibilities, carved out resources, and defined your tech-empowered goals, it's time to identify potential service providers who can help address your needs and goals. It isn't just about picking a vendor; it's about finding a *partner* who understands your mission, values, and operational challenges. **As a nonprofit leader, you need providers who align with your strategic goals, offer the right solutions, and have a proven track record of supporting organizations like yours.** This will help ensure your AI and tech investments are practical, sustainable, and impactful.

Start by researching vendors who have experience working with nonprofits or organizations of a similar scale and focus. **Use peer networks, forums, and nonprofit technology resources to gather recommendations.** Be sure to vet each provider's offerings against your needs by asking key questions: Do they understand the nonprofit sector? Can they demonstrate case studies or examples of past successes with similar organizations? Does their solution align with your technical requirements and budget constraints? **Nonprofit Technology Network (NTEN)** (https://www.nten.org/) **and TechSoup** (https://www.techsoup.org/) **are excellent starting points for finding potential providers and gathering real-world insights.** AI tools and online searches will also help you quickly compile and analyze a list of appropriate vendors.

Pick Your Partner

With a list of potential technology solutions in hand, it's time to share your technology plan, or more likely a subset of the information included in the form of a request for proposal (RFP), as detailed in the inset, "Guidelines for AI Vendor Selection." Be sure to review all responses critically, as this is a big decision that will be difficult to reverse. **Evaluate each solution based on factors such as cost, ease of implementation, scalability, and alignment with your organizational goals.**

Involve key stakeholders in this review process to ensure that the chosen solutions meet the needs of different departments and functions within your nonprofit. **Use AI to help create a decision matrix or rubric, clarifying your criteria and assigning values to each priority.** By systematically comparing the pros and cons of each option, you can make informed choices that best align with your priorities and resources.

Evaluate Outcomes and Integrate Tech

It's go time! Ensure any new tools integrate with your existing systems, and that you're able to enjoy the benefits of seamless data sharing that are key to aligning new technology with your overall strategy and planning. ***Revisit your milestones, timelines, and metrics for success now that you have a partner, updating your tech plan accordingly.*** It's important to understand how quantitatively and qualitatively AI tools compare to your organization's legacy tools; if the AI tools cannot perform at least at parity, reconsider deploying them. Then, of course, track progress. Did the new tech increase donations? Did it help you serve more clients? Successful tech integration ensures your new tools enhance rather than disrupt your existing operations, leading to improved outcomes and greater mission impact.

Pitfalls and Solutions

Underestimating the Investment

Implementing any new technology can be challenging, especially when your nonprofit is likely juggling a million other balls in the air at the same time. Success with adoption across your entire organization, not just a few early adopters, requires time and careful planning. ***Add a healthy cushion to your plans—typically, a 50% buffer is advisable given the early stage of this technology.*** And be prepared for an iterative process, where initial implementations may need adjustments based on feedback and performance. By acknowledging the complexity and dedicating sufficient time and resources to implementation, you will increase the likelihood of successful AI adoption and integration.

Not Engaging Middle Management

They say middle management is where good ideas go to die. But in nonprofits, that's rarely true. More often than not, it's the bridge between high-level vision and on-the-ground realities. ***Listen to mid-tier leaders intently to ensure a smooth transition and facilitate execution, as they often understand on-the-ground realities*** *alongside executive considerations.* Engaging middle management ensures that your technology plans are realistic and actionable. Once you adopt new technology, middle management can provide valuable feedback on the practical implications of new solutions, helping to identify challenges and opportunities for improvement. By involving them in the planning and implementation process, you foster a sense of ownership and commitment, leading to smoother transitions and more successful outcomes.

Staying in Your Silo

Failing to engage your community and clients when adopting AI can lead to tools that miss the mark, wasting resources and alienating those you aim to serve. That's why it's key to actively involve stakeholders—whether program beneficiaries, donors, or partners—in identifying needs and priorities. Use surveys, focus groups, or AI tools to gather insights, ensuring your solutions address real challenges and enhance impact. By centering your community's voices, you'll create equitable, inclusive, and effective technology that truly aligns with your mission.

Over-Automation and Ignoring Data Security

Over-relying on AI without proper safeguards can lead to inaccurate results, data breaches, and a failure to fully integrate AI into your team's workflows. *Instead of human-in-the-loop (HITL) strategy, adopt an AI in the decision-making loop approach where AI tools support—not replace—human decision-making.* This ensures outputs are reviewed critically and used appropriately. Be vigilant about the data you input into AI tools—avoid sharing sensitive or confidential information like Social Security numbers or other personally identifiable information that could compromise security or privacy. Simultaneously, evolve job roles to incorporate AI effectively, enabling staff to leverage AI insights in their decision-making processes.

Road Map to the Future

Looking ahead, expect more AI-integrated products, especially in GenAI. *The distinction between procuring new tools and adjusting processes to fit embedded AI*

will continue to blur. This evolution will affect how nonprofits research and adopt new technologies, emphasizing the importance of staying adaptable and informed. As AI technology advances, nonprofits must remain agile and responsive to leverage new opportunities and address emerging challenges.

Invest in ongoing education and training for your staff to ensure that they are equipped with the skills and knowledge needed to navigate the rapidly changing technology landscape. By fostering a culture of continuous learning and innovation, your nonprofit can stay ahead of the curve and effectively leverage new technologies to drive mission success.

Dos and Don'ts

Do

- Engage your team early in the process by involving staff across all levels, including middle management, to ensure buy-in, gather practical insights, and foster a sense of ownership over new technology initiatives
- Anchor your technology plan in your mission and strategic goals, ensuring that every tool you adopt directly supports your nonprofit's purpose and aligns with your long-term objectives
- Conduct a thorough review of your current tech stack, workflows, and internal processes to identify gaps, redundancies, and opportunities for improvement, creating a clear foundation for decision-making
- Vet potential providers by researching their experience working with similar nonprofits and evaluating their ability to align with your technical requirements, budget, and mission-driven needs
- Test new tools with small-scale pilot programs before implementing them organization-wide to identify potential issues, refine processes, and build confidence in your solutions
- Allocate sufficient resources for implementation and long-term maintenance, including a detailed budget that accounts for ongoing expenses and considering personnel allocations

- Stay future-focused by investing in scalable, cloud-based tools and regularly reviewing your technology plan to adapt to new advancements and the evolving needs of your organization

Don't

- Undertake any AI or technology initiatives without first articulating clear, measurable outcomes, indicators, and milestones against which progress can be evaluated
- Assume that what works for another nonprofit will work for yours; avoid adopting one-size-fits-all solutions without assessing how they align with your unique needs and workflows
- Ignore integration needs; ensure that new tools work seamlessly with your existing systems to avoid creating inefficiencies or extra work for staff
- Rely entirely on AI tools without implementing an HITL process to maintain accuracy, accountability, and oversight for AI-generated outcomes
- Overlook ethical considerations, such as biases in data or algorithms, which can unintentionally disadvantage certain groups or undermine trust in your initiatives
- Neglect to include adequate time and resources for staff training, as this will help ensure smooth adoption and effective use of new technologies
- Overlook data security risks that can lead to breaches of sensitive information; instead, remember to audit your existing data for accuracy and consistency, standardize data entry and management practices, and implement robust security measures to protect sensitive information

Conclusion

Technology planning for AI adoption is not just about tools—it's about aligning your nonprofit's mission with the right systems to enhance impact and efficiency. By starting with clarity on your goals, engaging stakeholders, and evaluating your existing tech stack, you will lay a strong foundation for success. Just remember to focus on creating a road map that balances your immediate needs with long-term goals. Thoughtful resource allocation, careful provider selection, and pilot testing will help ensure your technology investments are practical and sustainable.

As you embrace AI, remember that this journey is iterative. Stay adaptable, continuously update your systems, and invest in your team's education to keep pace with evolving technologies. ***By following the actionable tips and strategies in this chapter, you'll not only position your nonprofit to leverage AI effectively but also create a culture of innovation and continuous improvement.*** Let your technology plan be the blueprint that transforms your vision into reality, one smart, intentional step at a time.

Interviewee Bio

Afua Bruce is a recognized public interest technologist, strategist, policymaker, and author dedicated to guiding organizations through the complexities of technology planning. From her leadership roles at the White House Office of Science and Technology Policy and the FBI to her service at IBM and DataKind, Afua has helped shape how organizations identify, assess, fund, and implement emerging technologies, including AI, in ethical and impactful ways. As the coauthor of *The Tech That Comes Next*, she provides a framework for organizations to align their technology investments with their values and build for long-term sustainability. Afua was also recognized with a statue in the IF/THEN exhibit of impactful women in STEM. https://www.linkedin.com/in/afua-bruce/

Resource Review

- *The Tech That Comes Next* (Afua Bruce and Amy Sample Ward, Wiley, 2022)—Explores how technology can be reimagined and built to serve the greater good, offering actionable insights for nonprofits, funders, and technologists to create a more equitable future.
- NTEN: https://www.nten.org/—A great starting point for your AI and #nptech journey, with a range of offerings including access to courses, research, and community events, plus their incredible annual NTC conference.

- TechSoup: https://www.techsoup.org/—Offers a wide range of technology resources and discounts for nonprofits, helping you access essential tools at lower costs.
- Beth Kanter's blog: https://bethkanter.org/—Insights on leveraging AI and other technology for social good, offering practical tips and case studies.
- AI Governance for Nonprofits Framework: https://cdn-dynmedia-1.microsoft.com/is/content/microsoftcorp/AI-Governance-Framework-for-Nonprofits-with-captions%20—Training videos, governance template for nonprofits to use, and AI talking points for conversations with nonprofit boards.
- AI for Good Global Summit: https://aiforgood.itu.int/—A conference exploring AI applications for social impact, offering insights into the latest advancements and best practices.
- Tech Impact: https://techimpact.org/—Provides technology services and support for nonprofits, helping you implement and manage tech solutions effectively.
- Digital Nonprofit Academy: https://www.thedigitalnonprofit.com—Offers online training, product reviews, and resources specifically designed for nonprofits seeking to enhance their digital strategies and technology planning.
- AI Now Institute: https://ainowinstitute.org/—A research institute dedicated to understanding the social implications of AI, offering reports and analysis relevant to nonprofits.
- Candid.org: https://candid.org—A resource for nonprofits looking for funding to implement or upgrade technology, offering a database of grant opportunities and practical advice.

Chapter 6.1

Guidelines for AI Vendor Selection

Based on insights from an interview with Alfredo Ramirez.

As a nonprofit leader, the pressure to stay ahead in technology while managing limited resources can be overwhelming. Consequently, it's quite common to look to third parties to help you adopt AI technology. Third-party support usually entails sifting through dozens of vendors and solutions to find the right one. *Adopting a clear framework for evaluating vendors enables you to make informed decisions that align with your goals, ensure compatibility with current operations, and ultimately drive your mission forward.*

A Framework for Mastering Vendor Selection

Clarify Needs

Before diving into the sea of AI solutions, it's essential to have a crystal-clear understanding of your nonprofit's specific needs. *Start by identifying the core challenge you aim to address, then break the problem into its parts, and finally map each component to measurable metrics or targets.* These metrics may be internal or dictated by funders. Are your goals programmatic, related to fundraising, content management, or operational efficiency? Reflecting on this and writing the results down in a document—to which others contribute ideas and feedback—will quickly establish a solid basis for your request for proposal (RFP) and ensure you avoid the common pitfall of chasing technology trends without clearly understanding their relevance to your work.

Assess Current Capabilities

A thorough assessment of your current technological landscape is vital. **Document the systems, processes, and tools you currently use to address your identified needs.** Update your RFP-in-progress accordingly, noting any associated metrics you are measuring today to ensure they will be accessible or even improved on after you adopt any new tools. A detailed understanding of your tech stack will also help you communicate your existing infrastructure effectively to potential vendors.

Finally, reflect on the resources—time, personnel, tools, and budget—you have available for implementing new technology. What staff capacity can you lend to support adoption during the build and ongoing, and what funds can you allocate to ensure initial and sustained success? **Think deeply about deadlines and timelines** as well. Is there a particular date before which you want to solve the problem or when you want to launch a new solution? Reverse engineering an achievement can be a helpful way to identify milestones that confirm you're headed in the right direction.

Craft a Comprehensive RFP

Now that you have the building blocks of an effective RFP, it's time to synthesize all those insights into one comprehensive document. When reaching out to potential vendors through formal RFPs or informal inquiries, ***it's important to overshare rather than undershare.***

At a minimum, your RFP should include:

- **Key needs/problem statement:** Clearly state the challenges you seek to address.
- **Requested scope:** Outline the project scope while allowing for vendor input.
- **Current solutions:** Describe how you currently address the issues.
- **Available resources:** Include budget and time constraints, even if they are just ballpark figures. ***Whether you're hiring a freelancer or a multinational agency, it's critical to include your budget in your RFP*** to narrow down your list of potential vendors.
- **Selection criteria:** Share your preferences and desired qualifications, such as relevant experience and required integrations.

- **Timeline:** Provide key dates for the project and the selection process, including milestones and outputs needed to meet funder requirements.
- **Organizational overview:** Offer context about your organization, the project, goals, and expected outcomes.

Leverage AI to Facilitate Selection

GenAI tools like ChatGPT or Claude can assist in sorting through numerous proposals, especially when you have an evaluation rubric against which to assess applications. ***Feed the proposals and your RFP into an AI system, then ask the AI to generate summaries and create an evaluation matrix*** based on your selection criteria. This helps quickly narrow down the field and unearth key concerns or highlights of each proposal.

Protect Your Investment

Finally, safeguard your organization's resources by negotiating proof of concepts or money-back guarantees with vendors. This enables you to validate the solutions on a small, "minimum viable product" scale before committing fully. ***Ask potential vendors if they offer full refunds within a set period if their solution fails to meet expectations.*** Think seriously about looking elsewhere if not, especially if you're being pitched a retainer agreement with no out.

Interviewee Bio

Alfredo Ramirez is a strategic advisor and technology expert with a proven track record of guiding nonprofits in adopting and implementing AI solutions to maximize impact. With extensive experience helping organizations evaluate and select technology vendors, Alfredo excels at identifying tools and platforms that align with each nonprofit's mission, goals, and operational needs. His deep understanding of AI applications in fundraising, program delivery, and back-office efficiency enables him to provide tailored recommendations that drive innovation while maintaining budgetary and ethical considerations. https://www.linkedin.com/in/alfredojramirez/

Chapter 7

Prompt Engineering: Asking AI the Right Questions

Based on insights from an interview with George Weiner.

In the digital age, nonprofits must harness the power of AI to stay relevant and effective. That means learning how to "speak computer" in this new age, so you can feed your AI tool instructions. **Prompt engineering is the process of crafting clear and specific instructions or questions to guide an AI system to produce the most accurate and useful responses.** If you're serious about mastering, or even just using AI, it is one of the most foundational skills you need to develop. In fact, **prompt engineering is the backbone of effective AI use, since without asking the right questions, the answers you receive will be incomplete or irrelevant.**

This chapter can help. In the pages that follow, we will guide you through the dos and don'ts you need to learn to master this craft, helping you leverage AI to achieve your mission more efficiently. Whether you're crafting donor appeals, generating reports, or engaging with your community, mastering prompt engineering will unlock AI's full potential for your organization.

Critical Skills and Competencies

Crawl-Walk-Run Approach

Prompt engineering starts with understanding basic principles, akin to learning the grammar of a new language. **You must provide clear, concise, and context-rich instructions to your AI tool; the more specific you are, the better the outcome.** Think of it as giving directions to a visitor in your city, whom you don't want to overwhelm or confuse, but you do want to ensure is clear and understands your directions.

So, how can you master this crucial skill? Well, just like learning to run, we'll start simple and then work our way up to more advanced prompt engineering techniques.

Crawl Phase (Understanding the Basics)

Start by familiarizing yourself with the types of prompts. ***Zero-shot prompts ask AI to generate responses with no prior context, while few-shot prompts provide examples to guide its answers.*** Few-shot prompts are useful for more complex or less familiar tasks, while zero-shot prompts work well for simpler or more generalized tasks, when you're safe to assume your AI tool understands what you want without any context. By providing examples, few-shot prompting helps it better understand the output you're looking for.

Zero-shot prompting can lead to inconsistent or underwhelming results, especially for complex or specialized tasks. For example, asking "*Write a grant proposal for our nonprofit*" without any context or examples will produce a generic response that doesn't capture your nonprofit's unique mission or voice, and that disregards the funder's goals and priorities. It's simple to ***level-up your AI outputs with few-shot prompting by uploading documents, sharing links, or directly pasting relevant samples into your prompts,*** for example, "*Here's an example of how we've started past grant proposals: '[Example text].' Using this as a guide, draft a new proposal for our program supporting youth mentorship.*" This approach helps your bot AI better understand the desired structure, tone, and content you're after. ***Few-shot prompting also allows you to reuse examples from successful past projects, ensuring consistency in the outputs across different tasks or team members.***

Familiarize yourself with the limits and abilities of the AI tool you are using. For example, some AI chats have access to the internet, which means it can pull from search results. Other AI chat tools may have access to custom databases of your nonprofit's information to provide useful context. Understanding these restrictions and what your system can do is critical to this early crawl stage.

When you're first starting out, ***begin with simple tasks and gradually move to more complex ones as you gain confidence.*** For example, you might start by asking the AI to draft an email, then progress to more nuanced tasks like drafting a comprehensive fundraising strategy for your nonprofit. This incremental approach helps build your skills progressively, ensuring you are comfortable and effective at each stage.

Here are a few basic concepts with which you should experiment to develop basic prompting skills:

- **Start simple:** Begin with clear and straightforward prompts. Avoid overloading the AI with unnecessary details or complex instructions.
- **Be specific and explicit:** Clearly state what you want the AI to do, including desired format, tone, length, and objective of the response. For example, *"Write a three-paragraph email in a formal tone aimed at convincing someone to volunteer for a food pantry."*
- **Experiment with variations:** Test different ways of phrasing your prompts to see which produces the best results. Small changes often make a big difference.
- **Incorporate few-shot prompts:** Include examples in the prompt to guide your AI, showing it exactly how you'd like the task to be completed.

Walk Phase (Intermediate Prompting)

Effective prompts require precision. Imagine you're a chef providing a recipe to an assistant. You wouldn't just say "make a cake"; you'd specify the ingredients, measurements, and steps. Similarly, when crafting prompts, strive to include your desired format, style, application, audience, and so on. One way to do this is to use what is often called a "sandwich prompt" to enhance clarity and coherence. ***A sandwich prompt is a structured approach to prompt engineering where you sandwich the main task or question between clear instructions or context at the beginning and specific guidelines or constraints at the end.*** This structure provides the AI with both context and boundaries, ensuring it produces a focused and accurate response.

Here's the structure of a sandwich prompt:

- **Top slice (context/setup):** Start by providing background information or setting the scene to help the AI understand its role as a "world-class" expert for the task.
  Example: *"You are a world-class expert in digital nonprofit fundraising."*
- **Filling (the task/question/context):** Clearly state what you want the AI to do and who it is doing it for.
  Example: *"List three creative donor engagement ideas for a small nonprofit organization based in New Jersey that serves the elderly."*

- **Bottom slice (guidelines/constraints/reminder):** Add specific instructions about the format, tone, or scope of the output.

    Example: *"Each idea should be under 50 words and actionable for a team of fewer than five people. Remember to stay in the role of a world-class fundraiser and do your best."*

Here is a full example of a sandwich prompt:

"You are a world-class digital marketing specialist for nonprofits. Suggest three social media strategies to boost donor engagement for a mid-sized nonprofit organization based in California that helps local pets. {add context about your org's brand voice and key information}. Each strategy should be concise, practical, and under 30 words. Stay in the role of a world-class digital marketing specialist and do your best."

Yes, we ended that last prompt with "*do your best*" because, believe it or not, the data shows that it actually improves AI outputs!

As you further strengthen your prompting skills, ***experiment with role-playing to refine prompts.*** For instance, instruct the AI to act as a world-class interviewer or a nonprofit governance consultant. This technique ensures the AI understands the context and produces more relevant responses. Role-playing can also help fine-tune your AI's responses to align more closely with your nonprofit's voice and style, making the generated content more authentic and useful. This works OK if you point it to your website and ask it to write in your style, but is especially powerful when you upload a range of documents and materials, as detailed in Chapter 21, so your bot gets to "know" your voice and goals.

As you move from crawling to walking, here are a few intermediate concepts to play around with to continue to refine your prompting skills:

- **Use constraints and boundaries:** Set clear rules for the AI. For instance:
    - *Respond in two sentences.*
    - *Only provide actionable advice.*
    - *Make responses rhyme.*

- *Make responses appropriate for an 8th-grade reading level.*
- *Add a section below your response with reasons why this may fail.*

- **Specify the audience:** Indicate who the response is intended for to shape tone and complexity. For example:
  - *Write this explanation for a 12-year-old student.*
  - *Make responses tailored for new potential donors that are parents between ages of 30 and 45.*

- **Encourage multiple outputs:** Request multiple ideas or variations at once, such as *"Provide 10 different ideas for our annual fundraising appeal."* ***It's often helpful to see several options and then to narrow in on those you like best and dive deeper.*** You can also ask it to break up the reply into categories or by audience cohort.

- **Leverage Iterative refinement:** *If the output isn't what you want, tell your AI tool what doesn't work for you and invite it to try again,* or experiment with tweaking your prompt to see if you get better results. Try asking the AI how it would improve the reply given your goals.

Run Phase (Advanced Optimization)

One of AI's standout features is its ability to retain context within a conversation, just like our short-term memory. Unlike a simple Google search, AI can build on prior interactions to provide more nuanced and informed responses. This capability depends on something called a "context window"—the amount of information the AI can remember. These windows are growing, enabling more detailed and comprehensive interactions. To leverage this effectively, ***familiarize yourself with your specific AI tool's context window by simply asking it and keep related information within the same session whenever possible.*** For example, if you're drafting a grant proposal, first share your organization's mission, audience, and goals, then ask the AI to build on that foundation to craft compelling narratives. Be mindful of the window's limits—if your conversation gets too long, earlier details will drop off. To avoid losing key context, ***summarize essential points periodically and reintroduce them as needed.***

Advanced Concept: Vector Databases

Vector databases make your organization's knowledge instantly accessible to AI without repetitive context-sharing in prompts. By converting your grants, donor interactions, and program outcomes into searchable formats, your AI can pull relevant details automatically when crafting responses. When writing a grant proposal, it can reference successful applications and metrics instantly. Though initial setup requires effort, the improved consistency and time savings make vector databases a valuable investment in your nonprofit's digital infrastructure.

Advanced Concept: Agents

AI agents can integrate with your nonprofit's existing tools and databases through application programming interfaces (APIs). This means your AI can directly access and act on data from your donor management system, email platform, analytics tools, and other internal software. For example, an agent could analyze donor giving patterns from your customer relationship management (CRM) system, generate personalized email campaigns, schedule sends through your email service, and track engagement metrics—all while maintaining appropriate permissions and security protocols. The agent coordinates these actions across multiple systems to complete complex workflows independently. To leverage this capability, identify your key systems that offer API access and document the specific actions you want automated. This groundwork ensures your agents will have the right connections and permissions to execute tasks effectively across your technology stack when the capability becomes available.

Now that you're running, it's time to apply your AI tools to more advanced tasks, including producing more robust outputs. ***When working on lengthy projects, break down the task into manageable sections.*** Start with an outline, have the AI generate content for each section, and then refine the output. This iterative process ensures coherence and completeness, especially when, as mentioned previously, you use feedback loops to refine the outputs and ensure each is exactly what you want.

Now that you're at the head of the class, there are only a few final frontiers to work toward your prompting black belt:

- **Ask for explanations or outputs in steps:** If the task involves reasoning, *instruct the AI to explain its thought process to ensure it aligns with your own and is based on sound thinking.* This is called "chain-of-thought" prompts and may not work with some AI tools like ChatGPT's o1-Preview. This can simply sound like "*Explain your answer before providing the final response*" or "*Explain your reasoning*" after you get a final output.
- **Test temperature and creativity settings:** Adjust AI parameters like temperature, logit bias, presence and frequency penalty, and top-p to control how creative or focused the responses are. For example, *lower temperature for precise answers, higher for brainstorming.*
- **Document successful prompts:** Keep track of prompts that work well for specific tasks. Over time, this will serve as a personal library of best practices.
- **Pay it forward:** Now that you've mastered prompt engineering, be sure to pass on what you've learned! Teaching is the best way to learn, and *aside from building your team's capacity to leverage AI, helping others will advance your own professional development.*

Pitfalls and Solutions
Vague Prompts

If your prompts are nebulous or broad, your AI is left to interpret your request on its own, which often leads to irrelevant or unhelpful responses. For instance, asking, "How can we fundraise better?" will result in generic advice that doesn't fit your nonprofit's specific needs or context. To avoid this, *be as specific as possible when crafting prompts, including providing details about the AI's role, the desired task and outcome, the audience, the tone, and the desired output format.*

So, instead of asking the generic question, you'd be *way* better off prompting, "You are a nonprofit fundraising expert. What are three creative fundraising strategies our small animal shelter can use to engage small-business owners in our local community, formatted as bullet points? Limit your output to ideas we can realistically implement with minimal staff." The more context you provide, the more likely you are to receive actionable, targeted responses that directly address your nonprofit's challenges. ***Save your most effective prompts as templates so you can reuse or adapt them for similar tasks in the future.***

Information Overload

On the flipside, ***providing too much information or competing requests in a single prompt will often confuse your AI and dilute the relevance of its response.*** For example, asking, "What should we include in a donor newsletter, and how can we better engage volunteers, and what's a good way to share program updates?" forces the AI to split its focus, often leading to scattered or unfocused answers. Instead, ***break your requests into separate, concise prompts, each addressing a single task or question.***

Similarly, ***to manage longer or more complex requests, use a step-by-step approach.*** Begin by asking the AI to generate an outline or organize the task into parts. For instance, "What are three key elements of a donor newsletter for a mid-sized nonprofit?" Once you have that, you can build on it with follow-up prompts to refine specific sections, such as "Expand on how to write an engaging opening paragraph for the newsletter." By keeping prompts focused, you'll get more actionable and higher-quality responses.

Failing to Validate Outputs

Throughout most chapters in this book, you'll hear tons of references to the critical importance of keeping a "human in the loop," which is so fundamental to AI success it's often abbreviated as HITL. That's because ***blindly accepting AI-generated responses leads to errors, omissions, or inappropriate content.*** This is due to the "hallucinations" that are endemic to AI, at least at this stage in its development, plus the fact that the tech doesn't always know your voice and goals. ***If you ask your AI to draft an email for a fundraising campaign and use it without review,*** *you might miss factual inaccuracies, inconsistent messaging, or phrasing that unintentionally alienates donors.* Validation is crucial to ensure that the output aligns with your organization's mission, values, and goals.

Always treat AI outputs as drafts rather than final versions. Review each response carefully and cross-check factual claims. When working on sensitive communications, such as donor appeals or beneficiary stories, involve a team member to ensure the content is appropriate and empathetic. By integrating a validation step into your workflow, you'll maintain the integrity and quality of your nonprofit's communications while still benefiting from the efficiency of AI.

Not Training Staff on Effective Prompting

If only a few individuals in your nonprofit understand how to create effective prompts, you risk missing out on the full potential of AI. For example, if your development director knows how to use AI to write donor letters but your program staff don't know how to leverage it for reporting, the organization's overall efficiency and impact will be limited. *Prompt engineering needs to be a shared skill across your entire team to maximize AI's benefits in your nonprofit.*

Invest in training sessions to teach staff the basics of crafting clear, specific, and actionable prompts. Provide examples tailored to shared tasks, such as how to draft program updates, schedule events, or summarize meeting notes using AI. Encourage cross-departmental sharing of successful prompts, and *work with your team to create prompt libraries to archive best practice prompts useful for executing recurring tasks.* By empowering your entire team with prompt engineering skills, you'll ensure that AI becomes a versatile and impactful tool throughout your organization.

Road Map to the Future

No doubt, prompt engineering will evolve significantly as AI becomes more advanced, intuitive, and integrated into nonprofit operations. In particular, the rise of agential AI, or AI systems that act autonomously to perform tasks based on broader, less specific instructions, will minimize the need for detailed prompts. Your future AI will know all about you and your affiliations, including "understanding" your nonprofit's mission, data, and workflows at a deeper level. Rather than requiring you to craft a detailed prompt for a fundraising appeal, ***future AI tools will autonomously analyze donor data, past campaigns, and your program impact reports to generate highly targeted communications.*** Your nonprofit can prepare by ensuring your data is well organized and accessible, which will help these systems optimize outputs.

Another key trend will be the deeper integration of AI into existing nonprofit tools, particularly in fundraising platforms, CRM databases, and program management systems. These tools will likely incorporate AI features that make prompt engineering almost invisible—enabling users to initiate powerful processes with minimal input. ***Imagine your fully integrated CRM system of the future simply offering you the ability to click a button labeled "Predict Top Donor Prospects," with AI handling the rest.*** To prepare, your nonprofit should focus on adopting tools that offer seamless AI integration and invest in training staff on how to maximize their capabilities. Additionally, as AI becomes better at working with unstructured data (like text-heavy grant applications or qualitative survey responses), you will need to develop workflows that feed this data into AI systems in useful formats. ***Mastering prompt engineering today will ensure your organization is at the forefront of AI innovation, maximizing the benefits to the clients you serve and driving your mission forward*** with greater impact and efficiency.

Dos and Don'ts

Do

- Provide clear, concise, and context-rich prompts with as many specifics as possible, including your desired role, format, tone, length, and objective
- Walk before you run and start to develop your prompting skills by focusing on simple tasks
- Include examples in the prompt to guide your AI's outputs
- Experiment with "sandwich prompts," when you start with background information or a role, then clearly state what you want the AI to do, and finally provide specific instructions about the format, tone, or scope of the output

- Learn your AI's context window and work within its short-term memory limits by keeping related information within the same session, summarizing and reintroducing key points periodically
- Adjust AI parameters like temperature to rebalance the creativity versus focus of its responses
- Learn the abilities the AI chat you are using has, like document upload, internet connection, other agent ability
- Save your most effective prompts as templates and create prompt libraries for recurring tasks
- Build prompt templates for recurring tasks such as grant reports or donor updates
- Break down robust projects into smaller components and use clear formatting instructions (bullet points, paragraphs, sections) to structure outputs

Don't

- Let staff bring their own AI for work tasks as it leads to security risks and poor outputs by untrained AI tools
- Leave prompt engineering to chance; invest personal and organizational capacity into mastering this fundamental skill
- Settle for one response to your inquiry versus requesting several variations at once so you can identify and refine the best ones, and asking your AI to try again and telling it what you like and don't about its last attempt to improve results
- Provide too much information or competing requests in a single prompt
- Treat AI outputs as final, instead of understanding they are drafts that all require human refinement
- Assume that just because some of your nonprofit's team members are fluent in prompt engineering you don't need to invest in training and support to build up this critical skill across your entire team

Conclusion

Mastering prompt engineering is absolutely essential if your nonprofit aims to harness the full potential of AI. By understanding the principles of effective prompting, walking before you run, avoiding common mistakes, and staying informed about future developments, you will unearth the many possibilities of AI and drive your mission forward. And while prompting may be seamlessly integrated into the AI of the future, leveling up your skills today will offer a huge advantage over counterparts who fail to learn how to converse with AI effectively, catapulting your work forward in ways that are sure to compound over time. So, start crawling, and before you know it, you'll be running an AI marathon!

Interviewee Bio

George Weiner is a recognized leader in leveraging technology and data to empower nonprofits, focusing on the critical skill of prompt engineering—formulating AI queries to yield actionable insights. As the founder and "Chief Whaler" at Whole Whale, he has guided countless mission-driven organizations in using digital tools and analytics to improve their impact. He is also the cofounder of PowerPoetry.org, a safe creative free platform for youth poetry that was a leader in using Machine Learning becoming a Google Cloud NLP case study in 2018. Previously, George served as the chief technology officer of DoSomething.org, where he helped design systems that harnessed data and technology to scale youth engagement. Drawing on these experiences, he now trains nonprofit professionals to ask AI the right questions, ensuring that Machine Learning models produce meaningful, context-rich results. His approach aligns technical strategy with organizational values, enabling nonprofits to navigate the AI era with greater clarity, effectiveness, and confidence. https://www.linkedin.com/in/georgeweiner/

Resource Review

- Cause Writer: https://causewriter.ai—Provides your nonprofit with AI-driven tools and templates for crafting effective prompts, in addition to offering access to a wide range of AI resources and low-cost access to custom large language model or generative pre-trained transformer (GPT) development, all specifically geared toward nonprofit leaders.

- GitHub's Prompt Engineering Guide: https://github.com/dair-ai/Prompt-Engineering-Guide—Get hands-on tips and best practices from this open-source guide to crafting better AI prompts.

- NTEN: https://nten.org—Offers AI resources such as webinars, guides, and blog posts, along with sessions at their annual Nonprofit Technology Conference, all designed to help nonprofits master technologies like prompt engineering to improve fundraising, marketing, and operations.

- The AI Alignment Forum: https://www.alignmentforum.org—Engage with a community focused on refining AI behavior, where you can learn about prompt crafting and best practices to ensure accurate AI responses in your work.

- OpenAI blog: https://openai.com/blog—Dive into OpenAI's blog to explore practical guides and updates on how to craft effective prompts for better AI responses in your nonprofit work.

- AI for Good Foundation: https://ai4good.org—Stay informed on AI's applications for social good and how you can use AI effectively to drive your nonprofit's mission and improve prompt engineering.

- AI for Everyone Course: https://www.coursera.org/learn/ai-for-everyone—Take this introductory course by Andrew Ng to understand the basics and dive into how prompt engineering fits into the broader landscape of AI in nonprofits; in addition to searching Coursera for other similar courses, you can also check out www.udemy.com and www.medium.com.

- AI Now Institute: https://ainowinstitute.org—Stay informed on AI ethics, applications, and research, with resources to help you build responsible prompt engineering practices in your nonprofit.

- Nonprofit Tech for Good AI Toolbox: https://www.nptechforgood.com/ai—Learn how AI is being used across the nonprofit sector, with a focus on tips for improving prompt engineering and ensuring you ask AI the right questions.

Chapter 7.1

Introducing Arnold, the StaffBot: Lung Cancer Foundation of America Case Study

Based on insights from an interview with Donna Whitney.

Background and Problem Statement

Lung Cancer Foundation of America (LCFA) is a small nonprofit organization with a powerful mission: to improve lung cancer survival rates by funding transformative scientific research. Despite their significant goals, the foundation operates with only four full-time employees, supplemented by key media consultants. As with most nonprofits, **their small team was continually challenged with the demands of program development, marketing, fundraising, and increasing their search engine optimization.** As a result, the team is always looking for new ways to leverage technology to amplify their bandwidth in the most efficient and cost-effective way.

AI-Driven Solution

To address these challenges, LCFA turned to their long-time consultants at Whole Whale (https://www.wholewhale.com/), whose CauseWriter.AI platform assists nonprofits with their AI development needs. With their help, **LCFA developed a custom large language model (LLM), essentially adding a digital staffer while ensuring data privacy.** They were excited to safeguard any sensitive information entered into AI, ensuring prompts wouldn't find their way into the public domain. They were also drawn to the concept since it would enable them to orient their bot properly with background information and materials, so any outputs were customized for their needs, written in their voice, and factored in a wide range of knowledge of their historic efforts.

Over a nine-month iterative process, the AI was trained using LCFA's style guide, branding documents, voice samples, proposals, grants, emails, newsletters, FAQs, and lung cancer facts. This extensive training ensured that the AI could produce content that was consistent with LCFA's voice and accurate in its information. LCFA also used this time to reflect on and document which tasks were best suited to automation and AI support, following the best practices detailed in Chapter 21. They also mandated AI training for all staff (including select patient advocates and vendors), starting with the basics of prompt engineering to enable them to communicate effectively with the AI and receive valuable outputs.

The AI, affectionately named Arnold (think Terminator), was designed to assist with repetitive and time-consuming tasks, such as podcast production, posting relevant research news articles, and drafting various types of content that is supported with evidence-based citations. LCFA ensured privacy by keeping all inputs within their system, preventing their data from being integrated into broader AI training datasets.

Results and Impact

The introduction of Arnold had a transformative impact on LCFA's operations. *Each team member now had their own virtual assistant, significantly reducing the time spent on routine tasks and allowing them to focus on higher-priority activities.* Arnold helped streamline the production schedule of LCFA's podcast episodes complete with scripts, show notes, summaries and suggested social media posts for program promotion and engagement. The AI also assisted in updating meta tags on the website—a tactic it suggested when asked how to boost traffic—which contributed to an increase in web traffic when other organizations were experiencing declines. Here are a few other ways LCFA used AI effectively:

- Increase operational efficiency with email communications
- Enhance marketing effectiveness:
  - 66.67% more emails were sent in 2024 versus 2023
  - 48.1% increase in online sessions to the website from emails

- Social media growth
- Content creation for multimedia educational and awareness messaging
* Scale their impact without significantly increasing overhead
* Program development research

Lessons Learned

LCFA's journey with Arnold offered several key lessons for other nonprofits considering custom AI solutions. First, **it's crucial to focus on customization to ensure the AI meets your nonprofit's specific needs.** Continuous improvement is essential, as ongoing training and refinement of the AI will enhance its effectiveness over time.

Another important lesson was **the value of a collaborative approach and specifically enlisting expert assistance with developing and adopting a custom AI platform.** Working closely with experts like Whole Whale helped LCFA maximize the benefits of their AI tool. Transparency is also critical; being open about the use of AI and ensuring staff were well trained in its application helped mitigate concerns about job security and fostered a culture of innovation within the organization.

Interviewee Bio

Donna Whitney, director of Digital Strategy and Web at Lung Cancer Foundation of America, brings 20 years of digital technology expertise and a decade of nonprofit health care experience to her role. Previously senior manager of Digital Strategy at National Stroke Association, Donna combines technical innovation with strategic vision to advance health care advocacy through digital solutions, driving the organization's mission to fund lung cancer research. https://www.linkedin.com/in/donnaraewhitney/

Part II

Fundraising: Strengthening Relationships, Not Replacing Them

"As artificial intelligence evolves, we must remember that its power lies not in replacing human intelligence, but in augmenting it. The true potential of AI lies in its ability to amplify human creativity and ingenuity."
—Ginni Rometty, executive chairman, IBM

Fundraising is the lifeblood of any nonprofit. But for many organizations, especially smaller ones with limited resources, development work can often be more transactional than relational due to limited capacity. The day-to-day demands of donor outreach, grant applications, and stewardship can overwhelm even the most dedicated teams, leaving little room to build and nurture the meaningful connections that lead to sustained support.

This is where AI can change everything. ***Imagine a not-too-distant future where AI tools help you identify the donors most ripe for follow-up, remind you of their personal interests and connection to the cause, draft a personalized email appeal to facilitate outreach, and include a suggested donation amount and custom language.*** Combine that with your newfound freedom to enjoy leisurely conversations and lunches, cultivating your most promising prospects with helpful intel fueling your efforts, and strategically stewarding your most loyal supporters. In fact, that bold future is right around the bend, and *now* is the time to prepare for it.

Ultimately, AI can never replace the human touch essential to fundraising success—but it can enhance it. ***By taking on repetitive, time-intensive tasks, AI enables your team to focus on what matters most: building relationships.*** It equips you with insights and tools to better understand your donors, tailor your approach, and foster deeper connections. With AI as your partner, you can move closer to the ultimate goal of relationship-driven fundraising, rather than being stuck in a cycle of transactional efforts.

Part II explores the key ways AI can transform your fundraising efforts, helping you raise more money with greater efficiency while staying true to your mission. We begin with "Prompting Next Gen Donors to Give," taking a deep dive into how to use AI to not only bolster fund development but also help to diversify your donor base with younger supporters primed to support your efforts well into the future. From there, "Donor Research" explores how AI can analyze vast datasets to identify prospective donors, enhance outreach, and align interests with your mission. Whether you're seeking individuals, foundations, or corporate partners, AI helps you prioritize prospects and focus your energy where it matters most. Within that chapter, you'll find a helpful inset on "Political Fundraising," complete with tons of tips and direction to support AI-powered fund development for campaigns. Building on this, "The Future of Philanthropy: AI and Donor Engagement" examines how AI-powered tools enable personalized outreach and tailored communication, fostering deeper donor connections. The inset "CRM 2.0: The Road Map Ahead" provides you with a peek at how this technology is evolving, the opportunities those changes present, and how they can equip fundraisers with actionable insights for engagement strategies.

From there, we turn to "Peer-to-Peer Fundraising and Ambassador Engagement," showcasing how AI can empower your most passionate supporters to amplify your mission and expand your donor database. For those pursuing institutional support, "Foundation Prospecting" highlights how AI simplifies grant research and helps you identify and pursue promising sources for institutional support. Finally, "Grant Writing and Reports" demonstrates how AI can assist in drafting compelling proposals and comprehensive reports, saving time while improving quality and funding results. The inset "Securing Funding for Your AI Upgrades" offers insights into positioning technology needs as mission-critical investments, ensuring you can fund adoption of the tools poised to help you thrive.

Each chapter provides actionable guidance to integrate AI into your fundraising efforts, empowering you to achieve more without losing sight of the human connections at the heart of philanthropy.

AI won't write thank-you notes with heartfelt sincerity or shake hands at donor events—but it will free up your time to do those things better and more often. By embracing these tools thoughtfully, your nonprofit can unlock new possibilities for funding while staying rooted in the relationships that drive true impact.

Chapter 8

Prompting Next Gen Donors to Give

Based on insights from an interview with Josh Hirsch.

When engaging next-gen donors—millennials and Gen Z—it's essential to remember that they expect more than just clever messaging. They demand transparency, value alignment, and personalized interactions that feel authentic and human. With their heightened digital literacy, ***younger audiences easily recognize generic content, making it critical to refine your AI prompts to craft experiences that resonate deeply with their priorities.***

Refining prompts for next-gen donors isn't just about improving word choice or tweaking tone; it's about designing a process that reflects their unique expectations. ***Younger donors are drawn to emotional storytelling, clear calls to action, and evidence of tangible impact.*** They're also attuned to inclusivity, sustainability, and collaboration—values that should be baked into the very structure of your prompts.

This generation also thrives on iteration. ***They value innovation and respond most positively to nonprofits that experiment with bold, creative ideas.*** In the same way, refining your prompts is an iterative process—testing, adjusting, and optimizing to ensure that your messaging lands with maximum impact.

So, let's explore best practices in prompt engineering specifically tailored for courting next-gen donors. ***By applying these strategies, you can ensure your AI-generated content feels personal, emotionally resonant, and aligned with the values of the next generation,*** creating a foundation for meaningful engagement and long-term relationships.

Critical Skills and Competencies

Humanize Your Messaging

Younger donors crave authenticity and connection. They're quick to dismiss content that feels robotic, overly polished, or disconnected from their values. ***To engage effectively, your prompts must encourage messaging that feels personal and relatable,*** reflecting the language and tone of your audience.

Practical Tips

- ***Mirror the conversational tone of younger donors.*** Start by analyzing the language they use on platforms like Instagram or TikTok. For instance, instead of "We are requesting your assistance in achieving our fundraising goal," opt for "We're counting on you to help make this happen!"
- Avoid formalities unless absolutely necessary. For a campaign targeting young professionals in tech, say, "Your $25 can bring clean water to a family for a month," rather than "We hope you will consider supporting our clean water initiative."
- Experiment with using emojis or playful language where appropriate for social media or SMS campaigns.

Example Refinement

Original: "Please consider supporting our initiative with a generous donation."

Refined: "Your $20 donation can be the reason a rescued pet finds a forever home this month."

Framing donors as mission partners makes the message more engaging and inclusive, empowering them to feel part of the solution.

Prove the Impact

Next-gen donors are data-driven and skeptical of vague claims. They want evidence that their contributions lead to real, measurable outcomes. ***Prompts should elicit messaging that combines compelling statistics with stories to create a balanced and impactful appeal.***

Practical Tips

- Use specific, tangible examples in your prompts to inspire confidence. For instance: *"Explain how $50 provides a week's worth of meals for a family of four and ties into the larger campaign goal."*
- *Incorporate time frames and progress metrics:* "Highlight that the $5,000 raised so far has provided clean water for 50 families and explain how their $50 can help us reach 100 families by next month."
- Encourage AI to include proof points or external validation (e.g., ratings on Charity Navigator or testimonials).

Actionable Strategy

Take the time to celebrate victory and congratulate your community for their support, while clearly conveying the impact they made possible. ***After the campaign ends, close the loop with follow-up content.*** Example: "Thanks to your generosity, we exceeded our goal! Together, we raised $10,000, which funded clean drinking water for 1,000 families. *You* made this happen!"

When donors, especially young ones, see the results of their support, it builds trust and increases the likelihood of continued engagement.

Include a Call to Action (CTA)

A strong CTA is essential for driving donor engagement. ***Younger donors respond best to concise, visually distinct CTAs that tell them exactly what action to take.*** Pair CTAs with emotional or aspirational language to create urgency.

Practical Tips

- Use action verbs and specific outcomes in your CTAs: "Donate Now," "Join Us," or "Make a Difference Today." Pair these with impact-driven statements such as "Your $10 provides a day's worth of food for a rescued animal."
- Experiment with creative CTAs for social media campaigns: "Tap the link to save a life today" or "Swipe up to help us build a brighter future."

- Ensure CTAs are prominent and easy to act on. For emails, include buttons or bold links. For social media, provide clickable links in your bio or Stories.

Advanced Strategy

> ***Test different CTAs to identify what works best for each audience.*** For example, A/B test "Donate Now" versus "Be a Hero Today" and track click-through rates to refine your approach.

A clear CTA not only removes friction but also empowers donors to act confidently and quickly.

Experiment and Iterate

AI-generated content often requires refinement to ensure it aligns with your goals. Iteration is essential for tailoring messaging to next-gen donors' preferences. ***Start broad, refine outputs through feedback, and tweak for maximum impact.***

Practical Tips

- With very few exceptions, ***never settle for AI's first output; instead, use subsequent prompts to upgrade the draft, and then manually take it over the finish line.*** "Rewrite this email for a Gen Z audience with a casual tone and a focus on the impact of small donations" or "Add a compelling call-to-action and a success story."
- Experiment with tone, structure, and specificity. For example, prompt your GenAI tool for variations of a social media post targeting younger audiences to find the most engaging option.
- Document successful iterations as templates for future campaigns to save time and maintain consistency. See "Next-Gen Fundraising Sample Prompt Library" for a starting point.

Actionable Strategy

> If any of your colleagues typically use only one prompt and then run with the results, instead of manually refining it or asking them to do so, show them how you can quickly, effectively use AI to upgrade the results. And be sure to regularly test and

review your AI workflows. ***Develop a feedback loop with your team to share insights and ensure outputs align with your nonprofit's brand and tone.***

Prioritize Inclusivity

Next-gen donors value inclusivity and expect organizations to reflect diversity in their messaging. ***Avoid assumptions or stereotypes, and craft prompts that emphasize belonging and respect for all identities.***

Practical Tips

- Encourage neutral language: "Support caregivers in providing meals for their families" instead of "Help mothers feed their children."
- Incorporate cultural awareness: "*Highlight how this campaign supports underrepresented communities*" or "*Create a message that acknowledges regional traditions while making a universal appeal.*"
- Test AI-generated outputs for unintended biases and refine accordingly.

Advanced Strategy

Use AI to adapt messaging for different cultural contexts or languages, ensuring your campaigns resonate globally.

Leverage Emotional Storytelling

While data builds trust, storytelling creates emotional connections. ***Younger donors respond strongly to narratives that illustrate how their support transforms lives.*** Prompts should inspire AI to craft stories with relatable characters, vivid details, and clear resolutions.

Practical Tips

- ***Ask for narratives that focus on one individual's experience,*** such as "*Write a story about how Maya's scholarship, funded by $50 donations, helped her become the first college graduate in her family.*"
- Use prompts to adjust tone for specific platforms. For Instagram: "*Summarize Maya's story in 280 characters with an engaging call-to-action.*" For email: "*Expand Maya's story with details about her journey and photos.*"

Actionable Strategy

Combine data and storytelling. Example: *"Show how our grassroots donors helped 100 students like Maya achieve their dreams."*

Refinement in Action: Sample Iterative Workflow

1. **Initial prompt**

    "Write an email to Gen Z donors about our upcoming fundraiser for clean water."

2. **First AI output**

    "Join our efforts to provide clean water for all. Donate today to make a difference."

3. **Refinement prompt**

    "Make it more casual and specific. Include a clear example of the impact of a $20 donation."

4. **Second AI output**

    "Hey there! Did you know just $20 can provide clean water to a family for a month? Help us reach our goal of 1,000 families by donating today!"

5. **Expanded refinement**

    "Add an emotional appeal and a thank-you message for past supporters. Highlight how $20 ties into the larger campaign goal."

6. **Third AI output**

    "Thanks to amazing donors like you, we've already provided clean water to 500 families! Just $20 can help us reach 500 more. Join us today and be part of this life-changing effort."

7. **Final manual edits**

    Adjust for brand tone, personalize salutation ("Hi Sarah"), and add a specific CTA button: "Click here to give water and hope."

Next-Gen Fundraising Sample Prompt Library

This sample library is designed to help you maximize the potential of AI in crafting tailored, impactful fundraising content. Each example focuses on a specific fundraising scenario, addressing the unique values and preferences of younger donors. Alongside each prompt, you'll find recommendations for refinement to help you take the AI-generated output from good to great. These recommendations encourage iteration and highlight areas to personalize, enhance tone, or clarify messaging.

Use this library as a starting point to spark creativity and streamline your fundraising efforts.

1. **Personalized email appeal for monthly giving**

    Prompt: *"Act like a fundraising strategist for [Your Organization and URL]. Craft an email appeal targeting millennial professionals in urban areas. Highlight how a $20/month donation supports clean energy projects that reduce carbon emissions. Include a success story from a previous campaign and emphasize the convenience of automated monthly giving."*

    Refinement recommendation: Ensure the success story feels authentic and specific, rather than overly generic. If AI provides a vague example, refine by prompting it with something like this: *"Make the story more detailed and emotionally engaging. Include a name, location, and a measurable impact, such as the amount of emissions reduced."*

2. **Social media post for peer-to-peer fundraising**

    Prompt: *"You are a social media specialist. Write an Instagram caption and suggest hashtags for a peer-to-peer fundraising campaign targeting Gen Z college students. The campaign supports scholarships for first-generation students. Include an inspiring call to action and emphasize how small contributions from their network can create a ripple effect of impact."*

    Refinement recommendation: Check that the tone matches the platform. If the output feels too formal, refine with: *"Make it more casual and conversational, suitable for Instagram. Use emojis and a playful tone to engage Gen Z."*

(Continued)

3. Donor thank-you email

Prompt: *"You're a nonprofit fundraising expert. Write a heartfelt thank-you email for a Gen Z donor who gave $25 to our animal rescue campaign. Highlight how their donation provided a week of care for a rescued puppy. Include an invitation to share their impact on social media with a personalized hashtag like #RescueHeroes."*

Refinement recommendation: If the tone feels generic, ask AI: *"Make the thank-you more personal. Use a warm and conversational tone and emphasize the unique connection between the donor and the cause."*

4. SMS campaign for micro-donations

Prompt: *"You're a mobile fundraising expert with a focus on social impact. Create a three-message SMS campaign targeting millennials. Message 1 introduces our emergency food drive and the $5,000 goal. Message 2 shows how a $10 donation provides five meals for a family. Message 3 shares a progress update and invites donors to help us close the gap by donating or forwarding the campaign link to friends."*

Refinement recommendation: Ensure the SMS messages are concise and action-oriented. If the AI output feels too wordy, refine: *"Shorten each message to under 160 characters and include a clear CTA for each step."*

5. Event promotion for a virtual fundraiser

Prompt: *"You are a nonprofit fundraising and communications guru. Generate an email invitation for a virtual fundraiser targeting young professionals in the tech industry. The event features a panel on climate change solutions and includes a networking session. Include a link to register and suggest a $25 suggested donation to support reforestation efforts. Highlight the value of participation beyond the donation."*

Refinement recommendation: If the output doesn't emphasize the unique value of the event, refine with: *"Expand on why this event is a must-attend for young professionals. Highlight exclusive networking opportunities and actionable takeaways from the panel."

6. **Recurring donor recruitment campaign**

   Prompt: "You're a nonprofit fundraising and marketing expert. Write a Facebook post encouraging millennials to join our monthly giving program. Show how just $15/month helps provide tutoring for underserved students. Include a testimonial from a current monthly donor about why they support our cause and add a direct link to sign up."

   Refinement recommendation: Check that the testimonial feels authentic. If the AI generates a generic quote, refine: *"Create a more specific testimonial with details about how long the donor has been giving and why they're passionate about the cause."*

7. **Crowdfunding campaign update**

   Prompt: "You're a nonprofit fundraising and crowdfunding expert. Draft a crowdfunding update targeting Gen Z donors. Explain that we've raised 75% of our $10,000 goal to build a community garden and need their help to cross the finish line. Include an emotional appeal about the impact the garden will have on local families and a call to action to donate and share the campaign."

   Refinement recommendation: If the appeal feels too generic, refine: *"Include a specific example of a family that will benefit from the garden and how their quality of life will improve."*

8. **TikTok video script for donor engagement**

   Prompt: "Act like a social media content creator. Write a 30-second TikTok script encouraging Gen Z donors to support our clean water campaign. Include a quick statistic about the number of people who lack access to clean water and show how $10 can make a difference. End with an upbeat call-to-action to visit the link and donate."

(Continued)

Refinement recommendation: Ensure the script flows naturally for video. If it feels too scripted, refine: *"Make the language more conversational and add suggestions for visuals or on-screen text."*

9. **Inclusive appeal for underrepresented communities**

    Prompt: *"You're a nonprofit email fundraising professional with 20 years' experience. Create a fundraising appeal email that emphasizes our work supporting underserved communities. The target audience is millennials passionate about social equity. Highlight how their $50 donation supports a program providing job training for individuals facing systemic barriers. Use inclusive language and share a success story to inspire action."*

    Refinement recommendation: Check that the language is inclusive and avoids stereotypes. If needed, refine: *"Ensure the appeal uses neutral and empowering language, focusing on strengths and opportunities rather than deficits."*

10. **Post-campaign impact report**

    Prompt: *"You are a nonprofit fundraising and major gifts expert. Write an email to donors summarizing the success of our youth mentorship campaign. Explain how their contributions helped 200 students receive guidance from trained mentors. Include a thank-you message, a link to a video highlighting the program's impact, and an invitation to join our next campaign."*

    Refinement recommendation: Ensure the thank-you feels warm and genuine. If the tone is too transactional, refine: *"Make the thank-you more personal. Include specific examples of student success stories from the mentorship program."*

The prompts and refinement recommendations in this library are a foundation for crafting impactful, next-gen-focused fundraising content. As you integrate AI into your strategies, remember that iteration is key. *Use these prompts to inspire your messaging but remember to refine outputs to align with your nonprofit's voice and the unique needs of your audience.*

Pitfalls and Solutions

Neglecting Personalization

Generic messaging can make donors feel like just another number rather than a valued supporter. This is particularly problematic with next-gen donors, who expect tailored, meaningful interactions that reflect their values and contributions. ***Use AI to analyze donor data and craft personalized messages that acknowledge past giving, interests, and engagement history.*** For instance, instead of "Thank you for your donation," use AI tools to personalize the message to "Thank you, Alex, for your $50 gift last month—it helped provide 25 meals to families in need!"

Data Overload

Overwhelming donors with facts and figures without an emotional connection will make your appeals feel impersonal and transactional, while excessive detail can overwhelm them and obscure your message. ***Next-gen donors resonate with impactful narratives that put faces to numbers, conveyed in concise, digestible formats.*** Encourage AI to integrate stories of real people or communities affected by your work, weaving in relevant statistics to reinforce the story. For example, "Your $30 donation helped Maria, a single mother, access nutritious meals for her three children last week—along with 200 other families this month." It's also critical to ***avoid information overload, which occurs when you throw too many facts and figures at young folks.*** To avoid this, balance data with personal storytelling to inspire action.

Sticking with One Approach

Using the same message format repeatedly without experimentation limits your reach and fails to engage diverse audiences, and it'll quickly get stale in the eyes of young supporters. Plus remember, different platforms or donor segments require distinct strategies and messaging. ***Regularly test variations of your AI-generated content by prompting different tones, formats, or CTAs.*** Analyze the results and use them to refine future prompts and outreach.

Neglecting Visuals

Failing to incorporate compelling visuals alongside your messaging weakens the emotional impact of your appeals, especially when posting on social media. In particular, **next-gen donors are highly visual and quickly get bored with text-only messages** since they're so used to platforms like Instagram or TikTok. Use AI to suggest or create ideas for visual content, such as *"Help me create a powerful image for this email fundraising appeal featuring a photo of volunteers distributing meals."* Pair text with relevant, compelling images whenever possible, ideally with faces clearly visible to drive action. And on the flipside, pair visuals with concise, impactful text that complements the imagery, ensuring your message resonates on both visual and emotional levels.

Working on Your Time Versus Theirs

Sending messages at inconvenient times results in missed opportunities for engagement. **Next-gen donors are particularly accustomed to real-time, contextual communication.** Use analytics to determine when your audience is most active and prompt AI to *"Draft a follow-up email to send two hours after our live fundraiser concludes"* or *"Create a morning SMS reminder for our afternoon event."* Similarly, **when news breaks, use AI to quickly send out relevant messages, demonstrating your relevance and focus** on the issues that matter to you and your supporters. Timely communication ensures your message lands when donors are most likely to respond, while giving donors a sense that you're paying attention and on the ball.

Road Map to the Future

As we press into the exciting near-term future of AI, fundraising is poised to become more advanced, with next-gen donors and other digital natives expecting to benefit and be treated accordingly. AI's ability to analyze unstructured data—such as social media posts, videos, and emails—will open new avenues for understanding donor behavior, motivations, and preferences. That means *if your messages aren't personalized, they'll be even more likely to fall flat than those you send today.* AI will also be increasingly, seamlessly integrated into existing fundraising platforms, such as

CRM systems and peer-to-peer fundraising tools, making it easier for your nonprofit to unify its data, automate workflows, and create comprehensive donor engagement strategies. These advancements will not only enhance the efficiency of your fundraising efforts but also create opportunities for deeper, more authentic connections with next-gen donors.

To prepare, ***experiment first with AI-powered tools that integrate with your existing systems to streamline your operations.*** Establish processes for continuous learning and iteration so your team can adapt to emerging trends and innovations. By taking these proactive steps, your nonprofit will be well positioned to leverage AI's evolving capabilities to drive next-gen fundraising success while maintaining trust and alignment with your mission.

Dos and Don'ts

Do

- Craft prompts that create conversational, authentic messaging to reflect the language and values of next-gen donors, making them feel personally connected to your mission
- Use AI to combine specific statistics with emotionally compelling stories that showcase the tangible impact of donor contributions
- Write prompts that call for strong, actionable calls to action
- Incorporate visual storytelling into your outreach by using AI to generate ideas for images, videos, or infographics to engage visually driven audiences
- Regularly test and refine your AI-generated messaging to find the most effective tones, formats, and CTAs for different donor segments
- Prioritize inclusivity by crafting prompts that reflect diversity and cultural awareness, ensuring all supporters feel represented and valued

Don't

- Use generic, one-size-fits-all prompts that fail to personalize the donor experience or reflect individual interests and behaviors

- Overload your messages with excessive data or lengthy explanations that obscure the main point and overwhelm your audience
- Send messages without considering optimal timing—use AI insights to determine when your audience is most likely to engage
- Neglect to follow up with donors to thank them and show how their contributions have made a difference, which is key to building trust and loyalty
- Rely solely on automation without human oversight—review AI-generated outputs to ensure they align with your nonprofit's tone and mission
- Use the same message format across all platforms—tailor your content to fit the medium and audience for maximum engagement

Conclusion

Engaging next-gen donors with AI provides an unprecedented opportunity to forge meaningful, authentic connections with millennials and Gen Z. By crafting personalized, impactful messages that resonate with their values and priorities, you can inspire action and build long-term relationships. The power of AI lies not just in automation but also in its ability to amplify the creativity and empathy at the heart of your mission.

As you adopt these strategies, ***remember that transparency, inclusivity, and iteration are key to maintaining trust and staying relevant in a rapidly evolving digital landscape.*** By combining the strategic use of AI with a human-centered approach, your nonprofit can inspire the next generation of donors to join your cause and make a lasting difference.

Interviewee Bio

Josh Hirsch is a forward-thinking expert in nonprofit innovation and digital engagement, with a career dedicated to helping mission-driven organizations prepare for the future of philanthropy. He empowers nonprofits to bridge the gap between traditional philanthropy and cutting-edge technology using AI through his consulting firm, The AI Dude. Josh is also the education and training strategist at Fundraise Up and serves as a faculty member for The Fund Raising School at Indiana University Lilly Family School of Philanthropy. https://www.linkedin.com/in/joshahirsch/

Resource Review

- Fundraise Up: https://fundraiseup.com—Streamline your online giving process with AI-powered donation forms that increase conversion rates and optimize donor experiences.
- Association of Fundraising Professionals (AFP): https://afpglobal.org—Access professional development opportunities, resources, and insights to strengthen your fundraising strategies and embrace AI innovations, including an annual international conference and webinars on AI-powered fundraising.
- Fundraising.AI: https://fundraising.ai—Join this collaborative initiative to explore responsible AI use in fundraising, with a focus on ethics, privacy, and impactful technology adoption.
- Bloomerang: https://bloomerang.co—Use this donor management software to leverage AI insights for improving donor retention and campaign effectiveness.
- CauseVid: https://www.causevid.com—Create personalized video messages at scale with AI tools to engage donors more effectively.
- Givebutter: https://www.givebutter.com—Simplify peer-to-peer and crowdfunding campaigns with AI features that enhance donor engagement and campaign visibility.
- DonorSearch: https://www.donorsearch.net—Identify and segment top prospects with predictive AI tools that analyze wealth and giving capacity.
- Charity Engine: https://www.charityengine.net—Maximize donor relationships with an AI-enabled platform that combines CRM, marketing, and fundraising tools.
- Kindful: https://www.kindful.com—Integrate AI tools into your donor database to automate workflows and enhance fundraising efficiency.
- OneCause: https://www.onecause.com—Access AI-powered tools for event-based fundraising and mobile giving to increase donor participation and contributions.
- The AI Dude: https://theaidude.ai—Interviewee Josh Hirsch's consultancy, with a focus on helping nonprofits implement responsible AI-driven strategies, plus you can find a range of workshops and tools to enhance your fundraising efforts, improve donor engagement, and empower your organization to embrace digital transformation.

Chapter 9

Donor Research

Based on insights from an interview with Nathan Chappell.

Welcome to the fascinating world of donor research, where the intersection of technology and philanthropy promises to revolutionize how nonprofits engage their supporters. In this chapter, we delve into the transformative potential of both generative AI (GenAI) and predictive analytics for nonprofits, providing you with actionable insights and practical tools to enhance your fundraising efforts. By leveraging these two complementary types of AI effectively, you will not only deepen your understanding of donor behavior but also foster more meaningful and lasting relationships with supporters, delivering both short-term results and long-term outcomes.

As a nonprofit leader, no doubt you're always looking for ways to maximize impact with limited resources. This chapter will show you how AI can be a game changer, helping you identify and prioritize prospects, cultivate donor relationships, and ultimately close more gifts faster and at higher amounts. Ready to unlock the power of AI for your organization? Let's dive in!

Critical Skills and Competencies

Phase 1: Readiness

Nonprofits ready to overcome their skepticism and put GenAI and predictive analytics to work for their cause need to first understand the difference between the two and how each can help. ***GenAI is great at generating personalized content,*** making it an excellent tool for crafting donor communications, creating compelling narratives for fundraising campaigns, and generating insightful reports. ***Predictive analytics predict donor behavior and help you identify patterns in giving,*** making it ideal for strategic planning and donor segmentation. It's crucial to use the right tool for the right job. Each AI type has its strengths and appropriate applications, and understanding these will help you maximize their potential. By mastering the basics, you lay the foundation for more advanced applications of AI in your nonprofit operations.

After ensuring a working understanding of the basics, your next step is to identify the AI tools you're already using—Adobe, Canva, a CRM system, ChatGPT, and so on. To the extent possible, ask peer organizations what they're using, as this comparison will help you recognize both efficiencies and gaps, providing valuable insights and inspiring innovative uses of AI.

Finally, shop around, with a focus on predictive analytics. GenAI adoption is already entering the mainstream, but too many nonprofits ignore the huge opportunities made available by platforms and providers who look at everyone who donated and didn't, and then use that data to help you identify which donors are ripe for follow-up, proper ask amounts, which messages are most likely to resonate, and exactly when to reach out. Typically, ***predictive analytics will score potential donors from 0 to 100, predicting when and why they'll give.*** These insights can then be leveraged by GenAI tools such as ChatGPT, Claude, and Gemini to help you personalize and engage donors based on their interests and preferences. ***Articulate a detailed, measured approach and set clear goals***—whether it's increasing donations, improving donor retention, or identifying new potential donors—as this will guide your AI-powered fundraising strategy and enable you to generate and measure success.

Phase 2: Adoption and Maximization

Now that you have a clear sense of your needs, goals, and some useful resources, select the most promising, appropriate tools and get to know them. Deepen your working understanding of these platforms to maximize their use, and be sure to also leverage publications and resources like those highlighted at the end of this chapter to increase your AI fluency. ***Avoid the temptation to sit around and wait for your current tools to get "AI-ified,"*** as even just a few months of lag will undermine your work exponentially over time.

Your focus as you dive in should be to go deeper versus wider with tools that build trust within and outside your nonprofit. As you do, maximize use of these tools by reprogramming your organization to leverage the things AI does well. Check in with a cross-section of your team over time to see how things are going, moving away from silos and encouraging collaboration. Predictive AI may identify likely donors who don't look like your typical donor, so plan for change and the need to overcome resistance. As you begin your journey together, there are three key use cases that will serve as your central focus.

Three Steps to Success: Finding, Engaging, and Activating Donors

1. **Prospect identification and prioritization:** Your goal here is to tighten your focus increasingly on a small group of people most likely to give generously over time. ***Start by using ChatGPT, Claude, Gemini, Co-Pilot, or other GenAI tools to help research prospects before calls and meetings,*** getting to know their interests, giving patterns to other causes and groups, and a sense of their financial capacity ("Hey Siri, what are the estimated monthly lease payments on her private jet?").

   Aside from creating donor profiles or dossiers, especially for major prospects, predictive analytics can further refine your focus. By uploading all your giving data, you can understand donor velocity—who is leaning in and likely to increase their giving over time versus those who might step away. This data-driven approach enables you to prioritize efforts on those most likely to become significant, long-term supporters. Be sure to explicitly prompt the system to ***pay special attention to recurring donors or planned givers to identify which of your loyal supporters are most ripe for deeper engagement.*** This strategic focus not only enhances efficiency but also ensures your donor cultivation efforts are directed toward those most likely to make a substantial impact.

Action Steps

- **Research and data enrichment:** Use AI to gather and analyze data on prospective donors, creating comprehensive profiles that include giving history, social media activities, and other relevant personal interests.

- **Predictive analytics:** Upload past giving data into AI models to identify patterns and predict which donors are likely to increase their contributions. Prioritize engagement with these individuals.
- **Focus and prioritization:** Use AI to highlight key prospects, especially recurring donors or planned givers, and tailor your strategies to engage them at an opportune time.

2. **Cultivate donor relations and increase retention and lifetime donor value:** Keeping donors engaged and feeling valued can be challenging, but AI can ease this burden. *Use GenAI to help you craft personalized messages, thank-you gifts, and other forms of appreciation that best resonate with each donor.* You can even build customized annual reports for major donors or create segmented communication strategies to better engage different donor groups.

   This kind of tailored approach significantly enhances donor retention and lifetime value, often abbreviated as LTV. However, it's crucial to remember that *while AI can help you sound authentic, genuine human connection should always remain at the center of your donor engagement strategies.* Segmentation is getting easier, and GenAI can help you put your donors into micro buckets so you're speaking in a personalized way and better able to identify new donors—similar to what many corporations are already doing. This ensures a more profound connection with each donor, fostering long-term loyalty and reducing attrition.

Action Steps

- **Personalized communication:** Deploy AI tools to craft personalized messages, thank-you notes, and event invitations that resonate uniquely with each donor.
- **Segmentation and tailoring:** Use AI to segment your donor base into micro groups for more targeted and effective engagement strategies.

- **Customized appreciation:** Create customized annual reports for major donors using AI to compile and present data that highlights their impact in a personalized way.

3. **Closing more gifts, faster, at a higher average amount:** This is where the return on investment of AI truly shines. When properly leveraged, *AI enables you to move prospects through the moves management cycle more quickly, secure higher quality donors faster, making the entire process easier for your team, while donors feel more personally connected and valued.* Beyond increased revenue, an important side benefit of identifying and closing more gifts, faster, and at a higher average dollar value is that this will help you increase your employee retention rates, especially with your fundraising staff and donor support teams.

   For instance, the DonorSearch AI team worked with the Children's Hospital of Philadelphia, who moved from prospect identification to securing a donation 17% faster thanks to predictive AI identifying the right donors at the right time. Aside from improving fundraising outcomes, *this also enhances the overall donor experience by helping personalize the donor experience through timing, approach, and communication styles, leading to higher average gift amounts and more sustained giving over time.* By streamlining the donation process and ensuring your team stays focused on high-value activities, AI helps you maximize fundraising potential both with your supporters and your team.

Action Steps

- **Efficient moves management:** Use AI to streamline this cycle, allowing for quicker progression from prospect identification to donation. Learn more about moves management via online searches or articles like https://neonone.com/moves-management-guide.
- **Enhanced donor interaction:** Apply AI to customize your approach for each donor, using insights gained from data analysis to personalize interactions and communications.

- **Increased donation amounts:** Leverage AI to predict the best times and methods for soliciting donations, ensuring that donors are approached when they are most likely to give generously.

Phase 3: Immersion

As your nonprofit reaches AI maturity, you'll increasingly employ AI to ensure ripe donors are proactively identified and stewarded in a personalized manner, with your entire team playing a role in the AI feedback loop. Collectively, you'll understand the data points used, which will enable your team to grasp the math behind scoring donors. To reach the head of the class at this advanced stage, ***the key is setting clear goals for staff efficiency and optimizing those over time.*** Your endgame gold standard, at least for the next few years, is to aim for 50% of all staff activities to be powered by AI. Imagine the power of having 2.5 free days every week to focus on building relationships and human-centric activities!

Pitfalls and Solutions

Not Documenting Your AI Strategy

One of the most common potholes nonprofits fall into when adopting new technology is not having a documented, clear strategy. As outlined in "Phase 1: Readiness," ***without a clear strategy, your AI initiatives will likely fail because you have no defined goals or metrics for success.*** Your strategy should outline your objectives, the tools you will use, and how you will measure success. It also helps in motivating your staff to embrace the cultural shift required for AI adoption. Having a clear governance approach and strategy is crucial, as this can undermine fundraising efforts if not properly managed.

Even if you have a strategy, if you treat AI as a one-time project rather than a core business strategy and don't commit to long-term integration, you'll likely see fragmented efforts and limited benefits. Creating a culture of curiosity, where experimentation is rewarded, is key. In the world of big data and algorithms, ***70% of AI success is not about the technology itself but about people and their adoption of it.*** Even with the best AI that money can afford, if people and the organizations for which they work remain hesitant to adopt the technology, success in using AI to support fundraising and other research will be greatly limited. AI is an ongoing journey, not a destination.

Being Paralyzed by Fear

Too many nonprofits are consumed by fear, afraid to take the first step into AI. This often stems from a lack of understanding and the perceived complexity of AI technologies, along with not wanting to make mistakes and concerns around potential costs. As a result, many nonprofits have fear of missing out yet remain on the sidelines, watching as others take the plunge. To address this, ***educate your team about AI and its potential benefits, start small with pilot projects to build confidence and demonstrate value, and promote professional development*** by carving out time for your team to leverage resources such as webinars, workshops, and newsletters to build AI literacy within your organization. By demystifying AI and showing its practical applications, you can reduce fear and encourage a more proactive approach to AI adoption.

Failing to Embrace Responsible AI

Nonprofits are all in the business of trust, and that has to extend to our transparent, ethical development, deployment, and use of technology and other tools. If done right, this builds trust with your donors and within your organization, ensuring AI enhances your mission rather than undermining it, while setting a standard for the industry. Responsible AI means being mindful of data privacy and security, ensuring that donor information is protected and used ethically, working to mitigate biases, and providing accountability. Your goal is to maximize the benefits of AI while minimizing potential harms, and this robust field of study and thought is an area worthy of your ongoing attention and consideration.

Road Map to the Future

As AI technology continues to evolve, there will surely be even more sophisticated tools that provide deeper insights and more personalized engagement strategies. Nonprofits that embrace AI will be able to operate more efficiently, engage donors more effectively, and ultimately raise more funds to support their missions. ***In the next few years, AI will become an integral part of every nonprofit's strategy.*** The focus will shift from simply adopting AI tools to mastering their use and integrating them seamlessly into everyday operations. The potential for AI to transform the nonprofit sector is immense, and those who are willing to invest in this technology will be at the forefront of this exciting evolution.

Dos and Don'ts

Do

- Develop a comprehensive AI strategy with clear goals, a detailed approach, and metrics to gauge your success
- Integrate AI into your fundraising and core business processes for long-term success
- Leverage GenAI to create personalized donor communications and reports, and use predictive analytics tools to identify which supporters and prospects are most ripe for deeper engagement, including recurring donors and planned givers
- Foster a culture of continuous learning and adaptation, including budgeting staff time for professional development and hosting regular meetings to swap notes
- Ensure transparency and ethical use of AI to build trust

Don't

- Let fear or assumptions your current tools will get "AI-ified" prevent you from adopting AI; start small with pilot projects to build confidence and demonstrate value and scale-up
- Rely solely on technology; human oversight is crucial
- Wait for perfect conditions to start; begin experimenting with AI now

Conclusion

AI is no longer a futuristic concept; it's here and it's transforming the way nonprofits operate, today. By understanding the basics, preparing your organization, and adopting AI tools strategically, you can unlock new levels of fundraising efficiency and effectiveness. Embrace this technology responsibly and continually adapt to stay ahead. The future is bright for nonprofits willing to innovate, and AI is the key to unlocking your organization's full potential.

Interviewee Bio

As a renowned thought leader, AI inventor, and award-winning author, **Nathan Chappell** is one of the world's foremost experts on the intersection of AI and generosity. In 2018, Nathan founded Fundraising.AI, a global advocacy organization to promote the responsible and beneficial use of AI for the nonprofit sector. He serves on the International Committee of IT Standards and is the coauthor of the award-winning book *The Generosity Crisis: The Case for Radical Connection to Solve Humanity's Greatest Challenges.* https://www.linkedin.com/in/nathanchappell/

Resource Review

- DonorSearch: https://www.donorsearch.net—Leaders in quantifying connection and predictive AI Deep Learning.
- Fundraising.AI: https://fundraising.ai—An open-source community of nonprofit professionals offering a framework for responsible AI and a glossary of terms.
- Nonprofit Technology Network (NTEN): https://www.nten.org—Provides education, networking, and resources to help nonprofits use technology effectively, plus they offer a free nonprofit technology readiness assessment to evaluate your tech capacity, including AI readiness.
- Microsoft AI for Good: https://www.microsoft.com/en-us/ai/ai-for-good—Offers AI resources and grants for nonprofits.

- Google for Nonprofits: https://www.google.com/nonprofits—Provides access to Google's AI tools and training for nonprofits.
- AI for Good Foundation: https://ai4good.org—Resources and support for nonprofits looking to leverage AI for social impact.
- TechSoup: https://www.techsoup.org—Offers discounted software, including AI tools, and training for nonprofits.

Chapter 9.1
Political Fundraising

Based on insights from an interview with Mike Nellis.

Whether you're advocating for policy changes, supporting political candidates, or driving voter registration initiatives, AI offers powerful tools to enhance your strategies and outcomes. While political fundraising might seem like a domain best left to the pros on Capitol Hill, the reality is that grassroots nonprofits benefit immensely from these technologies. ***AI can help you personalize your outreach, increase your efficiency, and make data-driven decisions—all without breaking the bank or burning out your team.***

While just about all the strategies and tactics shared throughout this book apply to nonprofits engaged in political fundraising, ***here are a few specific tips and tricks that can help you best leverage the transformational potential of AI to kick your political fundraising efforts into high gear.***

The AI Advantage
Microtargeting and Enhanced Ad Targeting

AI empowers you to deliver highly specific and impactful messages by analyzing donor behaviors and segmenting your audience into actionable categories. While we've detailed these AI applications elsewhere, in political fundraising this capability is especially important since this ensures your appeals reach individuals most likely to donate, advocate, or amplify your campaign. ***By pairing microtargeting with enhanced ad targeting, you can strategically place digital ads for maximum reach and efficiency.***

Your first step when moving forward is cleaning and organizing your donor data and enriching it with AI-driven insights. Use tools like NationBuilder (https://nationbuilder.com/) or Bonterra (https://www.bonterratech.com) to build audience segments, and platforms like Meta Ads Manager (https://www.facebook.com/business/tools/ads-manager) to deploy targeted ad campaigns. Google AdWords is also another powerful platform, and **nonprofits can apply for $10,000 per month of free ads on Google by applying for a Google Ad Grant** (www.google.com/grants). Once campaigns are in place, be sure to regularly review performance analytics and adjust based on AI-generated recommendations.

Dynamic Geo-Targeting

AI's ability to target specific audiences also applies to the geographic level, making it a natural extension of microtargeting and enhanced ad targeting. ***While audience segmentation helps you refine whom you're speaking to, dynamic geo-targeting focuses on where—helping prioritize regions where your political fundraising and outreach efforts are most likely to succeed.*** In political fundraising, this approach ensures you're directing resources to communities with the highest potential for impact, whether it's areas with a history of strong voter turnout, communities most affected by your cause, or regions critical to an election or policy outcome.

To get started, collect and analyze location-based data from your donor management system, voter outreach initiatives, or public data sources. Use tools like Mapbox (https://www.mapbox.com/) or CivicEngine (https://www.civicengine.com/) to visualize and analyze geographic trends. These tools enable you to identify hotspots for engagement or regions that require additional support. Tailor your messaging to address local concerns and values and consider running geo-specific campaigns through Google AdWords or Meta Ads. For further learning, explore Esri's nonprofit tools (https://www.esri.com/en-us/industries/nonprofit/overview) and Google Maps Platform tutorials (https://developers.google.com/maps/documentation). ***By layering geographic insights on top of your microtargeting strategy, you can create a more comprehensive, data-driven approach to political fundraising.***

A/B Testing and Optimization

Once you've identified your target audiences and prioritized key geographic regions, the next critical step is ensuring your messages resonate. This is where A/B testing with AI becomes invaluable. ***Traditional A/B testing enables you to compare two versions of a message to see which performs better, but AI elevates this process by automating experiments, analyzing results in real time, and identifying patterns across multiple variables.*** In political fundraising, where campaigns evolve quickly and attention spans are short, this capability ensures your outreach is as effective as possible. Especially when combined with AI's powerful content creation tools—like Quiller (https://quiller.ai/), which helps you generate engaging proposals, reports, stories, email appeals, and marketing materials in minutes by combining customizable templates with AI-driven writing assistance and seamless design integration—this enables you to quickly adapt to changes in the political or media landscape, ensuring your messaging remains relevant and timely.

To implement, define specific elements to test, such as subject lines, calls to action, or visuals in your email campaigns, ads, or landing pages. **Use tools like Optimizely** (https://www.optimizely.com/) **or HubSpot** (https://www.hubspot.com/) **to set up automated tests and analyze results.** Pay close attention to key metrics like open rates, click-through rates, and conversion rates to determine what resonates most with your audience. Integrate these learnings into future outreach and run iterative tests to continuously refine your approach. For a deeper dive into testing best practices, explore Campaign Monitor's A/B testing guide (https://www.campaignmonitor.com/) and Optimizely's resource library (https://www.optimizely.com/resources/).

Predicting Voter Turnout and Campaign Fundraising

Now that AI has helped you refine your approach, it's time to leverage its crystal ball capabilities so you can gauge how your efforts will pan out, including leveraging its "butterfly effect" ability to see how small changes today may lead to vastly different outcomes. These insights can shape where you focus your efforts and how you allocate resources, ensuring you stay proactive. This capability is especially important in political fundraising, where timing, strategy, and optimal allocation of resources make the difference between hitting and missing your goals.

Step 1 is to use AI tools like Civis Analytics (https://www.civisanalytics.com/) or Ecanvasser (https://www.ecanvasser.com/) to analyze historical data from previous campaigns or elections, such as voter turnout rates, demographic trends, and key engagement moments. Then, you'll combine this with real-time inputs like social media activity or email click-through rates using tools like Microsoft Power BI (https://powerbi.microsoft.com/). ***These platforms enable you to create data-driven forecasts that guide decision-making, helping you determine which regions or audiences on which to focus.*** Finally, you incorporate these insights into your overall strategy by aligning them with your microtargeting and geo-targeting efforts.

Fraud Detection and Donor Compliance

As your fundraising campaigns gain momentum, ensuring compliance and preventing fraud becomes a top priority. ***AI plays a critical role in monitoring donation patterns, flagging anomalies, and ensuring adherence to campaign finance laws.*** By maintaining integrity and transparency, you build trust with your supporters and avoid costly legal or reputational risks.

For starters, integrate fraud detection systems into your donation processes. Tools like Sift (https://sift.com/) or Kount (https://www.kount.com/) analyze transaction patterns in real time and alert you to suspicious activity. You should also regularly audit your donor database using compliance tools like NGP VAN (https://www.ngpvan.com/) to ensure adherence to relevant regulations. Be sure to ***establish internal protocols for addressing flagged donations, including immediate follow-ups with donors or legal teams*** as necessary.

Interviewee Bio

Mike Nellis is a leading authority in political fundraising and donor research, specializing in leveraging technology to build impactful campaigns and strengthen donor relationships. As the CEO and founder of Authentic, a full-service digital agency, Mike has driven groundbreaking strategies for some of the most high-profile political and non-profit organizations. His expertise lies in blending data-driven insights with innovative digital tools to identify, engage, and cultivate donors effectively. Under his leadership, Authentic has played a pivotal role in raising millions of dollars for progressive causes, setting a new standard for modern fundraising. https://www.linkedin.com/in/mikenellis/

Chapter 10

The Future of Philanthropy: AI and Donor Engagement

Based on insights from an interview with Allison Fine.

Welcome to the brave new world of philanthropy, where AI is not just a futuristic concept but a present-day game changer. As nonprofit leaders and technologists, **understanding and leveraging AI will revolutionize how you engage with donors, enhance your fundraising strategies, and amplify your impact.** This chapter will provide you with tips and tools to harness the fundraising power of AI effectively. From gaining a bird's-eye view of your fundraising operations to retraining your staff and focusing on donor retention, we'll detail the skills and knowledge that will help you navigate this new landscape.

Ultimately, ***AI presents an incredible opportunity to break the long-time pattern of frantic, transactional fund development and to replace it with relationship-based fundraising at scale.*** Ask any development person if they are good at relational fundraising and the answer is, "Of course!" But what they mean by this is taking a single major donor out to lunch.

Regular, everyday donors are subject to an onslaught of impersonal mailings, emails, and reports they are unlikely to read. ***AI can help you customize messages based on donors' interests and previous actions.*** It can take the steam out of the pot of administrative pressure by reducing paperwork and low-value, repetitive tasks. This frees staff up to actually ask your donors questions and get to know them more deeply, instead of sending yet another laundry to-do list as an appeal. Your donors want to know how you're changing the world, especially in the ways they care about, and when you can do that, true fundraising magic ensues. ***AI makes it possible for every donor, regardless of the size of their wallet, to feel like a million-dollar contributor.***

Critical Skills and Competencies

Gain a Bird's-Eye View

Your willingness to pull your fundraising operation apart and think through the entire donor experience, from the first communication through all the touchpoints that follow, will be one of the most critical factors of your success with unlocking AI's fundraising potential. This will enable you to ***identify areas where you can use AI to personalize communications, making each donor feel seen and valued.*** This also will help build more authentic relationships with your supporters instead of treating them as mere entries in a funnel. The ultimate return on investment is newly freed-up time that can be used to do things only *people* can do: build relationships, listen to one another, solve complex problems. By automating routine tasks such as summarizing long email chains or drafting donor acknowledgment letters, AI can free up your time to focus on more valuable activities, like talking with donors and prospects.

Your goal is to better understand who your donors are and their interests. ***It is critically important to talk to donors, not just survey them, and listen closely to learn which components of your work are of interest to them and how they want to be treated*** and invited to participate. Then you can make informed decisions about ways AI can be used to streamline your operations and free up time to build stronger relationships with donors and increase the likelihood they will give again to your cause.

Get Your Team's Hands Dirty

Your team needs a reboot to thrive in an AI world, and it starts with understanding the difference between data and people. While data can provide valuable insights, it's the human touch that builds lasting relationships. As almost every other chapter has pointed out, training your staff to use AI tools effectively is essential; when it comes to fundraising, this is all about letting them try the tools on for size. ***Challenge your development team to use AI to create dynamic donor profiles that go beyond basic demographics to include interests, past interactions, and preferred communication channels.***

For instance, invite anyone helping with fundraising to create a donor profile of a particular mid-range donor and compare results. Then charge one person with sending a personal note to ask why they feel connected and give to your organization: what makes them feel like their contribution matters, and how does your work bring them joy? ***By understanding what makes your donors tick and entering those insights into any AI-accessible database, your team can then easily craft personalized messages that resonate at scale.*** This approach not only enhances the donor experience but also makes fundraising more friction-free.

Focus on Donor Retention

Too many nonprofits focus more on acquisition at the expense of keeping existing donors engaged. AI helps you flip this script by providing tools to track donor engagement and predict future giving. For example, ***after a donor makes their first gift, AI can help you identify what actions or messages are most likely to encourage a second gift,*** as well as provide insights on the optimal timing and gift size request.

Consider the powerful example of the American Cancer Society, which leveraged AI to determine the most effective communication channels and messaging strategies for their donors. By analyzing donor data and preferences, they were able to customize their outreach in ways that resonated more deeply with supporters. The results were remarkable—this personalized approach led to an astounding 400% increase in donor conversion rates! Their success demonstrates how ***understanding individual donor preferences and using AI to deliver tailored communications can transform engagement outcomes.***

Think of it this way: donors come for lunch, but what gets them to stay for dinner? What do you need to say or do differently to secure that second gift? By focusing on retention and leveraging AI to personalize your outreach, you can build stronger, more lasting donor relationships.

Segment Your Donor List

By segmenting your donor list, you can ensure that your communications are timely, personalized, and aligned with each donor's unique interests. This targeted approach leads to higher engagement rates and stronger donor relationships. ***To get started, use your CRM or donor database and decide which tags are most helpful to provide a customized, personalized experience for every donor.*** This will vary by organization, but your goal is to segment supporters based on past responses, interests, and points of personal connection to the organization. For example, you might tag donors who are moved by video appeals, willing to become ambassadors, or open to joining a local giving circle.

When you know when, who, and how to reach out to donors, you can create more effective engagement strategies. What questions can you ask new donors to understand their interests and preferences? AI can help customize messages based on these insights, making your outreach more relevant and impactful.

Engage Your Board

When properly motivated and equipped, your board can play a crucial role in building and nurturing donor relationships. They can add that special touch that helps separate you from the vast majority of other causes sending boring, standardized messages. But we all know how challenging this can be. ***The key is finding low-touch, high-value ways that directors can make donors feel special and appreciated, while deepening their own connection to the work.***

Keep it simple and start small. ***Ask the board if they'd be open to each stewarding a group of 50–100 donors each.*** The details of what this includes are open to discussion, but ideally start with a personal thank-you call after a first gift, which Bloomerang found increased lifetime giving by 50%. From there, suggest other quick but powerful tactics like handwriting thank-you notes to repeat donors, adding in short personal notes when forwarding generic updates or newsletters to supporters, and personal invites to events and campaigns.

One last note: as you engage your board in fundraising, ***it's critical you regularly update directors on fundraising progress and especially the impact of their efforts.*** Sharing the credit will keep them motivated!

Keep the Conversation Active

Schedule regular meetings with your team to review and refine your donor engagement and AI fundraising strategies. You want to **avoid letting your team work in silos, so shoot for a weekly meeting to discuss what's working, what to improve, and how else you can leverage AI to enhance your efforts.** This is also a great time to review any dashboards or analytics, brainstorm new strategies, and to discuss trends and opportunities.

By continuously refining your efforts, you will ensure that your donor engagement strategies remain effective and relevant. This ongoing process of evaluation and adjustment is key to maintaining strong relationships and achieving fundraising goals.

Pitfalls and Solutions
Turbo Charging Outdated Practices

If you use AI to supercharge transactional fundraising, you'll likely just produce more spam without increasing effectiveness. This alienates donors, making them feel like they're just another number in your database. Instead of using AI to send more generic appeals, use the technology to help personalize and enhance donor engagement.

Go Slow to Go Fast

Nonprofits, especially grassroots organizations, are constantly in motion and all-too-often frantically busy, whether it's effective or not. Do you really need to send out that monthly newsletter or appeal that no one reads? **Examine your existing activities and determine which ones you do because you have always done them (e.g., sending out a newsletter) and which ones actually build stronger ties to your donors.** This is not an activity to be done by staff alone, but in concert with boards and donors.

Overautomating

Nick Hamlin once quipped, "AI is like hot sauce"—you don't want to layer this powerful tech into all aspects of your operation without careful consideration and clarity about your goals. **Relying too heavily on automation can make it difficult for**

donors to connect with an actual person, leading to frustration and disengagement. Instead of creating a chatbot to answer every FAQ, ensure there is an easy way for would-be donors to connect with a human. Balance automation with personal touchpoints to maintain the human element in your donor interactions.

Road Map to the Future

Looking ahead, AI will continue to evolve and become even more integrated into fundraising practices. ***Any fundraising product you use will soon have the ability to customize communication and integrate predictive analytics, helping you determine when and how to best communicate with your supporters.*** Fundraising products will soon offer customized communication and integrated predictive analytics to help you determine when and how to best communicate with your supporters. This will help you more easily identify donors with untapped capacity and optimize the timing and content of your messages. And no doubt in the years that follow, we'll see more and more case studies of nonprofits that have successfully gone all-in on relational fundraising at scale, eliminating some of the fear of more tentative groups struggling to move past increasingly outdated models.

Dos and Don'ts

Do

- Track and tag donor info in your CRM system or database to ensure donor profiles are as accurate and comprehensive as possible
- Personalize your communications using AI insights to make each donor feel seen and valued
- Segment your donor list to provide a customized, personalized experience for each supporter
- Talk to your donors about what they want from your organization (e.g., how often they want to hear from you and how) and focus on making them feel seen and heard

- Engage your board in donor stewardship, encouraging them to handwrite thank-you notes, personal updates, and other light touches
- Schedule regular meetings with your team to review and refine your AI and donor engagement strategies

Don't

- Think of donors in a transactional way; your goal is to build relationships with this key audience
- Make it difficult for donors to connect with a human

Conclusion

AI is not just a buzzword; it's a powerful tool that can transform how you engage donors and enhance fundraising strategies. By gaining a bird's-eye view of your operations, leveling up your staff, ensuring you have the right data to work with, and then engaging your staff and board in building lifelong, meaningful relationships with your donors, you can leverage AI to take your fundraising efforts to the next level. Take the time to be mindful about what practices no longer serve you or your donors as things evolve and stay focused on the human touch that makes philanthropy so impactful. As AI continues to evolve, the opportunities for your nonprofit to expand impact will only grow, making it an exciting time to embrace this technology.

Interviewee Bio

Allison Fine is a trailblazing force in the area of technology for social good. She has been at the forefront of leveraging digital networks to ignite social change. As the president of Every.org, she is working to scale online generosity and transform fundraising to a deeply relational model that brings causes and donors closer together. She has written four books on technology for social good including the groundbreaking *The Smart Nonprofit: Staying Human Centered in an Automated World* coauthored with Beth Kanter, and the award-winning *Momentum: Igniting Social Change in the Connected Age*.

Resource Review

- Every.org: https://www.every.org/—Helps nonprofit leaders leverage AI to advance donor engagement by automating administrative tasks, enabling organizations to focus on building genuine connections with supporters.

- *The Smart Nonprofit: Staying Human Centered in an Automated World* (Wiley, 2022)—This helpful book, written by our interviewee and coauthor Beth Kanter, is designed to help you learn how to embrace AI responsibly by focusing on human-centered strategies that enhance donor relationships and ensure technology aligns with your nonprofit's mission.

- NTEN's Nonprofit Technology Readiness Assessment: https://www.nten.org/learn/nonprofit-tech-readiness—A free tool to evaluate your organization's tech capacity, including AI readiness.

- TechSoup: https://www.techsoup.org/—Provides nonprofits with technology solutions, skills, and resources to enhance their tech capacity.

- Beth Kanter's blog: https://bethkanter.org/—A great resource for insights on nonprofit technology, including AI and data-driven strategies.

- Nonprofit Tech for Good: https://www.nptechforgood.com/—Provides technology and social media resources for nonprofits, including a great newsletter and an active LinkedIn social presence.

- AI for Good Foundation: https://ai4good.org/—Focuses on leveraging AI for social impact, offering resources and case studies.

- *The Chronicle of Philanthropy*: https://www.philanthropy.com/—Offers news and insights on the latest trends and technologies in the nonprofit sector.

- Classy blog: https://www.classy.org/blog/—Provides articles on fundraising, technology, and nonprofit management.

- Bloomerang: https://bloomerang.co/resources/—Offers webinars, guides, and articles on donor management and engagement strategies.

- HubSpot for Nonprofits: https://www.hubspot.com/nonprofits—Provides resources and tools to help your nonprofit improve marketing and donor engagement efforts.
- Salesforce.org: https://www.salesforce.org/—Provides technology solutions and resources to help nonprofits scale their impact, including 10 free nonprofit licenses for their leading CRM platform, which usually requires customization.

Chapter 10.1

CRM 2.0: The Road Map Ahead

Based on insights from an interview with Lori Freeman.

Customer relationship management (CRM) systems have been foundational in helping nonprofits both big and small manage relationships with donors, volunteers, and other stakeholders. But these critical contact databases are being transformed by their integration with AI. This evolution—let's call it ***CRM 2.0—reshapes how you engage with your supporters, streamlines your operations, and ultimately, enhances your organization's impact.***

The Evolution of CRM: From 1.0 to 2.0
Next-Gen Data Management and Personalization

In the world of CRM 1.0, data management was primarily about keeping track of donor information—names, addresses, donation history, and maybe a few notes on interactions. It's where you stored your information so your team could try and figure out what to do with it, whereas the next generation of CRM does this for you. ***CRM 2.0 turns data into knowledge by not just storing data but also actively analyzing it to provide insights, and in many cases, automating the best next steps for each donor.*** These new systems can predict which donors are most likely to give based on past behaviors. They can personalize communication at scale, tailoring messages to individual donor preferences and thereby significantly increasing engagement and retention rates. For example, a CRM system might identify that donors who respond to direct mail or volunteer are also likely to attend in-person events, enabling you to plan hybrid engagement strategies for increased impact.

Keys to Progress

- **Pick your platform wisely:** When selecting a CRM system with AI capabilities, prioritize one that offers detailed data analytics and supports personalized engagement strategies.
- **Experiment with personalization at scale:** Test AI-generated personalized messaging, like tailored appeals based on donor interests (e.g., mentioning a recent event they attended or a program they supported).

Predictive Analytics Transforms Donor Engagement

Gone are the days of guesswork in fundraising. ***With CRM 2.0, AI algorithms analyze vast amounts of data to forecast donor behavior, identifying trends and patterns that humans might miss.*** This means you can anticipate donors' needs, preferences, and likelihood to contribute, enabling you to tailor your engagement strategies more effectively. For example, predictive analytics could identify lapsed donors likely to return with a targeted email campaign or reveal which new donors are most likely to become recurring contributors or would prefer updates on specific programs they've supported, for example, a donor who recently gave to a youth program might appreciate tailored updates about its impact rather than general organizational news.

Keys to Progress

- **Leverage predictive analytics to prioritize efforts:** Use your CRM system to segment your donor base, focusing on high-potential groups like lapsed donors, recurring donors, or major donor prospects.
- **Incorporate predictive insights into strategy meetings:** Schedule monthly reviews of AI-generated forecasts with your development team to refine campaign plans.

Automation of Routine Tasks

From sending out thank-you emails to updating donor records, ***CRM 2.0 can handle many of the administrative duties that consume valuable staff time.*** This not only increases efficiency but also reduces the risk of human error.

Keys to Progress

- **Identify repetitive tasks:** Implement automations through your CRM system to free up your team's time for more strategic activities.

Donor Journey Mapping

By tracking interactions across multiple touchpoints, from social media to email campaigns, ***CRM 2.0 provides a comprehensive view of how donors interact with your organization.*** This helps you identify pain points and opportunities to enhance the donor experience, enabling you to more deeply engage your supporters. An example of a pain point could be a confusing donation portal with high abandonment rates, whereas an opportunity might include automating personalized thank-you emails for first-time donors, with follow-up messaging that shares impact stories tied to their contribution.

Keys to Progress

- **Use data to create donor journey maps:** Visualize how donors move from first contact to recurring giving and identify areas where they drop off.
- **Focus on actionable insights:** For example, if donor journeys reveal a low response rate to generic appeals, implement personalized follow-ups tailored to their giving history or interests.

Integration with Other AI Tools

CRM 2.0 is not just a stand-alone tool; it's part of a larger ecosystem of AI-driven solutions. ***Integrating your CRM with other AI tools, such as chatbots for donor support or marketing automation platforms, ensures that all aspects of your donor engagement strategy are aligned and optimized.*** This internal connectivity also helps promote a more seamless and efficient operational environment, streamlining tasks and data entry while disseminating useful insights, instead of requiring you to manually connect the relevant dots. For example, syncing your CRM system with an AI-powered chatbot could provide personalized responses to donor inquiries based on data stored in the system, enhancing real-time engagement.

Keys to Progress

- **Build an integrated tech stack:** Identify key AI tools your team already uses or could benefit from, such as chatbots or social listening tools, and ensure seamless integration with your CRM system.
- **Streamline donor interactions:** Use integrations to reduce friction, such as ensuring donor information from your chatbot flows automatically into your CRM system for follow-up.

Interviewee Bio

Lori Freeman is a trailblazer in the field of philanthropy, with deep expertise in leveraging AI and advanced CRM systems to revolutionize donor engagement. Serving as Salesforce for Nonprofits' global general manager and VP after more than a decade of leadership at the world's leading CRM provider, Lori has led numerous high-impact projects aimed at integrating technology into the social sector, developing innovative engagement strategies, and driving growth for mission-driven organizations. Lori is a passionate advocate for CRM 2.0, where AI and predictive analytics empower nonprofits to personalize outreach and deepen relationships at scale. https://www.linkedin.com/in/loridfreeman24/

Chapter 11

Peer-to-Peer Fundraising and Ambassador Engagement

Based on insights from an interview with Jennifer Ybarra.

Let's kick things off with a little nugget of wisdom: **people don't give to organizations; they give to people.** This age-old truth is the bedrock of peer-to-peer (P2P) fundraising success and speaks to why recruiting ambassadors to support outreach is key to putting numbers on the board. AI is perfectly suited toward supercharging these efforts. So buckle up, because that's exactly what we're diving into in this chapter!

Why should you, as a busy nonprofit leader, care about this? As we've shared in many other chapters, AI offers you the ability to personalize your outreach like never before. **Even small nonprofits with limited resources can now identify top donors and potential ambassadors who amplify your campaigns to their networks with precision.** AI helps you understand when, why, and how to engage these individuals, creating tailored messages that resonate. Whether you're leveraging platforms like LinkedIn or Facebook, or crowdfunding sites like Classy, AI is your secret weapon for effective fundraising and engagement.

Critical Skills and Competencies
Define Goals and Boundaries

First things first: you need to build a strong foundation. Start by understanding the basics of AI and its potential applications for your nonprofit. **Set clear goals and objectives, and ensure they align with your nonprofit's mission and operational needs.** Remember, your North Star–level objectives must guide your AI journey. Bring an ethical lens to this process; transparency and integrity are crucial when implementing

AI tools, so map out any limits or constraints you need to keep in mind to ensure these tools advance your work and don't cause problems.

When thinking about these goals, do your best to be as clear as possible. ***Consider these foundational questions as a starting point: what are you aiming to achieve, how, and how exactly will you measure success?*** Begin with the end in mind. Whether it's increasing donor retention, improving engagement, or driving more donations, having concrete goals will help you measure success. Equally important is ensuring alignment with your organizational values. AI should enhance your mission, not detract from or undermine it, so ***taking the time to plan for success will be critical to your efforts.***

Map AI Capabilities to Your Goals

Next, conduct an audit of your current tools and their AI road maps. Many existing platforms have AI capabilities you may not be fully leveraging. But ***just because something is possible, doesn't mean you need to put those features to use.*** Again, once you're clear on your goals, you'll have a simple framework to apply against these options to see if they serve you, so take the time to align technology use cases with your organizational goals. This ensures that your tech investments drive value and don't just add complexity.

Form an AI task force to oversee implementation. This team should include representatives from different departments and perspectives to ensure a holistic approach. They will be responsible for communicating objectives, use cases, and timelines across the organization. Clear communication and collaboration are key to successful AI integration.

Build Data Literacy

Before diving into AI, you must get your data in shape. Data literacy is essential—your team needs to understand how to collect, clean, and analyze data. This starts with data hygiene. Ensure your donor databases are up-to-date and free from duplicates. Once this is done, ***use AI tools to help your team maintain proper data hygiene after you've built a strong foundation,*** automating data cleaning, saving time, and reducing human error.

Cultivate strategic data skills within your team. This includes analytics, clean data collection, and interpretation. This will enable you to much more easily review your data and identify key donor archetypes, which in turn enables you to optimize outreach and engagement strategies. *Focus on reverse-engineering data needs to facilitate analysis.* Do you already have access to the data needed to achieve the goals you laid out, what's missing, and are you taking time to collect data that you don't actually need? Clean, accurate data is the foundation of effective AI use.

Clarify Calls to Action

Before identifying or especially contacting potential ambassadors, it's critical you clarify exactly what you're hoping to achieve with their support. That means being crystal clear about what you're asking them to actually *do* and taking the time to think about how to facilitate their support to honor their time and increase the likelihood of engagement. Whether it's sharing your campaign on social media, hosting a fundraising event, or connecting you with potential supporters, think "low touch, high value" and have the ask in your back pocket before you send an email or call a prospect. Especially if you're emailing or DMing your request, *be sure to get right to the point and map the ask to impact to make their support tangible,* for example:

> I see you're connected to [NAME] on LinkedIn and we'd like to connect with them to explore expanding our vocational training program, with the goal of helping another 500 unhoused individuals get off the street and back into the workforce. This appears perfectly aligned with [NAME]'s history of providing marginalized members of the Oakland community with a hand up, versus a hand out. Would you be open to connecting us, and if so, would an email template be helpful to facilitate your outreach?

By providing specific, actionable requests and connecting the dots between your request to the associated impact, you make it easier for ambassadors to say yes and feel motivated to contribute. Strong calls to action and clear next steps encourage immediate action and demonstrate the value of their participation.

Identify, Prepare, and Engage

Identify. Effectively engaging community leaders in a strong position to support your work and drive donations requires a strategic approach. AI can help you identify potential ambassadors by analyzing social media activity and other digital footprints. So, **step 1 is to use AI to interpret a dataset and identify your top prospects.** This can entail, for example, researching which key data points and interactions most clearly led to peer-to-peer campaign donations, then using those insights to find more people to replicate or expand those efforts, or it could be as simple as prompting your GenAI tool to do the following:

> "Review our social media followers and suggest 20 people who are in a strong position to serve as ambassadors of our work, as defined by having a close connection to our organization and a large audience of their own followers. Give me a sentence each about how to best engage them, and what it is that connects them to our mission and programs."

AI tools like Zapier (https://zapier.com/) can be used to automate tasks and funnel data from diverse sources (social media, email campaigns, website interactions) into platforms like Google Sheets (https://docs.google.com/spreadsheets) for comprehensive analysis. This setup allows the AI to scrutinize donor data to derive actionable insights for engagement preferences, donation patterns, and content interaction in a low-cost and simple way. Tools like DonorSearchAI (https://www.donorsearch.net/donorsearch-ai/), HubSpot CRM (https://www.hubspot.com/), and MailChimp (https://mailchimp.com/) can also play a helpful role by streamlining your efforts to identify and segment high-impact donors based on their engagement levels, interests, and past involvement, plus they help tailor personalized email journeys that encourage deeper involvement and advocacy.

Finally, in addition to looking for ambassadors in your current base, consider creating special forums to enable them to self-select. **Set up a private group on whichever social media platform is most popular with your supporters, then use the platform's analytics and insights platform to identify the most active members.** Plan live Q&A sessions, workshops, and case study reviews there, which you can invite the group's emerging ambassadors to help lead and coordinate. Success stories and fundraising tips shared by these ambassadors are highlighted, fostering a culture of empowerment, learning, and mutual support.

Prepare. Now that you've identified these prospects, you can once again use AI to craft personalized, tailored engagement messages, as detailed in other chapters, especially in Parts II and III. AI is an incredible tool to help you identify the best times to contact potential ambassadors and to develop the types of messages to which they are most likely to respond.

Use content tools like Jasper AI (https://www.jasper.ai/), WriteSonic (https://writesonic.com/), and Grammarly (https://www.grammarly.com/) to help draft customized email copy and social media posts in the donor's tone of voice, enabling a personalized approach to ensure messages resonate deeply, foster stronger connections, and provide more effective peer-to-peer fundraising campaigns. More robust tools like Salesforce for Nonprofit Success (https://www.salesforce.com/nonprofit/) enable you to funnel data into predictive analytics platforms, which process vast datasets to identify behavior patterns and predict future engagement levels. This enables you to strategically plan your outreach efforts, ensuring they occur when supporters are most receptive. Other new data-driven fundraising tools worth investigating include Wisely (https://fundraisewisely.com/); Dataro (https://dataro.io/), which enhances nonprofits' understanding of their P2P donors; and Hatch (https://hatch.ai/), which uses data and AI to grow peer-to-peer campaigns.

Engage. OK, the time has come to press play! That means using the messaging you've generated as part of an integrated campaign. ***Plan to send three to four messages to each prospect to secure their support, because one-off outreach rarely yields results.*** These folks tend to be busy, so keep your initial message brief and focused on the impact they can enable with their efforts, and the specific ask and call to action. Subsequent messages should be limited to one to two sentences, where you simply reply to your own message and ask for a reply to the initial email, or to schedule a call or meeting to discuss the opportunity.

Remember to ***treat each ambassador as an individual and communicate in THEIR language, with a focus on THEIR priorities, to maximize engagement.*** Personalizing your communications with ambassadors not only increases response rates and support but it also shows them you know them, especially when combined with custom outreach toolkits like we'll share shortly, and empowers them to launch their own fundraising campaigns with authentic, compelling, ready-to-use content. That maximizes engagement by aligning outreach efforts with supporters' readiness and interests, significantly boosting the effectiveness of your fundraising initiatives and long-term donor engagement.

Convert Donors to Ambassadors

Aside from the supporters, celebrities, and influencers unearthed in your research using the tips provided earlier in this chapter, once you launch a campaign be sure to ***keep an eye out for generous donors and passionate supporters who you can engage in deeper ways.*** After someone makes a generous gift, proactively shares your campaign, or otherwise raises their hand to demonstrate support, embrace the following two-part framework.

Send a Personalized Thank-You

Strike while the iron is hot. No more than two days since the potential ambassador took their action, send them a message expressing sincere gratitude for their support. Acknowledge their specific contribution and its impact on your cause to ensure they realize it's not a template. ***After thanking them, introduce the idea of taking on a more active role by clearly outlining what being an ambassador entails and how they can contribute further.*** Include the specific calls to action, activities, and timelines associated with participation, and once again reinforce the campaign's overall impact goals. Then, make it personal again and dive a level deeper to speak to how their specific, deeper involvement stands to amplify the impact of your work by clarifying how their efforts will lead to tangible results. Don't be afraid to cater to their ego a tad, for example, "Your influence and passion are powerful tools in driving change."

Finally, make it easy to respond. Encourage them to confirm their interest in joining you as an ambassador, but make yourself available for any questions. Consider signing off by saying something like, "If this sounds like something you'd like to be a part of, please reply to this email or call me directly at [phone number]. I'd be happy to discuss how we can work together to make an even greater impact."

Follow Up Respectfully

If they don't respond within one week, send a brief follow-up message to keep the conversation going without pressuring them. It's often easiest to simply reply to your own previous message so you can keep the subsequent message to two to three sentences, along the lines of

> Hi [Name],
>
> I hope this message finds you well. I'm following up on my previous email to see if you'd like to become an ambassador for our cause. Your [summary of past support] meant a lot to us, and we'd be thrilled to have you on board in a larger capacity as we work to [impact summary].
>
> In Community,
>
> [Your Name]

By taking these steps, you acknowledge their existing support and open the door for deeper engagement. This personalized approach not only strengthens your relationship with them but also increases the likelihood that they will become active ambassadors for your mission.

Celebrate Support

Foster community engagement by sharing impact stories and celebrating ambassadors who help put numbers on the board. Everyone loves to be recognized, and this is critical to getting your most effective champions to sustain outreach. **P2P campaigns where the organizer sends at least five emails are 80% more effective,** so when sending updates to your supporters and ambassadors, highlight top donors and ambassadors, along with your progress toward topping off your campaign thermometer, and always, always be sure to underscore the impact the campaign will unlock once successful.

Help Them Help You

Provide ambassadors with tools, templates, and playbooks for outreach, including draft emails and social media posts. Your goal is to make it as easy as possible for them to tap their networks and leverage their social capital on your behalf; that means giving them everything they need to copy and paste, facilitating outreach with "marketing toolkits" containing sample messages and posts, imagery, and other assets so key supporters can focus on the most valuable contribution they can make: inviting their networks to follow them in supporting your campaign. Send personalized reminders and updated toolkits regularly, ensuring you remain top of mind and sustaining their support.

Use AI to help you tailor these toolkits and resources to fit the preferences and behaviors of your ambassadors, optimizing engagement. AI-powered storytelling tools like ShortlyAI (https://www.shortlyai.com/) can quickly generate a short script you can upload into Lumen5 (https://lumen5.com/) to create a video in seconds, while content creation platforms like WriteSonic (https://writesonic.com/) and Canva (https://www.canva.com/) can help you craft compelling narratives and designs. These tools can help you engage high-impact ambassadors by aligning creative elements with their interests and motivations, enriched with AI-generated stories, infographics, and videos that narrate your nonprofit's mission and achievements.

To the extent possible, ***encourage ambassadors to donate first, since the most powerful form of ask is a peer ask,*** meaning I'm inviting you to do something I've already done myself. This enables incredibly powerful language like, "I invite you to *join me* in supporting this critical campaign to (insert impact here)."

Pitfalls and Solutions

Over-Reliance on AI

Over-relying on AI often leads you to lose the human touch so critical to the success of your outreach efforts. ***While AI can automate many processes and provide valuable insights, it cannot replace the empathy and connection that human interactions bring.*** Balance automation with interaction and maintain quality control and oversight on AI-generated content. Ensure that your communications still reflect the personal touch that donors and ambassadors appreciate.

Settling for One Tool

Depending too much on a single technology or tool limits flexibility and will leave your nonprofit vulnerable to disruptions if that tool fails or becomes obsolete. ***Embrace an ecosystem approach, exploring multiple AI tools and platforms to diversify your technological portfolio.*** And engage people from across various parts of your nonprofit to ensure a healthy range of perspectives, priorities, and sensibilities. This not only mitigates risk but also leverages the strengths of different best-of-breed tools and points of view to enhance fundraising and engagement, instead of relying on a one-size-fits-all approach.

Forgetting to Seed the Tip Jar

Everyone wants to be part of a winning team, which is the reason you'll never walk into a cafe and see an empty tip jar. When that happens, nobody gives. The same is true for P2P and crowdfunding campaigns. So, ***kickstart your campaign before going live to the public by securing at least 15–20% of your goal from board members, existing donors, and other members of your inner circle.*** This will dramatically increase donations and deliver more traction to your efforts, further inspiring ambassadors. If potential donors show up and see an empty thermometer, odds are they'll move on instead of being the first to break the seal.

Road Map to the Future

Looking ahead, the integration of AI in P2P fundraising and ambassador engagement will continue to evolve. As AI technologies become more advanced and accessible, nonprofits of all sizes will be increasingly able to drive more effective and personalized outreach and supporter experiences, competing more effectively for donor attention and resources. Expect AI to become a standard part of successful nonprofit operations, enabling organizations that use it strategically to attract donors much more effectively than their counterparts over time

As a result, ***the key to successful fundraising and donor engagement will shift from nonprofits that merely adopt AI to those that optimize its use strategically across all levers of the organization for maximum impact.*** Nonprofits that proactively embrace this technology will be better positioned to deepen supporter relationships, increase operational efficiency, and amplify their mission's reach and meet their audiences' expectations.

By staying adaptable and continuously learning, your nonprofit can not only keep pace with technological advancements but also set new standards in the sector. The organizations that thrive will be those that view AI not just as a tool, but as an integral component of their strategy to create meaningful change.

Dos and Don'ts

Do

- Take the time to crystallize and document your goals with AI and any P2P campaigns, along with associated success metrics
- Prioritize data hygiene and ensure your databases are clean and up-to-date
- Leverage predictive analytics to target the right donors and ambassadors
- Segment your audience so you can personalize outreach for more effective engagement
- Develop toolkits to facilitate ambassador outreach; make it quick and easy for them to support your campaign

Don't

- Assume one email will suffice to recruit ambassadors or launch a successful P2P campaign; plan a series of messages to maximize results by taking prospects on a journey to see it, feel it, and, ultimately, to believe it
- Forget to invite your ambassadors to donate to the campaign before reaching out to their network, enabling a peer ask
- Launch a P2P campaign without first securing 15–20% of your goal from your inner circle of supporters
- Over-rely on AI and neglect the human touch in your communications
- Fail to measure and assess the effectiveness of your AI initiatives regularly

Conclusion

As you embark on your journey to integrate AI into your P2P fundraising and ambassador engagement strategies, remember the key to your success lies in balancing technology with human insight. By developing your team's knowledge of what AI can and can't do, mapping those possibilities to your fundraising and other goals, keeping your data clean, and personalizing your outreach, you can unlock the full fundraising potential of AI.

Stay adaptable, keep learning, and always prioritize ethical considerations. With these strategies in place, you'll be well equipped to elevate your fundraising efforts and deepen your connections with donors and ambassadors. The future of AI in the nonprofit sector is bright, and by embracing these tools, you can drive meaningful impact and further your mission.

Interviewee Bio

Jennifer Ybarra has helped raise over $3 billion for more than two million nonprofits worldwide and is a seasoned nonprofit strategist with a focus on helping mission-driven organizations amplify peer-to-peer fundraising efforts and engage ambassadors to expand their impact. She does that now via her consultancy, The Good Human Group (www.goodhumangroup.co), but has worked with nonprofits big and small and across some of tech's biggest organizations, including Facebook and Yahoo. During her tenure at Facebook, Jennifer helped grow Social Impact Partnerships, spearheading groundbreaking initiatives and programs with organizations like GivingTuesday that transformed digital philanthropy. https://www.linkedin.com/in/jennifer-d-ybarra/

Resource Review

- Zapier: https://zapier.com/—Automates workflows to seamlessly connect peer-to-peer fundraising platforms with CRM, email marketing, and social media tools for improved ambassador coordination.
- Google Sheets: https://docs.google.com/spreadsheets—Acts as a real-time data hub for tracking and analyzing ambassador performance and donor engagement metrics.
- DonorSearchAI: https://www.donorsearch.net/donorsearch-ai/—Identifies high-potential donor prospects within peer-to-peer networks to focus ambassador efforts effectively.
- HubSpot CRM: https://www.hubspot.com/—Provides insights and engagement tracking to help ambassadors personalize donor outreach and strengthen

relationships, plus their Nonprofit Marketing Hub offers marketing resources and tools for nonprofits, with a focus on data-driven strategies.

- MailChimp: https://mailchimp.com/—Automates email campaigns, enabling targeted communication and engagement with fundraisers and their networks.
- Jasper AI: https://www.jasper.ai/—Generates compelling fundraising copy and ambassador outreach scripts to maximize donor engagement.
- WriteSonic: https://writesonic.com/—Produces engaging social media posts and email templates to inspire ambassadors and their networks to take action.
- Grammarly: https://www.grammarly.com/—Ensures professional, clear, and error-free communications for ambassadors and nonprofit staff alike.
- Salesforce for Nonprofit Success: https://www.salesforce.com/nonprofit/—Centralizes donor and ambassador data to streamline engagement and measure the success of peer-to-peer campaigns, plus it integrates with their Einstein platform to process vast datasets to identify behavior patterns and predict future engagement levels, enabling you to plan outreach when supporters are most receptive.
- Wisely: https://fundraisewisely.com/—Uses AI insights to predict donor giving capacity and guide ambassadors toward strategic asks.
- Dataro: https://dataro.io/—Predicts donor behavior and provides data-driven recommendations to optimize peer-to-peer campaigns.
- Hatch: https://hatch.ai/—Offers AI-powered conversational tools to engage ambassadors and donors through text and chat.
- ShortlyAI: https://www.shortlyai.com/—Helps create concise and persuasive fundraising appeals for ambassadors to share within their networks.
- Lumen5: https://lumen5.com/—Converts written content into engaging video stories for ambassadors to promote campaigns on social media.
- Canva: https://www.canva.com/—Empowers ambassadors to create visually appealing graphics for their fundraising efforts, ensuring a cohesive brand presence.
- Classy blog: https://www.classy.org/blog—Features articles and insights on fundraising, including the use of AI in P2P campaigns.
- LinkedIn for Nonprofits: https://nonprofit.linkedin.com—Provides resources and tools for leveraging LinkedIn to engage donors and ambassadors.

Chapter 12

Foundation Prospecting

Based on insights from an interview with Ann Mei Chang.

In the fast-paced world of nonprofit fundraising, it's easy to feel overwhelmed by the sheer volume of potential funders and the complexities of engaging them. This chapter will guide you through leveraging AI to transform your institutional prospecting efforts. By the end, you'll understand why AI isn't just a buzzword but a powerful tool that can streamline your work, help you make data-driven decisions, and ultimately strengthen your fundraising strategies.

Critical Skills and Competencies

Dial in Your Digital Footprint

In the world of AI, data is king. The volume and accuracy of your data will underpin your AI efforts. Just as you're using technology to find funders, they may find you digitally. Therefore, it is crucial to **ensure your digital footprint is accurate and comprehensive.** This means keeping your information up-to-date on your website and other online platforms that syndicate information to funders, including Candid.org (formerly GuideStar).

To maintain a robust digital presence, you should regularly audit your online profiles and ensure they reflect your current projects and achievements. Taking a proactive approach to confirming that your digital footprint is both discoverable and compelling is vital in attracting and securing funding.

Pick Your Platform

There is a proliferation of AI platforms that can be used for foundation prospecting. In selecting one, it's important to consider both the quality of the data and how well the tool is tailored to your needs, ultimately helping you easily identify and even connect with likely funders. This is far more effective than using generic AI tools like ChatGPT, which lack the specific data about charitable giving. ***When choosing a prospect research platform, look for one that offers a large, relevant dataset that supports your needs, including information on how much funders are giving, to whom, and for what purposes.***

You should also look at how potential platforms align with your current and future needs. For example, does the platform only search through open requests for proposals (RFPs), which represent less than 1% of total foundation funding, or also help you research foundations that don't have an open application process? Is grant data tagged using a taxonomy that adequately represents the nature of your work? Does it help you identify potential contacts at a foundation of interest? Finally, given the cost can range anywhere from free to thousands of dollars a year, are you getting the data, features, and sophistication you need for the right price? Taking time to select the right platform will streamline your research, outreach, and efforts, and increase the likelihood of securing funding.

Prioritize Prospects

If you really want to maximize outreach, no doubt you can find hundreds of potential prospects if you look broadly enough. But ***the key to your success is using AI to identify and focus on the most promising funders, by honing in on the 20–30 prospects who are best aligned*** on three elements: cause alignment, geographic focus, and grant size. By focusing your efforts on the most appropriate funders, you will create more meaningful connections and increase your chances of success. You can get a good sense of all of these by researching funders' publicly stated priorities, the nature of their grants historically, and how similar other nonprofits they have funded are to yours. Many research platforms are now offering AI-driven recommendation engines that can vastly speed up this process. Even simply rating these three dimensions subjectively on a small scale will help you quickly identify the most fertile fundraising ground, enabling you to cull your list.

Once you have your ideal prospect list, you'll likely want to *prioritize the funders where you already have an entry point you can leverage* to secure a call or meeting. For the rest, use AI and social media tools like LinkedIn to identify contacts in your network whom you can leverage to get a foot in the door.

Take Deep Dives on Top Prospects

Once you've narrowed your prospect list down to the top two to three dozen prospects, use AI to gather detailed information about each. Specifically, look into their previous giving history, including amounts and grant size, the specific types of organizations supported, and any insights you can unearth about their intentions and goals. You should also *ask AI to summarize recent news, announcements, highlights from annual reports, and public speaking topics of potential funders.* This enables you to gain a comprehensive understanding of each prospect before delving deeper into your research and outreach.

This custom research will help you tailor communications, maximizing results with personalized messaging. By understanding the specific interests and priorities of each funder, you can prepare for calls and meetings, and also ensure any communications convey your clear appreciation of their objectives. Remember, *the key to foundation fundraising is demonstrating a clear understanding of the funder's goals, and then conveying how you can help advance those,* so always take the time to prepare before any sit-downs.

Secure Calls Versus Submitting Proposals

Now comes the counterintuitive part. Even though you've now identified a couple dozen perfectly suited funders aligned to your work with deep pockets, *avoid the temptation to use AI to submit unsolicited proposals, even if it's to the right prospects.* A spray-and-pray approach is unlikely to be successful without first building relationships and gaining insights to better target your ask. That means first and foremost leveraging any existing relationships you or your inner circle have with the prospect, and if there are none, finding other ways to get in the door.

Direct engagement, either through a call or in-person meeting, is your best bet to identify or hopefully confirm the fit between your work and the foundation's priorities, and for securing invitations to apply for funding. Never forget: *your foundation outreach will*

be exponentially more successful if you do as much of your fundraising in calls and meetings, where you can ask questions and engage in dialogue to dial in the details of your partnership, instead of by submitting unsolicited proposals without any ability to validate assumptions. This may not always be possible, especially if funders refuse to meet or you're responding to a public RFP, but any chance you get to build the relationship and work through key aspects of the grant request in advance of putting thoughts on paper will increase your chances. To secure those invitations, once you've succeeded at getting a call or a meeting, plan for a four-part agenda:

- **Small talk.** Relationships matter in fundraising, so develop your connection if you don't already know the funder or strengthen it if you've spoken before. Use AI to identify points of intersection and shared interest, like where you went to school, your pets, or anything else you can use to break the ice in the first couple minutes of your meeting. Just a question or two will suffice.
- **Ask "level 2" questions.** Level 2 questions combine basic research about the funder with thoughtful inquiries to better understand their giving strategy and how they think about measuring grantees' success; ***prepare two or three open-ended questions designed to subtly demonstrate you've done your homework, while enabling you to better understand their goals and priorities.*** The advice to secure calls instead of submitting proposals isn't new, so most funders have tons of nonprofits asking for their time. When funders agree to a chat, make sure you never disrespect their time by asking simple questions you could've answered with a few minutes of research. Instead, use AI, their website, and recent annual reports to learn as much as possible about their funding goals, and then prepare a few questions to get a better sense of their priorities, how they measure success, and their intended outcomes. Typically, these sound like a statement followed by an open-ended question, and you can definitely ask AI for some suggestions. For example, "I know that the X Foundation has been funding climate change work since your inception in 1992, but can you please tell me a bit about why you chose to devote your resources to this critical cause?" or "Your work in solving homelessness is so exciting, especially given your commitment to supportive housing. But given the complexities, how do you measure success and exactly what changes are you looking to create in your work?"

- **Make your pitch, their way.** Now that you have a solid working understanding of the funder's goals and strategy, present your work at the elevator pitch level, and listen for interest and resonance that calls you to dive deeper. Start out with the big picture about your organization and any programs or initiatives you believe are aligned to their goals, as this will help ensure you're on the same page and have an interested audience. Use AI to bolster your commonsense thinking about which components of your work are best aligned, and what framing may prove most fruitful. But whether you get your storytelling suggestions from bots or your head, be sure to *frame as much of your work as a solution to their challenges and goals as possible,* even explicitly calling out how "Given your goals of X, we may be in a unique position to support your efforts given Y."

- **Close the deal.** Hopefully, while you were making the pitch, at least some parts of what you shared resonated with your audience, ideally even leading them to say what they'd consider supporting, and why. But often, they don't volunteer this, so be prepared to ask explicitly about anything where you felt like there was interest, again framing it as a solution to their needs. *You will get the best foundation fundraising results if you do your fundraising in the call or meeting versus the grant application or proposal, enabling you to engage in dialogue and problem-solve together, and then using the application to document what was already discussed.* That means using the meeting to ask things like, "Thanks so much for your interest in our vocational training program, which I agree aligns perfectly with your goals of providing people with a hand up, not a handout. Is that something you'd consider inviting a grant to support?" Your goal is to secure an invitation to submit a proposal for support, but if you're successful, you'll also want to ask them for a few additional, crucial pieces of information, all of which you should've used AI in advance to research the most likely responses to:
    - **Why?** Now that you've confirmed *what* they want to support, be sure you take the time to confirm exactly *why* it's aligned with their goals. Listen carefully during this portion of the meeting and take detailed notes, as you'll want to include this language word-for-word in your proposal.

- **How (much)?** For every single item the funder has expressed an interest in supporting, each of which will be outlined in your proposal or grant request, you should ask what funding level is realistic. AI can typically give you a solid estimate here, but it's always helpful to ask something like, "Thanks so much for your interest in X, given our shared focus on Y. Our budget for the program next year is $250K, which will enable us to impact Z. Do you think the foundation could underwrite the program completely next year, or would a $125K request be more realistic given we'd be a first-time grantee?" *Any ask should include a specific figure or two, the associated impact, and end in a question mark, not a period.* And after you finish making an ask, the prospect needs to be the next person to speak. Again, you'll need to make a series of asks for each point of intersection, and unless there's a good reason, *never ask for more than a quarter of your total annual budget from a funder,* as they'll be unlikely to want to create that level of dependence. Finally, when quoting a program budget, be sure to quote the true cost of delivery, including the overhead costs critical to your ability to execute. And if possible, consider asking for general operating support or lightly restricted funding to give your nonprofit the flexibility you'll need to adapt your activities based on both learnings and a changing environment.

- **When?** Asking a funder if they'd be willing to review a draft of your proposal somehow leads them to have a deeper sense of ownership over your proposal, championing it when the grantmaking council is deciding what to support. As counterintuitive as it sounds, *asking if they'd be willing to review a draft of your proposal before you formally submit it will improve fundraising results,* even though most funders won't ever take the time to do so. Nonetheless, if they agree ask them what deadline would enable them to take the time to review it, but assume they won't actually do it, so whatever you submit should be a final draft. Either way, the goal is for them to adopt your proposal as it's shared upstream.

Simplify Outreach

Chapter 13 dives into how to use AI to draft and submit proposals and streamline outreach, including useful tools like Candid's AI-powered letter-of-intent (LOI) generator (https://candid.org/labs). Use AI tools to draft emails when following up with your prospects and to help draft any requested documents or materials. If you're still at the stage of getting in the door, see if your foundation research platform can help you identify the right contact, typically a program officer or director, making your outreach even more targeted and efficient. As always, human oversight is essential. This combination of AI efficiency and human touch is key to ensuring your communications are both effective and authentic.

Pitfalls and Solutions

Building with No Foundation

AI is a tool, and you should only use it if you have a clear problem in mind that needs to be solved, and if you're clear that AI can help in a specific way. Many nonprofits are underinvested in their technology infrastructure, including hardware, software, training, and so on, which is essential before moving on to the latest AI tool. Without the proper foundation, AI can become more distracting than helpful.

Garbage in, Garbage out

Data is the lifeblood of AI and technology, so if you don't take the time to ensure data quality on both your side and that of your research platform, your cause will pay the price. Ultimately, ***the value you receive from any AI platform will be directly proportional to the quality, comprehensiveness, timeliness, and accuracy of the data it is trained on.*** So, be sure any providers regularly update their databases and integrate data from multiple reliable and robust sources. Equally important is ensuring your nonprofit's work and interests are accurately represented in online profiles and your website on an ongoing basis, so that AI systems have the most accurate information to base their analysis and recommendations.

Beware Bias

With the way most search algorithms work, research platforms typically surface the largest, best-known nonprofits first in their search rankings. While not much can be done about the inherent confirmation biases in data, there are a few steps you can take. Ensuring you earn any certifications you can on data platforms like Candid (https://www.candid.org) and getting rated well on sites like Charity Navigator (https://www.charitynavigator.org) will help you separate your cause from others. Candid offers Seals of Transparency, there's the Better Business Bureau's Accredited Charity Seal (https://give.org), and Charity Navigator provides ratings based on their proprietary algorithm. All of them are essentially acknowledgment of a nonprofit providing information about how they operate across various categories, but they aren't all ratings or approvals. Just be sure to ***take the time to provide as much information as possible in your online profiles,*** including things like the demographics of the community served, since that will enable funders searching for lesser-known grantees that fit a particular profile to more easily find you.

Road Map to the Future

As AI continues to evolve, its applications in foundation prospecting will become even more sophisticated. Nonprofits can look forward to more personalized and predictive tools that streamline the fundraising process, optimizing the timing and content of your outreach. In the future, customized ***AI agents will be able to learn the ins and outs of your nonprofit, your funding needs, and the philanthropic landscape—then autonomously be on the lookout for news, funding patterns, and website updates that indicate a new opportunity worth exploring.*** And as generative AI systems mature, hallucinations will become increasingly rare, making LOI and grant application drafts more robust. However, a human eye and touch will always be necessary.

Dos and Don'ts

Do

- Ensure your digital footprint is accurate, current, and comprehensive
- Select an AI platform with a large, relevant dataset
- Prioritize quality over quantity when identifying prospects, taking the time to zero in on 20–30 top prospects
- Take the time and spend the money to select a prospect research platform that offers a large, relevant dataset including how much funders give, to whom, and to what end
- Always keep a human in the loop (HITL) to verify AI-generated content

Don't

- Fall into the trap of sending unsolicited proposals to perfectly targeted funders—take the time to secure calls and meetings and get invited to apply
- Show up to calls or meetings with funders without thoroughly researching their work and identifying one or two ice breaking questions and two or three level 2 questions
- Rely on cookie-cutter outreach; take the time to conduct custom research on top prospects and tailor your communications
- Fail to collect any data that you can use now *or in the future* to support fundraising, programs, and operations

Conclusion

AI offers transformative potential for foundation prospecting in the nonprofit sector. By dialing in your digital footprint, selecting the right tool, prioritizing prospects, and then taking the time to secure calls and meetings with the best-suited funders, you can maximize results, especially if you leverage AI throughout the process. Remember to keep human oversight in the process to maintain accuracy and authenticity. With these strategies, your nonprofit will be well equipped to navigate the evolving landscape of fundraising and secure the support needed to achieve your mission.

Interviewee Bio

Ann Mei Chang is the CEO of Candid, a nonprofit that provides the most comprehensive data about the social sector—where money comes from, where it goes, and why it matters. Ann Mei leads Candid in increasing the social sector's ability to do good using data, technology, and compassion. She is a social innovator and author of *Lean Impact: How to Innovate for Radically Greater Social Good*. Ann Mei served as chief innovation officer at the USAID and executive director of its US Global Development Lab. She was chief innovation officer for Pete Buttigieg's presidential campaign, chief innovation officer at Mercy Corps, and senior advisor for women and technology at the US Department of State. https://www.linkedin.com/in/annmei/

Resource Review

- Salesforce's Einstein: https://www.salesforce.com/artificial-intelligence/—An AI tool that integrates with Salesforce CRM to provide predictive insights and recommendations.
- Candid.org: https://www.candid.org—Access to the world's largest collection of high-quality data on philanthropic funding and nonprofits. Claim and update your nonprofit profile to have accurate information available; their data powers a network of over 200 giving platforms, corporate giving programs, donor-advised funds, foundation grantmaking software, and AI-informed donation decisions.
- Candid labs: https://candid.org/labs—Test drive the newest AI technology for nonprofits, including an AI-powered LOI generator (a free tool that helps you draft letters of inquiry using AI), plus access funder recommendations, a philanthropy chatbot, and more.
- Blackbaud'sNXT: https://www.blackbaud.com/products/blackbaud-raisers-edge-nxt—A cloud-based fundraising and donor management solution with AI capabilities.
- DonorSearch: https://www.donorsearch.net—A prospect research tool that provides detailed profiles and wealth indicators for potential funders.
- WealthEngine: https://www.wealthengine.com—A data-driven platform that helps your nonprofit identify and understand your best prospects.
- OpenRefine: http://openrefine.org—An open-source tool for cleaning and transforming data.
- Dedupely: https://www.dedupely.com—A tool that helps you clean up duplicate records in your CRM system.
- Charity Navigator: https://www.charitynavigator.org—An organization that evaluates nonprofits and provides ratings to help donors make informed giving decisions.
- NTEN's Nonprofit Technology Readiness Assessment: https://www.nten.org/learn/nonprofit-tech-readiness—A free tool to evaluate your organization's tech capacity, including AI readiness.

Chapter 13

Grant Writing and Reports

Based on insights from an interview with Susan Mernit.

In today's fast-paced world, nonprofit leaders are often overwhelmed by the sheer volume of work when writing and managing grants. The grant writing process can be daunting, from crafting compelling narratives to compiling data and adhering to strict guidelines. This chapter explores how **AI can revolutionize grant writing and reporting for nonprofits, streamlining your workflow, enhancing proposals, and ultimately increasing your chances of securing funding.** By leveraging AI effectively, you can save time, reduce stress, and focus on what truly matters—advancing your mission.

AI can automate work, analyze data, create templates and ways to structure reports in line with best practices, and it's great at editing. When AI is used to write a case for support to request general operating and/or programmatic support, it can save you tons of time. AI serves as a smart assistant, but it's essential to remember that it isn't always perfect and still requires human oversight.

Critical Skills and Competencies

Craft Shared Agreements on Use

Before diving into the technical aspects of using AI, it's crucial to establish shared agreements on ethics and use. We've discussed the need for an explicit policy governing your nonprofit's AI use extensively in many other chapters, and again, mapping out the most critical use cases is a core component of any effective acceptable use policy. Regarding your fundraising efforts, **AI should never produce the final copy** *of grant proposals or reports.* Instead, use it as a drafting tool that requires human oversight and input. Ensure your team understands the importance of not copying material from other sources and that you provide clear guidelines to help maintain the integrity of your work.

Consider Privacy

Privacy is a significant concern when using AI, especially when dealing with sensitive information like budgets and evaluations. **Opt for AI tools that do not integrate your data into their training models.** Custom large language models (LLMs) or generative pre-trained transformers (GPTs), which offer this benefit and allow you to control data input, offer a more secure solution—see Chapter 21 for details. By being mindful of privacy issues, you can protect your nonprofit's confidential information while benefiting from AI's capabilities.

Master Prompting

Effective use of AI starts with asking the right questions. As detailed in Chapter 7, **be specific in your prompts to get the most valuable outputs, including telling your bot its role, intent, desired outcome, and format while offering context for the request.** For example, instead of asking your AI to simply *"write a grant proposal,"* you'll generate far superior results by prompting it with

> "You are a seasoned nonprofit grant writer. Please draft a proposal for a $50,000 grant to https://kelson.foundation/ to support the after-school programs of https://www.thecrucible.org/, focusing on our impact on local youth and detailing how and why we are in a strong position to advance their goals of enabling marginalized youth to reach their full potential. They have funded similar organizations in our region, and we have been invited to submit this request by XXX."

The more detailed your request, the better the AI can tailor its response to meet your needs. And often, grant writing is something you'll do over and over again. If so, **create a template case for support for each program you want to fund,** resulting in a useful toolkit that ensures you have valuable points of reference when drafting a new, custom request with specific grant requirements.

Upload your core materials and direct your AI by specifying the angle or approach you believe will be most effective, with an overarching focus on what the funder is most likely to find attractive, instead of trying to apply a cookie-cutter approach to all grants. Ultimately, *success with grant writing and institutional fundraising is less about your ability to compellingly share your work uniformly and more about clearly understanding the funder's priorities and helping them understand how and why you're in a unique position to advance their goals.*

Iterate and Refine Outputs

AI is not a one-and-done solution, and it's rarely the case that you should take your bot's first output and run with it. Instead, *take the time to converse with your GenAI platform, telling it how to enhance its draft and get you closer to a B+ or even an A−, after which you can manually review and finalize the content to ensure it aligns with your organization's voice and goals.* This iterative process enables you to refine the output and get closer to a polished final proposal or report, saving you time and ensuring it meets the funders' expectations and highlights your nonprofit's strengths.

Take the time to share each question from the application and ask your AI, "Are we missing anything in this answer? Is there anything else we should be highlighting?" This can be incredibly helpful, especially for complex grants. Finally, ask any other specific or general questions you think may strengthen your draft, including whether your responses can benefit from data provided by your nonprofit or public sources, personal accounts of your impact, and so on.

Leverage AI for Data Analysis

AI excels at analyzing large datasets, making it an invaluable tool for identifying trends and insights from your donor database. As detailed in other chapters in Part II, *use AI to segment your donors, track engagement patterns, and predict future giving behaviors.* Aside from directly helping you bring more donations in the door, this data-driven approach can also inform your grant proposals, helping you craft compelling narratives backed by solid evidence.

By leveraging AI for data analysis, you can make more informed decisions and increase your chances of securing funding. Aside from asking AI to review your private data and public sources for trends, invite it to assess your funding prospects. Upload data and reports and then ask, *"What are the trends among previous grantees, and what made them competitive?"*

Final Editing and Proofreading

AI can also serve as a powerful editing tool. After drafting your proposal or report with AI and then manually getting it to the point where you're ready to submit, embrace AI as a resource one last time. ***Run your final draft through an AI-powered editor like Grammarly*** (https://www.grammarly.com)***, Quillr*** (https://quillr.ai)***, or Writer*** (https://writer.com) ***to catch grammatical errors, improve readability, and ensure consistency in tone and style.*** While AI editing tools are incredibly efficient, always perform a final review to catch any nuances the AI might have missed. This dual approach ensures that your documents are polished and professional.

Pitfalls and Solutions

Insufficient Collaboration with Teams

AI tools are useful for generating content based on data inputs, but they cannot replace your program staff's insights, knowledge, and expertise or key stakeholders. ***Without involving your team, there's a risk that AI-generated content will be incomplete or even inaccurate.*** For instance, a grant proposal might misrepresent program outcomes or overlook crucial details about how a specific initiative operates. This can lead to misalignment between what you submit and what your nonprofit can realistically deliver.

To mitigate this, treat AI-generated drafts as collaborative documents. ***Share drafts with relevant team members who can validate the accuracy of the information included in your submission and add helpful details.*** Program staff should be encouraged to add real-world examples or success stories. Finance and administrative staff should be tapped to ensure accurate budgets and projections align with your proposal. A collaborative approach will ensure your final product is comprehensive and reflects your nonprofit's work.

Failing to Fact-Check, Address Redundancies, and Ensure Alignment

AI-generated content often includes repetitive language, inaccurate data, or details that don't align with your nonprofit's key priorities, undermining the quality and effectiveness of grant applications and reports. Restating the same points multiple times without adding depth will make your content appear unpolished. **AI-generated fabricated or outdated data points or citations will seriously call your credibility into question.** Bots can also miss the mark when emphasizing secondary programs instead of the initiatives most relevant to the funder's interests. **It's up to you to ensure your final product is streamlined, factually correct, as specific and targeted as possible, and focused on the key points that will speak to your prospective funder.**

To address these issues, take the time up front to guide AI tools with prompts that emphasize your nonprofit's strategic priorities. Once you have a solid draft you're ready to bring home, thoroughly review AI-generated content to eliminate redundancy and ensure each sentence contributes meaningfully to the narrative. **To maintain accuracy and credibility, cross-check all facts, figures, and claims against reliable sources, such as internal data, recent research, or funder guidelines.** Be sure to review outputs to ensure alignment with both your mission and the funder's expectations. This comprehensive approach ensures your proposals and reports are concise, accurate, and reflective of your strengths and goals, increasing the impact and competitiveness of your submissions.

Relying on a Single AI Tool

Different AI tools excel at various tasks, and **relying on a single platform will limit the quality and scope of your content.** For instance, one tool might be great at generating ideas, while another excels at improving tone and style. Using only one tool will prevent you from leveraging the strengths of different platforms, resulting in less refined or compelling outputs.

So, integrate multiple AI tools into your writing process. For example, **ChatGPT can brainstorm ideas, Grammarly can do grammar and style checks, and ProWritingAid** (https://prowritingaid.com/) **can be used for readability analysis.** Combining the capabilities of several tools will give you the best of all worlds, helping increase the likelihood that your final content is comprehensive, polished, and aligned.

Road Map to the Future

The rapid evolution of AI is poised to reshape how nonprofits approach grant writing and reporting, transforming these tedious, labor-intensive tasks into dynamic, data-driven collaborations between humans and intelligent tools. ***As AI becomes more sophisticated, nonprofits will move beyond basic drafting assistance to leveraging systems that analyze funder priorities, organizational performance metrics, and program outcomes*** with unparalleled speed and accuracy. This shift will enable nonprofits to craft more targeted and persuasive grant applications while significantly reducing the time required to produce comprehensive and impactful reports.

Over the next couple of years, "agential" AI, capable of independently researching, synthesizing, and adapting to specific grant requirements, will change everything. ***Your AI of the not-so-distant future will integrate seamlessly with your donor management platforms and CRM, drawing insights from structured and unstructured data.*** That means beyond feeding your AI tools well-organized information to help them help you, you'll be able to easily, if not automatically, share unorganized meeting notes, emails, program evaluations, proposals, and just about anything else, and the system will decipher it and internalize the relevant insights, enabling you to focus on high-value tasks, like refining narratives and building relationships with funders. To prepare, invest in organizing your data (for now, this is still key) and training staff to position your nonprofit at the forefront of AI-powered grant writing and reporting innovation.

Dos and Don'ts

Do

- Establish shared agreements for ethics and use, spell out acceptable use for grant and report writing, and note that AI should never produce the final copy of anything submitted to a funder
- Take the time to master prompt engineering; always using prompts that include the bot's role, intent, desired outcome, format, and any useful context
- Create a template case for support for your nonprofit and each of your programs, but don't ever share these as-is instead of taking the time to customize the templates based on funder requirements and objectives

- Use AI to assess funding prospects by asking for insights on trends among previous grantees
- Share proposal drafts with your team to validate accuracy and provide details
- Invest in organizing your data and training staff to make the most of the AI revolution

Don't

- Use AI tools that integrate your data into their training models instead of custom LLMs or GPTs
- Forget that success with grant writing depends on clearly understanding the funder's priorities and helping them understand how and why you can help them achieve their goals
- Ever rely on AI's first outputs versus taking the time to iterate and refine initial results to get a quality starting point before you dive in manually to get it across the finish line
- Skip the final step of running your final draft through an AI-powered editor to catch grammatical errors, improve readability, and ensure consistency in tone and style
- Send out a proposal or report without a final, manual review, when you make sure whatever you submit is streamlined, correct, specific, and focused on the right points
- Rely on a single AI tool; for grants and other fundraising documents, consider one tool for brainstorming ideas, another for grammar and style reviews, and a third for final readability analysis

Conclusion

Incorporating AI into your grant writing and reporting processes can transform your nonprofit's efficiency and effectiveness. ***You can save valuable time and resources by establishing ethical guidelines, protecting privacy, and leveraging AI's strengths for data analysis, template creation, and editing.*** Remember, AI is a powerful tool that complements your expertise and intuition, not a replacement. Use it wisely to enhance your proposals, streamline workflows, and ultimately secure more funding to advance your mission. AI can be incredibly helpful, but it's not a silver bullet. It requires human oversight and refinement to ensure the best results. Embrace AI as an ally in your quest to make a positive impact, and you'll find yourself better equipped to tackle the challenges and opportunities that lie ahead.

Interviewee Bio

Susan Mernit is a nonprofit consultant, seasoned leader, and innovator with extensive experience leveraging technology and storytelling to drive nonprofit and social impact. As CEO of The Crucible, a nonprofit arts education organization, and cofounder of Hack the Hood, Susan demonstrated her ability to harness data, technology, and creative strategies to advance fundraising, community engagement, and program delivery. Her expertise lies in combining practical tools with visionary leadership to help organizations thrive, including implementing AI-powered systems to improve grant writing, reporting, and operational efficiency. http://linkedin.com/in/susanmernit

Resource Review

- Grammarly: https://www.grammarly.com—An AI-powered writing assistant that helps grant writers catch grammatical errors, enhance clarity, and maintain consistent tone and style through real-time suggestions.

- Quillr: https://quillr.ai—Offers AI-powered editing tools that help you identify grammatical errors, improve sentence structure, and ensure a consistent and engaging tone tailored to your nonprofit's storytelling approach.

- Writer: https://writer.com—Tailors AI writing assistance to organizational style guides, ensuring that grant proposals align with your nonprofit's unique tone and branding.

- ProWritingAid: https://prowritingaid.com/—Helps nonprofits with AI-powered grant and report writing by providing advanced grammar checks, readability enhancements, and style suggestions tailored to create clear, compelling, and professional content.

- Candid: https://candid.org—Offers you access to a wealth of data and insights on foundations, grants, and funding trends, helping you identify top prospects and craft more informed and targeted grant proposals.
- Grantable: https://www.grantable.co—Offers AI-powered grant writing tools designed to simplify the proposal creation process and improve the clarity and competitiveness of your submissions.
- Foundant Technologies: https://www.foundant.com—Delivers grant management and writing software that streamlines workflows and integrates AI features to enhance proposal development and reporting.
- Instrumentl: https://www.instrumentl.com—Combines grant discovery, tracking, and management with AI-driven insights to help your nonprofit identify and secure the best funding opportunities.
- Grants.gov Learning Center: https://www.grants.gov/learn-grants.html—Offers a comprehensive resource hub for understanding the US federal grant application process, with guides and tips to help nonprofits succeed in securing government funding.
- Beth Kanter's blog: https://www.bethkanter.org—An excellent resource for how-to content on AI and nonprofit technology.
- Susan Mernit's blog: https://susanmernit.com/blog/—Our interviewee offers practical tips on using AI for fundraising and development.

Chapter 13.1

Securing Funding for Your AI Upgrades

Based on insights from an interview with Michael Belinsky.

Thanks in part to this book, you've heard about all the amazing things AI can do for your nonprofit—boosting fundraising, enhancing marketing efforts, streamlining operations, and even improving program delivery. But **here's the million-dollar question: how do you actually pay for AI upgrades?** If you're like most nonprofit leaders, your budget is tight, so new AI projects might seem unaffordable. The good news is, many funders, from the Gates Foundation to Google.org, are funding AI. And *all* funders are still trying to figure out this new technology, just like you. So, let's dive into some tried-and-true methods to get those AI dollars flowing your way.

Lead with Impact

First things first: start with the impact, not the tool, which often is a means to an end. Funders will want to understand how AI will help increase your organization's impact, not just that you're using a shiny new technology. You are probably already prioritizing projects that are most likely to advance your programmatic goals. So, when you talk to funders, frame the conversation accordingly. For example, instead of saying, "We need funding for AI to improve our back-office operations" (which may be exactly true!), say, "AI can help us reach more beneficiaries on the front end through more efficient operations on the back end." This will **help funders draw the connection between your organization's mission and impact—the ultimate reason they are funding you—and how your use of their funds in this project will enable that impact.**

Follow Fast and Embrace Community

It's tough to be a pioneer, but you don't have to always blaze a new trail. Look at what other organizations are doing with AI and learn from their successes and mistakes. You can do that by *joining communities of practice and virtual networks where you can exchange ideas and learn from your peers.* Then you can turn around and share these insights with your funders. Your funders will appreciate learning alongside you and view you as a thought partner. Remember, many of your funders are wrestling with similar challenges in understanding AI and its potential opportunities and risks. Also, it will show funders that you've done your homework and are ready to implement proven strategies. This not only helps you stay informed and gather new ideas but also derisks your project in the eyes of potential supporters.

Start with Core Funders, Then Expand

More and more funders are launching capacity-building funds to support AI upgrades for nonprofits. Research these opportunities on platforms like Candid.org and apply where appropriate. However, since these funders are getting flooded with requests, *your best bet is likely to turn first to your existing funders who already understand your organization and believe in your mission.* They are one of the most probable sources of support for your AI initiatives, typically funded as part of their ongoing commitment to your organization. Think of it as a capital campaign—small planning or seed grants can lead to larger opportunities down the road.

Right-Size Your Projects

Many program officers have small discretionary funds they can allocate to projects they find compelling. *Consider breaking down big AI ideas into bite-sized concepts that your specific counterparts at the funding organization can approve more easily and quickly.* That way, you have the potential to secure funding faster, while at the same time painting a picture of how this initial funding can lead to significant, broader impact—and set the stage for a larger fundable project down the line. Most AI applications are inherently scalable, so show how a small investment now can lead to major benefits later.

Convey Responsible Use

Because AI is a rapidly evolving technology, its risks and downsides are still being understood. In this environment, many funders want to have confidence that they are funding responsible uses of AI. And you'll certainly want to have similar confidence yourself! Once you've done your own diligence on responsible use of AI in your project, ***be prepared to discuss with funders how you will safeguard data, reduce potential bias, and ensure ethical use of AI.*** Highlight your policies and strategies for responsible AI use in your funding applications. This not only reassures funders but also demonstrates that you are a thoughtful leader who takes the ethical implications of AI seriously.

Interviewee Bio

Michael Belinsky is an expert in nonprofit strategy, fundraising, and grant development, with a track record of helping organizations secure transformative funding. Michael is an accomplished leader and social entrepreneur with more than 15 years of experience making investments and leading teams focused on topics spanning AI, philanthropy, impact investing, and global development. Currently, he is a director in the AI and Advanced Computing Institute at Schmidt Sciences, a philanthropy cofounded by Eric and Wendy Schmidt to foster the advancement of science and technology. His work there builds on his previous roles as director at Schmidt Futures, principal at the Bridgespan Group, and cofounder of the social enterprise, Instiglio. https://www.linkedin.com/in/michaelbelinsky/

Part III

Marketing and Community Engagement: Building More Meaningful Relationships Through AI

"Connection is why we're here; it's what gives purpose and meaning to our lives."
—Brené Brown, researcher and author

Outreach and engagement are the lifelines of any mission-driven organization, connecting your purpose with people who share your vision. Yet, ***in a world overflowing with information and competing priorities, cutting through the noise to reach your audience has never been more challenging.*** Fortunately, AI offers tools that can amplify your message, foster deeper connections, and inspire action.

AI is reshaping the way organizations connect with their audiences, bringing precision, scalability, and insight to the forefront of engagement strategies. Imagine creating dynamic audiovisual content tailored to diverse languages and cultural contexts, or using advanced AI-powered social listening tools to anticipate your community's needs and sentiments in real time. ***AI doesn't just enhance your reach—it provides the means to build relationships that are more personal, more relevant, and ultimately more impactful.*** With AI tools handling data analysis, trend forecasting, and even content generation, your team can focus on creativity and strategy.

This section explores how AI can revolutionize your marketing and engagement efforts while keeping your nonprofit's mission at the center. We begin with "Audiovisual (AV) Content Creation," where we share how AI-powered tools can enable your nonprofit to produce compelling graphics, videos, podcasts, and more with unparalleled efficiency.

AI doesn't just expedite production; it also personalizes content delivery, tailoring it to audience preferences and optimizing engagement. The "Translation" inset demonstrates how AI-powered solutions can break down language barriers, making your message accessible to a global audience and fostering inclusivity.

Next, the "Social Listening" chapter delves into how AI analyzes vast amounts of online data to track trends, gauge audience sentiment, and uncover opportunities for authentic engagement. This chapter includes three key insets—"Using Machine Learning to Segment Your Lists," "Social Media Analysis," and "Volunteer Recruitment and Management"—covering how to segment your lists and leverage behavioral and demographic data to create hyper-targeted communication. We also look at how to use AI to quickly, effectively analyze your social media efforts and to recruit and engage volunteers.

"Community Engagement" examines how AI can deepen relationships with supporters by enabling personalized interactions, predicting community needs, and measuring the impact of engagement efforts with precision. By using AI-driven sentiment analysis, chatbots, and predictive modeling, your nonprofit can build trust and responsiveness into its engagement strategies. Finally, "Lobbying and Advocacy" demonstrates how AI tools can empower policy-driven initiatives by mapping networks of influence, analyzing legislative trends, and crafting targeted advocacy campaigns that resonate with decision-makers and communities alike.

Throughout this section, you'll discover actionable strategies, useful tools and tactics, and ethical considerations to guide your approach. ***Each chapter offers a road map for integrating AI into your marketing and engagement strategies in a way that enhances, rather than replaces, human ingenuity.*** AI is not a substitute for the empathy and authenticity that drive effective engagement; instead, it's a force multiplier, equipping your nonprofit to make smarter decisions, foster deeper connections, and inspire greater action.

By thoughtfully integrating AI into your marketing and engagement strategies, your organization can break down barriers, extend its reach, and build a community that feels heard, valued, and motivated to support your mission. AI isn't just a bridge to your audience—it's a foundation for creating lasting, impactful relationships in an increasingly digital world.

Chapter 14

Audiovisual (AV) Content Creation

Contributed by Darian Rodriguez Heyman and Cheryl Contee.

In today's fast-paced digital landscape, capturing attention is more challenging than ever. Your nonprofit needs to cut through the noise to get your message heard. AV content has become a powerful tool for engagement, but here's the kicker: traditional methods of creating AV content can be time-consuming and expensive.

Here's where AI is your new best friend. ***Imagine creating stunning videos, images, presentation decks, and even podcasts without breaking the bank or pulling your hair out over tight deadlines.*** This chapter is your golden ticket to understanding how AI can revolutionize your AV content game. Whether you're a seasoned technologist or a nonprofit leader dipping your toes into the tech pool, you'll find some helpful tips and tools in the pages that follow. By the end, you'll be equipped to create eye-popping, attention-grabbing content that'll make your audience sit up and take notice.

Critical Skills and Competencies

Whether you're creating images, videos, audio files, or slide decks, these best practices will help you produce high-quality content that meets your nonprofit's goals—and stays future-proof. We'll start with media-specific tips and then share other critical considerations, including example prompts you can adapt.

Images

- **Iterate and refine:** Don't settle for the first image generated. ***Test multiple prompts, tweaking variables like style, color palette, and composition.***
- **Review for inclusivity:** ***Carefully examine AI-generated images for representation and bias.*** Ensure they accurately reflect the diversity of your audience.
- **Transparency:** ***Clearly label AI-generated images*** as such to maintain trust and authenticity with your audience.
- **Maximize relevance:** Make sure the images align with the message or campaign goals. ***Avoid generic visuals that lack context.***
- **Experiment with styles:** Use AI to generate various artistic styles, from photorealistic to abstract, to find the best fit for your needs.
- **Use editing tools:** Refine AI-generated images with human editing to enhance quality and ensure they meet your standards.

Sample Prompt

"Act like a creative designer for a nonprofit helping refugees. Generate five AI image options that combine elements of warmth and resilience. Each image should feature diverse people in empowering poses and use a color palette of blues and greens. Keep the style photorealistic."

Refinement Recommendation

If the images feel too generic or lack diversity, try this:

"Rewrite to focus on a specific region (e.g., Middle East). Add more detail to clothing style, emotional expressions, and background elements that convey hope."

Video

- **Storyboard first:** Before generating videos, ***outline the key scenes and messages you want to convey.*** This will help you craft precise prompts for your AI tool.
- **Mix media types:** Combine live footage with AI-generated animations to create dynamic, engaging videos. ***Use AI to add subtitles, animations, or transitions.***
- **Quality assurance:** Thoroughly review videos for visual glitches, incorrect information, or unintended messaging.

Sample Prompt

"You are a nonprofit video producer. Create a 60-second video script that blends live-action testimonials from volunteers with AI-generated animation. The theme is environmental cleanup, emphasizing urgency. Include text overlays showing stats on reduced plastic waste."

Refinement Recommendation

If your script is missing a strong emotional hook, refine:

"Make the script more emotionally compelling. Add a personal story of one volunteer's experience and highlight how a single cleanup day can remove over 500 pounds of trash."

Audio and Music

- **Experiment with iterations:** As with images, don't settle for the first result. ***Use iterative prompts to refine the tone, mood, and complexity of the audio.*** Ask questions like "*Can you make this sound more uplifting?*" or "*Can you reduce the tempo for a calmer effect?*"
- **Ethical sourcing:** ***Ensure that the AI tool you're using respects copyright laws and only generates music free of intellectual property (IP) conflicts.***

- **Test for emotion:** Use feedback from your team to ensure the audio evokes the desired emotional response, then adjust the AI prompts accordingly.
- **Explore customization:** Use tools that allow fine-tuning of generated audio to better align with your organization's branding or thematic goals.
- **Blend human creativity:** Consider combining AI-generated music with human input for a unique touch. This could involve layering AI-produced sounds with recorded voices or instruments.

Sample Prompt

"Act like a sound designer. Generate a 30-second, upbeat instrumental track suitable for a youth-focused nonprofit's Instagram reel about school supply donations. Aim for a playful, modern pop vibe with light percussion, and keep the volume levels consistent for voiceovers."

Refinement Recommendation

If the final track is too busy, refine:

"Reduce background percussion and simplify the melody to emphasize spoken narration. Keep the mood energetic but not overwhelming."

Podcasts

Podcasts are a powerful way to connect with your audience through long-form storytelling, interviews, and discussions. ***AI can streamline the podcast creation process—from scripting to editing***—making it easier for nonprofits to produce high-quality audio content.

Scripting and Storyboarding

Use AI to draft podcast scripts based on your topic, tone, and audience. For example:

"Write a 10-minute podcast script discussing the impact of our clean water initiative, aimed at engaging young professionals."

Refine the script with human input to ensure it aligns with your nonprofit's voice and mission.

Voiceovers and Audio Generation

AI tools can generate realistic voiceovers for intros, outros, or even entire episodes. For example:

> "Generate a warm, conversational voiceover for our podcast intro, emphasizing our mission to empower underserved communities."

Experiment with different voices and tones to find the best fit for your podcast.

Editing and Post-Production

Use AI-powered tools like Descript (https://www.descript.com/) or Adobe Audition (https://www.adobe.com/products/audition) to edit audio files, remove background noise, and add effects. For example:

> "Edit this podcast episode to remove pauses, add background music, and enhance audio clarity."

Ensure the final product is polished and professional.

Accessibility and Distribution

Use AI to generate transcripts and captions for your podcast, making it accessible to a wider audience. For example:

> "Create a transcript for this podcast episode and format it for our website."

Distribute your podcast on platforms like Spotify (https://open.spotify.com/) or Apple Podcasts (https://www.apple.com/apple-podcasts/), using AI tools to optimize metadata and reach your target audience.

Ethical Considerations

Clearly disclose when AI-generated voices or content are used in your podcast to maintain transparency with your audience. Ensure that any AI-generated music or sound effects comply with copyright laws.

More Sample Prompts for Podcast Creation

- *"Draft a five-minute podcast segment explaining our new youth mentorship program, aimed at engaging donors aged 35 to 65."*
- *"Generate a list of interview questions for a podcast episode featuring a community leader discussing climate change solutions."*
- *"Edit this podcast episode to remove background noise and add a professional intro and outro."*

Slide Decks

- **Define the narrative:** Use AI to draft slide content, but ***be clear about your goals, the intended audience, and any calls to action.*** For example: *"Create a slide deck summarizing our 2025 impact goals, aimed at encouraging previous donors to once again support our animal shelter."*
- **Human oversight:** ***Always review AI-generated slides for accuracy and branding alignment before sharing.***
- **Incorporate multimedia:** Use AI tools to embed relevant images, animations, or videos that enhance the message.
- **Focus on accessibility:** Ensure AI-generated slides are accessible, with features like alt text for images and readable fonts.

Sample Prompt

"You are a presentation designer for a nonprofit. Draft a five-slide deck that outlines our homeless outreach strategy for 2025. Use bullet points, relevant stock images, and a bold color scheme. Include data on our goal to reduce unsheltered homelessness by 20%."

Refinement Recommendation

If the slides look cluttered, refine with:

> *"Make the design minimalist. Limit text to key points on each slide and replace some text with infographics or icons."*

Find the Right Tool

Settling on the right AI tool is like dating—you might have to kiss a few frogs before finding your prince. ***Look for tools that are user-friendly, offer robust support, and can grow with you.*** Tools like Lumen5 (https://lumen5.com/) for video creation, Descript for audio and video editing, and RunwayML (https://app.runwayml.com/) for all sorts of cool video effects are a great place to start. Look for tools that offer a free trial or a nonprofit discount. Test multiple tools to compare their features and performance. Involve your team in the evaluation process to get diverse perspectives and ensure that the chosen tool meets your organization's requirements.

The AI tool landscape is constantly evolving, with new tools emerging regularly. It's essential to stay informed about the latest developments and trends. ***Assign a team member to keep track of new AI tools and evaluate their potential for your nonprofit.*** Attend webinars, read industry blogs, and participate in online communities to stay in the loop. And finally, don't be afraid to switch tools if something better comes along. The cost of switching is typically low, and the potential benefits can be significant.

Master Prompting

Think of mastering prompting as learning a new language—only this one talks to robots. The clearer and more detailed your prompts, the better the AI output. ***Get specific about tone, audience, and key messages.*** And note that different tools require different approaches to prompting, so experiment to find out what works best and create a prompt library for your team to share successful prompts and fast-track everyone's learning curve. Trust us, a little effort here goes a long way in making your AI-generated content shine, so we even devoted all of Chapter 7 to this crucial, foundational skill that is key to enabling you to get the most out of AI.

Refinement in Action: Sample Iteration Workflow

Initial Prompt

"Generate a 30-second video script about our nonprofit's food drive."

First AI Output (Summary)

"Support our food drive. Your donations feed the hungry. Act now."

Refinement Prompt

"Make the script more emotionally compelling. Include a short personal story, a clear call to action, and mention we aim to collect 1,000 canned goods."

Second AI Output (Refined)

"Meet Maria, a single mother who depends on your generosity. With just a few donated cans, you help families put dinner on the table. Help us reach our goal of 1,000 canned goods by next Friday—together, we can make a difference."

Expanded Refinement

"Add a closing scene that thanks volunteers and includes our website URL for more info."

Final AI Output

"Thanks to caring people like you, Maria and hundreds of others have meals tonight. Visit www.OurFoodDrive.org to learn more and volunteer. Let's feed hope, one can at a time."

This final script is now stronger, more emotional, and more specific. From here, add your human touch to personalize language, align it with your brand voice, or incorporate real footage of Maria (with her permission) for authenticity.

Create Custom Large Language Models

Creating custom large language models (LLMs) involves training AI models on your organization's data, voice, goals, and specific use cases. This enables the AI to generate content that is tailored to your brand and audience. By using the same AI model for similar tasks, you ensure that your content has a cohesive tone and style. ***Identify repetitive tasks that can be automated using custom LLMs.*** This could include drafting email newsletters, creating social media posts, or generating reports. By automating these tasks, you free up your team to focus on more strategic and creative work. Once again, see Chapter 21 for details.

Pitfalls and Solutions

Stepping on IP

IP issues can arise when using AI tools to create AV content. AI-generated content may inadvertently infringe on the rights of artists, photographers, and other creators. That's why it's key to establish clear guidelines for using AI tools. ***Avoid using specific names or trademarks in your prompts.*** Always obtain proper licenses and permissions for any third-party content used in your creations.

Transparency is crucial when using AI-generated content. ***Clearly label and disclose any content created using AI tools.*** This builds trust with your audience and ensures that they are aware of the source of the content.

Disinformation

The rapid creation and dissemination of AI-generated content can lead to the spread of disinformation. This can harm your organization's credibility and erode public trust. To combat this, prioritize accuracy and truthfulness in all your content. ***Implement strict fact-checking protocols to verify the information before publishing.*** Use reliable sources and cross-reference data to ensure that your content is accurate and trustworthy. And finally, provide your team with training on fact-checking techniques and ethical considerations.

Content Bias

AI tools can inadvertently perpetuate biases present in their training data. This can lead to the creation of content that lacks diversity and representation. To mitigate this, ***use images of AI-generated people sparingly and always review them for potential biases.*** Non-photorealistic images, such as illustrations or animations, are generally safer and can reduce the risk of bias.

Ensure that your AI tools are trained on diverse datasets that represent a wide range of demographics and perspectives. This helps create more inclusive and representative content.

Road Map to the Future

The rapid advancement of AI technology promises exciting opportunities for AV content creation. AI tools are becoming more accessible and affordable, making it easier for nonprofits to leverage their capabilities. As AI continues to evolve, it will offer new features and functionalities that can enhance your content creation process, enabling your nonprofit to produce high-quality content more efficiently.

This includes creating personalized and interactive content that engages and resonates with your audience. This ability to generate content quickly and at scale will increasingly enable your organization to respond to emerging trends and opportunities in real time. But only if you stay on top of things, so be sure to stay informed and prioritize ongoing training and professional development to stay at the head of the pack to stay competitive.

Dos and Don'ts

Do

- Experiment with multiple prompts and settings in AI tools to refine outputs, exploring variations in tone, style, and composition to achieve the most effective results
- Ensure all AV content aligns with your nonprofit's goals, brand identity, and audience needs, incorporating accessibility features like captions, alt text, and user-friendly layouts

- Clearly disclose when content is AI-generated to maintain transparency and build trust with your audience, especially for visuals, audio, and video that represent your organization
- Review AI-generated outputs for potential biases, factual inaccuracies, or misrepresentations, combining them with human oversight to ensure high-quality, inclusive content
- Take advantage of nonprofit discounts, free trials, and team collaborations to identify cost-effective tools and optimize your AI investments

Don't

- Publish AI-generated content without thorough reviews, risking glitches, errors, or messages that conflict with your nonprofit's values or mission
- Rely entirely on AI tools to create content without adding human creativity and personalization, which are essential for engaging and resonating with your audience
- Neglect to address copyright and IP concerns, ensuring all AI-generated elements comply with legal requirements and respect the rights of others
- Overlook training your team in using AI tools effectively, leaving staff without the skills or knowledge needed to maximize their potential
- Assume AI tools will automatically produce inclusive or representative content without carefully reviewing outputs for diversity and relevance to your audience

Conclusion

AI transforms the way your nonprofit can create audiovisual content, offering tools that save time, reduce costs, and elevate the quality of your storytelling. By using AI strategically, you can produce compelling videos, images, and other multimedia content that resonate deeply with your audience, amplifying your mission and increasing engagement. However, success lies in balancing the speed and efficiency of AI with the creativity, oversight, and authenticity that only your team can provide.

To make the most of these opportunities, ***adopt AI thoughtfully—align its use with your goals, train your team to use it effectively, and ensure every piece of content reflects your organization's values and inclusivity.*** By combining the power of AI with a clear vision and ethical approach, your nonprofit can stand out in a crowded digital landscape, inspiring action and driving meaningful change. The tools are ready; it's your turn to make them work for you.

Contributor Bios

Darian Rodriguez Heyman is an accomplished fundraising and philanthropy consultant. He is the bestselling author of *Nonprofit Management 101*, the former executive director of Craigslist Foundation, and a sought-after keynote speaker at social impact events around the world. He can be reached directly via his website, https://helpingpeoplehelp.com/, and is happy to offer any readers a pro bono coaching session if helpful. http://www.linkedin.com/in/dheyman

Cheryl Contee is a pioneering technology entrepreneur and digital transformation expert. She is the bestselling author of *Mechanical Bull: How You Can Achieve Startup Success*, a trailblazing startup founder, and a trusted advisor on digital innovation and social impact. She inspires audiences globally as a leading voice on inclusive entrepreneurship and social enterprise. http://www.linkedin.com/in/cherylcontee.

Resource Review

- Lumen5: https://www.lumen5.com—Transform written content into engaging videos with ease, perfect for telling your nonprofit's story in a dynamic format.
- Descript: https://www.descript.com—Edit audio and video seamlessly, from creating podcasts to refining your video content with minimal technical expertise.
- RunwayML: https://app.runwayml.com—Experiment with AI-powered video effects, animations, and enhancements to elevate your nonprofit's video production.
- TechSoup: https://www.techsoup.org—Access discounted software, webinars, and guides that help your nonprofit implement technology solutions like AI effectively.

- Loom: https://www.loom.com—Create and share quick video updates or tutorials for your team, stakeholders, or audience to enhance communication and engagement.
- Pexels: https://www.pexels.com—Source high-quality, royalty-free stock images and videos to supplement your AI-generated content.
- Canva: https://www.canva.com—Design eye-catching presentations, social media graphics, and more with easy-to-use templates and AI features.
- Adobe Express: https://www.adobe.com/express—Produce stunning graphics, flyers, and short videos with this free and intuitive design tool ideal for nonprofits.
- Otter.ai: https://otter.ai—Use AI to transcribe and caption audio and video files, making your multimedia content more accessible to all audiences.
- VideoAsk: https://www.videoask.com—Engage donors, beneficiaries, or partners with personalized, interactive video messages that can include responses.

Chapter 14.1
Translation

Based on insights from an interview with Nicholas Martin.

Whether you're expanding services to marginalized communities, engaging a global network of volunteers, or soliciting donations from international benefactors, the ability to translate your content into multiple languages can open up a world of possibilities. But historically, offering multilingual content has been cost prohibitive for most nonprofits, and even then, only when they were trying to reach a huge audience to make it worth it.

AI offers a robust solution to the often-daunting task of translation, allowing you to bridge language gaps more efficiently than ever before. In the past, translating something like a comprehensive digital health course could cost up to $200,000 and take up to six months. With AI, that cost and time can be substantially reduced, with only a small amount of staff support required. While the quality of AI translations might not be perfect yet, it's rapidly improving, especially for the major languages. Even now, leveraging AI for translation can save you time and resources while breaking down language barriers and expanding your nonprofit's impact. The tools are here, the technology is improving, and with a little intentionality, your organization can expand your reach across borders and cultures.

Breaking Language Barriers with AI
Shop the Shelves

There's no need to reinvent the wheel when it comes to AI translation. ***Start by exploring one of the existing large language models (LLMs) like ChatGPT, Gemini, Claude, and Perplexity, which have built-in translation engines.***

The major GenAI platforms already translate content into over 100 languages with varying levels of fluency, covering most widely spoken languages, regional dialects, and even some lesser-known ones. And they're adding more every day.

You may also want to consider specialized platforms like DeepL (https://www.deepl.com/) or Lokalise (https://lokalise.com/), which offer more robust accuracy, contextual understanding, and adaptability for translation than the mainstream LLMs. Many of these tools have cost structures that are more affordable than hiring translation firms. Either way, it's critical to recognize that any ***AI-generated translations are generally good but not perfect, offering 80% accuracy and climbing.*** As such, you either need to accept some errors and be OK with that or have someone fluent in the target language review translations if precision is critical to your work—think legal documentation or health care information.

Safety First

When using AI for translation, data privacy and bias are key concerns. Ensure you implement guardrails around data protection and ethical use. While we cover these considerations extensively in other parts of the book, it's particularly important here since you might be translating content into languages you don't fully understand. ***Make sure your chosen AI tools comply with your organization's data privacy policies and you understand some of the potential biases that could skew your translations.***

Invite Intentionality and Look Inside

Be clear about your use case, audience, and desired outcomes. Are you creating multilingual FAQs, program overviews, or chatbot responses? How can these translations better serve your clients and stakeholders? ***Internally, consider integrating AI translation tools with your learning management or HR system, allowing team members to communicate in their preferred languages.*** This not only enhances internal communication but also ensures that your translated content is accurate and contextually appropriate.

Rinse and Repeat

AI is an evolving field, and staying updated with the latest advancements will keep your translation efforts on the cutting edge. *Keep an eye on new features like real-time voice-to-voice translation, sign language translation, and improvements in soft skills,* which are crucial for areas like mental health support. Regularly reassess your tools and processes to incorporate these advancements and continue improving your translation quality.

Just Do It

Dive in and start experimenting! Upload documents, input text for translation, and see how the AI performs. Continuously monitor the quality of translations and have native speakers review outputs if accuracy is paramount. *For less critical communications, spot checks might suffice, but for high-stakes content, thorough reviews are essential.*

Expand the Base

If your work involves indigenous or endangered languages, consider helping "AI-ify" these languages by incorporating them into LLMs. This can be a long-term goal, requiring significant data input (about 17 million datapoints), but it's a vital step in preserving and promoting linguistic diversity. Collaborate with experts and communities to gather the necessary data and ensure these languages are represented in the AI landscape. Organizations like XRI Global (https://www.xriglobal.ai/) are working with nonprofits and communities to bridge language gaps by developing AI tools and curating datasets for low-resource and endangered languages, aiming to enable speakers of every language to flourish through language technology.

Interviewee Bio

Nicholas Martin is a visionary leader in audiovisual content creation, with a focus on using technology to amplify nonprofit storytelling and global impact. As the founder and CEO of TechChange, Nicholas has pioneered innovative approaches to training and education, producing high-quality multimedia content that engages diverse audiences worldwide. Under his leadership, the organization has developed transformative e-learning experiences for organizations such as UNICEF, USAID, and the World Bank. https://www.linkedin.com/in/nicholascmartin/

Chapter 15

Social Listening

Based on insights from an interview with Julia Campbell.

Social listening is akin to having a giant ear to the ground. It involves monitoring blogs, news sites, and other platforms to understand what people are saying about your cause and organization. Community engagement, however, is the lifeblood of your marketing and social presence. Are you authentically reaching your community and inspiring them to action? Are you empathetic and do you understand and address their needs? Are you responding to disinformation and misconceptions?

In the hustle and bustle of daily nonprofit work, it's easy to lose sight of what's happening on the ground. AI can serve as a neutral party, enabling you to keep your fingers on the pulse. ***AI helps you understand people's sentiments, address their concerns, track important trends, uncover and engage nonobvious partners and supporters, and build meaningful relationships.*** In this chapter, you'll learn how to leverage AI for effective social listening and community engagement, ensuring your nonprofit remains relevant and responsive to community needs.

Critical Skills and Competencies

Experiment with Tools

Your first step as you begin tipping your toes in the AI waters should be experimenting with free or low-cost tools. ***Free tools like Google Alerts*** (https://www.google.com/alerts) ***support social listening by enabling you to get a free notification anytime a phrase or word appears online.*** It's also a great way to track celebrities, influencers, and funders you're looking to track. These tools are easy to set up and use, making them perfect for nonprofits with limited resources. Platforms like Hootsuite (https://hootsuite.com), Buffer (https://buffer.com), or Sprout Social (https://sproutsocial.com) are typically only used to preschedule social media posts on ideal dates and times. These ***often-underused scheduling resources are also great for social media monitoring, plus they offer nonprofit discounts*** and can be a great starting point.

Don't be afraid to try out different tools and strategies, as this will help you find what works best for your nonprofit. Start small, and as you gain confidence and understanding, you can explore more advanced tools and techniques.

Focused Monitoring

In the game of social listening, less is more. ***Instead of trying to monitor everything, identify a handful of the most relevant keywords or topics, and then keep a close eye on those over time.*** As mentioned, free tools like Google Alerts are perfectly suited to this task. Your list of keynotes will likely include your nonprofit's or program's name, key issues you address, and the names of other like-minded or similar organizations. Focused monitoring enables you to dive deeper into specific conversations, making your efforts more effective and manageable.

By narrowing down your focus, you can allocate resources more efficiently. This targeted approach ensures that you are not overwhelmed by the data and can derive meaningful insights that are directly relevant to your mission.

Dive Deeper with Sentiment Analysis

Usually, it would be impossible to comb through the entire information and media landscape to assess what people are saying and thinking about you and things you care about, but no longer. ***AI enables you to gauge public opinion and emotions about your nonprofit, programs, or the issues you champion by analyzing social media posts, reviews, comments, and other textual data.*** Then it quickly, easily helps you discern whether people are expressing positive, negative, or neutral sentiments, which can guide your communication strategies, identify potential crises, and inform decisions about messaging and engagement efforts. If these numbers tank, it's cause for alarm, and if you see an uptick, it not only causes celebration but also invites reflection so you can learn from what's working. ***By incorporating sentiment analysis into social listening, your nonprofit can proactively address concerns, amplify positive feedback, and better align your efforts with stakeholder expectations.***

To implement sentiment analysis effectively, start by selecting a tool that integrates with the platforms where your audience engages most—be it Instagram, TikTok, or forums like Reddit. Use keywords and hashtags relevant to your organization or campaign to monitor conversations, similar to what you'd do on Google Alerts but going a level deeper to gauge the emotion behind relevant posts. Tools like Hootsuite Insights (https://hootsuite.com/products/insights), Brandwatch (https://www.brandwatch.com/), or MonkeyLearn (https://monkeylearn.com/sentiment-analysis/) help automate sentiment tracking and generate actionable insights. ***Establish a process to review and interpret the data regularly, combining it with contextual understanding—like recent events or cultural nuances—that might influence sentiment.*** Training your team to recognize sentiment patterns and integrate these insights into strategic planning can make this effort even more impactful.

Track Trends over Time

Now that you're successfully using AI to monitor key references and gauge how folks feel about you, it's time to turn that photograph into a movie. Instead of just getting a glimpse at these things, ***trend analysis and tracking involves monitoring patterns in conversations, keywords, and topics OVER TIME to identify emerging issues or shifts in public interest.*** This helps your nonprofit stay ahead of developments that matter to your mission—whether it's a new policy affecting your community, a viral campaign aligned with your cause, or a budding partnership opportunity. ***By identifying trends early, you can adjust your strategies to remain relevant, respond to audience needs, and capitalize on momentum.*** For example, tracking an uptick in discussions about environmental sustainability might prompt your nonprofit to highlight its related programs or launch a timely awareness campaign.

Start by using tools that specialize in trend monitoring, such as Google Trends (https://trends.google.com/), Sprout Social, or BuzzSumo (https://buzzsumo.com/), to track keywords and hashtags tied to your mission. Regularly review these tools for patterns, spikes, or changes in volume over time. **Set alerts for relevant topics to receive real-time updates when there's a surge in interest.** To go deeper, analyze your own digital metrics—such as website visits, email open rates, or social media interactions—to detect internal trends that may correlate with external conversations. Finally, align these insights with your strategic goals, ensuring your nonprofit is positioned to lead or respond to critical developments in your sector.

Measure, Analyze, and Adapt... Regularly

At least weekly, you should review what your social listening tools uncover. Look for patterns and trends, and adjust your strategy accordingly. Simplify this by avoiding ad hoc meetings, instead scheduling something regular that people can plan around. **Weekly check-ins to review AI insights will help you stay on top of emerging trends and shifts in sentiment.** And more robust monthly reports are a great forum to help you and your team identify successful engagement tactics and areas where improvement is needed.

Adapting to what you learn is key to staying relevant and responsive. **As you gather insights from your social listening efforts, use them to refine your strategies, always ensuring they align with your nonprofit's goals and the needs of your community.** By continuously reviewing and adapting your approach, you can maintain a dynamic and effective engagement strategy.

Pitfalls and Solutions

Lack of Clear Objectives

Without knowing what you want to accomplish, your social listening efforts will be unfocused, leading to data that's irrelevant or difficult to act on. Without context or intention, monitoring every mention of your nonprofit without knowing whether you want to track sentiment, measure campaign effectiveness, or identify influencers can overwhelm your team and dilute your insights. So, **start by identifying specific questions you want to answer or goals you want to achieve,** such as improving donor engagement, quickly responding to negative public comments before they escalate, or identifying emerging trends in your field. Clear objectives will guide your keyword selection, tool configuration, and analysis, ensuring your efforts are purposeful and impactful.

Exclusive Focus on Quantitative Metrics

While the number of times your nonprofit is mentioned online or the reach of your social media content is important, they don't tell the full story. Tracking only what are sometimes called "vanity metrics" causes you to miss deeper insights, such as the context or sentiment behind audience conversations. A spike in mentions could indicate a controversy rather than positive engagement. To avoid this, ***pair quantitative metrics with qualitative analysis, digging into the content of posts, comments, or conversations to understand audience emotions and motivations.*** This balanced approach ensures your strategies are based on a complete picture.

Tracking Too Much

Trying to monitor an excessive number of keywords or topics can inundate you with irrelevant data, making it difficult to extract meaningful insights. If you track every variation of a common term related to your mission, it will clutter your dashboard with noise. Instead, ***focus on a concise, high-impact list of keywords that reflect your priorities, campaigns, and organizational goals.*** Regularly review the relevance of these and adjust them based on emerging trends or shifting conversations. Starting small and refining your approach ensures your data remains manageable and actionable.

Not Monitoring Competitors and Partners

If you limit your focus to posts and conversations about your own organization, you'll miss out on valuable insights. ***Observing competitors can reveal gaps in their strategies that your nonprofit can fill, while monitoring partners can highlight collaboration opportunities or shared challenges.*** Competitors' unsuccessful campaigns offer valuable lessons in what to avoid without you having to pay the price, whereas successful efforts can inspire innovation and ideas. Incorporate competitor and partner analysis into your social listening strategy by tracking their keywords, mentions, and audience engagement patterns, ensuring you're always informed about your broader ecosystem.

Failing to Act on Insights

Social listening data is only valuable if it drives action. If your nonprofit collects insights but doesn't translate them into meaningful strategies or adjustments, you're wasting time and resources. Noticing a rise in negative sentiment without addressing the root cause will likely lead to a hit to your reputation. ***Create a clear process for acting on insights, such as assigning team members to analyze data, present findings in actionable formats, and recommend specific next steps.*** Establishing this workflow ensures your social listening efforts lead to tangible improvements in your campaigns, messaging, and stakeholder relationships.

Road Map to the Future

There are two disruptive advancements about to seriously change now nonprofits practice social listening and community engagement: voice recognition and agential AI. Within a very short time, the new normal will involve simply speaking to AI just like you do with Siri today, but accessing vastly more functionality. ***Imagine donors watching a commercial or hearing a story on the radio and then simply telling their bots to donate to the highlighted nonprofit,*** streamlining the giving process and removing barriers to engagement. It'll all be easier than the touch of a button before you know it.

As AI technologies evolve, they will also offer deeper insights and more precise predictions, with more and more features baked in. Whether that means ***your chatbot will automatically refine its language and approach in real time based on user interactions,*** or increasingly not only analyzing data but also providing actionable recommendations tailored to specific organizational goals, the results will be mind-blowing. No more looking over social media analysis reports that only tell you what happened, but with vastly more insights around why, along with a list of the top five trends you should pay attention to, what similar people were talking about last year or the election cycle at this time, and with automated suggestions accessible via a simple "make this post better" button. Not only that, but you also may not even need to regularly read reports, since the bots will always be on the lookout and will automatically feed you useful updates and recommendations whenever there are noteworthy developments.

To leverage these advancements, your nonprofit needs to stay adaptable and continuously update your strategy. By embracing AI and integrating it thoughtfully into your operations, you can enhance your impact and better serve your community. The organizations that thrive will be those that balance technological innovation with the irreplaceable value of human empathy and connection.

Dos and Don'ts

Do

- Experiment with free or low-cost social listening tools to get started without significant financial investment
- Focus on monitoring specific keywords and topics to make your social listening efforts more effective and manageable
- Use AI-powered sentiment analysis tools to enable you to gauge whether people are sharing positive or negative thoughts on your work and organization
- Monitor trends over time, so you can adjust strategies and maximize relevance
- Schedule weekly check-ins and monthly reports to stay on top of trends and act on insights, with specific team members assigned to analyze data, present findings, and recommend action
- Establish clear AI policies that include guidelines on data privacy, consent, and transparency to ensure ethical and effective use of AI tools
- Combine the power of analyzing quantitative metrics with qualitative insights to really understand your audience's emotions and motivations

Don't

- Commence social listening activity without first identifying specific questions you want to answer or goals you want to achieve
- Track every variation of a common term related to your mission, which leads to information overload and makes it difficult to discern what information is actually useful

- Focus social listening efforts solely on your nonprofit and work, neglecting the critical importance of also tracking competitors and partners
- Stick your head in the sand and wait for AI to go mainstream: it already has, and the longer you wait, the further behind the pack you'll find yourself!

Conclusion

Embracing AI for social listening and community engagement can revolutionize the way your nonprofit interacts with its audience. By leveraging AI tools effectively, you can gain deep insights into your donors and stakeholders, address any concerns promptly, and build stronger, more meaningful relationships. However, it's crucial to balance AI with a human-centered approach, ensuring that your interactions remain personal and empathetic.

Remember, ***the key to success lies in experimentation, focused monitoring, ongoing trend analysis, regular team check-ins, and taking the time to create clear policies.*** Equip your team with the right tools and guidelines, and you'll be well on your way to harnessing the power of AI to amplify your nonprofit's impact. As you move forward, stay adaptable and responsive to the evolving needs of your community, and let AI be a valuable ally in your mission to create positive change.

Interviewee Bio

Julia Campbell is a renowned digital marketing strategist and author specializing in helping nonprofits harness the power of social listening and community engagement to amplify their impact. With a deep understanding of AI-driven tools, Julia equips organizations to monitor online conversations, analyze audience sentiment, and identify emerging trends that inform strategic decision-making. Her expertise lies in blending technology with storytelling to create meaningful connections between nonprofits and their supporters, fostering stronger communities and driving mission-focused growth. A sought-after speaker and educator, as well as the producer of the hit *Nonprofit Nation* podcast, Julia regularly shares her insights through workshops, webinars, and her podcast. https://www.linkedin.com/in/juliacampbell/

Resource Review

- The *Nonprofit Nation* podcast: https://nonprofitnation.buzzsprout.com/—Empowers nonprofit leaders to harness AI for social listening and community engagement, offering actionable insights and tools to understand and respond to their audiences more effectively.
- Google Alerts: https://www.google.com/alerts—A free tool to track mentions of your nonprofit or relevant topics online.
- Sprout Social: https://sproutsocial.com/—Combines social listening and analytics, enabling your nonprofit to monitor conversations, identify trends, and meaningfully engage your audience across various platforms.
- Hootsuite Insights: https://hootsuite.com/products/insights—Provides real-time social listening and sentiment analysis, helping nonprofit leaders monitor conversations and measure audience sentiment across multiple social media platforms.
- Brandwatch: https://www.brandwatch.com/—Offers advanced analytics and trend tracking, enabling your nonprofit to identify emerging topics, understand audience perceptions, and tailor your engagement strategies effectively.
- Google Trends: https://trends.google.com/—Tracks search interest over time for specific topics or keywords, providing insights into audience behavior and emerging trends relevant to their mission.
- BuzzSumo: https://buzzsumo.com/—Enables you to analyze trending content, track topic popularity, and discover influencers, helping you amplify campaigns and stay ahead of relevant discussions.
- Buffer: https://buffer.com—A user-friendly tool for scheduling and monitoring social media posts.
- Talkwalker: https://www.talkwalker.com—A robust social listening and analytics platform.
- Mention: https://mention.com—A real-time media monitoring tool to track mentions across the web.
- Meltwater: https://www.meltwater.com—A media intelligence platform offering social listening and analytics.

Chapter 15.1

Using Machine Learning to Segment Your Lists

Based on insights from an interview with Brian Young.

As your nonprofit looks to adopt AI and unlock the myriad benefits outlined in this book, odds are the idea of sending custom messages to vastly improve response rates and fuel donor engagement has caught your attention. After all, wouldn't it be great if your messages could cut through the noise, reach the right people at the right time, with content that speaks directly to them?

Sure, that all sounds great, but does the implementation required seem daunting? ***Especially if you have lots of contacts and a small staff, segmenting your list to enable mass personalization likely seems an insurmountable task.*** But Machine Learning (ML) can help by taking a lot of the heavy lifting off your plate, making this undertaking more realistic. Ready to learn how to make it happen in five simple steps?

AI-Driven List Segmentation

Choose the Right Email Messaging Service Provider

Your first step is selecting a provider that's not just good, but *great* for your specific needs. Here's what to keep in mind:

- **Relevance to your work:** Ensure your provider has experience with nonprofits like yours, whether you're an advocacy or activism-based organization, a think tank, or a food pantry, ***take the time to find a provider that understands the nuances of your work*** and won't have to learn on your dime. Enlisting your GenAI platform's help can support this research with a simple prompt like, "*You are a nonprofit technology and marketing expert with deep experience in AI, ML, and email marketing. Please share a bulleted list of five email messaging service providers who have lots of nonprofit clients, especially groups who share our focus on XXX, and who offer AI-powered list segmentation as part of their services, with links for each.*"

- **Training opportunities:** Opt for a provider that offers training on deliverability metrics and industry developments, as trends and features are constantly evolving.
- **Turnkey AI solutions:** Ideally, *your provider should offer AI-driven segmentation and list optimization as part of their package.* This means the heavy lifting is done for you, making the process seamless and integrated.

Set Realistic Goals

Now that you have your provider lined up, it's time to dive in, right? Nope! **Before beginning any segmentation efforts, set clear, realistic goals.** Are you looking to deepen engagement with a smaller, more dedicated group, or broaden your reach to a wider audience? Understanding your priorities will help you set achievable targets and avoid the pitfalls of overpromising and under-delivering. AI can provide useful context and insights to integrate into your thinking, but ultimately human judgment here is still crucial.

Identify Meaningful Criteria

For your segmentation efforts to produce the most benefits, you need to *think beyond demographics and consider a wide range of other attributes, including donor behavior, engagement history, peer influence, programmatic alignment and interests, predicted lifetime value, location, and communication preferences.* Consider what types of messages your supporters respond best to, when supporters are most likely to engage with your messages, past interactions that help predict future behavior, and how different segments of your audience respond to various senders and styles. If your AI-driven CRM system identifies that a certain subset prefers text message updates over emails, use that insight to tailor your outreach. Incorporate behavior-based criteria like predicted lifetime value or programmatic alignment to create hyper-targeted campaigns.

Once you've identified your criteria, it's time to put ML to work. If your email messaging service provider offers AI-driven segmentation, you can input your goals and criteria, and the system will analyze your data to create segments automatically, saving your team significant time and effort. For example, it can group donors who respond best to end-of-year campaigns or those who prefer impact-driven messaging, ensuring your outreach aligns with their preferences. If your provider doesn't offer this capability, you can still leverage ML tools like Google Cloud's AI capabilities or stand-alone platforms like RFM segmentation tools to process your data and create actionable segments. Either way, the key is to let the machine do the heavy lifting, while you focus on tailoring strategies for engagement.

Test and Refine

Testing is your friend, since you shouldn't expect to get this right out of the gate. ***Start by sending test messages to a small subset of your list, using the insights gained to refine your approach before rolling out to your larger audience.*** This iterative process helps you continually improve and ensures your messages hit the mark. Once again, depending on your email provider, they may offer AI tools that streamline this process by quickly interpreting results and adjusting strategies in real time.

Maintain Human Oversight

AI can be an incredibly powerful tool for creating draft messages, analyzing donor data, and suggesting tailored communication strategies. However, it's crucial to remember that AI should serve as an assistant, not a substitute for human connection. ***Use AI to generate insights and draft content but always ensure a human reviews and personalizes messages before they reach your supporters.*** This not only helps maintain the authenticity and trust that are essential to your donor relationships but also ensures that your messaging aligns with your organization's voice and values.

Interviewee Bio

Brian Young is the founding executive director of Action Network, a nonprofit organization dedicated to providing cutting-edge technology to the progressive movement. Under his leadership, Action Network has become a pivotal platform for progressive organizations, offering tools that have powered major mobilizations such as the Women's March and various anti-Trump resistance efforts. Brian is also a board member of Netroots Nation, where he contributes his expertise in digital strategy and grassroots advocacy to foster online activism and community organizing, and previously served as the managing director of technology and digital services at the United Nations Foundation and directed John Kerry's digital operations, overseeing fundraising and organizing efforts. https://www.linkedin.com/in/brian-young-0973035/

Chapter 15.2
Social Media Analysis

Based on insights from an interview with Robin Sukhadia.

If your nonprofit has been on social media for a while now, as most of us have, you may be wondering which topics, timing, days, hashtags, and post length delivered the best engagement. What content generates likes, comments, and shares most consistently? **Before AI, it was difficult if not impossible to conduct real, detailed data analysis to figure out what worked and why.** But now, it's quite simple to invite AI to review historic data and make important inferences, using data-driven metrics to optimize your investments in awareness building and communications moving forward. The good news is, this isn't rocket science, and all you have to do is follow a simple step-by-step process to unearth eye-opening insights.

Your Blueprint for Decoding Social Data
Scrape Your Social Data

First up, you need to gather, or "scrape," your social data so the bots have something to analyze. ***Apify*** (https://apify.com) **offers a clearinghouse of third-party tools focused on data extraction across Instagram, Facebook, TikTok, YouTube, and many more platforms.** These tools, also known as "actors," can scrape all your public posts, including hashtags, date/time, content, media, calls to action, and so on. Most are free, but depending on the scope of the data or history of posts you analyze, there may be a cost. In most cases, these are quite nominal. In minutes, you'll have a comprehensive comma-separated values (CSV) file of your social media history. This is the gold mine that AI will sift through to extract valuable insights. You don't need to be a tech wizard to use them, as most of these tools are user-friendly and often come with trial options to get you started.

Ensure Data Quality

Before diving into analysis, take a quick peek at your data to confirm it's clean and consistently formatted, which can save you hours of frustration later. ***Verify your data has proper column headers, labels, and accurate data entries.*** Consistent formatting is crucial for AI tools like ChatGPT to process and analyze your data effectively, although this is likely to be less true in future years as unstructured data is more easily digested by AI tools.

Prompt and Upload

Now that you have your clean CSV file, it's time to upload it to ChatGPT or your preferred GenAI platform. Here's a sample prompt to ensure your bot both understands the relevant context and is teed up to deliver insights tailored to your needs, paving the way for you to upload your CSV file:

> "You are a social media analysis expert. I am going to upload data about the Instagram profile @NAME. This account is for my nonprofit, with a focus on the impact the organization is making to support foster care youth. Please analyze the data and provide insights to help us optimize social media posts moving forward, as we continue posting to build a larger audience and engagement. Please share actionable, tactical suggestions for what topics most resonate with our followers, when to post, how frequently, and any other insights that can help maximize engagement."

Drill Down

Once you receive the initial output from your AI tool, ***ask for visual breakdowns of the most useful data points and request any specifics not offered.*** Here are some questions that may be useful to ask as you dive deeper into the data:

- *Which posts were most engaging and why?*
- *What percentage of posts were fundraising focused? What about focused on our programs and impact?*

- *Which hashtags are most relevant to our work and have proven most effective?*
- *What days and times are best to post?*
- *What's the impact of photos, videos, and links on engagement?*
- *Which influencers and celebrities were most effective in supporting our work?*
- *If we were to consider a small advertising budget, how would you suggest we best allocate those funds in hopes of [goal]?*

Some of this may be volunteered in the initial output, but **conversing with your bot to refine and iterate its answers will provide deeper insights.** It may also be helpful to ask why some of these things may be the case, as the technology may propose ideas you hadn't considered. And to the extent you upload data across multiple social platforms, ask your AI tool to look for trends across those, as well as help with identifying what kind of content and posts you should consider across platforms. Finally, **consider boosting your most effective posts with a small ad budget to expand your impact and reach, but if a post isn't working, don't waste ad dollars to show it to even more people.**

Compare, Contrast, and Respond

Finally, **ask your AI platform to compare your analytics and insights against similar organizations and industry averages.** How do your efforts stack up, and what would your bot recommend to help you close any gaps or expand your lead? Are any of these like-minded groups talking about your organization or posting any inflammatory remarks? If so, ask for tips on counter-messaging and consider how to best respond.

Follow this framework once a quarter or semi-annually to transform your social media strategy from a shot in the dark to a data-driven powerhouse. Share insights internally with your staff and board to encourage organization-wide dialogue on how to strengthen your nonprofit's social media engagement and fundraising efforts. Embrace the power of AI to streamline your social media analysis and make smarter, more impactful decisions about how to best steward your organization's precious resources and good name in the community.

Interviewee Bio

Robin Sukhadia has more than 20 years of social media communications, nonprofit fundraising, and technology leadership experience. He is a nonprofit consultant who most recently served as the interim director of development for the Los Angeles Chamber Orchestra and major gifts officer at the Colburn School in Los Angeles, overseeing a successful $10 million endowment fundraising campaign to double scholarships for the school's neediest students. His focus is on helping mission-led clients responsibly implement technology solutions, including using those to assess and optimize social media efforts, as well as to advance fundraising goals. https://www.linkedin.com/in/tablapusher/

Chapter 15.3

Volunteer Recruitment and Management

Based on insights from an interview with Geng Wang.

Just about every nonprofit starts as a 100% volunteer-led endeavor. But as you know, managing volunteers can be overwhelming, especially for smaller organizations. The good news? ***AI can make recruiting and engaging volunteers smoother, more efficient, and ultimately more impactful.*** All it takes is five simple steps to unlock the potential of tech tools to streamline this critical aspect of nonprofit management, plus we'll share one bonus tip to convert these supporters to some of your top donors!

Unlock AI's Potential for Volunteer Management

Reinforce Recruitment

Managing and engaging your volunteers is next to impossible if you don't start by getting the right volunteers on board. Use AI to streamline the creation of volunteer job descriptions, ensuring they're engaging and comprehensive. ***Use GenAI tools like ChatGPT to draft multiple versions of position descriptions and then synthesize the best parts of each to create the final product.***

Provide a detailed prompt with as much context as possible to start your process, for example, "*You are a nonprofit volunteer expert at our nonprofit animal shelter (link). Write a volunteer job description for a position that includes responsibilities for [scope of work, hours, etc.]. Ensure the overview is written in our voice and speaks to our overall work and impact as an organization, connecting the dots to clarify how this position directly supports our mission.*"

After each output, refine AI's drafts by inviting it to iterate responses until you get something spot-on. Then, simply ask it to try again a few times, tell it to combine the parts you like best from each, and voila! You've got a solid starting point that covers all bases, even those you might have overlooked, and from there it should be quite simple and quick to manually review the final draft and get it ready for use.

See the full chapter on AI-powered board recruitment and engagement for more, as directors are really a special form of high-powered volunteers. As detailed there, ***using AI to create an evaluation rubric and assess candidates can save time and mitigate bias.*** And be sure to use tools like Zoom, Otter.ai, or Fathom.ai to record interviews, and then feed those transcripts into your AI tool to give it more data on which to draw conclusions and recommendations.

Identify Trends

Next, it's time to invite AI to analyze your volunteer data. Share your anecdotal experiences and any data sources you have—surveys, applications, timesheets, and so on. ***Use AI to identify patterns and trends, asking it to help you identify your best volunteers, common complaints, and any ideas to improve your volunteer engagement efforts.*** AI can help you spot insights more efficiently. For instance, you may discover that volunteers aged 60–65 with flexible schedules are your most reliable helpers. Focus on these personas and tailor your recruitment strategies accordingly.

Identify Interests

Understanding your volunteers' motivations and availability is crucial, especially your most important contributors. With the data entered in the last step, you can ask your bot what specific volunteers love about their experience and what may be motivating them. Then, take the time to ask them, too. ***Create a simple Google Form or survey to ask volunteers about their goals, preferred duties, availability, and what inspired them to volunteer.*** Civic Champs (https://www.civicchamps.com/) and other volunteer management software can help with this, as they offer volunteer application templates that capture all this information and store it in each volunteer's profile.

Use this information to tailor their experience and ensure they feel valued and engaged. If you have a diversity, equity, and inclusion (DEI) policy, consider asking about race, gender, and location—but handle this sensitively and only if you plan to act on the information. Use AI to help you manage this data and schedule follow-ups and check-ins. As you move forward, remember your focus needs to not only be on meeting your nonprofit's needs but also supporting your volunteers in achieving their personal goals.

Facilitate Feedback

Finally, don't forget to gather feedback after every volunteer session. Keep it simple—*use a range of smiley faces or stars to make it easy for volunteers to rate their experience, always inviting but not requiring more comments and context.* This not only provides you with valuable insights into their satisfaction but also gives them a voice, helping to foster a sense of community and engagement. This also generates valuable data that you can leverage to identify what your organization is doing well and where you can improve.

Communicate Consistently

Engaging your volunteers continuously is key. *Use AI-powered predictive analytics to identify which volunteers are ripe for follow-up and what messages will resonate most with them.* With data points such as volunteer satisfaction, their historical donations, and volunteer history, AI tools can also help identify high potential donors from your volunteer pool. As detailed in Parts II and III, *tools like ChatGPT can help you craft personalized messages at scale, maintaining a personal touch even when communicating with a large group.*

The key is segmenting your list. So, look at where your data pools—Facebook groups, LISTSERVs, CRM systems, and so on. Feed this data into your AI tools to get a better understanding of what makes your volunteers tick, and how to group similar personalities. Integrating your volunteer management platform with your CRM and donor database can make this even more powerful, giving you a comprehensive view of your community.

Convert Volunteers into Donors

Now that you've got your volunteers deeply engaged and connected, it's time to turn them into some of your most valuable donors. *Most nonprofits don't realize that volunteers are some of their most valuable donor prospects.* The data is clear: aside from volunteers being 14.5% more likely to donate to the nonprofits they support per Do Good Institute's Social Connectedness and Generosity study in 2024, Fidelity Charitable found that fully 50% of them donate more because of this connection ("Time and Money: The Role of Volunteering in Philanthropy," 2024). And per Giving Pulse's 2024 report, they're also loyal and more likely to continue donating, even when others drop off. So, whether you realize it or not, *your volunteer and fundraising strategies are intertwined, as these supporters have a strong, firsthand appreciation of your work that directly translates to increased likelihood to give, to give more, and to sustain their generosity over time.*

Interviewee Bio

Geng Wang is the CEO of Civic Champs, a volunteer management and engagement platform that delivers software for nonprofits to empower them and their volunteers to more easily serve their communities. Geng currently serves on the board of directors for Westminster Neighborhood Services, a local youth service and hunger relief organization. Prior to Civic Champs, Geng cofounded and sold two companies, RentJungle.com (an apartment search engine) and Community Elf (a social media management firm). https://www.linkedin.com/in/gengwang/

Chapter 16

Community Engagement

Based on insights from an interview with Eli Pariser.

Imagine your nonprofit is launching a pedestrian safety campaign to ensure a local school remains a safe place for children. That's not a goal one person or organization can achieve alone; it requires a communal approach to solving a community challenge. But activating networks and mobilizing action can be challenging. AI to the rescue! **By leveraging AI, you can gather input from various sources, distill this information, and elevate the voices of affected communities.** AI acts as a catalyst for aligning diverse groups and amplifying collective voices. This chapter will guide you through the effective use of AI to facilitate collaboration and harness the strength in numbers to advance impactful change.

Critical Skills and Competencies

Synthesize and Personalize Collective Voices

Understanding how a wide range of stakeholders feel about an issue is a crucial first step to inspiring shared action. **Use AI tools like SurveyMonkey Analyze** (https://www.surveymonkey.com) **and Amazon Comprehend** (https://aws.amazon.com/comprehend) **to aggregate and analyze sentiments from diverse inputs, whether from surveys, digital comment boxes, or transcribed voicemails.** Then you can easily upload this data into your GenAI platform to further help you cluster and summarize similar ideas.

It's often helpful to illustrate and personalize this, so **ask AI to identify the largest subgroups, give them catchy names, and provide representative comments.**

This is exactly like how the Zagat guide provides snippets of different voices in its restaurant summaries. Ultimately, this process helps you visualize what the community collectively thinks and ensures no voice goes unheard, while creating a richer and more nuanced understanding of collective sentiment. By synthesizing these voices, you can create a more inclusive and representative picture of the community's needs and desires.

Engage the Group

If you hope to lead any group to action, it will be critical to talk with, not at, them. Your community needs to feel heard, understood, and aligned for it to be engaged. **Use AI platforms like Zoom AI Companion** (https://www.zoom.com/en/ai-assistant) **or Twilio** (https://www.twilio.org) *to facilitate real-time conversations and feedback loops, inviting stakeholders to share thoughts and participate in decision-making.* AI-driven chatbots and forums also help ensure everyone has a voice, making the engagement process inclusive and dynamic.

Try not to be set in your approach, but practice deep listening and refine your strategy and tactics based on what you hear. Reflect the results back to the group and invite them to share their ideas about next steps to foster a communal sense of ownership and commitment. This participatory approach ensures that the group feels heard and valued, which leads to higher engagement and better outcomes. A hundred heads are better than one! Use AI to facilitate input by helping you collect, analyze, and present feedback in real time.

Map Ideas to Action

Once you have gathered and synthesized input from your stakeholders, it's time to connect the dots between ideas and concrete plans for action. Use the same AI tools that helped you identify common input themes and priorities to clarify the most popular and promising approaches to achieving your goals. *By using AI to cluster proposed strategies and tactics, you can create a clear road map of actionable steps that address your community's most pressing concerns.*

This approach ensures people feel heard and generates critical buy-in, ensuring your actions align with the community's needs and desires. And while it may take some work to invite all the various stakeholders to contribute their thoughts and ideas, doing so, especially with the support of AI, will oftentimes actually make your planning more efficient. But either way, it will help guarantee you maximize impact and help unearth the most promising solutions, turning collective input into tangible outcomes that drive social change.

Uncover Overarching Narratives

Beyond specific action plans and policy suggestions, shared stories—about how the world is, why it's that way, and how it ought to be—can reveal your community's shared values and aspirations. These narratives provide a powerful foundation for shaping your content, marketing, and organizing efforts. **AI tools, especially large language models (LLMs), can help uncover these deeper stories by analyzing stakeholder comments, policy proposals, or survey responses.** With prompts like *"Identify three to five overarching narratives from this input,"* AI can surface recurring themes, such as justice, innovation, or collective responsibility. These insights help you go beyond individual suggestions to understand the broader perspectives driving your community's sentiments.

By weaving these narratives into your communications, you can **align your campaigns with the values and aspirations of your audience,** significantly expanding their resonance with those you wish to engage. Whether highlighting stories of innovative solutions or emphasizing equity and fairness, tapping into these overarching themes ensures your efforts feel authentic, relevant, and deeply resonant with your stakeholders.

Pitfalls and Solutions

Unclear Directions

For AI tools to be effective, they need clear and specific instructions. This is why **prompt engineering is one of the most critical, fundamental skills to master if you want to effectively leverage AI.** Be precise about what you want your AI tools to do and how you want them to do it. Provide detailed prompts and guidelines to ensure your AI tools advance your goals and objectives. To the extent you're creating a custom LLM, generative pre-trained transformer (GPT), or chatbot, regularly review and adjust its instructions to keep your AI tools on track and ensure they continue to meet your needs.

Spotting the Skew

AI algorithms inadvertently perpetuate biases present in the data they analyze. This can unfairly disadvantage certain groups, reinforce stereotypes, or exclude individuals from opportunities, thereby perpetuating systemic inequities. ***Be vigilant about the potential for bias in your AI tools and take steps to mitigate it.*** This includes regularly auditing your AI processes, using diverse training data, and being transparent about how your AI tools work. By being proactive about identifying and addressing bias, you can ensure your AI-driven insights are fair and equitable.

Seeing What You Want to See

Even when your AI tools and data are unbiased, your own assumptions and expectations can lead you astray. ***Too many nonprofits unconsciously interpret AI-generated insights or survey results in ways that confirm preexisting beliefs, rather than reflecting the reality of what your community is saying.*** This is known as "confirmation bias" and can lead to misaligned strategies, lost trust, and missed opportunities to meet the true needs of your stakeholders.

To avoid this, take deliberate steps to ground yourself in the actual data, not just your interpretation of it. ***Regularly cross-check findings with raw input, involve diverse voices in interpreting results, and remain open to conclusions that challenge your assumptions.*** Encourage your team to ask "What might we be missing?" and use AI to surface less prominent but potentially important trends. Staying rooted in what the data truly reflects ensures your decisions are both accurate and aligned with the community you serve.

Road Map to the Future

As AI technology continues to evolve, its potential to engage the masses, facilitate collaboration, and drive social change in communities will only grow. In the coming years, ***expect AI to become even more integrated into nonprofit work, offering***

new ways to engage stakeholders, gather insights, and drive action. Imagine a future not too far away where you'll be able to give an AI agent a goal and ask it to map out the best path to fixing it, including which stakeholders to target, the best places and ways to target them, the messages that will most resonate, and the messengers whose voices are most likely to be heard. It's closer than you think.

Embracing AI is not just about adopting new tools—it's about rethinking how we approach collaboration and community engagement. By leveraging AI to amplify collective voices, engage stakeholders, map ideas to action, and identify compelling stories, your nonprofit will unlock new levels of impact and drive meaningful social change. The future of AI in the nonprofit sector is bright, and by embracing these technologies, you can help shape a more inclusive, equitable, and effective approach to social innovation.

Dos and Don'ts

Do

- Use AI to synthesize a wide range of stakeholder inputs, aggregating and analyzing sentiments, identifying and naming the largest subgroups, and sharing representative comments for each
- Ensure your community feels heard and represented: use AI, chatbots, and online forums to invite stakeholders to share thoughts and participate in decision-making

Don't

- Try to figure out how to best meet community needs on your own; use AI to review stakeholder input and identify the most promising strategies and tactics, creating a blueprint with actionable steps to address any challenges faced
- Expect vague instructions and directions will generate quality AI outputs, instead of embracing best practices in prompt engineering
- Rely solely on AI without human validation: use AI to gather insights, but always ensure final decisions are made by humans, evaluating suggestions from AI to make informed decisions

Conclusion

AI offers powerful tools for facilitating collaboration and harnessing the strength in numbers. By synthesizing collective voices, engaging groups effectively, mapping ideas to action, and identifying collective stories, AI helps nonprofits, social entrepreneurs, and philanthropists drive meaningful social change. Remember to use AI as a tool to augment human efforts, ensure data quality, and remain vigilant about potential biases. Embrace the potential of AI to transform your approach to collaboration and community engagement, and unlock new levels of impact for your organization.

Interviewee Bio

Eli Pariser is a distinguished author, activist, and entrepreneur dedicated to aligning technology and media with democratic values. As the cofounder and codirector of New_ Public, he leads efforts to create inclusive digital public spaces that foster meaningful community engagement. Eli's leadership experience includes serving as executive director of MoveOn.org, where he pioneered online citizen engagement, and cofounding Upworthy, a platform designed to amplify socially significant content. His extensive work examines the ethical implications of AI in digital environments, advocating for technologies that promote civic discourse and community well-being. https://www.linkedin.com/in/eli-pariser-5847491/

Resource Review

- SurveyMonkey Analyze: https://www.surveymonkey.com/—Enables nonprofits to consolidate responses from digital surveys and automatically generate sentiment insights for improved decision-making.
- Amazon Comprehend: https://aws.amazon.com/comprehend/—Processes diverse inputs, such as transcribed voicemails and digital comments, using natural language processing (NLP) to analyze sentiment and detect emotional tones.
- Zoom AI Companion: https://www.zoom.com/en/ai-assistant—By integrating AI-powered features, Zoom helps nonprofits foster interactive webinars and meetings with live feedback tools like Q&A sessions and sentiment polls.

- Twilio: https://www.twilio.org/—Enables nonprofits to set up real-time, AI-enhanced messaging systems where stakeholders can share feedback and participate in decision-making via SMS or chat applications.
- Qualtrics XM: https://www.qualtrics.com/xm—Helps nonprofits centralize feedback from surveys and voicemails while applying AI-driven sentiment analysis to uncover actionable insights.
- Sprout Social's AI social media tools: https://sproutsocial.com/—Use AI-powered tools to analyze engagement metrics, schedule posts, and foster meaningful community interactions.
- Community Roundtable: https://communityroundtable.com/—Access resources and reports on how AI is shaping community engagement and collaboration across sectors.
- Mighty Networks: https://www.mightynetworks.com/—Learn how to use AI-powered platforms to create and manage online communities that amplify your nonprofit's mission.
- CauseVox blog: https://www.causevox.com/blog/—Explore fundraising and marketing strategies that incorporate AI to better engage donors and volunteers.
- *The Community Manager Newsletter:* https://thecommunitymanager.com/—Subscribe to stay updated on AI tools and techniques for building and managing thriving nonprofit communities.

Chapter 17
Lobbying and Advocacy

Based on insights from an interview with Brian Rubenstein.

In today's fast-paced world, AI is revolutionizing how nonprofits approach generating public support and effecting policy reform. The blend of technology and grassroots activism opens up incredible opportunities for enhancing your impact, whether you're a small community-led organization or a larger nonprofit. By leveraging AI, you can streamline your efforts, engage more effectively with stakeholders, and drive meaningful change. *This chapter will explore how AI can transform your lobbying and grassroots advocacy campaigns and provide practical tips to harness its power.*

Critical Skills and Competencies
Automate Legislative Awareness

AI can help automate and streamline the process of monitoring the introduction of new legislation and the progress of existing bills. *Creating an automated search based on keywords related to your nonprofit's mission will provide you with regular reports and proactive alerts to ensure you stay on top of important shifts in the policy landscape* while saving you time and effort. This proactive approach ensures you stay informed and ready to act.

AI-driven platforms like FiscalNote (https://fiscalnote.com/) track legislation and regulatory changes across different jurisdictions, ensuring you are always up-to-date. That means you don't have to reinvent the wheel each time. *It's about leveraging the power of AI to enable your team to focus on higher value tasks while ensuring you never miss a notification about important legislation.*

Identify Legislative Champions

Finding and engaging the right members of Congress to introduce and sponsor your legislation can have a profound impact on the prospects of your bills passing. The key is to look at who's already on your side and who's likely to be swayed by your arguments. ***Use AI to monitor and analyze lawmakers' floor statements, press releases, and social media posts.*** This intelligence will help your lobbyists prioritize their time, enabling them to focus on supportive lawmakers while also exposing officials who might stand in opposition to your issue. AI tools like Quorum (https://www.quorum.us/) are a great resource for helping you identify and track the activities of potential champions.

Microtarget Social Media Activists

In addition to attempting to recruit elected officials to your cause, there are a range of other potential ambassadors you can recruit to amplify your efforts. ***Use AI to comb social media and identify passionate community and issue leaders, with a focus on those who are vocal and highly active on your issue and who have large groups of followers.*** Dive deeper to zero in on the prospects with followers that align with you or are in the key communities of your legislative targets. Your goal isn't to find the mega social media influencers; instead, look to recruit the most impactful, complementary people to your campaign based on your needs and goals.

As shared in the ambassador engagement and peer-to-peer fundraising chapter, customize your research and outreach strategies using AI tools like Zapier (https://zapier.com/) to analyze data from social media and other diverse sources to assess how to best engage and communicate with these prospects.

Policy Innovation and Research

AI excels at processing vast amounts of data quickly, making it an invaluable tool for policy research and innovation. ***Use AI to analyze policy documents, summarize key points, and even draft policy proposals.*** This saves you time and helps ensure your advocacy is backed by solid research, making your arguments more persuasive. If properly and regularly leveraged, AI can identify trends and patterns in policy development, enabling you to stay ahead of the curve and propose innovative solutions.

Tools like PolicyMap (https://www.policymap.com/) let you take a mountain of data and filter it down to actionable insights, visualizing data trends that inform your policy positions. Platforms like this enable you to easily ***analyze extensive datasets by overlaying demographic, economic, and social indicators to identify areas of need, thereby informing targeted advocacy strategies.*** By visualizing these data trends through maps and reports, you can more effectively communicate complex information to policymakers, influencers, and stakeholders, strengthening your lobbying efforts with evidence-based insights.

Build Alliances

"The rope is stronger than the thread," and this is especially true with lobbying and advocacy, where like-minded partners can amplify your efforts, enabling you to pool resources, share knowledge, and create a more powerful collective voice. ***AI can help you efficiently, effectively identify potential collaborators, analyze their strengths, and suggest how you may be able to best work together.*** Use AI to analyze social media interactions to find nonprofits and community-based efforts with similar goals and values.

Tools such as Meltwater (https://www.meltwater.com/en) help with all this. But when conducting your research, always remember that building alliances is about finding common ground and leveraging each other's strengths. So, use AI to help you pinpoint those opportunities quickly and effectively.

Convert Narratives into Digital Content

There is no longer a need to manually write every piece of campaign content. ***Upload your campaign strategy and email narrative into AI and ask it to draft emails to your campaign volunteers,*** customizing messaging to hit each recipient's hot buttons and likely creating different segments that respond best to specific framing, whether it's more data-driven or anecdotal. Once that content is finalized, have AI convert that into social media content, text messages, and web articles. Working with AI, you can create an entire digital campaigns series in under an hour.

Many of the major email platforms like MailChimp (https://mailchimp.com/) facilitate this, helping with mass customization by identifying and segmenting subscribers based on what folks have responded to previously and the level of their engagement, enabling you to more effectively enlist their support with your advocacy efforts.

Optimize Subject Lines and Content

Now that we have the content for our messages, it's time for the cherry on top. **Subject lines are one of the keys to driving more email opens and the first step toward driving engagement, so taking the time to optimize those will directly boost any email outreach.** And while you're at it, let's refine your messages to ensure they hit home and maximize response rates.

Upload your email and social media performance data into a privacy-protected AI system. This can be as simple as a personal generative pre-trained transformer (GPT) on ChatGPT or a paid Anthropic Claude account. Your spreadsheet should include typical measurements, especially open rates, clickthrough rates, and action-taking rates/conversions, as well as the related subject line and email or social media content. **Ask your AI tool to analyze your historic performance data to detect trends in the subject lines and content that drive the greatest metrics.** Upload the batch of emails you're looking to send and ask your GenAI platform to recommend five subject lines that maximize open and action-taking rates, in addition to inviting its suggestions to fine-tune any of the content in the body of your messages.

Identify Your Super Volunteers

The true legislative power in any grassroots campaign comes not from digital actions like sending messages to lawmakers, but from your volunteers or members who carefully and deliberately develop relationships with key lawmakers and their staff. Identify people who can serve in these crucial, longer-term roles by determining who has consistently taken action across issues, especially those who have completed higher-barrier tasks like making phone calls and participating in local events. While some grassroots organizations think they may be able to do this intuitively, most nonprofits, especially larger ones, benefit by enlisting AI's help. Specifically, ***ask AI to analyze your data and identify the most likely campaign captains.***

See Chapter 11 or the volunteer engagement inset in Chapter 15 for a detailed breakdown of useful tactics and platforms to support this effort.

Audience Targeting and Engagement

Now that you've built out the inner circle of your operation, engaging legislators, influencers, ambassadors, and key campaign volunteers, it's time to expand your efforts and work to engage your entire community. ***To be successful, lobbying and advocacy campaigns need to translate often-complex policy issues into emotionally driven, locally intensified stories that affect the constituencies of key lawmakers or society as a whole.*** Nonprofits see the greatest success when they can not only identify the people within their database who will be interested in an issue but are also able to spot those most likely to take action. As noted in the "Convert Narratives into Digital Content" section we just shared, now it's time to ***use AI to help you segment your general audience based on various criteria, such as demographics, interests, and past behaviors.*** That then enables you to customize messaging for various segments, maximizing engagement just as you did with campaign captains.

Tools like HubSpot (https://www.hubspot.com/), AdvocacyAI (https://advocacyai.com/), and other AI-powered customer relationship management (CRM) platforms enable you to easily analyze your audience data and suggest the best ways to engage them. As detailed in Part III of this book, this allows you to tailor your messages to different segments, increasing the likelihood of engagement and support by ensuring your advocacy efforts are not only broad-reaching but also deeply impactful.

Create an Internal AI for Public Policy Information

Multiple chapters have addressed the benefits of creating your own large language model, custom GPT, or personalized GenAI tool. Nonprofits engaged in advocacy work, especially across multiple states, too often waste lots of time and resources trying to align state legislation throughout the country to promote best practices. They also regularly invest lots of effort ensuring proposed policies are consistent with their goals and don't cross any red lines that would lead the organization to oppose the bill. ***For nonprofits with multiple staff working in state legislatures, an internal AI will streamline the usually laborious process of answering key questions***

about proposed policies, drafting template legislation, and editing bill proposals. AI can automate this manual, time-intensive work, and because it's internal only, you don't have to worry about hallucinations or uncertain responses.

Educate Your Board on AI

Strategic use of AI can exponentially increase your capacity and campaign sophistication, but it requires at least minor investments, including subscription costs, staff time, and training. Sharing the benefits and potential of AI in advocacy is crucial for securing board support and involvement for these efforts, unlocking a key source of resources and institutional support. Just as with fundraising, ***directors are typically some of the easiest people to engage at the beginning of a campaign, bolstering credibility by generating traction in the critical early stages and enabling peer-to-peer advocacy among board members,*** which is much more powerful than staff pitches.

To get your board on board, present data-driven insights and forecasts that demonstrate the value of AI-powered advocacy. By showing how AI enhances your campaigns, you can build a compelling case for its ongoing use. Tools like Tableau (https://www.tableau.com/) automatically create visual presentations to highlight AI's impact on your work, enabling your board to appreciate its tangible benefits.

Trust but Verify

While AI is a powerful tool, it is essential to verify the information it generates. As we've shared in many chapters throughout the book, hallucinations are all too common in the early stages of AI development, since the underlying technology can't separate fact from fiction yet. As a result, ***AI sometimes produces inaccurate or biased results, so it's crucial to have a human in the loop (HITL) to review and validate AI outputs.*** This ensures that your advocacy efforts are based on accurate and reliable information.

Typically, the first draft that comes out of AI is not great, so ***instead of relying on AI's first attempt to help, use further prompts to refine outputs and then edit your results to give them that human touch.*** And always double-check facts and statistics generated by AI to avoid potential errors.

Pitfalls and Solutions
Ignoring Data Security

AI systems often handle sensitive information, so whether you're managing Health Insurance Portability and Accountability Act (HIPAA)–compliant health records or other data you don't want to enter the public domain, it's crucial to implement robust security measures to protect sensitive data. ***Ensure that your AI tools comply with data protection regulations and that you have protocols in place to safeguard against breaches.*** One common way to do this is to create your own private chatbot or GPT, as covered in Chapter 22 and the case study on the Lung Cancer Foundation of America in Chapter 18. This approach enables you to train a bot on your mission, programs, activities, voice, and more, so you don't have to start from scratch each time you ask AI for help, while at the same time providing you with the security of ensuring anything you share or ask does not get integrated into your platform's training data and made public. Aside from legal and other liability concerns, making sure your data is secure avoids harm to both your nonprofit and the people you serve.

Not Confirming Sources

As already mentioned, double-checking any statistics or "facts" generated by AI is an absolute must. But it's also critical to dive a level deeper and ***ask AI to cite its sources, so you can confirm they are legitimate and avoid any copyright concerns.*** At this early stage in AI's development, you'll frequently find fake or entirely made-up sources, while also helping ensure any AI-generated content you use complies with copyright laws and includes proper attribution and permissions to avoid potential legal issues.

Road Map to the Future

Looking ahead, AI will increasingly be integrated with nonprofit lobbying and advocacy efforts. As AI technology continues to advance, it will offer new opportunities for enhancing your efforts. Nonprofits can expect AI to become an intrinsic part of their operations, enabling them to achieve greater efficiency and impact. In a few short years, ***AI tools will not only automatically monitor legislative changes but also accurately predict the likelihood of policy outcomes and craft tailored advocacy messages in real time.*** These technologies will empower nonprofits to engage policymakers with unprecedented precision, amplify grassroots movements, and build coalitions based on data-driven insights, transforming the landscape of social impact advocacy.

Realizing these benefits won't just be one person's job; instead of having an AI person at your nonprofit, these functions will be integrated into the activities associated with *everyone* on your team. So, embrace AI and stay ahead of the curve to ensure your efforts remain effective and relevant by standing out in the increasingly crowded marketplace of ideas.

Dos and Don'ts

Do

- Create a regular practice of checking legislative updates and running AI prompts to identify relevant bills and policy changes
- Use AI to identify and engage with champions, especially lawmakers and social media influencers, who are well positioned to support and amplify your cause
- Leverage AI for policy research and innovation, using it to analyze and summarize documents, draft proposals, and identify policy trends
- Build strong alliances with like-minded organizations by using AI to find potential partners and crystallize potential opportunities to collaborate
- Use AI to segment your audience and tailor communication and engagement strategies for maximum impact
- Bolster your writing capacity by having AI create the first drafts of your digital campaign content
- Educate your board about the benefits and potential of AI-powered lobbying and advocacy to secure their support and involvement
- Invest the time needed to become a prompt engineering expert, as fluency in this skill is fundamental to optimally leveraging AI

Don't

- Rely solely on AI without human oversight; always have an HITL to interpret and apply AI insights, ensuring accuracy and relevance
- Forget to check AI's sources, asking it to cite its reference points to ensure they're valid and avoiding any copyright concerns
- Fail to appreciate the importance of data security; implement robust security measures and consider setting up your own chatbot or GPT to protect sensitive information

Conclusion

Incorporating AI into your lobbying and advocacy efforts can dramatically enhance your nonprofit's impact. By creating regular practices; identifying and engaging campaign champions; and leveraging policy research, alliances, and your board you can harness the full potential of AI. Remember, AI is a tool that, when used wisely, can streamline your processes, provide valuable insights, and amplify your voice. As you move forward, embrace these strategies to unlock the benefits of AI, ensuring your advocacy campaigns are not only efficient but also deeply impactful. The future of advocacy lies in the seamless integration of technology and human effort—don't get left behind.

Interviewee Bio

Brian Rubenstein, president of Rubenstein Impact Group, is a digital and grassroots strategist with two decades of experience leading high-impact advocacy campaigns and volunteer programs. His expertise in strategy, writing, and technology has enabled him to develop record-breaking advocacy programs for some of the nation's most respected nonprofit organizations and companies. He is passionate about using AI-powered tools to optimize advocacy campaigns, increase volunteer and member engagement, and enable nonprofits to achieve their policy goals. https://www.linkedin.com/in/brianrubenstein/

Resource Review

- FiscalNote: https://fiscalnote.com/—A comprehensive platform for tracking legislation and regulatory changes that may affect your advocacy efforts.

- Quorum: https://www.quorum.us/—A tool for identifying and engaging key influencers and decision-makers to support your advocacy campaigns.
- Zapier https://zapier.com/—Helps nonprofits leverage AI for lobbying and advocacy by automating workflows that integrate AI tools with data monitoring, email outreach, and social media platforms, enabling real-time responses to legislative changes and stakeholder engagement.
- PolicyMap: https://www.policymap.com/—Visualize data trends to inform your policy positions and advocacy strategies.
- Meltwater: https://www.meltwater.com/—Helps you monitor social media and identify potential partners for building strong advocacy alliances.
- MailChimp https://mailchimp.com/—Supports outreach with AI-powered segmentation and predictive analytics to deliver personalized, targeted email campaigns that engage stakeholders and mobilize supporters effectively.
- HubSpot: https://www.hubspot.com/—Enables you to easily analyze audience data and create personalized engagement strategies for effective advocacy.
- AdvocacyAI: https://advocacyai.com/—Empowers your nonprofit to maximize advocacy impact through AI-driven supporter targeting, message optimization, and legislative analysis that increases engagement rates while reducing staff workload.
- Tableau: https://www.tableau.com/—A great tool to help you create visual presentations to demonstrate the impact of AI in your advocacy efforts to your board and stakeholders.
- NTEN's Nonprofit Technology Readiness Assessment: https://www.nten.org/learn/nonprofit-tech-readiness—A free tool to evaluate your nonprofit's tech capacity, including AI readiness.
- TechSoup for Nonprofits: https://www.techsoup.org/—Offers technology solutions, including AI tools, at discounted rates for nonprofits.
- *The Chronicle of Philanthropy*: https://www.philanthropy.com/—Stay updated with the latest trends and insights in the nonprofit sector, including AI advancements.

Part IV

Programs: Redefining Mission Delivery with AI

"In the end, it's not the technology itself, but the way we use it that defines its impact."

—Satya Nadella, CEO, Microsoft

Nonprofit programs are the heartbeat of the social sector's work in the world; it's where we translate vision into tangible impact. But today, the modern nonprofit operates in a landscape defined by increasing complexity: from balancing resource constraints and growing demand for data-driven insights to addressing the ever-evolving challenges of misinformation. In this dynamic environment, **AI offers a transformative opportunity to elevate program design, execution, and evaluation**.

AI isn't merely a tool; it's a strategic enabler. **Imagine real-time impact dashboards that transform raw data into actionable insights, custom large language models fine-tuned to your mission, or public-facing chatbots that create a seamless interface between your nonprofit and the communities you serve.** These possibilities aren't distant—they're here. The question is how to harness them responsibly, effectively, and ethically.

Part IV explores how your nonprofit can implement AI to redefine how your programs are envisioned and executed. It starts with "Preparing for AI Integration," outlining practical strategies for assessing readiness, ensuring organizational alignment, and taking the first steps toward adoption. Within that context, the "Leveraging Emerging Technology: Save the Children Case Study" demonstrates how emerging technologies can be deployed at scale to drive programmatic innovation.

In "Strategic Planning," we delve into how AI can refine decision-making, helping your nonprofit navigate uncertainty while maximizing its impact. The chapter includes lots of sample prompts and clear advice to guide your efforts. "Dashboarding: Impact Measurement and Data Visualization" unveils how AI-powered tools can translate complex datasets into compelling, actionable insights, turning data into knowledge. Complementary insets on "Program Evaluation" and "Ensuring Data Quality" provide solid tips for building robust systems that ensure accuracy and accountability.

If your organization is ready to dive in the deep end of the AI pool, "Developing Your Own Custom Large Language Model" showcases how mission-specific AI can drive innovation tailored to your needs. Beyond internal optimization, "Public-Facing Chatbots" explores the potential of AI as a bridge to enhance community engagement, while "Dealing with Mis/Disinformation" will equip your nonprofit to navigate one of the most pressing challenges of the digital age.

Throughout this section, you'll find actionable strategies, forward-thinking frameworks, and ethical considerations to guide your journey. ***AI is not a replacement for the empathy, ingenuity, or dedication of your team—it's a force multiplier, enabling you to amplify your impact and scale your mission with precision and confidence***.

By approaching AI integration thoughtfully, your nonprofit can not only meet the challenges of today but also position itself as a leader in shaping a more adaptive and equitable future.

Chapter 18

Preparing for AI Integration

Based on insights from an interview with Kim Ghatalia and Noah Halton.

Integrating AI can revolutionize your nonprofit's programs and services, unlocking efficiencies and enabling you to better serve more clients in need. However, diving in headfirst without proper preparation can lead to a wide range of problems that undermine instead of expand your impact. ***As you prepare to adopt AI and transform your programs, this chapter will guide you through the essential steps to prepare for AI integration,*** ensuring you maximize the benefits while avoiding common mistakes. The key is to start with understanding the unique systemic barriers your clients and communities face, and ensuring your approach and use of technology addresses, or at least takes into consideration, these challenges while striving to maximize outcomes. As you'll see, the other key to a thoughtful approach is clean, well-organized data; otherwise, even the best-intended AI initiatives will go sideways, leading to biased results, inconsistent outcomes, and unexpected costs. Let's get to it.

Critical Skills and Competencies

Team Alignment

For any AI or technology initiative to succeed, your team needs to be on board and fully engaged with the process. Chapter 5 provides a range of helpful details to guide this effort. But especially ***as it relates to integrating AI into your nonprofit's programs, it's absolutely critical that you lead with impact: how will AI expand your impact and streamline operations?*** Educate your team by conducting workshops and training sessions to build knowledge and enthusiasm. Share case studies and examples of successful AI implementations to illustrate the possibilities and inspire your team. Highlight how AI can help advance specific outcomes and meet clients where they are, fostering a sense of excitement and commitment.

Encouraging collaboration across departments is also key. Foster a culture of teamwork and ensure that everyone is working toward a common goal. ***Create cross-functional teams to oversee AI projects and leverage diverse perspectives.*** In addition to building buy-in, this will also help address privacy considerations and other challenges that may arise. Create open forums for discussions and feedback, listen to staff input, and actively address any concerns your team may have. ***Honoring diverse viewpoints and tackling reservations head-on at the onset of your AI adoption process will build trust and support, paving the way for a smoother integration process.***

Dial in Your Data

Access to clean, well-organized, scalable, and secure data forms the bedrock of any successful AI integration. That's why we've emphasized tactics for ensuring data accuracy, scalability, and cleanliness throughout this book, particularly in Chapters 20 and 30. ***Begin with a comprehensive audit of your current data assets, identifying gaps, inconsistencies, and inaccuracies*** that could undermine your AI systems. Implement regular data cleaning routines to maintain accuracy and reliability, leveraging automated processes to detect and correct errors. ***Standardize your data structure by categorizing, labeling, and documenting clear protocols for data entry and management.*** This ensures your AI tools operate efficiently while delivering accurate insights and predictions to support your program goals.

Equally critical is the protection of sensitive data, a non-negotiable aspect of AI adoption. Safeguard sensitive information, such as Health Insurance Portability and Accountability Act (HIPAA)–protected records or donor and beneficiary details, through robust privacy and security measures. ***Invest in encryption, access controls, and compliance systems to adhere to regulations.*** Regularly review and update your data protection policies to address emerging security threats. ***Incorporate cybersecurity training for staff and conduct security audits*** to proactively mitigate risks. By combining diligent data management with strong security practices, you ensure your AI initiatives are built on a trustworthy foundation, fostering confidence among your stakeholders while upholding the integrity of your mission.

Now that you've organized and cleaned your data, and ensured its security, it's time to move on to the final, more advanced consideration of planning for growth. As your nonprofit and programs expand, so will the volume and complexity of the data you handle. ***Consider scalable, cloud-based data management solutions that offer flexible storage and processing capabilities to efficiently steward large volumes of data,*** including those offered by Google (https://cloud.google.com), Microsoft (https://azure.microsoft.com), and Amazon (https://aws.amazon.com). Use AI and Machine Learning tools to streamline data collection, cleaning, and analysis, such as deploying automated data validation tools from providers in the "Resource Review" at the end of this chapter, to ensure ongoing accuracy and consistency. ***Regularly review and update your data management practices to keep pace with technological advancements and evolving best practices.*** By focusing on scalability alongside security and cleanliness, you future-proof your AI initiatives, ensuring they continue to deliver value as your organization evolves.

Consider Bias and Ethics

When integrating AI into your nonprofit's programs, biases in your data and algorithms can be especially destructive, especially if you're not aware of them. Regularly review and update your systems to minimize bias and ensure fairness. Conduct bias audits and implement corrective actions as needed. ***If your AI is used to prioritize recipients for program resources—such as determining which community members receive access to housing support, job training, or scholarships—make sure the algorithm doesn't unintentionally disadvantage certain groups based on biased data.*** This can happen due to historical inequities embedded in data, incomplete or unrepresentative datasets, or poorly designed algorithms that amplify existing disparities, and can lead to preferences for specific zip codes or socioeconomic backgrounds, as well as other biased outcomes. By actively addressing bias, you uphold the integrity and equity of your AI initiatives, ensuring they benefit all stakeholders fairly.

Establishing ethical guidelines for AI use within your organization is also essential. ***Develop an AI code of ethics that aligns with your nonprofit's values***

and mission, including explicitly connecting the dots to any commitments to equity and social justice and possibly leveraging templates and tips found from various free resources to get you started. Incorporate ethical considerations into your decision-making processes and regularly review your practices to ensure compliance.

Crystallize Outcomes

Now that you've laid a solid foundation for your AI adoption efforts, including enlisting your team's input and buy-in, plus ensuring access to quality, unbiased, and secure data, it's time to build your AI dream home! That means we need a blueprint to ensure everyone involved knows what we're building and has a clear reference point against which to gauge progress and outcomes. Said another way, setting clear, achievable objectives is fundamental to successful AI integration. ***Define specific outcomes you want to achieve with AI and align these goals with your organization's mission and strategic plan.*** For example, if your goal is to enhance service delivery, identify key performance indicators (KPIs) to measure success. See Chapter 20 for more on this important topic.

Now that you've set your goals and metrics, it's time to flesh out the checkpoints that will ensure progress against those. ***Develop a detailed road map outlining the steps and milestones for AI integration, breaking down the process into manageable phases with realistic timelines.*** This road map will keep your team focused and on track, ensuring a structured approach to AI implementation. Your plan should speak to the necessary resources, including budget, personnel, and technology, required to support your AI initiatives. It also presents a helpful forum to start identifying potential funding sources, now that you've clarified what you're building, why, and how. By prioritizing and clearly defining your objectives, you create a solid foundation for your AI projects, ensuring they are well supported and aligned with your overall goals.

Pitfalls and Solutions

Diving in the Deep End

Skipping a pilot phase can lead to costly mistakes or disruptions in your program's operations. ***When AI tools are deployed without proper testing, you risk encountering unexpected technical issues, inaccurate outputs, or poor user adoption.***

These challenges can delay your progress, waste resources, and even erode trust among your team and stakeholders. Instead, when possible, ***start with a small-scale pilot project before rolling out an AI tool organization-wide.*** Use these insights to refine the tool and address any issues before full implementation. See Chapter 3 for a simple framework to support this iterative process.

Disconnected Tools

AI tools that don't integrate seamlessly with your existing systems will often create inefficiencies and create more work for your staff, undermining your AI adoption goals. ***If your new tool doesn't connect with your program management software, staff may have to manually transfer data, which is both time-consuming and prone to errors.*** And even though our focus here is on adopting AI to enhance program delivery, AI may be used across a variety of other applications including chatbots or fundraising and marketing activities.

Before adopting AI, evaluate your current technology stack and identify gaps that the new tool should fill. ***Look for AI solutions that are compatible with the systems you already use, or consider platforms that offer integration capabilities like application programming interfaces (APIs).*** Work closely with your IT team or technology vendors to ensure a smooth integration process. Additionally, ***provide training to your staff on how the new AI tool fits into existing workflows to maximize its potential.*** These steps will ensure any AI integrations build off existing systems and are properly leveraged by your team, maximizing benefits to you and those you serve.

Insufficient Budget Planning

AI adoption requires a financial investment, and failing to plan for these costs creates challenges that can affect both your nonprofit and clients. Many nonprofits underestimate not only the initial costs of acquiring AI tools but also the ongoing expenses for training, maintenance, and upgrades. Without a realistic budget, you risk overspending or running out of funds before you see the full benefits of your AI initiative.

To prevent this, ***create a comprehensive budget that accounts for all phases of AI adoption, including the cost of software licenses, data storage, training*** *for staff, and regular system updates.* Don't forget to include room for unexpected costs, such as technical issues or additional training needs.

Thinking Short Term

Treating AI as a one-and-done project is a mistake that quickly leads to outdated or ineffective systems. *AI tools require regular updates to adapt to changing program needs, stay current with advancements in technology, and address emerging security threats.* To ensure sustained impact and benefits, develop a long-term maintenance plan as part of your AI adoption strategy. *Schedule regular system updates, monitor performance metrics, and conduct periodic reviews to ensure any AI or tech tools continue to meet your nonprofit's needs.* By adopting a proactive approach to maintenance and staying informed about new developments in AI, you can future-proof your AI initiatives and ensure they continue to deliver value over time.

Road Map to the Future

The role of AI in enhancing nonprofit program delivery will evolve rapidly in the years ahead, driven by advancements in agential AI, the ability to process unstructured data, and deeper integration with other nonprofit tools like donor management and program tracking systems. Agential AI, which can autonomously execute tasks based on predefined objectives, will transform how nonprofits manage program logistics, from automating beneficiary outreach to optimizing resource allocation in real time. Additionally, *breakthroughs in AI's ability to analyze unstructured data—like social media posts, audio recordings, and video transcripts—will enable nonprofits to extract insights from previously untapped sources, enhancing their ability to identify community needs and maximize program impact.* As these technologies become more accessible, nonprofits that embrace them will gain a competitive edge in delivering smarter, more responsive programs.

To prepare for tomorrow, your nonprofit should focus on building a strong foundation for AI adoption *today*. *Invest in tools and training that enable your team to leverage AI effectively and ensure your data is clean, secure, and well organized to take advantage of future advancements.* Stay informed about emerging trends in AI and evaluate how these tools can be integrated into your existing systems, particularly in program management and fundraising platforms. And ***pay special attention to the evolution of customer relationship management (CRM) and donor databases, both of which will soon incorporate AI features for predictive analytics and personalized engagement,*** making it easier to align fundraising efforts with program delivery. By adopting a proactive, iterative approach to AI integration, your organization will position itself to leverage these advancements, delivering greater impact to the communities you serve.

Dos and Don'ts

Do

- Start by building excitement with your team for any AI adoption efforts, leading with how any proposed tools will advance your goals and mission, and creating cross-functional teams to solicit input, build buy-in, and oversee adoption
- Develop a detailed road map outlining the steps and milestones for AI integration, including specific timelines and budgeted resources
- Ensure data cleanliness and accuracy by conducting a data audit, standardizing data structure and protocols, investing in data security measures, and offering cybersecurity staff training
- Develop an AI code of ethics to ensure a responsible approach to AI that aligns with your values and mission
- Remember AI isn't a one-time investment: to maximize long-term impact, schedule regular system updates, monitor performance metrics, and conduct periodic reviews to ensure tools continue to meet your needs

Don't

- Undertake any AI or tech initiatives without first articulating clear, measurable outcomes, indicators, and milestones against which you can gauge progress
- Forget to create a budget before adopting any new AI tools, including the cost of software licenses, data storage, training for staff, and regular system updates

- Assume what works for you today will keep pace with growth: explore scalable, cloud-based data management solutions to support future growth and regularly review and update your data management practices to identify any potential gaps or opportunities
- Ignore considerations about ethics and bias since AI tools can disadvantage certain populations based on skewed data
- Deploy full-scale AI initiatives without first running pilot programs to test the waters
- Integrate any AI tools without first ensuring they integrate with your existing systems
- Disregard the need to provide training to your staff on how any new AI tools fit into existing workflows

Conclusion

Preparing for AI integration requires a strategic approach and careful planning. ***By ensuring team alignment, prioritizing data cleanliness, setting clear objectives, and addressing privacy and ethical considerations, your nonprofit can successfully leverage AI to enhance your programs and services.*** Continuous learning and adaptation are crucial to staying ahead in the rapidly evolving AI landscape.

As you embark on this journey, remember that the ultimate goal is to use AI to drive greater impact for your organization and the communities you serve. By following the practical tips and strategies outlined in this chapter, you will unlock the transformative potential of AI, making your nonprofit more efficient, effective, and capable of addressing the unique challenges faced by your clients. Embrace the opportunities AI offers, and let it propel your mission forward!

Interviewee Bios

Kim Ghatalia is a seasoned leader with extensive experience in strategic development and implementation, across for-profit and nonprofit industries. She currently serves as a strategy and operations consultant for Larkin Street Youth Services in San Francisco, where she applies her expertise to enhance organizational effectiveness and program delivery. Kim is a graduate of Harvard Business School, and her expertise in strategic planning, data analysis, and innovation has been honed over years of leading transformative projects across various industries, equipping her with the insight to guide organizations in adopting AI responsibly and effectively. https://www.linkedin.com/in/kim-ghatalia-450007b0/

Noah Halton is the senior director of impact at Larkin Street Youth Services, where he leads strategic development and innovation. Noah leverages technology, including AI, to advance their mission and create data-informed solutions that enable its impact. Noah's career includes impactful roles with the United States Peace Corps, AmeriCorps, Juma Ventures, and the United Way, where he honed his skills in community development, capacity building, and program evaluation. Through Noah's career, he has led the design of new programming, systems of leadership, directed the implementation of multiple randomized control trials, and led evidence-based program development. https://www.linkedin.com/in/noah-halton-15100a4a/

Resource Review

- Google Cloud Platform: https://cloud.google.com—Provides powerful AI and data analytics tools, enabling your nonprofit to manage large-scale data efficiently and generate actionable insights for program enhancement.

- Microsoft Azure: https://azure.microsoft.com—Offers scalable cloud computing services, including AI and Machine Learning tools, your nonprofit can use to analyze large datasets, automate processes, and deliver personalized program insights.

- Amazon Web Services: https://aws.amazon.com—A suite of AI services like Amazon SageMaker and data storage solutions designed to help nonprofits build, train, and deploy Machine Learning models to improve program delivery and decision-making.

- Talend Data Fabric: https://www.talend.com—Provides automated data validation and cleansing tools that help nonprofits ensure the accuracy, consistency, and reliability of their data for seamless integration with AI systems.

- DataRobot: https://www.datarobot.com—Includes automated data validation and preprocessing features that enable nonprofits to prepare high-quality data for AI models, improving predictions and program outcomes.

- OpenRefine: https://openrefine.org—A free, open-source tool designed to clean and validate messy datasets, making it easier for your nonprofit to maintain data consistency and readiness for AI-driven analysis.

- NTEN: https://nten.org—Offers resources, webinars, and articles on ethical AI adoption, including guidance on developing AI codes of ethics that align with your nonprofit values and promote transparency, equity, and accountability in AI use.

- Fundraising.AI: https://fundraising.ai—Provides a collaborative platform for nonprofit leaders to explore ethical AI practices, offering tools, frameworks, and thought leadership to help organizations create responsible AI strategies and ethical guidelines.

- Fast Forward: https://www.ffwd.org—Offers a range of nonprofit tech resources, including case studies and insights, to showcase how tech-savvy nonprofits are using AI to maximize program delivery impact.

- Kaggle Datasets: https://www.kaggle.com/datasets—Free datasets you can use to support your AI applications and build tools to enhance your nonprofit's program insights and operations.

- TechSoup: https://www.techsoup.org—Discounted technology offerings, webinars, and articles that will help you explore AI and other technology tools that can enhance program scalability and delivery.

Chapter 18.1

Leveraging Emerging Technology: Save the Children Case Study

Based on insights from an interview with Ettore Rossetti.

As a nonprofit leader, you're always on the lookout for ways to amplify your mission and make a tangible impact with limited resources. So, how can you walk the line and navigate the balancing act between embracing innovation and too easily getting distracted by the shiny new object on the block? To help illustrate helpful best practices, **let's look at how Save the Children, a leading global nonprofit, successfully leveraged AI and blockchain to address critical challenges, expand impact, and enhance program delivery.** By understanding and mastering the integration of emerging technologies, you can unlock new efficiencies, enhance your reach, and, most important, better serve your community.

Background and Problem Statement

Save the Children operates in more than 100 countries, striving to provide health, protection, education, and a healthy start in life for children. In the Philippines, they face a significant challenge: **many youth are trapped in poverty and lack the digital literacy skills needed to thrive in the modern workforce.** This dual problem of economic and digital inclusion was ripe for an innovative solution. Enter AI and blockchain, which in this case came together to present a transformative solution that created lasting impact.

AI-Driven Solution

Through a partnership with Stak (https://stakwork.com/), ***Save the Children initiated the Mobile Microwork Program to provide youth with the opportunity to earn money and develop digital skills by completing micro-tasks on their mobile devices.*** The program included four interrelated components:

- **Task atomization:** Stak specializes in taking large, complex projects and breaking them down into bite-sized tasks that can be completed on a mobile phone. For example, participants photographed items in local supermarkets to support corporate supply chain oversight and inventory control.
- **AI integration:** AI played a crucial role in the project, since once the youth submitted their photos, AI algorithms took over to count and organize the data, ensuring accuracy and efficiency.
- **Blockchain payments:** To compensate participants, Save the Children used Bitcoin, leveraging blockchain technology to provide a digital, transparent, and secure payment method. Youth earned Bitcoin, which they could redeem with vouchers locally or use for online purchases in the form of e-gift cards.
- **Training and oversight:** Save the Children provided mobile phones and digital literacy training to the participants, mitigating two critical barriers while supporting technology skill building for the young participants. They also involved parents and local community organizations to ensure oversight and safety, ensuring alignment with their values and mission.

Results and Impact

- **Empowerment and earnings:** The pilot program in the Philippines generated positive results. Fifteen teenagers were trained and supported by 17 adults. Youth not only earned and learned but also they learned *how* to earn. Participants earned a total of 1.865,845 sats (the smallest unit of account on the Bitcoin blockchain). When converted to local currency, that was about 28,000 Philippine pesos, which is about US$500. In addition to the financial earnings, youth also gained valuable digital and financial literacy skills, including mobile app use, transacting with Bitcoin, saving, and responsible spending. For instance, Juanito was initially reluctant, but embraced the program and used his earnings to support his family and continue his education.

- **Community engagement:** The local community and Save the Children's country office were enthusiastic about the program and expressed interest in expanding it further, both within the pilot region and elsewhere throughout the country.

Lessons Learned

- **Embrace emerging technologies:** Don't shy away from new technologies. Learn about them and understand how to apply their potential to your mission and pressing community needs. ***Whatever you might be afraid of, learn about it!***
- **Implement guardrails:** If you are going to drive innovation, you also need safety measures to protect your cause and constituents. This starts with ensuring ethical use of technology and maintaining transparency. ***Organize a focus group on the responsible use of AI as it relates to data and privacy.*** Seek out internal stakeholders, external thought leaders, and subject matter experts across different disciplines to benefit from diverse perspectives.
- **Freedom to fail:** Innovation requires the ability to experiment, which isn't always going to work out the way you hope. Not every initiative will be a home run, but each failure brings valuable lessons that can lead to future success. Strive to ***create a culture where your team and partners feel comfortable tinkering at a small scale with the right protections in place.***

Interviewee Bio

Ettore Rossetti is a visionary leader in digital innovation who has guided some of the world's most impactful nonprofits through transformative technology shifts. He worked at Save the Children for two decades, most recently serving as head advisor of emerging technology, marketing, and innovation partnerships. In that capacity, Ettore has played a key role in spotting trends and adopting emerging technologies—including AI—to advance fundraising, advocacy, and program delivery. His strategic approach to preparing for AI adoption centers on collaboration, experimentation, and results-oriented implementation, ensuring that every new tool serves the greater purpose. https://www.linkedin.com/in/ettorerossetti/

Chapter 19

Strategic Planning

Based on insights from an interview with Sam Azar.

All too often, nonprofits fail to ask and answer one of the most important yet underused questions in our work: "What does success look like?" Beginning with the end in mind is key to any successful endeavor, including guiding nonprofits toward achieving their mission with clarity and purpose. ***AI introduces powerful new opportunities to enhance strategic planning, making it more efficient, data-driven, and insightful.*** This chapter offers tactical, practical tips and tools for nonprofit leaders looking to embrace and unlock those opportunities. By the end of this chapter, you'll be equipped with the knowledge to leverage AI effectively, ensuring your strategic plan is both robust and adaptable to future challenges.

Critical Skills and Competencies
Get Your Feet Wet

Before you can harness the full potential of AI in strategic planning, it's crucial to get comfortable with the technology. ***Start small by experimenting with basic GenAI tools and applications, especially multipurpose GenAI large language models (LLMs) like Anthropic's Claude (https://www.anthropic.com/claude), Google Gemini (https://deepmind.google/), and OpenAI's ChatGPT (https://chatgpt.com/).*** This initial phase is about building your confidence and understanding how GenAI works and how it can fit into your processes. Think of it as learning to drive—you need to get behind the wheel and practice before you can navigate complex terrains. Engage with GenAI tools to understand their capabilities and limitations. By getting more miles on the road, you'll gain the proficiency needed to use AI effectively.

As you level up your proficiency, experiment with tools that offer helpful functionality out of the box. ***Test AI-powered features available in software tools you already use*** (or AI-powered alternatives to software tools you use most often) and be prepared to invest a little time into learning how to use them effectively. ***Consider using AI-powered tools to perform basic, routine tasks, such as Superhuman (https://superhuman.com/) for email, Fathom (https://fathom.video/) for note-taking during virtual meetings, and Perplexity (https://www.perplexity.ai/) for internet research.*** You should also see if there are any AI-powered solutions built specifically for your industry, function, or any repetitive and time-consuming tasks you're trying to accomplish. For nonprofit strategic planning, consider Google Gemini's Deep Research feature (https://blog.google/products/gemini/google-gemini-deep-research/) to support benchmarking, Miro (https://miro.com/) for meeting facilitation with AI-assisted summaries and synthesis of participant input, Consensus (https://consensus.app/) for an initial summary of academic research relevant to your programs and impact goals, or the *Harvard Business Review*'s AI tool (a Beta version is available to subscribers) that provides instant AI-powered strategy and leadership insights based on years of articles from their publications.

As you become more adept at using these tools, you can gradually explore more advanced applications of AI. ***Ongoing experimentation will ensure you continue to try new tools and applications on for size, ideally combined with online resources and training programs to build your AI skills.*** By investing time in learning and experimenting with AI, you'll be better prepared to integrate it into your strategic planning efforts.

Tell Your Bot What You Need

Once you're comfortable with the basics, the next step is to communicate clearly with AI tools. Just like instructing a new staff member, you need to be explicit about your requirements. See the prompt engineering chapter for helpful tips here, but ***to support AI-powered strategic planning, start by providing your GenAI tool of choice with comprehensive background information, including your nonprofit's***

mission, core programs, past successes, and challenges. If you get stuck, think about how you'd provide guidance to a new intern at your organization. In addition to referencing your website, **upload annual reports, impact statements, grant reports, and previous strategic plans** to round out its understanding of your work. The more context you provide, the better the AI can generate relevant and accurate outputs. This step involves iterative communication, refining your prompts to ensure the AI understands your needs. Ask your GenAI tool to explain your work to you in various ways and levels of depth to ensure its output is accurate and provide feedback to correct any errors. Think of it as an ongoing conversation where clarity and context are key.

Produce and Refine Your Plan

With a solid foundation and clear channels for communication, you can now leverage AI to assist with each stage of your strategic planning process. ***Following the discover, design, plan, act framework ensures that your efforts are structured, iterative, and aligned with your mission.*** Figure 19.1 shares how AI can support each stage.

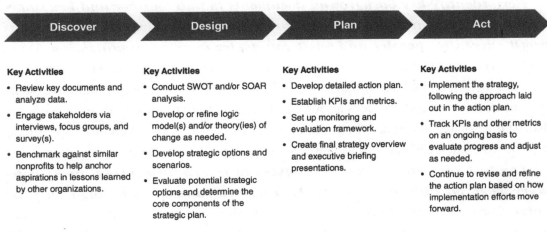

Figure 19.1 Strategy Development Process

Now, let's dive deeper and look at each of the four steps to provide you with an effective road map to maximize your AI-powered strategic planning efforts, including sharing some quick tips for each juncture.

Discover: Lay Your Foundation

Before you construct a building, you start with the blueprint and a team. The same is true for your strategic plan, so **work with your board and team to create a strategic planning committee to guide your process and regularly review your AI-powered progress.** As you'll see in the following steps, human oversight and judgment will provide critical guardrails for all aspects of this process, and the goal isn't to automate or outsource the whole thing, but to make it more efficient and effective, as with most applications of AI.

Work with your committee and GenAI platform to develop the table of contents for your plan and an overview of how you will manage your strategic planning process, iterating with prompts and conversations until you land on the right flow for your nonprofit, along with a one- to two-sentence description of the purpose and contents of each section. Even if you like your AI's first stab at this, hit refresh a few times to see what else comes up, as some of the less common options may be a good fit for your needs. When you feel good about the draft, circulate it with your committee, ensuring everyone is on the same page about the journey to come.

Next, **identify key background documents to pull together and key stakeholders to interview to provide a comprehensive perspective on how your nonprofit currently operates and what you aspire to as an organization.** Don't just focus on the good news and slick materials; at this point in the process you want to consider the good, the bad, and the ugly. Ask your GenAI tool to help summarize background documents and for ideas about which perspectives to include in your interview list. Your AI platform can also help draft interview questions and even develop a guide for how to conduct effective interviews to support your strategic planning effort.

Conduct your interviews, get consent to record them using an AI notetaker when possible, and use the AI-generated summaries to augment your notes. Consider using AI-powered analytical tools to support the synthesis of stakeholder interviews if you have a lot of them. Tools like Coloop (https://www.coloop.ai/)

can be helpful here, sorting through raw video recordings to synthesize findings across all interviews, while still enabling you to go back to the original video snippets when needed.

Finally, ***integrate all interviews and background documents into a current state assessment using your GenAI tool.*** Use that and background research to help generate potential priorities and strategic options, and to support benchmarking research. Identify organizations and gather background information using tools like Perplexity (https://www.perplexity.ai/) and Google Gemini Deep Research.

Design: Draft and Refine Your Plan

Now it's time to put digital pen to paper. ***The design phase is when you start building the structure of your strategic plan by translating the insights from your discovery process into clear objectives, priorities, and strategies.*** Start by using AI tools to help draft initial sections of the plan. For example, prompt your GenAI tool to structure content on key findings, using inputs from your current state assessment and stakeholder interviews. Feed the AI prompts such as *"Draft a section on our top three challenges and the opportunities they create for our nonprofit, based on the following notes."* Iterative refining will help tailor outputs to align with your mission and values.

One of the most valuable ways to use AI here is to brainstorm and refine strategic objectives. ***Prompt your AI tool to propose SMART (specific, measurable, achievable, relevant, and time-bound) objectives based on your data.*** For example, *"Propose three SMART objectives for our after-school program based on these community needs and past performance metrics."* Review and adapt these suggestions in collaboration with your strategic planning committee, ensuring they resonate with your nonprofit's mission and the priorities of your stakeholders.

After outlining strategic objectives, use AI to draft logic models or theories of change for each. Ask, *"Map the inputs, activities, outputs, and outcomes for this objective,"* and provide your AI tool with context or examples to guide its output. These models will clarify how your activities will achieve intended outcomes, helping stakeholders visualize the connections between your work and its impact. Share these drafts with your committee for feedback and refinement.

Finally, ***draft strategies to achieve each objective, incorporating AI suggestions for innovative approaches.*** Invite AI to suggest potential collaborations, funding opportunities, or programmatic tweaks that align with industry trends. Throughout this process, maintain a balance between AI's inputs and human judgment, ensuring the plan remains mission-driven and realistic.

Plan: Build an Actionable Road Map

The plan phase focuses on turning your strategic vision into concrete actions, ensuring every goal is backed by a clear road map for execution. This step involves detailing the specific actions, resources, timelines, and metrics needed to execute your strategies. Start by using AI to create implementation plans. For example, ask your AI tool, "*Break down this strategy into specific tasks with suggested timelines, responsible parties, and resource needs.*" Refine the output with input from your team to ensure feasibility and alignment with organizational capacity.

Next, use AI to create a comprehensive resource plan. ***Tools like ChatGPT or Claude can analyze your financial and human resources data to estimate the cost and capacity required for each strategy.*** Prompt AI to recommend ways to allocate resources efficiently, considering potential funding sources or partnerships to fill gaps. For example, "*Suggest cost-effective ways to expand our community outreach program using existing staff and potential grants.*"

Establishing key performance indicators (KPIs) is another critical component of this phase. ***Use GenAI to identify relevant metrics based on your strategic objectives,*** with prompts such as "*What metrics should we track to measure success in increasing student enrollment by 25% over three years?*" ***AI tools can also help identify data sources and design dashboards for tracking progress.*** Tools like Tableau (https://www.tableau.com/) or Power BI (https://www.microsoft.com/en-us/power-platform/products/power-bi/), with AI integrations, can be used to visualize your KPIs and make data accessible to stakeholders.

Last, ***create training materials to ensure that staff and stakeholders understand their roles in executing the plan.*** AI can draft onboarding guides, FAQs, or explainer documents tailored to different audiences. For example, "*Write a one-page explainer for board members about their role in supporting the new strategic plan.*"

These resources help bridge the gap between strategy and execution, fostering a shared understanding and commitment.

Act: Implement and Iterate

Aaaaand action! The act phase is the exciting culmination of the process, when your strategic plan comes to life. This step involves integrating your strategies into daily operations, monitoring progress, and iterating as needed. ***Begin by using project management tools with AI features, like Asana (https://asana.com/) or Monday.com, to assign tasks, track timelines, and monitor completion rates.*** AI can also generate automated updates, ensuring that everyone stays informed on progress without additional manual effort.

To maintain momentum, ***establish regular checkpoints to review progress.*** Use AI to analyze data, generate performance reports, and highlight areas that need attention. For example, prompt your tool, "*Summarize this month's program outcomes and identify any deviations from our strategic objectives.*" This continuous feedback loop enables your nonprofit to adapt quickly to challenges and capitalize on emerging opportunities.

Evolving job functions to integrate AI into workflows is another critical element of this phase. ***Train staff to use AI tools effectively, ensuring they understand how to combine AI-driven insights with their expertise.*** For example, program managers might use AI to analyze community feedback and adjust activities in real time, while fundraisers could leverage AI to refine donor engagement strategies.

Last, evaluate the impact of your plan and celebrate successes. ***Use AI tools to help create compelling impact reports for funders, donors, and stakeholders, showcasing quantitative and qualitative achievements.*** Ask your AI tool to help, with a prompt like "*Generate a report highlighting key milestones, successes, and testimonials from our first year of implementing this plan.*" Sharing these stories reinforces transparency, builds trust, and motivates your team to continue driving impact.

Develop an Action Plan

It's been said that "a plan without action is just a dream." ***Too many nonprofit strategic plans suck up a huge amount of time and energy, only to sit on a shelf*** *and collect dust after they're approved.* This is typically a factor of nonprofits producing plans that attempt to address a 5- to 10-year window, when the world is changing too quickly to justify those kinds of long-range plans. ***Consider keeping your plan's timeline to three to five years.*** Whether you agree with the increasingly popular premise that traditional strategic planning is dead and nonprofits are best served leveraging a more adaptive approach to strategy, setting your sights on what's around the bend is certainly increasingly important to impact. One option for this is a rolling plan, where you continuously add another quarter or year, as outlined in Chapter 3.

In addition to being more realistic about your time frame, ***the other big reason why too many strategic plans are immediately obsolete is because they fail to include an action plan detailing roles and responsibilities.*** For each strategic objective and activity, identify an owner of the related KPIs. If you're struggling to clearly identify who exactly on your team is charged with execution, ***use tools like RACI Matrices (responsible, accountable, consulted, informed) and Gantt Charts to help clarify different levels of engagement.***

As you develop and refine your action plan, use AI to assist with scenario planning and prototyping. ***Develop multiple strategic scenarios and use AI to iterate on these options in real time with your team.*** Frame critical assumptions and potential failure points within each scenario. These insights and possibilities can inform efforts to test plans at a smaller scale to validate assumptions, akin to the lean startup model. AI can help frame and direct these tests, interpret results, and refine your strategy based on real-time feedback. By leveraging AI in these ways, you will create a more robust and adaptable strategic plan.

Bring It Home Manually

It may be helpful to think of your strategic plan as a living, breathing organism. You have engaged AI's help to inhale a lot of ideas and insight throughout the process outlined in this chapter. But now that you've crystallized your strategies and bolstered them with data-driven insights, industry trends and benchmarks, and a concrete plan of action, it's time to exhale and streamline your plan, ensuring everything in the final product is aligned and trimming any unnecessary or irrelevant content. ***Less is more, and for the*** *final product, it's critical to ensure your strategic plan focuses exclusively on critical components to clarify your course.* Once again, AI can help.

Invite your GenAI tool to identify and flag any extraneous content in your updated draft, and also to help point out anything that needs to be fleshed out. Then, you're ready to do your final pass. *The human touch is best suited to covering the last mile so you can personalize your strategic plan; plus, it gives you a chance to correct any errors and optimize the tone and voice of the document.* Of course, you'll also want to familiarize yourself with the document inside and out to prepare for any questions and to ensure you keep the plan's insights top of mind as you move forward with your good work in the community.

Remember, AI is a powerful tool that can enhance your strategic planning, but it should complement human judgment and expertise. *At each step of the outlined process, the key to your success is continuously refining AI's outputs through iterative feedback and manual edits,* and using AI's capabilities to streamline and improve your planning process.

Pitfalls and Solutions

Assuming AI Can Do It All

AI is a powerful tool, but it's not a panacea. Your nonprofit needs to understand the strengths and limitations of AI to use it effectively. For example, *AI excels at data analysis and pattern recognition, provided you check for potential bias and address it, but it may struggle with tasks requiring deep contextual understanding or creativity.* Recognizing these limitations and engaging AI in ways that play to its strengths help you set realistic expectations and employ AI where it adds the most value. Complement AI with human expertise to fill in the gaps and ensure a balanced approach to strategic planning.

Not Looking Before You Leap

Implementing AI can be resource-intensive, both in terms of time and money. It's essential to *conduct a thorough assessment of your organization's readiness before diving in.*

Evaluate your existing infrastructure, staff capabilities, and budget to ensure you're prepared for the integration process. Frameworks like the AI adoption life cycle shared within the inset in Chapter 2 can help you ***identify where you are, set realistic goals for advancement, and define a plan to get there,*** including the relevant allocation of resources. This proactive effort will help mitigate risks and sets the stage for a smoother implementation. Additionally, consider starting with pilot projects to test AI applications on a smaller scale before rolling them out organization-wide. The prescribed approach to incorporating GenAI tools into your strategic planning efforts is designed to help highlight relatively simple and cost-effective ways to leverage GenAI tools without a substantial investment in GenAI as a strategic capability.

Neglecting Security and Privacy

AI systems often handle sensitive data, so ***nonprofits must prioritize data protection to maintain trust with their stakeholders and ensure you don't run afoul of regulations and laws,*** such as Health Insurance Portability and Accountability Act (HIPAA) compliance. Implement robust security measures, such as encryption and access controls, to safeguard your data. And always do your best to stay informed about relevant regulations and ensure your AI practices comply with legal requirements. By prioritizing security and privacy, you can mitigate risks and build a strong foundation for ethical AI use. If yours is a smaller nonprofit, ***look for model policies developed by peer organizations or associations to determine appropriate steps and precautions.***

Road Map to the Future

AI will continue to evolve, offering even more sophisticated tools and applications for strategic planning and a wide range of other helpful use cases. Nonprofits that stay ahead of the curve by continuously learning and adapting will be well positioned to leverage these advancements. ***The future of AI in strategic planning promises increased efficiency, deeper insights, and more innovative solutions.*** By embracing AI and integrating it thoughtfully into your processes, your organization can navigate the complexities of the future with confidence and agility.

Dos and Don'ts

Do

- Start with simple GenAI tools to build confidence, and then work your way up to dedicated scheduling, data entry, and data analysis tools when ready
- Begin your AI-powered strategic planning effort by ensuring your AI tool understands your nonprofit's mission, core programs, past successes, and challenges and goals by feeding it relevant documents, KPIs, desired outcomes, and other information as needed
- Iterate! At each step of the strategic planning process, ask AI for multiple outputs to find the gems you need, in addition to updating your plan and inviting AI to weigh in on new drafts and spot any room for improvement or inconsistencies
- Leverage AI outputs and stakeholder input to identify three to five strategic objectives in your plan, each of which should be mapped to activities, outputs, outcomes, KPIs, milestones, and roles and responsibilities
- Use AI to strengthen your plan by layering in data analysis and industry benchmarks
- Conduct a thorough assessment of your nonprofit's readiness before adopting AI tools

Don't

- Assume you have to create your nonprofit's strategic plan manually and by yourself; leverage AI and your board by mapping out a compelling outline and creating a committee to oversee the planning process
- Forget that "less is more" and your strategic plan should likely be limited to three to five years, and map to an action plan to guide implementation and assess performance
- Let AI produce your final draft, ignoring the value of the human touch to ensure the plan maintains your voice and style, and eliminating any errors
- Neglect to take data security and privacy measures to protect any sensitive information

Conclusion

AI offers immense potential to enhance strategic planning for nonprofits. ***By starting small, communicating clearly, and leveraging AI to strengthen and streamline your planning efforts, you will enjoy a more efficient and effective process.*** Remember to balance AI capabilities with human expertise and prioritize security and privacy. As AI continues to evolve, staying informed and adaptable will enable your organization to navigate future challenges with confidence. Embrace the opportunities AI presents and use it as a powerful tool to drive your mission forward.

Interviewee Bio

Sam Azar is a seasoned nonprofit executive with almost 20 years of experience in strategic planning, program evaluation, and organizational development. He is the founder and CEO of Ascend Impact Advisors, a consulting firm that brings a human-centered approach to strategy, data, and AI for social impact. His nonprofit leadership experience includes establishing the US Research and Measurement function for Habitat for Humanity International, scaling Compass Working Capital's evidence-based financial coaching program model nationally through training and technical assistance, and serving as director of strategy at United Way Worldwide. https://www.linkedin.com/in/sampazar/

Resource Review

- Anthropic's Claude: https://www.anthropic.com/claude—A GenAI LLM that excels at providing conversational insights, drafting content, and answering complex queries, making it a helpful partner for brainstorming and generating sections of your nonprofit strategic plan.
- Google Gemini: https://deepmind.google/—An AI tool offering capabilities like deep research for gathering and synthesizing information, enabling your nonprofit to benchmark performance and uncover trends relevant to strategic priorities.

- ChatGPT by OpenAI: https://chatgpt.com/—A versatile AI assistant that can support nonprofits with content creation, data synthesis, and stakeholder engagement, streamlining the planning process by generating drafts, summaries, and innovative ideas.
- Superhuman: https://superhuman.com/—An email management tool powered by AI that enhances productivity by prioritizing important communications, freeing up time for more strategic priorities.
- Fathom: https://fathom.video/—AI-powered meeting software that records, transcribes, and summarizes virtual discussions, making it easier to capture stakeholder input and integrate insights into your planning process.
- Perplexity: https://www.perplexity.ai/—A research assistant that uses AI to quickly answer questions and summarize complex topics, enabling your nonprofit to gather benchmarking data, identify trends, and generate insights for strategic planning.
- Miro: https://miro.com/—A collaborative platform that uses AI to assist with meeting facilitation, brainstorming, and synthesizing participant input, making it a valuable tool for workshops and planning sessions.
- Consensus: https://consensus.app/—Summarizes academic research using AI, helping you identify evidence-based strategies and gather supporting data for your plans.
- *Harvard Business Review* AI tool: https://hbr.org/ (Beta access for subscribers)—Provides AI-driven strategy and leadership insights based on HBR's extensive knowledge base, helping nonprofits align their planning efforts with proven best practices.
- Coloop: https://www.coloop.ai/—AI software that analyzes and synthesizes interview data, enabling nonprofits to process and distill stakeholder feedback for use in strategic planning.
- Tableau: https://www.tableau.com/—A powerful data visualization tool with AI integrations, enabling your nonprofit to monitor KPIs, track progress, and identify trends to support data-driven decision-making.

- PowerBI: https://www.microsoft.com/en-us/power-platform/products/power-bi/—An analytics platform that leverages AI to visualize data and generate actionable insights, supporting nonprofits in aligning resources with strategic goals.
- Asana: https://asana.com/—A project management tool with AI features that simplify task assignment, workflow automation, and timeline tracking, helping your nonprofit stay organized as you implement your strategic plan.
- Monday.com: https://monday.com/—A flexible project management platform that uses AI to automate workflows, monitor tasks, and provide updates, making it easy for nonprofits to track the execution of strategic objectives.

Chapter 20

Dashboarding: Impact Measurement and Data Visualization

Based on insights from an interview with Rachel Ward and Rajesh Naik.

AI-driven dashboards are powerful tools that transform how nonprofit leaders make data-informed decisions and measure impact, improving organizational effectiveness. These ***dashboards aggregate and analyze data from multiple sources—such as fundraising platforms, social media, volunteer management systems, program tracking tools, and, of course, bookkeeping and financial platforms—and can combine it with publicly available data to provide impactful insights.*** When designed and maintained with the proper care and tools, dashboards transform complex data into actionable insights, helping you track and optimize progress, identify patterns, and support decision-making.

By leveraging AI, dashboards go beyond static reports, offering predictive analytics to identify trends, uncover opportunities, and flag potential challenges before they escalate. This enables you to allocate resources more effectively, measure program performance, communicate progress to stakeholders with compelling data visualizations, and ultimately drive greater impact. By integrating AI-driven dashboards into your operations, you will turn raw data into actionable insights that support mission-critical goals while saving time and effort.

Critical Skills and Competencies

Clean and Organize Your Data

Conducting a thorough data audit is the first step in ensuring your data is accurate and reliable. To do this, *first develop your action plan by identifying any useful sources of data (e.g., databases, spreadsheets) and evaluating the quality of information found in each, including its accuracy, depth, consistency, relevance, and timeliness.* Then, ensure compliance with relevant data protection and security regulations, remove any inappropriate sources, and upgrade any on the edge by identifying solutions to address data quality concerns, including detailing any cleansing and validation processes. Data cleansing involves removing duplicates, correcting errors, and standardizing formats to ensure consistency. This process can be time-consuming but is crucial for the accuracy of your dashboards. *Investing time in cleaning your data up front will save you headaches down the line and improve the overall quality of insights generated.*

Ensure your plan includes assigned roles, responsibilities, and timelines so it's clear who is doing what by when, and *establish a schedule for ongoing data quality checks and audits to continuously refine processes, maintain data integrity, and ensure alignment with organizational goals.* Moving forward, regularly cleaning and organizing your data helps prevent errors and ensures that your dashboards reflect true and actionable insights. Ongoing data hygiene is essential and provides the foundation for any dashboarding effort.

Develop Data Literacy

Fostering data literacy across your organization is crucial. Everyone, from the executive team to frontline staff, should understand the basics of data interpretation and its significance. To maximize success, *ensure your entire team develops a practical understanding of relevant data sources and outputs, particularly as they relate to each individual's role.* By empowering your team with these skills, you ensure that data-driven decisions are made at every level of your nonprofit. Data literacy enables staff to ask the right questions and uncover the story behind the numbers.

To develop data literacy, offer frequent, regular training sessions and resources that teach staff how to read, analyze, and interpret data effectively.

Foster a culture of curiosity and continuous learning about data. When everyone in your nonprofit is data literate, you create a shared understanding of the numbers underpinning your work, making it easier to align on goals and make informed decisions that propel your mission forward.

Know Your Audience

Creating an effective dashboard involves balancing functionality, clarity, and user-focused design. By understanding your audience, setting clear goals, and using intuitive visuals, you can develop a dashboard that simplifies information and enhances decision-making. ***Identifying and involving the right people early on ensures your dashboard meets the needs of those who will use it most, as well as those it's meant to inform.*** This collaborative approach fosters buy-in and increases the likelihood of successful adoption, while also ensuring your reporting goals are realistic and that the outputs generated by your dashboard will in fact support informed decision-making and expand your impact. So, ***ask any key stakeholders for their input on what metrics are most important and how they should be presented.***

As you move forward with the steps outlined in this chapter, regularly ***update your stakeholders during the development process to manage expectations and enable you to address any concerns or suggestions.*** Their ongoing input will help guide the design and functionality of the dashboard, making it a more useful tool for your nonprofit and its end users. Simply put, a dashboard created with stakeholder input is much more likely to be embraced and used effectively.

Crystallize Metrics

It's easy to get overwhelmed by the sheer volume of data available, so zeroing in on the most critical key performance indicators (KPIs) helps maintain clarity and align your dashboard with your organization's objectives. ***KPIs should be specific, measurable, achievable, relevant, and time-bound (SMART), and convey progress against predetermined operational and financial goals, as well as your programmatic impact.*** While businesses may be fine only looking at the numbers of dollars made and products sold, mission-led nonprofits have a double bottom line, needing to both maintain sustainability while measuring and maximizing the impact of the services and programs delivered, so your dashboard must speak to this.

Selecting the right KPIs is crucial to ensure that you are tracking what truly matters, so *focus on metrics that align with your strategic goals or theory of change.* Once you've identified your KPIs, make sure they're clearly defined and understood across the organization, so everyone works toward the same objectives. For every KPI, it's critical to establish not only annual targets but also shorter-term projections (typically monthly or quarterly) to enable meaningful comparison between actual performance and goals. For example, knowing you are at 13% of your annual target is typically not as actionable as recognizing that you're at 102% of your year-to-date (YTD) target. This level of insight can quickly inform decision-making, so *one of the cornerstones of dashboards is a simple algorithm for categorizing performance within specified ranges (e.g., green, yellow, and red), typically calculated as a percentage: YTD goal divided by YTD actual.*

Develop the Dashboard

Choose user-friendly and scalable tools for developing your dashboard. Unlike manually creating dashboards in Microsoft Excel, which is oftentimes a good starting point, *AI-powered tools like Tableau (https://www.tableau.com/), MicrosoftPower BI (https://www.microsoft.com/en-us/power-platform/products/power-bi), and Google Looker Studio (https://lookerstudio.google.com/) automate data integration, offer advanced analytics, and enable automatic updates and interactive visualizations, significantly reducing effort and enhancing insights.* Depending on your needs, you may need to explore custom-built dashboards developed in-house if you have the technical expertise or by data analytics specialists.

Whatever tool you use, your dashboard's design should be intuitive, enabling users to easily navigate and interpret the data presented. Organize data visually to highlight the most critical information, using charts and graphs to clearly, compellingly showcase trends and insights. *A well-designed dashboard transforms complex data into actionable insights, flagging causes for concern, celebrating success, and highlighting critical discussions for staff and board.* When developing your dashboard, consider the end-user experience. Ensure the most important information is easily accessible and that visualizations are clear and engaging. Testing the dashboard with a small group of users before full deployment will help you identify any usability issues and ensure it meets the needs of your team.

Supplement Data Sources

External data sources can fill gaps in your own data and provide a more comprehensive view of your impact. Government databases, public records, and the like can all be valuable additions to your data pool. ***Integrating third-party datasets can enhance the accuracy and depth of your analysis, providing helpful North Star–level indicators and benchmarks against which you can compare your efforts.*** Tracking changes in community-level metrics like total homeless population or food insecurity rates provide useful context, especially if your figures are heading in a different direction. For example, reporting a grade point average increase for your program's students is helpful, but knowing that the general student body experienced a decrease at the same time makes your work even more compelling to donors, partners, and clients.

Exploring and integrating diverse data sources can also uncover new insights and opportunities. For instance, ***combining internal program data with American Community Survey census data will help you better understand the communities you serve and tailor your interventions more effectively.*** This holistic approach to data significantly enhances strategic planning and impact measurement.

Organize Ownership

Clearly defining data ownership and responsibilities within your team is essential. ***Assign specific roles for data collection, maintenance, and analysis to ensure accountability and consistency.*** And consider your approach to data sharing carefully, taking time to document your approach and updating any relevant AI policies. This helps maintain data integrity and streamlines the dashboard development process. When everyone knows their role, the process becomes smoother and more efficient. Having designated data stewards also ensures data management practices are consistently applied across the organization. These lieutenants serve as points of contact for any data-related queries and ensure your data governance policies are followed. Clear ownership and accountability are key to maintaining high-quality data and effective dashboards.

Maximize Relevance with Frequency

Outdated data can lead to misguided decisions and missed opportunities. AI tools can facilitate automated, near real-time access to data, but you may also rely on some sources that require manual entry or third-party updates. For any sources not automatically integrated, update your dashboard data at appropriate and consistent intervals. Whether it's daily, weekly, or monthly, *setting a regular schedule for data updates ensures any information presented remains current and actionable.* This consistency helps in making timely decisions based on the latest data.

Establishing a clear update schedule also helps manage expectations and ensures everyone knows when to expect new data. *Communicate your schedule to all dashboard users and provide reminders as needed to ensure anyone charged with inputting data does so on time.* Consistent updates are key to maintaining the relevance and usefulness of your dashboard.

Keep an Eye on Adoption

Provide ongoing training and support to ensure effective dashboard use. Regular feedback sessions and training workshops will help users become more comfortable with the dashboard, increasing its use and impact. *Update your dashboard and reporting templates over time to maximize usefulness.* Occasionally reviewing and updating your KPIs will keep them aligned with your evolving strategy and objectives.

This iterative process helps ensure your dashboard continues to meet your nonprofit's needs and remains a valuable tool for decision-making. Monitoring adoption rates and addressing any barriers to use is crucial for long-term success. *The most well-designed dashboard is ineffective if it isn't used, making continuous improvement and user engagement essential parts of your ongoing impact measurement and visualization strategy.*

Pitfalls and Solutions

Neglecting Buy-In

Too many nonprofits fail to secure buy-in from key stakeholders during the dashboard development process. Without their support, your dashboard will likely struggle to gain traction. ***Involve stakeholders from the outset, clearly communicate the benefits, and address any concerns*** to ensure successful implementation. Stakeholder buy-in is crucial for your dashboard's success. So, take the time to embrace open communication and invite input, and to regularly update them on your efforts over time. Being able to showcase how the dashboard can solve specific problems or enhance decision-making will help reinforce its utility in your organization.

Fearing the Truth

It's human nature to shy away from uncomfortable truths, even those revealed by data. However, acknowledging and addressing the cold, hard facts is essential for growth and improvement. Put your mission first: embrace the insights provided by your dashboard, even if they highlight areas that need significant change. ***Facing the truth head-on often leads to meaningful progress and stronger impact.***

Creating a culture that values transparency and continuous improvement is key. Encourage your team to see data as a tool for learning and growth, rather than a source of judgment. By fostering an environment where data is openly discussed and acted on, you will drive positive change and enhance your nonprofit's effectiveness.

Road Map to the Future

The future of dashboarding and AI in nonprofits is incredibly exciting. As these technologies advance, data will increasingly be at our fingertips, directly accessible to our AI tools. In the years ahead, your nonprofit will have even more powerful tools to drive impact and harness real-time insights to make data-informed decisions. Moreover, ***the integration of predictive analytics and Machine Learning will further enhance your nonprofit's ability to anticipate trends and allocate resources more effectively, providing powerful fodder to dashboards.*** Staying abreast of these technological advancements and continuously adapting your strategies will be key to maximizing their potential.

Nonprofits that embrace these innovations will be better positioned to achieve their missions and drive meaningful change. By investing in the right tools and fostering a data-driven culture, organizations can unlock new levels of efficiency and impact. The future holds immense potential for those willing to explore and leverage the power of AI and advanced analytics.

Dos and Don'ts

Do

- Conduct a thorough data audit and clean your data regularly, including removing duplicates, correcting errors, and standardizing formats
- Provide training sessions and resources that teach staff how to read and interpret data to foster data literacy across your organization
- Develop SMART KPIs that speak to both operational/financial health and progress against your mission
- Design your dashboard to report against not only annual targets but also YTD values and projections
- Integrate third-party datasets into your dashboard to enhance the accuracy and depth of your analysis with useful benchmarks and shifts in community-level conditions
- Establish and communicate the frequency with which your dashboard integrates updated data to properly manage expectations
- Revisit KPIs and reexamine underlying datasets regularly to maintain relevance

Don't

- Neglect to secure buy-in from key stakeholders during the development process: invite their input on what to measure and how to present it, and provide regular updates to unearth more suggestions and concerns
- Rely on Excel or manually created dashboards: AI-powered tools automate data integration, offer advanced analytics, and enable real-time updates and interactive visualizations
- Depend too heavily on third-party providers for AI solutions instead of building up your internal capacity to enable control and adaptability
- Assume any data you manually collect for your dashboard will magically appear, instead of assigning team members to collect, maintain, and analyze any required data inputs
- Discount the importance of continuous improvement and user engagement to inform your dashboarding efforts

Conclusion

By embracing data and leveraging AI-driven dashboards, nonprofits can revolutionize their approach to impact measurement and visualization, unlocking the ability to make data-informed decisions that propel your mission and impact. By taking the time to begin with the end in mind, invite and integrate input from a range of audiences, and develop and refine your dashboard, your organization will enjoy access to the tools once only available to the Fortune 500. And it will all be at your fingertips! Just don't be afraid to confront the hard truths when they arise; *if you create a culture within your nonprofit that embraces the facts and uses data-driven insights to make better decisions, your clients and community will enjoy the benefits.* And after all, isn't that why we're all here?

Interviewee Bios

Rachel Ward is a dedicated servant leader, child advocate, and public service professional committed to enhancing the well-being of communities, families, and children. As vice president of Omega Community Development Corporation in Dayton, Ohio, she leads the nonprofit's strategic, place-based efforts, including the Hope Zone Promise Neighborhood and the Hope Center for Families. Rachel's extensive career spans youth program development, regional leadership in child abuse prevention, and collaborative initiatives in early childhood education and food equity. A participant in the EdRedesign Lab's inaugural Cradle-to-Career Leaders Fellowship program at the Harvard Graduate School of Education, she also serves on the boards of the Miami Valley Child Development Centers and Miami Valley School. https://www.linkedin.com/in/rward27/

Rajesh R. Naik is the chief operating officer for Mined XAI, an explainable AI data analytics startup based in Dayton, Ohio. He is responsible for leading their socioeconomic modeling efforts to support nonprofit clients, in addition to building the company's business verticals, cultivating partnerships, and driving client engagement. Rajesh previously held technical leadership positions at the Department of Defense, where he managed several large science and technology programs. In these roles, developing metrics and measuring performance were crucial to ensuring the successful delivery of technological solutions. https://www.linkedin.com/in/rajesh-naik-044276ab/

Resource Review

- Dr. Michelle Ewy's blog: https://minedxai.com—A blog on leveraging AI and data analytics for the nonprofit sector.
- Tableau: https://www.tableau.com/—Empowers nonprofits to create visually compelling, AI-enhanced dashboards that simplify complex data, enabling leaders to uncover actionable insights and communicate impact effectively.
- Microsoft Power BI: https://www.microsoft.com/en-us/power-platform/products/power-bi—Enables nonprofits to leverage AI-driven analytics to generate dynamic, real-time reports that integrate data from multiple sources, providing a comprehensive view of your operations and outcomes.
- Google Data Studio: https://lookerstudio.google.com/—Offers nonprofits an intuitive, AI-powered platform to build customizable dashboards and real-time reports, making it easier to track performance and share insights with stakeholders.
- Data.gov: https://www.data.gov—A comprehensive resource for accessing US government datasets to supplement your nonprofit's internal data.
- Board.Dev: https://board.dev/—Currently limited to the San Francisco Bay Area, this platform helps place tech leaders on nonprofit boards, thereby strengthening tech governance and empowering organizations to effectively adopt and leverage AI-powered dashboards and other technology tools.
- Beth Kanter's blog: https://bethkanter.org—A blog by a nonprofit technology expert with valuable tips and strategies for using data and technology effectively.
- NTEN: https://www.nten.org—Helps nonprofits adopt and leverage AI-powered dashboards and other technology tools by providing training, resources, and a supportive community to build digital literacy, foster ethical tech use, and enhance organizational impact.
- TechSoup: https://www.techsoup.org—Offers technology products and services at discounted rates for nonprofits to support tech capacity building.
- *Nonprofit Quarterly*: https://nonprofitquarterly.org—Offers insights and analysis on nonprofit management and governance to help you stay informed.

Chapter 20.1

Program Evaluation

Based on insights from an interview with Chaitra Vedullapalli.

AI-powered program evaluation enables you to leverage data for strategic insights, making it infinitely easier to navigate the complexities of assessing program performance and ultimately amplifying your nonprofit's impact. Instead of just crunching numbers, with a few tips and tools you'll be able to automatically transform data into actionable insights.

By integrating AI into your evaluation processes, you can streamline data collection, enhance real-time monitoring, and make informed decisions that propel your mission forward. To guide you through this transformative process, consider the RISE framework—research and evaluation, innovate, sustain, and engage. This framework encapsulates the critical components needed for an AI-driven evaluation strategy, providing you with a road map to enhance your program's effectiveness and impact.

The RISE Framework: AI-Powered Evaluation

Research and Evaluation: Set the Foundation

Lewis Carroll once quipped, "If you don't know where you're going, any road will get you there." *The first step in evaluating your program is to identify the right data parameters and key performance indicators (KPIs) you can use to gauge your progress.* Are the dollars deployed driving maximum impact and value? Where are you getting the best social return on investment? Use AI tools to analyze program effectiveness by geography, audience, and partners.

Keys to Progress

- **Identify KPIs:** Determine what success looks like for your program. Are you looking at participant engagement, outcome achievement, or community impact? Tools like Power BI (https://app.powerbi.com/) and Airtable (https://airtable.com/) can help visualize these metrics.
- **Create dashboards:** Use AI to create instant dashboards that track program performance in real time, or at least that automatically update. As detailed in Chapter 20, this visual representation enables you to monitor trends, identify areas of improvement, and make data-driven decisions. Download your data into spreadsheets, upload them into AI tools, and prompt them to generate the reports you need.

Innovate: From Creation to Launch

Embracing change is key to staying relevant and effective, and AI is a great tool for developing intellectual property to help your nonprofit distinguish its unique offerings in the community. ***AI-powered micro innovations can help not only with dashboards and evaluation but also enable you to quickly, effectively collaborate with communities and stakeholders to implement new ideas and map out potential strategies.*** And once you've done that, use tech tools to streamline the process of developing and refining materials to bring them into the world.

Keys to Progress

- **Program creation:** Use AI tools to streamline the development of program materials, messaging, and audience frameworks. Tools like Canva (https://www.canva.com/) make it easy to create impactful one-pagers and case studies that highlight your program's success.
- **Go-to-market strategy:** Plan your program launch with precision. Use project management tools like Monday.com or Asana (https://asana.com/) to organize resources and manage timelines. Use AI to facilitate content creation, design, and even video production, ensuring a smooth and efficient launch.

Sustain: Monitoring and Decision-Making

Once the train leaves the station, it's critical to keep it on the rails. That means minding the store and keeping an eye on progress and optimizing your approach on an ongoing basis.

Keys to Progress

- **Real-time monitoring:** Use AI to set up dashboards that provide a weekly review of your program's progress. Once again, Power BI (https://app.powerbi.com/), Airtable (https://airtable.com/), and similar tools allow you to track data, identify issues, and adapt strategies accordingly.
- **Decision-making protocols:** Document your decision-making processes and ensure they are data-driven. Regularly review your scorecard metrics and use AI insights to adjust your approach, ensuring your program remains on track and impactful.

Engage: Partner and Funder Relationships

No program is an island. *For your program to maximize impact, it's critical to work with key stakeholders to identify pressing needs and ensure potential solutions are welcome.* AI can help!

Keys to Progress

- **Data transparency:** Be proactive in defining the parameters of any data exchange. Clearly communicate what can and can't be done with the data, ensuring privacy and compliance with funder requirements.
- **Collaborative planning:** Work with your funders to set up systems that align with their goals without compromising your organization's integrity. Use AI to provide detailed reports and updates that demonstrate your program's impact and value.

Interviewee Bio

Chaitra Vedullapalli is an award-winning entrepreneur, thought leader, and strategic go-to-market expert recognized for her contributions to technology, economic inclusion, and digital transformation. As the cofounder and CMO of Meylah, she led billion-dollar expansions at Microsoft and Oracle, leveraging AI to drive innovation. A passionate advocate for economic access, Chaitra cofounded Women in Cloud, a community-led organization empowering women in technology through AI and cyber skilling, entrepreneurship, and leadership initiatives. https://www.linkedin.com/in/chaitrav/

Chapter 20.2

Ensuring Data Quality

Based on insights from an interview with Nick Hamlin.

Data is the currency in today's AI-powered information economy. And whether you're using off-the-shelf free tools or custom, state-of-the-art platforms, AI is only as good as the data you feed it. Think of it like cooking a gourmet meal; even the best chef can't create a masterpiece with spoiled ingredients. ***Without a reliable data foundation, your AI initiatives can go awry, exacerbating biases and producing unreliable outcomes.***

As a nonprofit leader, you juggle countless responsibilities, and data hygiene might not always be top of mind. So, try to remember this to help you keep things in perspective: ***high-quality data not only enhances your AI's effectiveness but also fortifies your decision-making process across all areas of your work.*** Ensuring data quality is not just a technical task; it's a strategic imperative for any nonprofit serious about leveraging AI. By following this framework, you can build a solid foundation that enhances the effectiveness of your AI tools and, ultimately, the impact of your organization.

Maximizing Accuracy and Reliability

Identify Your Data Guardians

Data quality isn't a one-time project; it's an ongoing commitment that requires buy-in from all stakeholders. ***Start by forming a team charged with overseeing data quality, regular updates and audits, and the identification and integration of new datasets.*** This team should be cross-functional, drawing members from different departments to ensure a holistic approach to data management. Members should also have a strong understanding of how the organization operates and delivers on its mission.

Ask Who's Missing

One of the most common sources of data bias is the omission of key stakeholders or data points. ***Adopt a habit of regularly asking "Who is missing?" from our data and stakeholder groups.*** This vigilance helps ensure that your data is representative and comprehensive. Pair this with the "five whys" technique—ask why something is missing, and then ask why again for each subsequent answer, until you uncover the root cause. This method helps you dig deep and address underlying issues that might not be immediately apparent, but of course, that's only helpful if you follow through and address any needs unearthed.

Automate Data Collection

Manual data collection and oversight is both time-consuming and error prone, so you need to strive to automate as much of your data collection process as possible. ***By integrating checks and validations into your operations, you can significantly reduce the chances of human error.*** For example, consider a traditional workflow wherein you create a report manually, copying numbers from one data source into another and then verifying totals yourself or via Excel, one at a time. Instead, consider tools like DBT (https://www.getdbt.com/) and Great Expectations (https://greatexpectations.io/) to streamline and automate this process, offering your nonprofit benefits not just once, but any time you repeat the process in the future. Not only does this save time and ensure accuracy, but it can also help you keep data sources more uniform and up-to-date, while flagging potential data quality issues proactively before they lead to further problems and confusion downstream.

Stay Alert

The landscape of your data sources and organizational goals is ever-changing. ***Regularly review your data collection processes, sources, and outputs to spot potential problems.*** Constant exploratory data analysis will help you identify changes that will enhance your processes. AI can assist here, too—ask it to monitor key performance indicators (KPIs) for consistency and accuracy over time, as detailed in Chapter 20, and to suggest data hygiene checks based on your specific needs.

Document Effectively

Your data quality efforts aren't complete until they're documented. Write down your processes—what you did, how you did it, and how it can be improved in the future. Be sure to also include who on staff will own these efforts on an ongoing basis; otherwise, it's very easy for data quality projects to suffer from the tragedy of the commons since they're rarely high-profile or directly revenue- or impact-generating tasks on their own. Remember to revisit your documentation regularly to keep it up-to-date as things change. This documentation not only helps with transitions if team members leave but it also creates a culture of accountability and continuous improvement within your nonprofit. An ounce of prevention is worth a pound of cure, and spending a few minutes on documentation can save you hours down the road.

Interviewee Bio

Nick Hamlin currently supports organizations at many different points on their data journeys as director of data strategy and innovation at DARO, a consultancy that seeks to improve information flows in the aid and philanthropy space. Previously, Nick led the data team at GlobalGiving, a nonprofit that helps trusted, community-led organizations around the world access the money, tools, training, and support they need to make our world a better place. He's also served as a data ambassador for Datakind's impact practice in community health, and his work has been featured in several TechChange courses on topics including Machine Learning, data visualization, and monitoring and evaluation. https://www.linkedin.com/in/nickhamlin/

Chapter 21

Developing Your Own Custom Large Language Model

Based on insights from an interview with Craig Johnson.

Welcome to the AI revolution! As a nonprofit leader and maybe even a technologist, you've probably heard the buzz about AI and how it can transform your organization. This chapter will guide you through creating your own large language model (LLM) or generative pre-trained transformer (GPT) specifically for project management and internal communications. At its core, this means you can feed your bot information, documents, and materials so it gets to know you: how your nonprofit speaks, its goals and programs, the relevance of key stakeholders, and your ultimate mission. Having your own LLM means you can upload this information once, instead of at the beginning of each prompt or request. By leveraging AI, you can supercharge your nonprofit's efficiency and effectiveness, making it easier to manage projects, communicate internally, and ultimately, achieve your mission. ***Imagine a tool that can draft emails, summarize long reports, and even generate new project ideas, all tailored to your nonprofit's unique needs.*** Let's dive into the nuts and bolts of setting up your own LLM and explore why it matters for your cause.

Critical Skills and Competencies

Create a Guidebook

Before diving into the AI waters, you need a solid plan. As covered in many of the other chapters, your first step is to develop guidelines that outline and underpin your AI strategy. ***Your AI-powered project management and internal communications policy should evaluate potential use cases, ensuring you're clear on how***

AI will benefit your organization and addressing data security by identifying which platforms and products best suit your needs while safeguarding sensitive information. Look into both online and offline models to find something that fulfills your data privacy requirements. Online models like GenAI tools ChatGPT, Claude, or Gemini use your conversations to train their models. So, ***if privacy is important to you, alternatives like the self-hosted Mistral (https://mistral.ai) model offers the same functionality without the data risk.*** Keep track of alternative platforms as a backup in case your primary choice becomes unavailable due to business, political, or other reasons.

Training on your policies is crucial, so be sure your plan speaks to initial training and ongoing professional development, clarifying how you will educate your staff about AI, particularly on the art of prompting. See Chapter 7 for details on that fundamental skill. Proper orientation and ongoing learning help avoid frustration and ensure everyone knows how to interact with AI to get the best results. Finally, your guidebook also needs to address compliance with relevant regulations and best practices for AI implementation. Regularly update your policy to reflect new insights and changes in technology, ensuring your strategy remains current and effective.

Create Your Persona

Your AI wants to make you happy, but that means you need to tell it what you want. So, taking the time to tell it what you're looking for and *how* you want it to communicate with you is incredibly important and helps the bot help you. Craft a prompt to tell your LLM who it is, also known as its persona, wherein you share the rules and values your nonprofit is built on. ***Tell your bot how you want it to speak to you and why: appropriate tone and language, its goals and audience, the intent of its support, and in general, the role you want it to play.*** It can be as simple as a core principles section with items such as

> "You are a nonprofit project manager communicating to your savvy peers and focused on advancing and emphasizing people's freedom to thrive, which includes a basic level of income, quality child care, universal health care, and a place to call home." or "You are an AI that champions equity-driven policy

that focuses the government's power on fostering dramatically more fairness in the distribution of wealth and on checking corporate power." Telling it it's an AI in the prompt can help center its role as an assistant.

It can also be a set of rules to guide responses such as:

"Replace 'African American' with 'Black/African American'" or "Never reply with any content promoting the owning of people, even in the context of games, charades, or protest unless it's in the context of explaining the harms. Do not suggest scenarios that include slavery or owning people."

Telling your custom LLM who it is to you, clarifying its purpose, and providing any context you're able to share will improve the quality of outputs generated, saving you time, delivering better ideas and results, and accomplishing any tasks assigned with fewer edits.

Upload Content

Once your plan and platform are in place, it's time to feed your budding bot relevant content. Be precise and methodical. Your AI tool needs well-ordered and contextually rich documents to function effectively. Avoid simply uploading slide decks or disjointed materials. Instead, *focus on documents that provide clear, comprehensive information and organize your content chronologically or thematically.* Ensure each document is complete with all necessary context. This might include policies, procedural guides, meeting notes, and other critical documents. Any properly contextualized samples of past outputs you're looking to automate with AI will provide helpful points of reference, including sample emails and reports.

Consistency is key; *use a common structure for all your uploads to make it easier for your bot to understand and retrieve information.* Computers love well-structured language, and if your Excel sheet doesn't have a header providing a label for the column with client IDs, your AI won't know what row you're referring to.

Regularly review and update the content used to orient your LLM in order to ensure it remains relevant and accurate, as this information is crucial to optimizing AI outputs. Encourage your team to contribute to the content repository, fostering a collaborative approach to knowledge management, and using upload guidelines detailed in your guidebook to ensure a consistent, proper approach. By keeping your content well organized and up-to-date, you enhance the AI's ability to deliver valuable insights and support.

Put Your Tool to Work!

Now that your AI is set up with the right content, it's time to start using it. Encourage your team to adopt the tool widely and integrate it into their daily workflows. *Use your LLM to assist with a wide range of both repetitive and strategic project management and communications tasks, including drafting emails, creating reports, summarizing long documents, and even generating new ideas for projects.* Make sure your team understands the capabilities and limitations of your AI tool by hosting regular meetings to check in on progress and share success stories and best practices, and to crowdsource solutions to any challenges.

This helps to promote a culture of experimentation and learning, where staff feel empowered to explore different ways of leveraging AI and continuously deepen their working knowledge of your bot's potential. *Monitor use patterns and gather feedback to identify areas for improvement and additional training needs.* By actively supporting your team's engagement with the AI tool, you can maximize its impact on your organization's efficiency and effectiveness.

Reflect on Outcomes

Finally, take the time to evaluate how your custom LLM improves efficiency and communication within your organization. Gather feedback from your team at and between your regular meetings and adjust as needed. *Conduct quarterly or semiannual reviews of your AI's performance and update its training data to ensure it remains relevant and effective.* Use both quantitative and qualitative measures to assess performance. Track key metrics such as time saved, error reduction, and user satisfaction. Collect anecdotal evidence and success stories to provide a more comprehensive view of impact. Share your findings with stakeholders to demonstrate the value of your bot and secure ongoing support for its use. Regular reflection and evaluation will help you continuously optimize your AI strategy and achieve even greater benefits over time.

Nonprofits and other organizations tend to think narrowly at first when it comes to new and revolutionary technology. That means your team may try a new tool on for size in the prescription manner but not think more broadly about how it can be applied, which undermines creativity and innovation. So, ***invite your team to play around and think of out-of-the-box use cases.*** For example, some experimenting nonprofits have used AI to great effect with social media meme generation. While many of them didn't think this was well suited to GenAI, with enough structure they have saved immense time brainstorming new and creative ideas. So, don't leave tech strategy and application to technical or engineering staff or consider it a one-time activity. Instead, ***engage your whole team on a sustained basis in envisioning how AI can be best used, including program staff and team members directly interacting with your clients and community.***

Pitfalls and Solutions
Accepting One Size Fits All

Too many nonprofits assume generic tools and data-sharing practices will meet their needs. Each organization and its work are unique, and using generic tools without customization can lead to inefficiencies and data security risks. To avoid this, carefully assess your specific requirements and select tools that can be tailored to meet those needs. ***Invest in tools that offer customization options and integrate well with your existing systems.*** Work closely with any IT staff and external vendors to implement these tools effectively. Regularly review and update your data-sharing practices to address emerging threats and compliance requirements. By choosing the right tools and implementing secure data-sharing practices, you can enhance your organization's efficiency and protect sensitive information.

Inadequate Training

As shared in many other chapters, one of the most common pitfalls is inadequate staff orientation and support. Without proper training, your team will struggle to use AI effectively, leading to frustration and suboptimal results. ***Invest in comprehensive training programs that cover the basics of AI, the specific functions of your LLM, and general best practices for interacting with technology.***

Regular refresher courses and ongoing support can also help ensure your team remains proficient in using the tool. And as shared already, foster a supportive learning environment where staff feel comfortable asking questions and seeking help, encouraging peer-to-peer learning and knowledge sharing.

Road Map to the Future

Nonprofits' use of AI will surely continue to evolve and expand. As technology advances, AI will become even more sophisticated and accessible, enabling nonprofits to leverage these tools in new and innovative ways. In the coming years, ***expect to see increased integration of AI with other technologies such as blockchain and the Internet of Things (IoT).*** These integrations will open up new possibilities for data management, transparency, and efficiency in nonprofit operations. To stay ahead, keep an eye on emerging technologies and continuously explore new ways to incorporate AI into your organization's strategy. By doing so, you can unlock new opportunities for growth and innovation.

Dos and Don'ts

Do

- Create a comprehensive AI guidebook that outlines your strategy and best practices, including detailing your most common use cases, preferred or exclusive platforms, and approach to data security
- Organize your content chronologically or thematically and upload it methodically, ensuring it is well ordered and supported with context, and including samples of whatever you expect to frequently ask AI to produce
- Encourage your team to use your custom LLM widely, while constantly monitoring usage patterns and gathering feedback

Don't

- Neglect regular reviews and updates of your AI tool and content repository
- Assume generic tools will meet your organization's unique needs without customization

- Overlook data security and compliance when implementing AI tools
- Think of crafting your AI strategy as a one-time task for your tech team, instead of consistently engaging your whole team, especially program staff and others interacting with your clients and community
- Skimp on investing in thorough orientation and training programs for your staff to ensure effective use of AI tools, in addition to regular team check-ins to celebrate wins, share best practices, and problem-solve

Conclusion

Creating your own LLM for project management and internal communications can transform your nonprofit's operations, making your cause both more efficient and effective. *By developing a comprehensive guidebook, uploading organized content, leveraging and iterating your tool, and providing continuous training and support, you can maximize the benefits of AI.* Reflecting on outcomes and addressing common challenges over time will ensure your AI implementation remains successful and impactful.

Interviewee Bio

Craig Johnson is founder and managing partner of Unfiltered.Media and president/chief technology officer of Change Agent AI. Craig combines his extensive experience in political and issue-based digital communications with his recognized thought leadership and practical experience in AI and technology. Over his decade-long career, he has strategized and executed digital campaigns for notable members of Congress, Community Change Action, Census 2030, the Feminist Majority, and Americans for Tax Fairness. Craig's unique blend of strategic acumen and technical expertise, particularly his leadership in AI and full-stack web development, empowers Unfiltered.Media and Change Agent to transform complex strategies into tangible digital innovations. https://www.linkedin.com/in/craig-johnson-4bb33195/

Resource Review

- Change Agent: https://thechange.ai/—Empowers nonprofits to develop custom LLMs and GPTs tailored for project management and internal communications, streamlining workflows, enhancing team collaboration, and saving time through AI-driven solutions.

- Mistral AI: https://mistral.ai/—Open-source models that enable nonprofits to develop custom LLMs that automate project management tasks and enhance internal communications, leading to improved operational efficiency and resource allocation.

- ClickUp: https://clickup.com/—Facilitates integration with AI-powered automation and task prioritization to help nonprofits streamline project workflows, ensuring teams focus on high-impact activities and stay aligned on mission-critical goals.

- Jira: https://www.atlassian.com/software/jira—Leverages AI for agile project management, enabling nonprofits to track progress, identify bottlenecks, and collaborate more effectively on complex initiatives.

- Airtable: https://airtable.com/—Offers AI-enhanced capabilities that enable nonprofits to organize, visualize, and analyze project data, fostering seamless collaboration and more informed decision-making across teams.

- Notion AI: http://notion.ai—Combines project management tools with AI capabilities to help nonprofits organize tasks, facilitate team collaboration, and streamline internal communications within a unified workspace.

- Zapier: https://zapier.com/—Enables nonprofits to connect LLM-powered tools with their existing apps and automate tasks across platforms, streamlining project updates and internal messaging.

- NTEN's Nonprofit Technology Conference: https://www.nten.org/gather/ntc—Premier nonprofit technology gathering, where you can learn about the state of the industry and new trends in AI and project management, and connect with a range of helpful vendors

- Nonprofit Hub: https://nonprofithub.org—A great resource for articles, webinars, and guides on nonprofit technology and management.

Chapter 22

Public-Facing Chatbots

Based on insights from an interview with Jim Fruchterman.

In the digital age, nonprofits are constantly seeking innovative ways to engage with their communities and streamline their operations. Meanwhile, people are increasingly looking for the information and support they need *right now*. With the speed of change only increasing, how are resource-strapped nonprofits to cope? **Community-facing chatbots can automate a variety of tasks, from answering common inquiries and providing support to gathering helpful client data.**

A chatbot is an AI-powered virtual assistant designed to simulate human conversation. It's one of the many breakthroughs made possible by natural language processing (NLP). For busy nonprofit leaders, understanding how to effectively implement and use chatbots can free-up valuable time and resources while enhancing the service experience for beneficiaries, donors, and more. This chapter will help quickly level up your understanding so you can decide if chatbots are right for you and if so, effectively deploy them while sidestepping common pitfalls.

Critical Skills and Competencies

Are Chatbots Right for You?

A public-facing chatbot can be an excellent solution for a nonprofit that needs to provide consistent, 24/7 engagement and support to its stakeholders. **Chatbots are particularly effective for organizations with a high volume of repetitive, relatively low-risk communication needs, such as community resource centers or advocacy groups managing outreach campaigns.** Additionally, if your nonprofit serves a tech-savvy audience that prefers digital interactions, a chatbot can enhance accessibility and improve user experience. If your nonprofit frequently receives inquiries about programs, services, donation options, or event participation, a chatbot can help automate responses to common questions.

However, ***chatbots are not a viable solution for every nonprofit, particularly smaller, grassroots organizations with limited budgets or those whose work requires a high degree of personalized or sensitive communication.*** If your audience needs tailored advice, emotional support, or human connection—for instance, in crisis intervention or counseling services—a chatbot might fall short and even risk alienating those you aim to serve. Bear in mind that ***the current state of the field for chatbots is only 70–90% accuracy,*** although of course this is improving every year. What happens to the other 10–30%? If you are going to implement a chatbot, you need to understand what the error path is. Is it sending someone to the wrong article? That is not as bad as answering their question wrong, because most people will quickly recognize if they end up on the wrong content. Additionally, ***implementing and maintaining a chatbot requires resources, typically in the range of six figures or more over three to five years, plus the necessary technical capacity,*** If your nonprofit lacks the necessary infrastructure or staff expertise, it could become a distraction rather than an asset. In such cases, investing in human-centered communication strategies might yield more meaningful results.

Start with a Clear Vision

OK, so you've decided to go for it. Before diving into the technical aspects of chatbot implementation, it's crucial to have a clear vision of what you aim to achieve, just as with any AI technology. Define the goals and objectives of the chatbot and clarify its key audiences. Are you looking to provide information to the public, gather patient data, support donors, or something else? ***A well-defined purpose and audience will guide the development process and ensure the chatbot aligns with your nonprofit's mission and values.*** For instance, if your goal is to provide 24/7 support to beneficiaries, your chatbot should be designed to handle a wide range of inquiries and escalate complex issues to human staff.

A clear vision also provides a useful foundation for setting realistic expectations and identifying measurable outcomes. It ensures that all stakeholders, from developers to end users, are on the same page regarding the chatbot's purpose and capabilities. This **consistent understanding of and alignment on needs and priorities is crucial for the successful implementation and adoption of the chatbot.** Regularly revisiting and refining your vision based on user feedback and technological advancements will help keep your chatbot relevant and effective over time.

Crystallize Your Needs with Input

Now that you've clarified your vision with internal input, your next step is to get feedback from a sample of potential end users to ensure your platform addresses their needs. **The goals and preferences of your audience, combined with data on common inquiries and issues, must inform your chatbot's design and operation.** For instance, analyzing past interactions and feedback helps you identify gaps in service and areas for improvement.

Use this data to train your chatbot to provide accurate and helpful responses. The more data you feed your bot, the better equipped it will be to serve your community. And just as it's important to regularly ask your team for input, external data collection must be an ongoing process. Continuously gather and analyze data to refine your chatbot's performance and adapt to changing user needs. **Implementing regular feedback mechanisms, such as surveys or user satisfaction ratings, provides valuable insights into how well your chatbot is meeting its goals.** This iterative approach ensures your chatbot remains responsive and effective, ultimately enhancing the user experience and achieving your nonprofit's objectives.

Many chatbot platforms include built-in tools for gathering and analyzing performance data, making it easier to track how well your chatbot is meeting user needs and goals. These features often provide analytics dashboards that show key metrics, such as user engagement rates, FAQs, conversation drop-offs, and overall user satisfaction. Platforms like Tidio (https://www.tidio.com/), Drift (https://www.salesloft.com/platform/drift), and ManyChat (https://manychat.com/) offer robust analytics and feedback collection tools, making it simple for nonprofits to monitor performance and make adjustments as needed. Some even integrate with survey tools or allow for custom scripts to ask users for feedback directly within the chat interface. **If your chatbot platform doesn't have built-in feedback mechanisms, you can use third-party tools** like

Google Forms (https://docs.google.com/forms), Typeform (https://www.typeform.com/), or SurveyMonkey (https://www.surveymonkey.com/) to collect insights from users after their interactions.

Clarify the Stakes

Do you expect your chatbot to handle simple information that folks aren't counting on, or life-or-death support that costs lives if it's inaccurate? Understanding the often high-stakes nature of implementing AI in a nonprofit environment is essential, and this is equally true for anyone involved with your technology initiatives. With your team, **think through and discuss the potential implications of misinformation, biases, ethical considerations, and privacy concerns as it relates to any information your chatbot will handle.** Ensure your chatbot is designed to handle sensitive information responsibly and that it escalates issues to human staff when necessary. For example, a chatbot providing mental health support must be equipped to recognize signs of crisis and connect users with professional help.

Maintaining awareness also involves continuous monitoring and auditing of the chatbot's performance to identify and mitigate any unintended consequences. **Set up protocols for handling data breaches and ensuring compliance with relevant regulations.** By staying vigilant and proactive, combined with training your team on these high-stakes issues, you will maintain your chatbot's quality and reliability.

Create an Owner's Manual

Most of this book's chapters include tips for creating an AI policy as it relates to any specific application or use case. In the case of developing chatbots, it's certainly helpful to make your needs and goals explicit, but when it comes to documenting its ongoing operation, it's critical to write things down. **Documenting your chatbot's development process, including its goals, functionalities, and decision-making criteria, provides a helpful reference point for your team, avoids confusion, and supports consistent operation.** It also allows for easier troubleshooting and updates in the future. Clear documentation, including user manuals and training materials for staff who will interact with or manage the chatbot, ensures that everyone involved understands the chatbot's purpose and how it should function.

Thorough documentation also helps maintain transparency and accountability. It provides a clear trail of decision-making and changes, which can be invaluable during audits or evaluations. ***By maintaining detailed records, you can quickly address any issues that arise and make informed decisions about future improvements.*** This practice not only enhances the chatbot's effectiveness but also fosters a culture of continuous learning and development within your nonprofit.

Iterate and Evolve

We've already spoken to the critical importance of soliciting ongoing feedback from both your team and external stakeholders. But as we alluded, ***if you don't bother to integrate input and evolve your approach over time, your chatbot's usefulness will fade.*** Implementing a chatbot is an ongoing process that requires regular maintenance, updates, and improvements. Monitoring your chatbot's performance, gathering feedback from users, and making necessary adjustments ensures your chatbot remains effective and continues to meet the evolving needs of your audience. Regular testing and user feedback loops are critical components of this process, helping you refine the chatbot's functionality and user experience.

Finally, there's a third source of insights beyond internal and external: industry developments. ***Staying abreast of technological advancements and nonprofit best practices is crucial for keeping your chatbot relevant.*** As AI and Machine Learning evolve, new features and capabilities will become available that enhance your chatbot's performance. Allocate resources for ongoing support and improvements to ensure your chatbot continues to deliver value. Ignoring this will quickly lead to outdated functionality and poor user experiences, undermining your chatbot's effectiveness. Bear in mind the cost of hosting, staff support, and maintenance to keep your chatbot running smoothly and efficiently. By committing to continuous learning and adaptation, you can ensure your chatbot remains a cutting-edge tool that effectively supports your nonprofit's mission.

Pitfalls and Solutions

Ill-Defined Boundaries

Without proper guardrails, your chatbot will go off-script and provide incorrect or inappropriate responses. As such, you need to establish clear guidelines and protocols for your chatbot's interactions to maintain the quality and reliability of the information provided, protecting your organization's reputation and the trust of your community. In particular, **predefined responses for common queries and escalation protocols for complex issues will prevent your chatbot from making critical errors.** Other key guardrails you should consider include having clear protocols for data security, privacy, and maintaining accessibility to ensure the chatbot is inclusive for users with diverse needs, such as those with disabilities or limited technological proficiency.

Skimping on the Human Touch

While chatbots can handle many tasks, they should not replace human interaction entirely. **Ensure there is a seamless way for users to escalate issues to human staff when needed,** and that your guardrails and protocols speak to exactly when this should occur. For example, the Roo chatbot by Planned Parenthood (https://www.plannedparenthood.org/learn/roo-sexual-health-chatbot) refers users to external mental health providers if they indicate suicidal thoughts. If you plan to regularly refer people elsewhere, be sure to reach out to the other provider to let them know and confirm they can support anyone sent there.

In addition, regular human oversight of your bot is critical. **Have people regularly review your chat logs, especially in the early stages, to identify common needs, problems, and any recurring errors or hallucinations from the bot.** Keeping humans in the loop allows for more personalized and nuanced responses, particularly for complex or sensitive inquiries. This hybrid approach leverages the efficiency of AI while maintaining the empathy and understanding that only humans can provide.

Unclear Limitations

Be upfront about what your chatbot can and cannot do. Transparency helps manage user expectations and builds trust. **Clearly communicate the chatbot's capabilities and limitations, and provide alternative options for users who need assistance beyond what the chatbot can offer.** This honesty can prevent frustration and ensure users feel supported, even if the chatbot cannot address their needs directly. Make sure users know when they are interacting with a bot and when they can expect human intervention if necessary.

Forgetting Who Is Boss

The ultimate goal of implementing a chatbot should always be to enhance the experience of your clients and community. Keep their needs and preferences at the forefront of your planning and decision-making. ***Regularly seek user feedback and adjust based on their input to ensure your chatbot remains a valuable tool.*** User satisfaction should be a key metric in evaluating the chatbot's success and guiding its development. By focusing on the client's perspective, you will ensure your chatbot genuinely adds value and supports your nonprofit's mission.

Road Map to the Future

The future of chatbots in the nonprofit sector is promising. ***As AI technology continues to advance, chatbots will become more sophisticated and capable of handling a wider range of tasks, all made possible by continuous improvement in understanding and responding to natural language, making interactions more seamless and intuitive.*** Additionally, the integration of chatbots with other technologies, such as Machine Learning and data analytics, will enable nonprofits to gain deeper insights into their communities and tailor their services more effectively. To leverage these new opportunities and address emerging challenges, it's crucial for nonprofits to stay informed about these developments and continuously adapt chatbot strategies as the landscape evolves.

Dos and Don'ts

Do

- Clearly define the purpose and goals of your chatbot before doing anything else, including specifying exactly which audiences you want it to serve and how
- Collect and use user input when designing and training your chatbot, and regularly check in with them after launch to assess performance identify room for improvement
- Proactively consider the impact of misinformation, biases, ethical considerations, and privacy concerns as it relates to any information your chatbot will handle

- Set up protocols for handling data breaches and ensuring compliance with relevant regulations
- Ensure your chatbot is designed to handle sensitive information responsibly and escalate issues to human staff when necessary
- Document your chatbot's goals, key functions, and decision-making criteria to avoid confusion and maximize performance
- Prevent your chatbot from making critical errors by creating predefined responses for frequently asked or other important questions
- Regularly review chatbot logs to better understand common needs and problems, and any recurring errors or hallucinations

Don't

- Neglect the importance of recordkeeping to maintain transparency and accountability by providing a clear trail of decision-making and changes
- Discount the importance of ongoing training and professional development to ensure you and your team stay on top of technological advancements and industry best practices
- Assume it's OK to refer chatbot users to a third party without first contacting them to confirm their ability to provide the necessary support
- Assume users know what your chatbot can and cannot do: share its capabilities and limitations clearly, offering alternative options for users who need deeper support

Conclusion

Public-facing chatbots offer significant potential for nonprofits to enhance service delivery and engage communities more effectively. ***By starting with a clear vision; ensuring awareness of the stakes; documenting your needs, audience, and process; soliciting input from a wide range of stakeholders; and committing to continuous improvement, you can successfully implement and use chatbots.***

Focusing on client-centric solutions will ensure your chatbot remains a valuable tool in achieving your nonprofit's mission. Embrace the opportunities that chatbot technology presents and stay informed about future developments to stay at the forefront of innovation.

Interviewee Bio

Jim Fruchterman is a renowned social entrepreneur and technology pioneer, dedicated to harnessing the power of technology for social good. As the founder and CEO of Tech Matters, he leads efforts to design and implement innovative, scalable tech solutions that address critical social and environmental challenges. With a background in engineering and decades of experience in the nonprofit and social enterprise sectors, Jim has been a trailblazer in leveraging technology to empower marginalized communities, from creating accessible tools for people with disabilities to advancing AI-driven solutions for mission-driven organizations. A MacArthur Fellow and Skoll Awardee, Jim is widely recognized as a thought leader in the intersection of technology, equity, and impact. https://www.linkedin.com/in/jimfruchterman/

Resource Review

- Tech Matters: https://techmatters.org—Focused on leveraging technology for social impact, they provide insights, tools, and case studies to help nonprofits and mission-driven organizations implement AI solutions like chatbots ethically and effectively.
- The Chatbot Summit: https://www.chatbotsummit.com/—A conference dedicated to chatbot and AI technologies, with sessions relevant to nonprofits.
- Tidio: https://www.tidio.com—Helps nonprofits enhance their public-facing chatbots with AI-driven features like intent recognition and automated responses, streamlining user support and improving engagement.
- Drift: https://www.salesloft.com/platform/drift—Enables you to leverage AI-powered conversational marketing tools, optimizing chatbots to drive meaningful interactions with donors, volunteers, and beneficiaries.

- ManyChat: https://manychat.com—Enables nonprofits to use AI for creating and managing highly interactive chatbots on social media platforms, improving outreach and engagement with a broader audience.

- Google Forms: https://docs.google.com/forms—Provides a simple, cost-effective way to collect post-chat feedback, enabling nonprofits to gather insights and refine their chatbot's performance.

- Typeform: https://www.typeform.com—An engaging and user-friendly platform to create dynamic surveys that capture detailed chatbot user feedback and satisfaction ratings.

- SurveyMonkey: https://www.surveymonkey.com—Enables you to design comprehensive feedback mechanisms for chatbot interactions, offering advanced analytics to identify areas for improvement.

- AI for Good Foundation: https://ai4good.org—A hub for learning about AI applications for social impact, offering webinars, case studies, and research on how technology like chatbots can drive change in nonprofit sectors.

- OpenAI Blog: https://openai.com/blog—A go-to resource for staying updated on cutting-edge AI developments, including advancements in conversational AI and strategies for responsibly using these technologies in mission-driven organizations.

- The Nonprofit Technology Network (NTEN): https://www.nten.org—A nonprofit-focused resource that provides training, reports, and discussions about leveraging AI and emerging technologies, with practical tips for chatbot implementation.

- Nonprofit Tech for Good: https://www.nptechforgood.com/—A blog that offers insights and resources on technology trends and best practices for nonprofits.

- TechSoup: https://www.techsoup.org/—Provides nonprofits with access to technology solutions, training, and resources, including updates on AI tools like chatbots and their applications for community engagement.

Chapter 23

Dealing with Mis/Disinformation

Based on insights from an interview with Adam Fivenson.

In today's digital, increasingly post-truth era, misinformation and disinformation spread like wildfire, creating significant challenges for nonprofits. Inaccurate information without the intent to deceive, or misinformation, quickly erodes the hard-won trust and credibility you've built with your supporters, volunteers, and stakeholders. Meanwhile, disinformation, or false information deliberately spread to mislead or manipulate, can be incredibly destructive and quickly escalate. Make no mistake, nonprofits are not immune to such attacks. In fact, nonprofits are increasingly the target of bad actors who may disagree with their work, feel slighted by exclusion or the loss of access to support services, or believe the work of the nonprofit would be better done by others.

With the rise of AI, combating these challenges simply cannot be ignored, and action requires a blend of technology and strategy. Combatting this manually isn't an option, as the internet is too broad, too fragmented, and too complex for any one individual or team to be able to monitor discourse at scale. The advent of AI exacerbates this challenge in part because it multiplies the amount of content online, since producing that content is so much cheaper and easier. So, **nonprofits need to understand how AI helps monitor, identify, and respond to false information.** Whether it's a coordinated attack or an innocent mistake, this isn't just about damage control; it's about staying ahead of potential threats and maintaining trust within your community.

Critical Skills and Competencies

Do Your Homework

GenAI tools are also great for evergreen research. ***Your first step is to use AI to prepare for likely challenges by identifying some of the most common objections to, and misconceptions about, your cause.*** For example, if your nonprofit is focused on combatting climate change, use AI to help you identify common false narratives about climate science and prepare responses in advance. If you regularly hear these concerns raised, consider adding an FAQ page to your website and using social media to combat frequent falsehoods.

Training your team to recognize and respond to misinformation is another helpful, proactive measure that helps lay the foundation for your movement. ***Ask your GenAI tool for help creating training modules and simulations that prepare your staff for real-world scenarios.*** Regularly updating these trainings ensures your team stays informed about the latest tactics used by bad actors and is ready to act quickly and effectively.

Keep Your Eyes Open

AI can help you monitor social media and online platforms for false information about your organization or cause. ***Advanced AI features like sentiment analysis and natural language processing (NLP) identify negative or misleading content in real time*** by tracking when there's a shift in people's perspectives of your work, deciphering online chatter with all its jargon and shorthand. This is baked into platforms like Hootsuite Insights (https://www.hootsuite.com/platform/listening) and Grammarly Business (https://www.grammarly.com/business). ***Use AI and tools like Google Alerts (https://www.google.com/alerts) to set up alerts and track mentions of your organization,*** enabling you to respond swiftly and accurately.

AI is also a great tool to identify patterns and sources of misinformation. By analyzing data, ***AI can detect coordinated disinformation campaigns and provide insights into how these narratives spread.*** Platforms like Graphika (https://graphika.com) and NodeXL (https://nodexl.com) enable you to develop a proactive response strategy, addressing potential issues before they escalate, and helping you pinpoint troublesome actors, networks, and narratives. Meltwater (http://meltwater.com) is an excellent tool for monitoring the information environment across the web, social media, and search, as are more specialized firms that provide AI-driven tools for nonprofits, such as Blackbird AI (https://blackbird.ai/), Logically (https://logically.ai/), or Alethea (https://alethea.com/). Exolyte (https://exolyt.com/) is especially useful for monitoring discourse on TikTok.

Play Defense

If your nonprofit is ever the target of disinformation, your first question should be whether and how to respond. If it's a single message by a voice with little audience, consider whether your response might ultimately amplify the original lie and give it legitimacy. If through your monitoring efforts, you detect the spread of that message or narrative and it's being reposted by other accounts or it appears on other platforms, then consider responding quickly in ways that do not amplify the original lie but that defend and secure your integrity and the legitimacy of your work. For example, some organizations have chosen to amplify video testimonials from their beneficiaries rather than engage directly with the original lie, though there are certainly instances when it is critical to engage directly with a mis- or disinformation narrative, especially if it continues to spread and metastasize.

If a response is needed, consider deploying *AI-powered chatbots and automated response systems to provide accurate information to your audience, helping to dispel falsehoods and reassure your supporters.* As detailed in Chapter 22, these tools can be quickly programmed to address common concerns and questions, ensuring your responses are timely, relevant, and impactful. Just be sure to maintain trust with your audience by proactively communicating transparently about the use of AI, and consider using tools to help you build your chatbot and integrate it into existing online and social channels, such as Chatbase (chatbase.co) or Chatfuel (chatfuel.com).

If you're the victim of disinformation, you should also *use AI to analyze the concerns raised by false narratives and help you create tailored responses that address these issues directly.* If your critics claim you're misusing funds, for example, consider proactively releasing your financials or audit results and directly addressing their false attacks. Crafting targeted, personalized messages in this way not only corrects misinformation but also strengthens your relationship with your audience, especially when bolstered by any relationships you're able to develop with journalists to strengthen credibility even further.

Enter the Lion's Den

Now that you've laid your foundation, positioned your lookouts, and prepared a daunting defense, the only thing left to do if you see a steady stream of attacks or fake news is to go to uproot the problem at its source. ***By understanding the platforms and channels where misinformation is spreading, you can strategically place helpful, true messages where they're most likely to be seen by those who need accurate information the most.*** This ensures your corrective efforts are both efficient and effective, while enabling you to reach a wider audience.

Identifying the source of misinformation also enables you to create accountability for those attacking you. If you can gather sufficient evidence to convince your audience a particular actor is behind attacks, you can highlight that and the underlying agenda to your supporters, making it easier for them to dismiss false accusations and deepen their trust in your mission.

Finally, ***consider raising the issue of misinformation attacks on your work within trusted industry associations or multi-stakeholder fora.*** It is entirely possible that other organizations doing related work are facing the same attacks and you may be able to (1) share data about what you are seeing that may help you better understand those attacks, their origins, and tactics; (2) jointly design and amplify responses; and (3) share resources and tools, such as AI-driven detection platforms and communications tools.

Pitfalls and Solutions

Head in the Sand

It can be overwhelming to face mis- and disinformation when you're trying to stay focused on your nonprofit's operations and mission. Too often, these attacks or falsehoods are viewed as an unnecessary distraction, and leaders mistakenly believe if they ignore them, they'll go away. ***Mis- and disinformation rarely goes away on its own and typically gets much worse over time as it builds on itself,*** especially if there's a bad actor behind it all actively working to undermine your credibility. Hoping these attacks will sort themselves out is not a strategy for success, and even though the tips outlined in this chapter may take an investment of time and effort, that pales in comparison to unwinding a mature campaign you let get away from you.

Keep the Keys

While AI tools are powerful, they're not infallible and sometimes miss contexts or nuances that a human reviewer would catch. It's essential to maintain a balance between automation and human intervention to ensure accurate and appropriate responses to misinformation. To address this, your nonprofit should ***implement a layered approach where AI handles initial monitoring and flagging of potential issues, and then human staff conduct deeper evaluations and craft responses.*** This hybrid model leverages the strengths of both AI and human judgment, ensuring a more comprehensive and reliable approach to managing misinformation.

Road Map to the Future

Looking ahead, the use of AI in combating misinformation and its more intentional cousin, disinformation, will continue to evolve. ***Nonprofits can expect more sophisticated tools that offer deeper insights and more accurate detection of false information.*** The integration of AI with other technologies, such as blockchain, will also provide new ways to verify the authenticity of information and ensure transparency and credibility.

To prepare for the future, stay informed about the latest AI and technology developments and continuously adapt your nonprofit's strategies. Invest in ongoing training and stay connected with experts in the field to continue to leverage AI effectively and maintain your sterling reputation. By staying proactive and embracing innovation, your nonprofit will remain resilient in the face of evolving challenges within today's information economy.

Dos and Don'ts

Do

- Start by researching your issue and identifying common misconceptions about your cause so you can proactively address legitimate concerns and be prepared to respond to false narratives
- Train your team to recognize and respond to mis- and disinformation
- Use AI tools and alerts to monitor social media and online platforms for false information using AI tools
- Detect coordinated disinformation campaigns and figure out where these start and how they spread using AI tools to develop a proactive response strategy and address potential issues
- Consider whether any attacks violate the law or the terms of service on platforms, and if so, consider a legal response and be sure to report them

Don't

- Expect problems to solve themselves: if you are the target of a disinformation campaign, act quickly, using chatbots and AI-powered automated response systems to provide accurate information and addressing false narratives directly with targeted, personalized messages
- Focus only on responding to attacks, especially if they keep happening; instead, research the platforms and channels where misinformation spreads, and then leverage those to share the truth and change hearts and minds.
- Rely solely on automated systems without human intervention

Conclusion

AI technology can provide a huge boost to your nonprofit's efforts to combat misinformation and disinformation, especially with judicious human oversight. By understanding the capabilities of AI and integrating it into your strategy, your organization can effectively address false information targeting your staff, partners, and operations and maintain the trust of your community. *AI tools provide powerful capabilities for monitoring, identifying, and responding to misleading narratives, but they must be used thoughtfully and transparently.*

As you navigate the complexities of misinformation, remember to be proactive, stay informed, and never ignore attacks. By leveraging AI effectively, you can protect your nonprofit's reputation, ensure your message remains clear, and foster a trustworthy relationship with your audience. Embrace these tools and strategies to safeguard your mission and continue making a positive impact.

Interviewee Bio

Adam Fivenson is a speaker, writer, and researcher focused on global trends in democracy, online information manipulation, and nonprofit responses. Most recently he led the research portfolio on authoritarian information manipulation at the National Endowment for Democracy, where he brought together nonprofit leaders defending civic space and human rights across more than 50 democracies to accelerate learning and publish whitepapers and articles on GenAI and other key trends. Adam is a non-resident fellow at the Center for Security, Innovation, and New Technology at American University, and previously served as lead designer for citizen engagement tools for local governments in Guatemala and Afghanistan. https://www.linkedin.com/in/afive/

Resource Review

- Hootsuite Insights: https://www.hootsuite.com/platform/listening—Enables your nonprofit to monitor social media for misinformation trends and analyze sentiment about campaigns in real time.
- Google Jigsaw's Perspective API: https://perspectiveapi.com/—Leverages NLP to detect toxic or misleading comments in online discussions, helping nonprofits moderate conversations effectively.
- Grammarly Business: https://www.grammarly.com/business—In addition to the core writing assistance functionality, this tool provides tone and sentiment analysis, helping nonprofits craft clear and trustworthy messaging to counteract misinformation.

- Google Alerts: https://www.google.com/alerts—A free tool that helps nonprofits and people combat misinformation and disinformation by automatically monitoring the web for specific keywords, enabling you to quickly identify and address false or misleading content related to your mission or campaigns.

- Meltwater: http://meltwater.com—Provides media monitoring and social listening tools to help nonprofit leaders identify and respond to misinformation and disinformation trends across news and social media platforms.

- Exolyte: https://exolyt.com—Offers in-depth TikTok analytics that nonprofits can use to track and counteract disinformation campaigns on this fast-growing social platform.

- Chatbase: chatbase.co—Enables nonprofit leaders to create AI-powered chatbots trained on their verified content, ensuring accurate information is shared and helping combat disinformation in real time.

- Chatfuel chatfuel.com—Enables nonprofits to build conversational AI chatbots for platforms like Facebook Messenger, providing a scalable way to address misinformation directly with their audience.

- Graphika: https://graphika.com/—Helps nonprofits map and analyze disinformation networks, revealing how coordinated campaigns spread across social media platforms.

- NodeXL: https://nodexl.com/—This tool enables nonprofits to visualize and analyze social media interactions, helping them identify patterns and clusters indicative of coordinated disinformation efforts.

- The Center for Humane Technology: https://www.humanetech.com—Promotes ethical technology use and provides resources on combating misinformation.

- AI Ethics Lab: https://aiethicslab.com—Provides guidance on ethical AI practices and strategies for combating misinformation.

- Alethea Group: https://www.alethea.com—Specializes in detecting and mitigating disinformation and online threats.

- First Draft: https://firstdraftnews.org—Offers resources and training to help nonprofits understand and address misinformation.

- Snopes: https://www.snopes.com—A reliable fact-checking website that can help verify or debunk information related to your cause.
- FactCheck.org: https://www.factcheck.org—Provides nonpartisan information and fact-checking to help combat misinformation.
- The Trust Project: https://thetrustproject.org—Promotes transparency and trust in journalism, offering resources to help verify information.
- The NGO Information Sharing and Analysis Center: https://www.ngoisac.org/—Enhances nonprofit cybersecurity by fostering a community of professionals who share best practices and threat intelligence, strengthening defenses against misinformation and disinformation attacks.

Part V

The Invisible Backbone: Transforming Back-Office Operations with AI

> *"Artificial intelligence is not just about efficiency gains, it's about opening up new possibilities, unlocking human potential, and solving some of society's biggest challenges."*
> —Yoshua Bengio, computer scientist and Turing Award laureate, 2021

The strength of a nonprofit lies not only in its programs and outreach but also in the unseen operations that keep everything running smoothly. ***From human resources to IT infrastructure, the back office is the foundation on which mission success is built.*** Yet, managing these essential functions can often feel like a juggling act—balancing efficiency, compliance, and capacity in an environment of chronically limited resources.

AI, when leveraged strategically and responsibly, has the potential to revolutionize your back office. ***By automating repetitive tasks, providing real-time insights, and enhancing decision-making, AI enables your nonprofit to reimagine the way it manages operations.*** Think of AI-powered tools that streamline recruitment and onboarding, automate financial reporting, and optimize IT systems for seamless AI integration—all while freeing up staff time for strategic priorities.

But just as the quote says, the power of AI isn't just about increasing efficiency. It's also about creating new opportunities to align your operational capabilities with your mission. ***AI offers insights and automation that can enhance accountability, improve collaboration, and elevate the overall impact of your work.***

By embedding AI into the foundation of your nonprofit, you can build a more resilient and adaptive infrastructure, better equipped to navigate change and scale your efforts.

In Part V, we explore how AI can transform back-office functions, enabling your nonprofit to build future-ready operational infrastructure. We begin with "Human Resources," examining how AI can enhance talent acquisition, support diversity and inclusion initiatives, and improve employee engagement. AI tools can assist with everything from analyzing job descriptions for bias to identifying candidates who are the best cultural and skill fit for your organization. Once onboard, AI-powered platforms can streamline workflows, monitor employee satisfaction, and even predict attrition, enabling HR teams to address challenges proactively.

Next, "Finance and Bookkeeping" showcases how AI simplifies everything from expense tracking to compliance, ensuring transparency and efficiency. By automating tasks like invoice processing and payroll, AI reduces errors and saves time. AI-driven analytics also provide real-time financial insights, empowering nonprofit leaders to make informed decisions and optimize resource allocation. For example, predictive modeling can help anticipate funding gaps and guide proactive financial planning.

For leadership and governance, "Board Recruitment and Engagement" delves into the potential of AI to identify and engage board members with the skills and networks needed to advance your mission. AI tools can analyze data from professional networks, social media, and organizational history to pinpoint individuals whose expertise aligns with your strategic goals. The "Recruiting Tech Executives to Your Board" inset offers targeted strategies for attracting tech-savvy leaders who can guide your nonprofit through digital transformation, ensuring your board remains equipped to navigate a rapidly evolving landscape.

Finally, "IT Infrastructure and Software: The Tech Stack Needed to Support AI Integration" takes a deep dive into the technical backbone required for successful AI adoption. From cloud computing to customer relationship management (CRM), this chapter outlines the tools and systems your nonprofit needs to scale operations and maintain resilience in a tech-driven world. Emphasis is placed on selecting scalable and secure solutions that align with your mission, ensuring that your technology investments deliver long-term value.

Each chapter offers actionable guidance to help you integrate AI into your operations with intention and foresight. Practical checklists, sample prompts, and expert insights ensure you can take immediate steps toward implementation. ***By modernizing your back office, you'll not only unlock efficiencies but also position your organization to respond dynamically to future challenges and opportunities.***

AI can't replace the human judgment and care that underpin effective operations, but it can enhance them. It can eliminate bottlenecks, provide clarity amidst complexity, and empower your team to focus on the high-value work that drives impact. With a solid foundation powered by AI, your nonprofit can focus on what truly matters: advancing your mission and driving meaningful change.

Chapter 24

Human Resources

Based on insights from an interview with Tierney Yates.

In today's fast-paced, tech-savvy world, the role of AI in human resources (HR) has become indispensable, especially for nonprofits looking to automate repetitive tasks and enjoy deep insights to guide strategic decisions. When properly leveraged, ***AI can help you quickly, effectively develop job descriptions; amplify outreach and sort through applicants to find the best candidates; support onboarding; and advance diversity, equity, and inclusion (DEI) initiatives.***

Whether it's refining your interview questions to attract a more diverse candidate pool or streamlining recruitment and retention strategies, AI can enhance all your HR tasks. Imagine reducing the time it takes to post a job from weeks to just a few days, or mitigating bias to ensure your recruitment process is as inclusive and equitable as possible. So, let's dive in and look at how you can harness technology to not only make your HR processes more efficient but also more inclusive and effective!

Critical Skills and Competencies

Crystallize Your Use Case

Before diving into AI, it's crucial to ***identify the specific limitations and pain points you want AI to address in your HR processes.*** This will often take the form of a dedicated section within the AI policy suggested in many other chapters of the book, but either way, the important thing is to ***take the time to document exactly how you hope to deploy AI and to what ends.*** Whether it's recruitment, retention, onboarding, or DEI initiatives, having a clear understanding of your objectives will help you choose the right AI tools and strategies.

Once your goals are clear, start small and scale up as you become more comfortable with the technology. ***Implement AI in one area, evaluate the outcomes, and then expand its use to other HR functions.*** This approach enables you to test and refine your AI strategies without overwhelming your team or resources. Now, with your intentions clear and your experimental mindset in place, it's time to put tech tools to work! So, let's explore some tips and tools for a range of the most common HR use cases.

Draft Job Descriptions

AI-powered tools can streamline the creation of job postings, saving you time and ensuring they are inclusive and aligned with your nonprofit's values. Developing job descriptions manually often leads to inconsistencies, unintentional bias, or a lack of clarity. ***AI tools can quickly, effectively analyze successful job descriptions, suggest role-specific language, and help you emphasize the skills and qualities most critical to the position.*** This ensures your descriptions are professional, accurate, and appealing to the right candidates.

AI tools like Textio (https://textio.com) or Grammarly (https://grammarly.com) can help you easily craft clear, engaging, and inclusive job postings. ***Ensure you include the key responsibilities and tasks, desired skills, and your organizational goals in your AI prompts to get tailored outputs that fit your nonprofit's needs.*** Review any AI-generated descriptions for tone, clarity, and adherence to your DEI goals. Finally, always validate AI outputs by involving hiring managers or HR leads to refine them further before publishing.

Amplify Outreach

If a job description falls in the woods and no one is there to read it…. Expanding the reach of your job postings helps you attract a diverse and qualified candidate pool. Posting on the same platforms each time limits your applicant pool, and manual outreach can be time-intensive and inconsistent. ***AI helps you identify the best***

distribution channels, optimize posting schedules, and tailor messaging to reach the right audiences at the right time. Here's a quick breakdown of how:

- Leverage tools like LinkedIn Talent Insights (https://business.linkedin.com/talent-solutions) to analyze workforce trends and target high-potential candidates.
- Use platforms like SmartRecruiters (https://www.smartrecruiters.com) to distribute postings across multiple job boards, nonprofit-specific sites, and professional networks.
- Optimize reach by promoting listings on platforms like Idealist (https://www.idealist.org) and regional job boards like the one from California Association of Nonprofits (https://jobs.calnonprofits.org/), which focus on mission-driven careers.
- Track engagement through Google Analytics (https://analytics.google.com) or built-in AI analytics within hiring platforms to refine your approach.

By strategically expanding your outreach, you increase the likelihood of attracting top talent who align with your mission.

Identify and Screen Applicants

Finding and evaluating candidates takes significant time, but AI can streamline the process by analyzing résumés, LinkedIn profiles, and other data sources to highlight strong applicants based on predefined criteria. ***AI-powered sourcing expands your talent pool while helping mitigate bias in early screening.*** However, relying solely on AI risks overlooking critical factors like mission alignment and lived experience, so always integrate human oversight into the process.

Start by developing a structured evaluation rubric to ensure fair, consistent assessments. AI can provide a useful starting point, but be sure to collaborate with hiring managers to define essential skills, experiences, and competencies for the role. Outline clear, measurable criteria for each stage—such as technical abilities, nonprofit experience, and alignment with DEI goals—and then consider how to weigh each characteristic based on what's needed to thrive in the new role. Then you can leverage a range of tech tools to advance your hiring efforts:

- Use Google Sheets (https://docs.google.com/spreadsheets) or Notion (https://www.notion.com/) to standardize scoring.
- Use AI-powered screening tools like HireVue (https://www.hirevue.com) and SeekOut (https://seekout.com) to assess skills and potential fit.
- Platforms like Rival (https://rival-hr.com/entelo-recruit/) prioritize diverse candidates.
- Résumé-parsing platforms like Workable (https://www.workable.com) and Zoho Recruit (https://www.zoho.com/recruit) automate ranking based on your rubric, ensuring objective comparisons.

The landscape of resources will change over time, as will your needs and the particulars of any given tool, so *regularly audit AI-generated recommendations and involve a diverse hiring panel in final decisions to maintain fairness and alignment with your nonprofit's mission.*

Draft Survey and Interview Questions

So, now you've got some solid candidates, but how do you whittle that list down as you work to find the right hire? *Asking the right questions consistently during interviews and surveys ensures you assess candidates fairly.* Poorly structured questions, or deviating widely from a script, can introduce bias or fail to evaluate essential skills and cultural fit. *Use GenAI tools to draft competency-based questions tailored to your nonprofit's hiring priorities,* ensuring a structured, unbiased process.

Use Qualtrics (https://www.qualtrics.com) or your GenAI platform of choice to generate role-specific interview and survey questions that evaluate both technical skills and mission alignment. Especially if you have a large field of applicants, *using tools like SurveyMonkey (https://www.surveymonkey.com/) to develop and analyze survey results can quickly help you weed out lesser qualified candidates.* Then, use those competency-based interview questions to work through the finalists, scoring each on your rubric and feeding any notes or recordings into your AI platform to equitably inform your final decision. But of course, actual people should always make the final call on new hires. Tools like SkillSurvey (https://www.skillsurvey.com) can help you in the final stages by automating reference-checking, in addition to offering another survey tool with a focus on behavioral-based questions to assess candidates' soft skills. Throughout the process, involve your hiring or executive team in refining AI-generated questions, ensuring they align with your nonprofit's values and specific job requirements. And if possible, test interview structures internally before rolling them out to confirm clarity and effectiveness.

Generate Offer Letters

Once you've selected the best candidate, crafting a clear, professional offer letter is the final step before onboarding. ***A well-structured offer letter sets expectations, outlines key details, and reinforces your nonprofit's culture.*** AI can streamline this process by ensuring consistency, reducing errors, and personalizing offer letters based on role-specific requirements. Using AI to generate these documents enables you to focus on refining key terms rather than drafting from scratch.

Use AI-powered HR platforms like DocuSign (https://www.docusign.com) or DropBox Sign (https://sign.dropbox.com/) to generate and manage digital offer letters efficiently. Pair these with AI writing tools like Grammarly or any of the major GenAI platforms like ChatGPT to refine language, ensure clarity, and tailor tone. Standardize templates within your HR software to include key components like salary, benefits, job responsibilities, and detailed, milestone-based expectations for the first 90 days. Always review AI-generated offer letters for accuracy and compliance, then personalize them with a final human touch before sending. By automating this step, you ensure candidates receive a seamless and professional hiring experience while maintaining alignment with your nonprofit's mission and values.

Optimize Onboarding

OK, it's go time! Your new hire just showed up, so now what? A well-structured orientation process sets employees up for success and improves retention. Manual onboarding processes often overwhelm new hires with paperwork and lack that personal touch, but ***AI can streamline and personalize onboarding by automating administrative tasks, customizing training materials, and ensuring a smooth transition into your nonprofit's culture.***

Tools like BambooHR (https://www.bamboohr.com) can automate document management and workflow approvals, while AI-powered platforms like Talmundo (https://www.talmundo.com) create personalized onboarding journeys with interactive guides, training recommendations, and key introductions. ***Supplement onboarding with AI-curated training modules tailored to individual learning needs,*** including 360Learning (https://360learning.com) as just one example. But don't set it and forget it; instead, regularly collect feedback from new hires to refine and improve the onboarding experience over time.

Bolster DEI

Now you've found the right employee and welcomed them to your ranks, set them up for success by including some of our previous tips to facilitate a diverse pool of candidates. But after their onboarding, how can AI tools help ensure an inclusive workplace, where people of all backgrounds and abilities are poised to support and advance your mission and one another?

While nonprofits often focus DEI efforts on recruitment, true equity requires ongoing analysis of retention, promotion, pay equity, and workplace dynamics. With their power of data-driven analysis, AI tools can help track such disparities, detect patterns of bias in decision-making, and provide actionable insights to create a more equitable workplace. However, AI should augment rather than replace human-led DEI strategies—transparency, continuous learning, and accountability remain critical.

So, what belongs in your AI-powered DEI toolkit? Start by using next-generation workforce analytics platforms like Diversio (https://www.diversio.com) to assess workplace diversity and identify inclusion gaps across your organization. For real-time sentiment analysis and feedback on workplace culture, tools like Plum (https://www.plum.io) and CultureAmp (https://www.cultureamp.com) will help analyze employee experiences and engagement trends. And finally, to support equitable performance evaluations and promotions, Textio (https://textio.com) helps reduce bias in performance reviews by flagging potentially exclusionary language.

Pitfalls and Solutions

Focusing on Quotas

Aiming for diversity metrics without fostering true inclusion leads to superficial progress and high turnover. ***When nonprofits focus solely on increasing representation without addressing workplace culture, new hires from underrepresented backgrounds often feel unsupported or isolated.*** This results in lower retention rates and a revolving door of diverse talent. AI can compound this issue if used carelessly; prioritizing demographic diversity without considering broader equity and inclusion factors may lead to performative hiring rather than meaningful organizational change.

To combat this, use the DEI tools and practices outlined in this chapter to assess inclusion gaps, including but also beyond hiring statistics. ***Look for patterns in employee retention, pay equity, and promotion rates to uncover systemic disparities.*** Finally, use AI-powered sentiment analysis tools to surface real-time insights into how employees experience workplace culture, informing leadership decisions and targeted DEI strategies that go beyond recruitment.

Assuming AI Is Set-and-Forget

AI tools are powerful, but they are not self-sustaining solutions—leaving them unchecked can lead to outdated, biased, or ineffective HR practices. ***Over time, hiring trends, DEI priorities, and workforce needs evolve, and AI models that aren't regularly updated may produce irrelevant or inequitable results.*** For example, an AI-driven résumé filter may unintentionally reinforce outdated hiring preferences if it continuously ranks candidates based on prior selections without reassessment. Similarly, employee engagement tools that don't incorporate ongoing feedback can lead to misaligned workplace strategies.

To prevent AI stagnation, schedule regular audits of your AI-driven HR processes. Use platforms like hireEZ (https://hireez.com/) to monitor hiring data and identify shifts in applicant trends, and ***leverage HR analytics dashboards to assess AI's effectiveness in areas like DEI, retention, and promotions.*** Regularly review AI-generated recommendations with human oversight, adjusting filters and training models as needed. By treating AI as an evolving tool rather than a fixed solution, you can maximize its benefits while maintaining alignment with your nonprofit's mission and values.

Road Map to the Future

As AI technology continues to evolve, its applications in HR will become even more sophisticated and impactful. In the coming years, ***we can expect AI to play a larger role in areas such as predictive analytics, employee engagement, and personalized learning and development.*** The workplace of the future isn't as far away as you'd think, and it's one where the following will happen:

- AI-driven career pathing tools will proactively identify skill gaps and recommend personalized training opportunities, ensuring staff members can advance their careers while supporting your nonprofit's evolving needs.

- Real-time workforce sentiment analysis will enable your organization to monitor employee engagement and well-being, automatically flagging areas of concern and suggesting proactive interventions before staff burnout or turnover occurs.

- Automated, bias-aware promotion tracking will help your nonprofit ensure equitable advancement opportunities by analyzing promotion patterns, identifying disparities, and providing leadership with data-backed recommendations to foster internal growth.

- Predictive hiring models will anticipate workforce needs months in advance, enabling HR teams to proactively recruit talent based on organizational growth trends and upcoming funding opportunities rather than scrambling to fill urgent vacancies.

- AI-powered retention strategies will continuously assess risk factors for employee turnover, using historical and real-time data to recommend targeted interventions like mentorship programs, workload adjustments, and professional development opportunities.

The future's bright, but you need your AI shades to see it! So, if you want to be well positioned to leverage these advancements to drive greater impact and innovation, embrace AI and lead the pack forward!

Dos and Don'ts

Do

- Use AI to streamline hiring and onboarding processes while maintaining human oversight to ensure mission alignment and cultural fit
- Regularly audit AI-driven HR tools to identify and correct biases in job descriptions, candidate screening, and performance evaluations
- Leverage AI-powered analytics to track retention, engagement, and pay equity, using data to drive more inclusive and equitable HR policies
- Implement AI tools that enhance professional development, offering personalized training recommendations based on employee skills and career goals
- Communicate openly with staff about how AI is being used in HR, fostering transparency and addressing any concerns about automation and data privacy

Don't

- Rely on AI-generated job descriptions, outreach, or screening decisions without human review, as unchecked automation can introduce or reinforce bias
- Overuse AI in the hiring process at the expense of personal engagement, risking a transactional candidate experience that fails to reflect your nonprofit's values
- Assume AI tools are infallible—neglecting to monitor and refine their outputs over time can lead to outdated, ineffective, or discriminatory practices
- Use AI for diversity hiring without a broader DEI strategy, as focusing only on numbers without addressing workplace culture can result in high turnover
- Ignore ethical and legal considerations when implementing AI-driven HR tools, as failing to comply with regulations around privacy and fairness can lead to reputational and legal risks

Conclusion

AI is transforming HR, offering nonprofits the ability to streamline hiring, enhance onboarding, and build more equitable workplaces. However, while AI can improve efficiency and provide powerful insights, it is not a replacement for human judgment, empathy, and ethical oversight. ***The most successful nonprofits will use AI as a tool to augment, not replace, people-centered HR strategies.***

By thoughtfully integrating AI into recruitment, retention, and professional development, your nonprofit can build a stronger, more diverse, and mission-aligned workforce. But ***success requires an intentional approach—one that combines AI's efficiency with human oversight, continuous learning, and a commitment to equity.*** The future of HR is here, and by embracing AI responsibly, you can create a workplace that is not only smarter and more efficient but also more inclusive and impactful.

Interviewee Bio

Tierney Yates is an accomplished HR strategist and consultant with extensive experience in nonprofit workforce development and operations. As the founder of Little Light Consulting, Tierney works with organizations to enhance their HR practices, leveraging technology, including AI, to streamline recruitment, onboarding, and employee engagement. He is also a recognized advocate for integrating DEI principles into human resource management, ensuring that talent strategies align with organizational values. https://www.linkedin.com/in/tierney-yates-a56a28a3/

Resource Review

- Given the resources referenced in the chapter are all shared in context, instead of providing more information on each, we've opted to highlight a range of other resources to advance professional development in AI-powered human resource management:
- HR Exchange Network: https://www.hrexchangenetwork.com/—You can explore their in-depth articles and resources on how AI is transforming talent acquisition, employee engagement, and workforce management in the nonprofit sector.

- SHRM (Society for Human Resource Management): https://www.shrm.org/—The primary professional association for HR professionals, SHRM produces an annual conference and a range of resources, including highlighting AI tools and techniques that streamline HR processes and improve workforce outcomes.

- LinkedIn for Nonprofits: https://nonprofit.linkedin.com/—Provides free resources and discounted products to help you hire and develop talent, connect with potential donors, build your professional network, and spread the word about your mission to attract new supporters.

- Spiceworks: https://www.spiceworks.com/hr/—This platform keeps you informed about the latest AI trends and tools to optimize your HR operations and talent management.

- People Managing People: https://peoplemanagingpeople.com/—Discover practical advice and case studies on using AI to enhance HR functions, including recruitment, onboarding, and employee development.

- HRCI (HR Certification Institute): https://www.hrci.org/—Access training and certification programs that integrate AI into modern nonprofit HR practices.

- AIHR Digital HR Transformation Program: https://www.aihr.com/—This program guides you through adopting AI to digitally transform your HR department for improved effectiveness.

- BambooHR Blog: https://www.bamboohr.com/blog/—Discover how nonprofit HR teams are leveraging AI for recruitment, employee analytics, and fostering a positive workplace culture.

- HR.com: https://www.hr.com/—Access webinars, articles, and toolkits to help you incorporate AI-driven solutions into your nonprofit's HR strategy.

- Workday: https://www.workday.com/—AI-powered platform that can help your nonprofit align its HR and finance efforts.

- PredictiveHR: https://www.predictivehr.com/—Explore their AI-powered workforce analytics tools to make data-driven HR decisions and improve team performance.

Chapter 25

Finance and Bookkeeping

Based on insights from an interview with Justin Muscolino.

As a nonprofit leader, your time and resources are precious, and every dollar saved or more effectively allocated goes directly toward advancing your mission. Leveraging AI in your bookkeeping and accounting efforts can revolutionize how you manage finances by automating repetitive tasks like data entry, categorizing expenses, and generating financial reports. AI-powered tools provide real-time insights, ensuring compliance with regulations and giving you a clearer picture of your financial health to make informed decisions. By reducing manual errors and freeing up time for more strategic work, AI enables you to focus on what matters most: serving your community and growing your impact.

Critical Skills and Competencies
Define Needs, Create a Policy, Pick a Platform

We've said it in just about every other chapter throughout this book, but it bears repeating. **Before diving into AI for any application, your first step should be clarifying your specific needs.** Identify the key areas where AI can make the most impact, such as automating repetitive tasks, enhancing data accuracy, or generating insightful financial reports. By understanding your pain points, you can tailor AI solutions to address them effectively.

Once you've identified your goals and preferences, take the time to write it down, including any data security, ethics, or other necessary guardrails. A well-defined policy ensures consistency, security, and compliance, while mitigating risks associated with AI use and clarifying which platforms are best suited to your needs. For bookkeeping and accounting specifically, your policy should outline the different types of data your AI systems will handle, who has access to this data, and how data will be stored and protected.

Using these insights, ***evaluate options based on your organization's needs, budget, and technical capabilities.*** Look for accounting platforms that offer scalability, user-friendliness, and robust support. Platforms like QuickBooks (https://quickbooks.intuit.com), Xero (https://www.xero.com), and Sage Intacct (https://www.sage.com/en-us/industry/nonprofit) offer features tailored to nonprofits, enabling you to enjoy the benefits of real-time insights into your organization's financial health.

Garbage In, Garbage Out

AI systems are only as good as the data they process. Ensuring the accuracy of your input data is paramount, as ***poor data quality leads to inaccurate outputs, which undermine financial decisions and reporting.*** So, make sure you verify your data is correct and timely out of the gate, and as you move forward, implement regular data audits to maintain data integrity. Train your staff on best practices for data entry and management, emphasizing the importance of accuracy and consistency. High-quality data input guarantees reliable AI outputs, enhancing decision-making and operational efficiency.

Automate Recurring Tasks

Streamlining regular bookkeeping and accounting activities significantly reduces the burden on your finance team, while enabling you to better see the big picture and analyze trends. ***Use AI to handle routine tasks such as invoice processing, expense tracking, and payroll management,*** freeing up your staff to focus on more strategic activities.

Instead of using a generic tool to do this, ***you're much better off selecting a platform that does what you need out of the box.*** Tools like Bill.com (https://www.bill.com/) and Expensify (https://www.expensify.com/) automate various financial processes, including paying vendors, collecting payments, and automating expense reimbursements. Integrating these tools with your AI platform will streamline your operations, increase productivity, and ensure timely financial reporting.

AI can also help with another critical, ongoing need: creating an annual budget that aligns with your nonprofit's mission and available resources. ***AI-powered tools can analyze historical financial data to identify spending patterns and project future expenses,*** helping nonprofit leaders build more accurate and data-driven budgets. Generating the regular financial reports reflecting on how actuals compare to these budgeted amounts is another essential task for nonprofits, whether for board meetings, grant compliance, or fundraising campaigns. ***AI can automate report creation, pulling in real-time data to ensure accuracy and reduce manual effort.*** Once again, QuickBooks, Xero, and Sage Intacct are great off-the-shelf options for both budgeting and generating ongoing reports.

Gaze into the Future

Predictive analytics provide valuable insights into your organization's financial health, using AI to analyze historical financial and operational data to forecast future trends. This is a great tool for making informed decisions and planning for potential challenges. As one example, tools like Dataro (https://dataro.io), Keela (https://www.keela.co), and Jirav (https://www.jirav.com) enable you to monitor donor contributions and uncover patterns that guide targeted fundraising efforts or highlight areas where expenses can be optimized. These targeted applications of AI can help your nonprofit not only manage its finances effectively but also enhance strategic decision-making capabilities. Once again, these features and functionality should be integrated into your platform of choice, seamlessly offering you the ability to ***harness AI to identify patterns in donor behavior, forecast cash flow, facilitate scenario planning, and anticipate expenses.*** This proactive approach enables you to allocate resources more effectively, optimize fundraising efforts, and ensure financial stability.

While many platforms offer robust predictive analytics capabilities, your nonprofit may find additional value in leveraging third-party tools or plugins to address specific needs. For example, donor management platforms like DonorPerfect (https://www.donorperfect.com/) and fundraising analytics tools like Fundraising Report Card (https://fundraisingreportcard.com/) can complement your primary system by providing deeper insights into donor retention trends and campaign performance. Similarly, integrating GenAI platforms can offer unique advantages by analyzing reports or datasets and generating actionable recommendations. Your nonprofit can ***use AI platforms to answer strategic questions, such as identifying at-risk donor segments, suggesting optimal timing for fundraising appeals, or proposing adjustments to budget allocations based on forecasted cash flow scenarios.*** By combining the core capabilities of your primary bookkeeping platform with specialized tools and AI-driven insights, you can create a comprehensive, future-focused strategy that addresses your unique challenges and opportunities.

Refine Outputs

Regularly review and refine AI outputs to ensure accuracy and relevance. AI systems continuously learn and evolve, but human oversight is essential to maintain quality and relevance. ***Establish a review process so your team always verifies AI-generated reports and insights, and update your nonprofit's AI policy with these details.*** This ensures that the language is appropriate, the data is accurate, and the outputs align with your organization's goals. Continuous refinement of AI outputs enhances their reliability and usefulness.

Pitfalls and Solutions

Over Automation

Almost every other chapter has spoken to the critical need to keep a human in the loop (HITL), especially during these early stages of AI development. ***In bookkeeping and accounting, errors—such as misclassifying transactions, inaccurately calculating tax liabilities, or failing to flag potential fraud—can have a huge impact on your finances and seriously ruffle feathers.*** if you incorrectly pay a staffer or vendor, fail to collect payment on a grant, or even insist you haven't been paid when in fact you have. While AI offers incredible efficiency gains, it's essential to maintain a balance between automation and human oversight, particularly in the sensitive realm of bookkeeping and accounting. AI systems can process vast amounts of data, but they often lack the nuanced understanding required for complex financial scenarios, such as handling restricted funds in nonprofit organizations or interpreting ambiguous expense categories. Ignoring the review process can lead to errors and misinterpretations.

To address this, **regularly review AI outputs not only for content, grammar, and tone but also for financial accuracy and compliance with regulatory standards.** Beyond keeping a HITL, your nonprofit needs to remain vigilant about overreliance on AI-generated insights. For instance, AI predictions based on historical data may fail to account for sudden changes, such as economic downturns or shifts in donor behavior, leading to flawed budgeting or cash flow planning.

Missed Anomalies

AI tools can be highly effective at automating repetitive tasks, but **one significant shortfall is AI's potential to overlook anomalies, such as duplicate payments, inconsistent reimbursement claims, or missing documentation.** This issue often arises because AI systems rely on training data to identify patterns and make decisions, and if that data lacks examples of irregularities, the system may fail to flag them. These overlooked anomalies can lead to financial discrepancies, compliance issues, and a loss of trust among stakeholders if errors go unnoticed.

To mitigate this, establish robust internal controls that complement your AI tools. **Conduct routine audits to manually review financial data and identify irregularities that AI might miss.** Implement "exception reporting" to flag unusual transactions for further review, and ensure your team is trained to recognize and address potential red flags, so you can leverage AI's speed and efficiency without compromising the accuracy and integrity of your financial operations.

Static Policies

Life is full of change, and especially in the age of AI, it seems to only be speeding up. All the more reason why your policies need to evolve with technology. Once you have a policy in place, it's essential to update it at least annually to reflect new developments and challenges in AI use. Ensure your team adheres to your policy, updating it as needed to enable you to remain flexible and adapt to new applications and issues. **Never invite your team to "color outside the lines" and ignore your policy, as**

that will quickly undermine all your guardrails, including those critical to maintain. This dynamic approach ensures that your AI practices remain relevant and effective.

Road Map to the Future

As AI technology continues to evolve, ***expect to see more advanced tools that integrate seamlessly with existing systems, providing deeper insights and more comprehensive automation.*** The future holds the promise of AI-driven financial strategies that not only streamline operations but also enhance transparency and accountability. Imagine a not-too-distant future when AI tools predict donor behaviors with pinpoint accuracy, optimize grant application strategies, and even suggest new revenue streams tailored to your nonprofit's mission. To take full advantage of what's coming, ***don't be afraid to play around with AI tools, but stay vigilant and adaptive, with a keen eye on data security and ethical considerations.*** By keeping abreast of technological advancements and continuously refining your nonprofit's AI strategy, you will leverage AI to drive your mission forward sustainably and ethically.

Dos and Don'ts
Do

- Define your nonprofit's specific AI needs as it relates to bookkeeping and accounting, write down your goals and key use cases in an AI policy, and then select the right platform that fulfills your requirements
- Ensure high-quality data input for accurate AI outputs
- Automate routine bookkeeping and financial management tasks like invoice processing, expense tracking, and payroll management to increase efficiency
- Use predictive analytics for informed decision-making to spot trends and concerns with donor giving, cash flow, and unanticipated expenses
- Review and refine your AI policy at least once a year, but with smaller updates made more regularly as needs evolve

Don't

- Try to hack an AI platform to get it to do what you want, instead of working with providers who offer necessary functionality out of the box
- Rely solely on AI without human oversight
- Invite your team to disregard your AI policy as your needs evolve; require updates so that your policy is always current and never ignored

Conclusion

AI has the potential to transform nonprofit finance and bookkeeping, offering new levels of efficiency, accuracy, and insight. By defining your needs, creating robust policies, choosing the right platforms, and ensuring high-quality data input, your organization will be able to automate a range of tedious but critical functions and unlock the full power of AI. Remember to maintain human oversight and continuously refine your AI strategies to keep pace with technological advancements. With thoughtful implementation, AI can help you achieve your mission more effectively and sustainably.

Interviewee Bio

Justin Muscolino is a seasoned compliance and training expert with over 20 years of experience in the financial services industry. His extensive background in regulatory compliance and training positions him as a valuable resource for nonprofits seeking to integrate AI into their finance and bookkeeping operations responsibly. He held senior roles such as head of compliance training at Bank of China, Macquarie Group, UBS, and JPMorgan Chase, where he developed and implemented comprehensive compliance programs. At FINRA, Justin established Examiner University, enhancing the proficiency of regulatory examiners. https://www.linkedin.com/in/justin-muscolino/

Resource Review

- QuickBooks Online: https://quickbooks.intuit.com—Enables your nonprofit to automate bookkeeping tasks like invoicing, expense tracking, annual budgeting, and financial reporting, with real-time insights tailored for nonprofits.

- Xero: https://www.xero.com—Leverage AI to reconcile transactions, generate accurate reports, and integrate with donation and expense tools for seamless nonprofit accounting.
- Sage Intacct: https://www.sage.com/en-us/industry/nonprofit—Use AI-driven budgeting, grant tracking, and reporting tools to ensure financial transparency and efficiency.
- Bill.com: https://www.bill.com—Streamline accounts payable with AI-powered invoice extraction and automation to save time and reduce errors.
- Expensify: https://www.expensify.com—Simplify expense tracking and reimbursements with AI-powered receipt scanning and compliance features.
- Dataro: https://dataro.io—Helps you uncover donor patterns and optimize fundraising strategies using predictive analytics.
- Keela: https://www.keela.co—Track donor behavior, manage budgets, and enhance campaign planning with AI-powered insights.
- Jirav: https://www.jirav.com—Enable smarter forecasting and financial planning with advanced analytics and historical data analysis.
- DonorPerfect: https://www.donorperfect.com—Complement your bookkeeping platform with AI-driven donor retention and campaign insights.
- Fundraising Report Card: https://fundraisingreportcard.com—Analyze donor trends and campaign performance to guide better financial planning.
- Aplos: https://www.aplos.com—Designed for nonprofits, this platform offers AI tools for fund accounting, donation tracking, and financial reporting.
- Jitasa: https://www.jitasagroup.com—Explore AI-powered bookkeeping and accounting solutions tailored for nonprofits.
- Charity CFO Blog: https://www.thecharitycfo.com/blog/—Learn how AI tools can improve nonprofit financial management and compliance.

Chapter 26

Board Recruitment and Engagement

Based on insights from an interview with Matt Strain.

Recruiting a solid nonprofit board and enlisting their support in truly helpful ways can often feel daunting and complex. Effective boards are the backbone of many successful nonprofits and can mean the difference between stagnation and significant impact for your organization. To help you close that gap, this chapter will break down how to leverage AI to ensure your board is not only filled with the right people but also that they're engaged and productive.

The mantra for board engagement is "low touch, high value." Anything you can do to clearly set and manage expectations—and in general to help board members help you—will enable you to get what you need from your directors. AI can help, whether it's ensuring an intentional approach to recruitment; running more efficient, productive board meetings, offsites, and retreats; or even just automating the time-consuming task of taking minutes and highlighting next steps and takeaways, the opportunities are endless. And it's not just for synthesizing information; you can use AI to inspire and frame new ideas and strategies, including crafting or updating a compelling mission and vision statement. AI can also be used as a strategic partner and help with analyzing future trends that might uncover new opportunities. It can also step in as a therapist and help suggest ways to reduce conflict and improve working relationships among board members.

So, let's get to it and explore how your nonprofit can use AI to not only better manage and engage your board but also save you time!

These are the basic stages for identifying, recruiting, and onboarding new board members. Today, AI can be applied at each stage. In the future, if AI continues down the path it's going, many of these steps will be linked together by AI agents (see Figure 26.1).

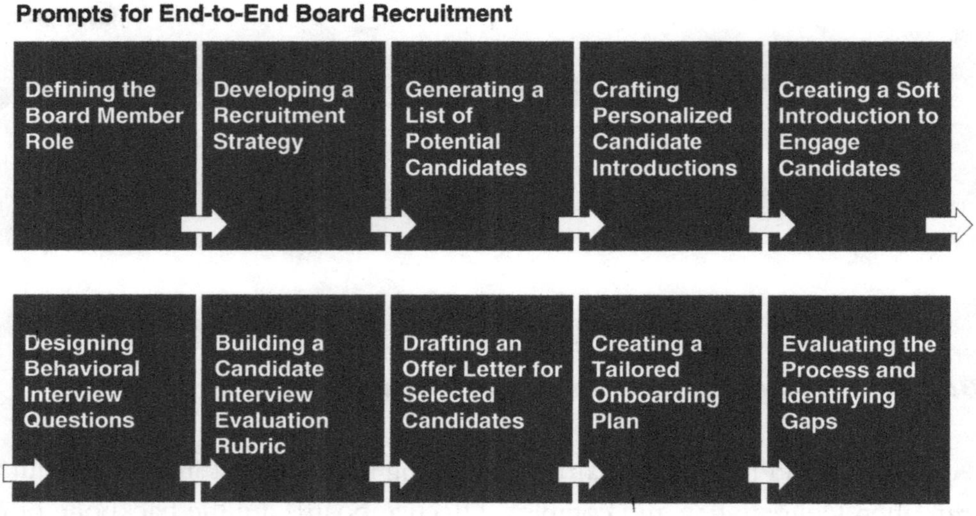

Prompts for End-to-End Board Recruitment

Defining the Board Member Role → Developing a Recruitment Strategy → Generating a List of Potential Candidates → Crafting Personalized Candidate Introductions → Creating a Soft Introduction to Engage Candidates → Designing Behavioral Interview Questions → Building a Candidate Interview Evaluation Rubric → Drafting an Offer Letter for Selected Candidates → Creating a Tailored Onboarding Plan → Evaluating the Process and Identifying Gaps

Figure 26.1 Prompts for End-to-End Board Recruitment

Critical Skills and Competencies

Tread Respectfully

AI adoption offers significant opportunities, but it's critical to approach its introduction with care, especially given the unique dynamics of any nonprofit board. Many board members, particularly those who are seasoned and well established in their careers, may be less familiar with AI tools than younger counterparts. This ***unfamiliarity can lead to hesitation, frustration, or even resistance—especially if the changes feel abrupt or inadequately explained.***

Adding to the challenge, board members often don't interact as frequently as employees do, which means they may lack the trust and rapport needed to navigate change together smoothly. ***Introducing AI effectively requires more than enthusiasm; it demands sensitivity to these dynamics and intentional relationship-building.***

In fact, an overly zealous AI champion—someone who dives in headfirst and pushes for rapid adoption—can inadvertently alienate board members. This not only undermines trust but also risks causing long-term relational damage that may hinder collaboration and progress.

To avoid this, it's essential to do the following:

- Acknowledge varying levels of familiarity: Meet board members where they are, offering reassurances and demonstrating how AI can enhance, not disrupt, their work and that of the nonprofit.
- Foster an inclusive approach: Emphasize collaboration, ensuring that all members feel heard, respected, and part of the journey.
- It's all about trust. **Start with small steps and focus on tasks that are low risk.** Trust is developed incrementally. Over time, as the board becomes comfortable with AI, you can move to more complex use cases

By prioritizing these steps, you not only smooth the adoption process but also lay a foundation for a confident, cohesive board that sees AI as an asset rather than a disruption. Change management isn't just about technology—it's about trust and relationships.

Enhance Recruitment

Successful board recruitment begins with clearly defining what your organization needs from a new board member. AI tools can simplify and clarify this process by guiding you in articulating your organization's mission, vision, strategic objectives, and the essential qualities desired in candidates. If you're uncertain where to begin, use AI to guide you. Prompt your AI tool of choice with questions like "*What specific information do you need to create a detailed board member job description?*" This approach ensures your initial description is rich in relevant context, even if it isn't perfect right away.

AI also plays a valuable role in identifying the board's current strengths and pinpointing areas of potential improvement—often called *asset mapping*. By analyzing this information, *AI can provide a detailed profile of the ideal candidate, focusing precisely on your nonprofit's gaps and needs.* Once you've drafted this candidate profile, engage your current board members openly to review and prioritize key traits and competencies. This human-in-the-loop (HITL) approach both ensures human oversight and engages your board in unlocking the benefits of AI, helping build confidence in and appreciation for its utility. Repeat this process regularly, especially when board membership changes or you update your mission or programs. This ensures ongoing alignment with your nonprofit's evolving strategic direction.

Finally, **AI can assist in creating a compelling, comprehensive job description** that draws on past board discussions, organizational history, and strategic goals. AI tools can quickly generate tailored communication, including engaging emails and social media content, enabling your board and staff to efficiently reach high-potential candidates.

As an example, consider this sample prompt, which you could use in ChatGPT, Claude, Gemini, or any of the other GenAI models:

"You are an expert in nonprofit governance and board recruitment."

"I need your help creating a job description for a new board member for our 501(c)(3) nonprofit organization."

Here's the context:

Organization overview: We are Fotokids, a nonprofit dedicated to empowering underserved youth through photography, arts, and digital media education. Our programs provide tools for creative self-expression and career skills, transforming lives in marginalized communities.

Role of the board: The board provides strategic oversight, supports fundraising efforts, and ensures the organization's financial and operational sustainability. Board members also serve as ambassadors for the mission, expanding Fotokids' network of partners and donors.

Key challenges and opportunities:

- Scaling our programs internationally, particularly in Latin America and beyond.
- Adapting to shifts in donor priorities and the growing demand for innovative fundraising approaches.

- Strengthening organizational impact tracking to communicate program outcomes effectively to stakeholders.
- Expanding capacity while ensuring operational sustainability.

Desired candidate profile: We seek candidates with deep expertise in one or more of the following areas:

- Digital transformation and innovation for nonprofits
- Fundraising and philanthropy, including experience with donor networks, foundations, and corporate sponsorships
- Nonprofit governance, financial acumen, and compliance expertise
- Global program development, particularly with experience in underrepresented communities
- Communications and advocacy expertise, with a focus on storytelling and social media strategies to amplify our reach

Additional information: The successful candidate will ideally have prior board or leadership experience with a nonprofit; a commitment to fostering diversity, equity, and inclusion (DEI); and a willingness to leverage personal and professional networks to support Fotokids.

Time commitment: Board members are expected to attend quarterly meetings (virtual or in person), participate in committee work, and engage actively in fundraising efforts. This is a volunteer position with the opportunity to make a profound impact.

"Please draft a professional job description that conveys Fotokids' mission, the board's role, and the desired qualifications for this position. You can learn more about the organization at https://fotokids.org."

Reel Them In

Once you've clarified your nonprofit's recruitment needs and identified an initial slate of promising candidates, AI can streamline the next steps by suggesting a targeted recruitment strategy. If outreach channels or tactics aren't already clear, AI tools can help pinpoint the most effective approaches to reach ideal prospects. Rather than relying on informal or generic job descriptions, **leverage AI to draft customized board member agreements or uniform board commitment forms,** providing clarity and consistency across your organization—as outlined in *Nonprofit Management 101* and *Nonprofit Fundraising 101.*

When you have your shortlist of recruitment prospects, **use AI to help craft personalized outreach messages tailored specifically to each candidate.** Leverage its analytical capabilities to develop messages that clearly communicate how your organization's mission aligns with their professional interests and personal impact goals, and that highlights why candidates would be a valuable addition to your board. Once candidates express interest and you arrange initial meetings, **use AI-generated behavioral interview questions and structured evaluation rubrics** to objectively assess each candidate. AI can even analyze interview transcripts to evaluate candidates systematically against your criteria, significantly reducing bias and enhancing transparency. Finally, it's helpful to **use AI tools to streamline the drafting of professional offer letters and personalized onboarding guides**, ensuring new board members smoothly transition into their roles and quickly become effective, engaged contributors.

Meeting Management

Board meetings often fail to rise to their potential, devolving into one-way updates rather than fully leveraging the expertise and strategic insight of members. Chapter 20 speaks to how dashboards can provide some useful tools to streamline updates, but aside from more quickly sharing those FYIs, **AI can facilitate more generative meetings by streamlining administrative processes and empowering your board to prioritize impactful discussions and high-level decision-making.**

Tools like Fireflies (https://fireflies.ai/) and Otter (https://otter.ai/) **use AI to automatically transcribe meetings, produce concise minutes, highlight key**

decisions and vote outcomes, and track action items. These AI-driven capabilities save valuable staff time, improve accuracy, and allow board members to remain fully engaged in strategic conversations rather than note-taking. For international or diverse boards, platforms such as Zoom (https://www.zoom.com) and Teams (https://www.microsoft.com/teams) provide real-time AI-powered translation, enhancing inclusivity and clarity during virtual meetings.

Scheduling tools like Calendly (https://calendly.com/) and Doodle (https://doodle.com/) analyze board members' calendars to propose optimal meeting times, boosting attendance and productivity. Once scheduled, ***collaborate with your board chair to refine AI-generated meeting agendas*** based on previous discussions and current organizational priorities, ensuring each session remains sharply focused and efficient.

Governance and Oversight

AI can help streamline board oversight by providing real-time data analysis and insights. Tools like Araize FastFund Accounting (https://araize.com) and Sage Intacct (https://www.sage.com/en-us/industry/nonprofit) analyze nonprofit financial reports, automatically flagging any discrepancies or areas of concern. This enables board members to focus on strategic governance rather than getting bogged down in the details. AI tools like LogicGate Risk Cloud (https://www.logicgate.com) and ComplyAdvantage (https://complyadvantage.com) help monitor compliance with regulatory requirements, ensuring that your nonprofit stays in good standing. By automating these tasks, you can reduce the risk of human error and ensure that your board is always operating with the most up-to-date information.

AI can also assist in drafting and updating governance documents. By analyzing best practices and current regulations, ***AI helps ensure your governance documents—including bylaws and policies—are comprehensive and compliant.*** The result is a more organized and effective governance structure that supports the overall mission and goals of your nonprofit.

Board Performance and Evaluation

Regular performance evaluations are incredibly helpful to maintaining an effective board, but all too often nonprofits and boards don't have the capacity to manage the process.

AI helps streamline board reviews by providing data-driven insights and recommendations, analyzing board meeting attendance, participation, and decision-making patterns to provide a comprehensive overview of each director's performance. AI tools like SurveySparrow (https://surveysparrow.com) and Typeform (https://www.typeform.com) help you easily create customized evaluation forms and surveys, ensuring you collect the most relevant feedback. They then analyze this feedback instantly, identifying areas for improvement and providing recommendations for individual board members and the board as a whole. And there are a range of tools like Asana.

AI is also a great tool for project management, helping you and the board track progress on action items and goals, ensuring that your trustees remain accountable and focused. Standard tools like Asana (https://asana.com) can help with this and may already be familiar to any directors with corporate backgrounds, but nonprofit-specific tools like Boardable (https://boardable.com) may also prove useful.

Pitfalls and Solutions

Ignoring Board Cohesion

When board members do not work well together, it often leads to inefficiency and conflict. *Use AI to facilitate team-building activities and identify potential areas of conflict.* AI can analyze communication patterns and suggest ways to improve collaboration and cohesion among board members. Ensuring strong board cohesion can lead to more effective decision-making and a more harmonious working environment.

Failing to Make It Easy

Just like donors, when working with your board you need to meet them where they are. That means not expecting them to take the time to figure out how to use an AI platform, or any other technology for that matter. *Failing to provide the necessary training and orientation, which AI can help direct and deliver, will impede adoption.* So, make it easy for them to understand and effectively use AI in their roles. Spoon-feed them whatever information they need, map the tools back to your mission and impact, and provide any support and troubleshooting needed to level up your board and unlock AI's full potential for your nonprofit.

Missing a Champion

Introducing new tools or processes to a nonprofit board can often be challenging, making it crucial to have an established board member serve as your AI champion. This champion helps generate enthusiasm and buy-in among their peers, facilitating smoother adoption and effective use of AI. Clearly define your champion's role, emphasizing responsibilities like promoting AI's strategic value, providing reassurance during adoption, and continually identifying innovative opportunities to leverage AI for greater organizational impact. ***Consider assigning an engaging, fun, honorific title to recognize and reinforce the importance of this role,*** encouraging consistent advocacy and support for AI integration.

Dos and Don'ts
Do

- Provide AI orientation and training to board members and staff to facilitate tool adoption
- Clearly communicate how AI contributes to recruitment, evaluations, and meeting management, embracing transparency to build trust and help your board gain confidence in leveraging AI effectively
- Use AI to generate prioritized board criteria and invite members to self-report to align recruitment needs
- Employ AI to craft comprehensive board job descriptions based on organizational data
- Leverage AI for personalized recruitment messaging, candidate identification, and outreach
- Use AI to develop unbiased interview questions and evaluation rubrics to ensure consistency
- Have AI transcribe meetings, highlighting decisions and automating actionable minute-taking

Don't

- Upload sensitive information into unsecured AI tools; always confirm data protection compliance
- Send AI-generated communications without human review for accuracy and appropriate tone
- Assume board members will adopt AI tools without clear training and ongoing support
- Rely solely on AI for recruitment; balance automation with human judgment to maintain diversity and alignment
- Allow AI outputs to complicate or detract from strategic discussions; focus on simplicity and utility
- Waste time manually scheduling meetings; use AI to streamline and optimize this process
- Neglect annual board reviews; regularly employ AI tools to manage evaluations effectively

Conclusion

AI can significantly elevate your nonprofit's board recruitment and management practices. By streamlining administrative tasks, AI empowers your board to focus more effectively on strategic decision-making and meaningful engagement. Implementing these practical AI-driven strategies will not only save your organization valuable time but also enhance your board's overall productivity and impact. By embracing these tips, you'll simplify routine tasks and enhance strategic governance, enabling your board to concentrate on what truly matters and moving your mission forward.

Interviewee Bio

Matt Strain is a distinguished technology leader and AI educator with over 30 years of experience in the tech industry, including strategic roles at Adobe and Apple. As the founder of The Prompt, a boutique AI training and consulting firm, Matt specializes in making AI accessible and actionable for impact executives and their teams. His expertise in AI implementation and innovation has been recognized by *Forbes*, which dubbed him the "AI Whisperer." Matt's commitment to social impact is evident through his board service with Fotokids, a nonprofit organization dedicated to empowering children in Guatemala through photography and education. https://www.linkedin.com/in/mattstrain/

Resource Review

- BoardSource: https://boardsource.org—A comprehensive resource for nonprofit board governance, offering tools, trainings, and best practices.

- BoardEffect: https://www.boardeffect.com—A platform providing board management software to streamline board processes and enhance board effectiveness.

- Araize FastFund Accounting: https://araize.com/—Designed specifically for nonprofits, this platform integrates AI to streamline financial management, automating transaction recording, categorization, and report generation.

- Sage Intacct: https://www.sage.com/en-us/industry/nonprofit/—This financial management solution incorporates AI to enhance data accuracy and compliance, offering real-time dashboards and reporting tools that flag irregularities.

- LogicGate Risk Cloud: https://www.logicgate.com/—This platform offers AI-powered solutions for risk and compliance management, enabling nonprofits to automate workflows, assess risks, and ensure compliance with various regulations.

- ComplyAdvantage: https://complyadvantage.com/—Uses AI to provide real-time insights into regulatory changes and potential compliance risks, helping nonprofits stay updated and mitigate issues proactively.

- SurveySparrow: https://surveysparrow.com/—Offers an AI-powered survey builder that enables the creation of engaging, conversational surveys, plus an analytics feature that provides in-depth insights, helping identify areas for improvement and offering recommendations for both individual board members and the board collectively.

- Typeform: https://www.typeform.com/—Provides an intuitive interface for creating interactive surveys, integrated with various AI tools to analyze responses, identify improvement areas, and generate tailored recommendations.
- Boardable: https://boardable.com/—Designed specifically for nonprofit boards, offers AI-driven tools to improve governance and decision-making, including features like automated scheduling, agenda creation, and real-time performance tracking, enabling boards to monitor key performance indicators (KPIs) and programs against strategic goals.
- Asana: https://asana.com/—A popular project management tool that incorporates AI to help teams organize, track, and manage their work; nonprofit boards can use Asana to set goals, assign tasks, and monitor progress through visual project timelines and dashboards, ensuring that action items are completed on schedule.

Chapter 26.1

Recruiting Tech Executives to Your Board

Based on insights from an interview with Aaron Hurst.

Effectively leveraging AI requires adopting technology more broadly across every level of your nonprofit, starting with your board. To approach this change both proactively and strategically, it's crucial to engage your board. Having **a seasoned tech strategist on your board can help guide your organization through the complexities of AI, ensuring your nonprofit makes informed decisions and remains competitive and impactful.**

Many of us are used to seeing lawyers and accountants on a board matrix, but what about tech executives? While it may sound obvious, this idea is new to most nonprofits. More important, to successfully recruit the right technology leaders, it's helpful to gain a working understanding of specific best practices, from which candidates to recruit to how to integrate them into your board's processes.

Your Five-Point Plan
Begin with the End in Mind

Before you start your recruitment journey, take a moment to reflect on the specific tech skills your board needs. **Consider the size and scale of your nonprofit and what kind of expertise would best support your mission and goals.** Are you a new organization that would benefit from the innovative spirit of a startup CEO, or are you more mature and in need of a seasoned enterprise leader? If you operate in sectors like health care or education, domain expertise, including familiarity with regulations such as the Health Insurance Portability and Accountability Act (HIPAA), can be particularly valuable.

Also, think about the areas where tech executives can make the most impact:

- **Strategic guidance:** A senior leader like a chief technology officer (CTO) can help you identify and consider possibilities, inform your long-term strategy, and help you stay ahead of tech trends.
- **Privacy, security, and compliance:** A CTO type or security specialist can help ensure your data and systems are secure.
- **Short-term technology planning:** Someone with a product background can assist in planning and implementing tech solutions.
- **Resource generation:** Most senior tech executives have robust social networks including high-net-worth colleagues, although setting expectations and engaging them in this way needs to be handled sensitively and generally shouldn't be the primary focus of their service.

Rank these needs in order of importance for the next four years and use this as a guide to profile your ideal candidate. ***Clearly defining success for the desired board member will make the opportunity more concrete and appealing, especially for those with an engineering mindset.***

Optimize Outreach

With clarity on your needs and a simple job description and evaluation rubric in hand, it's time to spread the word. Follow the detailed tips for maximizing recruitment and outreach shared in this chapter and be sure to ***share the job description with your current board members, staff, corporate partners, and funders to tap into their networks.*** LinkedIn is also a powerful tool for finding potential candidates. Search by experience, location, and interest in board service to identify and connect with suitable tech leaders.

If you have a board matrix, make sure to integrate tech expertise into it and use the results to inform your outreach efforts. Keep in mind that the tech industry is predominantly composed of white males, so while pursuing diversity, be aware of the demographic realities. Ideally, **aim to recruit at least two tech experts to avoid a single point of failure and to benefit from diverse perspectives.**

Intentional Onboarding

An effective onboarding process is crucial for integrating new tech leaders into your board. **Encourage a three-month discovery phase to help new entrants understand your nonprofit's tech landscape.** This should include structured onboarding sessions, interviews with key stakeholders, and a review of your current tech stack and policies. This period will help them provide informed and tailored advice rather than premature suggestions.

Encourage them to use AI tools to identify surprising trends and insights, separating hype from reality, and helping your organization make data-driven decisions. This structured approach will ensure they are well prepared to contribute meaningfully from day one.

Create a Shared Plan

As your tech directors complete their discovery phase, collaborate with them to articulate clear technology goals for the year ahead and the duration of their term. Document these goals to create accountability and a shared vision. This plan should **include an analysis of your current tech state; existing policies, tools, and gaps; as well as the vision moving forward, including key objectives as well as the timelines, milestones, metrics, and indicators against which you can both gauge success over time.**

Evaluate any highlighted gaps to determine if they are problems or opportunities and factor in return on investment calculations to prioritize investments. You might also consider creating a responsible, accountable, consulted, and informed chart to clarify roles and responsibilities within technology initiatives. This will avoid confusion and ensure tech directors' contributions align with your strategic objectives.

Keep the Fire Lit

Just as with any board member, it's crucial to keep your tech directors engaged and motivated. Regularly revisit the shared plan, celebrate milestones, and address any challenges that arise. Providing ongoing opportunities for them to contribute and recognizing their efforts will help sustain their commitment to your organization.

Interviewee Bio

Aaron Hurst is a globally recognized social entrepreneur and expert in purpose-driven leadership, with a strong focus on building meaningful connections between technology executives and nonprofit boards. As the founder of Board.Dev, he created a platform to help nonprofits strategically recruit and onboard board members with the skills and expertise needed to drive innovation and impact. Aaron is also the founder of the US Chamber of Connection, an organization leading the movement to reverse the decline in social connection and trust across the nation. Earlier in his career, Aaron founded the Taproot Foundation, where he pioneered the pro bono service movement, connecting skilled professionals—including tech leaders—with nonprofits. https://www.linkedin.com/in/aaronhurst/

Chapter 27

IT Infrastructure and Software: The Tech Stack Needed to Support AI Integration

Based on insights from an interview with Tim Lockie.

To harness the power of AI, your nonprofit needs the right tech stack: the collection of tools, software, and systems that work together to support your organization's goals. Without the right infrastructure, even the most promising AI tools will fall flat, leading to inefficiencies or missed opportunities. ***While any nonprofit can start using generative AI tools in simple, out-of-the-box ways, unlocking advanced functionality—like predictive modeling, personalized donor engagement, or automated reporting—requires a solid tech foundation.*** A well-constructed tech stack ensures that your data is clean, accessible, and actionable; your workflows are streamlined; and your team has the resources they need to maximize the value of AI. Think of it as building a strong foundation for a house—without it, everything else risks collapse.

The good news is that you don't need to be a tech expert to build this foundation. What you do need is clarity about your organization's goals and challenges, coupled with an understanding of the core components of an AI-ready tech stack. From a reliable customer relationship management (CRM) system to manage donor data, to integrations that connect your systems, to tools for data visualization and predictive analytics, each piece plays a role in enabling your team to work smarter, not harder. So, let's look at a few of the most essential elements of an AI-enabled tech stack, thereby helping you evaluate tools that fit your needs and budget, and setting the stage for a road map for implementation.

Critical Skills and Competencies

Let's take a look at several key elements of your tech stack, with tips and resources shared for each in kind.

Custom LLMs and GPTs: Your Own Secure AI

As nonprofits increasingly adopt AI tools, concerns about data privacy and confidentiality are becoming more important. Using general-purpose AI models poses risks, as prompts and data shared with public systems may not be fully secure, potentially exposing sensitive information. As detailed in Chapter 21, **custom large language models (LLMs) and generative pre-trained transformers (GPTs) enable nonprofits to deploy AI solutions that are trained on their specific data while remaining entirely private.** These models operate within secure environments, ensuring that donor information, program data, and organizational details stay confidential and do not leave the organization's control.

Implementing a custom LLM or GPT provides additional advantages beyond privacy. **These tailored models can be fine-tuned to understand your nonprofit's unique mission, language, and data, enabling them to deliver more accurate, context-specific insights and recommendations.** A custom LLM can generate grant proposals based on your past submissions, craft personalized donor communications, or assist with program reports, all while keeping sensitive data secure. To adopt these solutions, your nonprofit should explore platforms like BoodleBox (https://boodlebox.ai), CauseWriter.ai (causewriter.ai), The Change AI (thechange.ai), or Mistral AI (mistral.ai).

And as agentic AI emerges, tools like Cassidy (https://www.cassidyai.com/) and Bedrock from Amazon (https://aws.amazon.com/bedrock/) will shift routine tasks from humans to AI agents, but these more advanced tools are best when paired with the rest of your tech stack.

Focus on establishing clear data governance practices that can adapt to future AI advancements while ensuring your existing systems maintain high-quality data standards, robust security protocols, and well-trained staff. Lots will change in the years to come, but these fundamentals remain essential regardless of which new AI tools emerge.

Customer Relationship Management System

Your CRM system is the backbone of your nonprofit's operations. It's where you store and manage data about your donors, volunteers, program participants, and other stakeholders. *A robust CRM system ensures that all your key information is centralized, organized, and easily accessible.* For AI adoption, a CRM database is essential because it provides the structured data that AI tools need to deliver insights and recommendations. Without a reliable CRM platform, your AI efforts will often be scattered, inefficient, or misaligned with your actual goals.

With an AI-ready CRM system, you can unlock advanced functionalities like donor segmentation, predictive analytics for fundraising campaigns, and automated donor engagement workflows. To maximize its potential, focus on ensuring your data is clean and up-to-date, integrating the CRM database with other tools in your tech stack, and using built-in AI features or integrations. Popular providers to explore include Salesforce Nonprofit Success Pack (Salesforce.org), Bloomerang (bloomerang.co), and Neon CRM (neonone.com).

CRM systems (and platforms) are increasingly integrating AI into their core features (like AgentForce by Salesforce, Copilot by Microsoft, and Gemini by Google), improving customer experience in these platforms and handling automations that would previously have required custom programing or third-party solutions. These integrated AI options are worth taking advantage of because of their access to data and built-in security.

Data Storage and Management Solutions

If your CRM system is the backbone of your nonprofit's operations, then *your data storage and management solution is the nervous system that ensures information flows smoothly and remains secure.* While your CRM system holds key stakeholder data, a reliable data storage and management system provides the infrastructure to store, organize, and access the vast amounts of additional data your organization generates—program outcomes, website analytics, marketing performance, and more. For nonprofits adopting AI, this component is essential because it ensures your data is not only safe but also structured and ready for analysis.

Your CRM system can't function effectively in isolation; it needs a seamless connection to your broader data ecosystem. *A robust storage solution enables you to centralize data from various sources, integrate it with your CRM database, and enable AI to deliver advanced insights like predictive modeling and trend analysis.* Explore options like Google Cloud (cloud.google.com), Amazon Web Services (AWS) (aws.amazon.com), and Microsoft Azure (azure.microsoft.com) to ensure your data infrastructure is scalable, secure, and AI ready.

Integrated Fundraising, Program, and Marketing Communication Tools

Building on the foundation of your CRM and data storage solutions, integrated tools for fundraising, program management, and marketing communication bring your nonprofit's operations to life. *These tools connect the dots between the structured data in your CRM system and the broader data ecosystem managed by your storage solutions, enabling seamless workflows and data sharing across functions.* By integrating these platforms, you ensure that fundraising campaigns, program delivery, and communications work together cohesively, driving greater impact. With AI, these tools can personalize donor outreach, predict campaign success, and analyze program outcomes, helping your organization engage supporters more effectively.

Fundraising tools like Classy (classy.org) and Bloomerang (bloomerang.co) sync with your CRM system to track donor behavior and optimize giving campaigns, while marketing platforms like Mailchimp (mailchimp.com) and HubSpot (hubspot.com) automate personalized outreach. Meanwhile, program management tools like Asana (asana.com) and Monday.com (monday.com) ensure your programs are efficiently tracked and reported. These platforms, when integrated, enable AI to uncover insights like which donor segments are most likely to support a specific program or how to optimize your communication channels for engagement. To maximize these tools, *prioritize systems that integrate seamlessly with your CRM system and data storage solutions, creating a unified, AI-ready ecosystem that strengthens every aspect of your nonprofit's operations.*

Internal Communication and Collaboration Platforms

Effective communication tools ensure your team can collaborate seamlessly and share critical information in real time, making them essential for leveraging AI across your nonprofit. *These platforms act as the central hub where insights, updates, and tasks come together, enabling your team to take quick, informed action.* By integrating internal communication tools with your CRM system, program management software, and AI-driven systems, you can ensure that everyone has access to relevant data and recommendations exactly when and where they need them.

Platforms like Slack (slack.com), Microsoft Teams (microsoft.com), and Zoom (zoom.us) can be enhanced with AI-powered workflows to automate routine updates and flag important insights. As one especially powerful example of what's possible, *AI can post automated donor follow-up reminders, program updates, or campaign analytics directly to your team's shared channels.* To unlock these benefits, configure integrations with your CRM system and analytics platforms, and set up notifications for key actions, like reaching fundraising milestones or identifying new donor opportunities.

Middleware and Workflow Automation Tools

These tech tools connect your nonprofit's various systems and streamline workflows, enabling AI to access and leverage data from across your tech stack. *These platforms enable you to automate repetitive tasks, such as syncing donor data between your CRM system and fundraising platform or generating reports from program metrics.* Solutions like Zapier (zapier.com), Make (formerly Integromat) (make.com), and MuleSoft (mulesoft.com) automate complex workflows, reducing redundancies and ensuring seamless integration across platforms. For example, you can *set up workflows that automatically notify staff when AI identifies new donor opportunities or trigger updates to your email lists based on donor behavior.* Start by identifying time-consuming, repetitive processes within your organization, then use middleware to connect your systems and automate those tasks.

Analytics and Data Visualization Tools

AI thrives on data, and analytics tools help you make sense of it. *These platforms transform raw data into actionable insights through dashboards, reports, and visualizations.* For nonprofit leaders, they make it easier to measure impact, track fundraising progress, and identify trends.

Integrating AI into analytics tools unlocks predictive capabilities, such as forecasting campaign outcomes or identifying at-risk donors. To make the most of these tools, focus on platforms that integrate with your CRM system and data storage solutions, including options like Tableau (tableau.com), Power BI (powerbi.microsoft.com), and Google Data Studio (datastudio.google.com). These tools are the final step in transforming your data into meaningful action.

Cybersecurity Solutions

As your nonprofit adopts AI and integrates more systems, safeguarding your data becomes non-negotiable. ***Cybersecurity solutions ensure the data powering your AI tools is accurate, uncompromised, and protected from breaches, while also maintaining compliance with privacy regulations.*** Without strong security protocols, your nonprofit risks eroding stakeholder trust and jeopardizing the sensitive donor and program data that fuels your operations.

To protect your systems, consider tools like CrowdStrike (crowdstrike.com), Norton (norton.com), and Okta (okta.com), which provide advanced features like data encryption, multifactor authentication (MFA), and real-time threat detection. Begin with a comprehensive security audit to identify vulnerabilities, then implement strict password policies, train staff on recognizing phishing attacks, and schedule regular updates for all software.

Pitfalls and Solutions
Using Outdated or Incompatible Tools

Legacy systems often lack the ability to integrate with modern platforms, creating silos where valuable data is trapped and inaccessible to AI-driven insights. This results in inefficiencies, missed opportunities, and wasted time trying to manually transfer information between systems. To avoid this pitfall, regularly conduct a thorough audit of your tech stack to identify tools that no longer meet your needs. ***Prioritize platforms with open application programming interfaces (APIs) that integrate seamlessly with AI tools, CRM core systems, data storage, and other essential systems.*** As you evaluate new tools, look for open APIs and robust integration capabilities to ensure your systems can evolve with your organization and support AI adoption as your needs grow.

Overloading Staff with Complex Tools

Introducing too many tools or overly complex systems can overwhelm your staff and lead to resistance, undermining your AI adoption efforts. Nonprofit teams are often stretched thin, and adding new technology without proper support can feel like a burden rather than a benefit. So, be sure to **roll out new tools gradually and focus on platforms with intuitive interfaces that are easy for your team to adopt.** Provide hands-on training, clear documentation, and ongoing support to build confidence and ensure your team feels empowered rather than frustrated. Start by introducing one or two high-impact tools, such as an AI-enabled CRM system or email marketing platform, and expand your tech stack as your team becomes comfortable. A phased approach ensures that your staff can integrate AI tools into their workflows without becoming overwhelmed.

Failing to Integrate Tools

Disconnected systems can undermine your efforts to streamline workflows and gain actionable insights from AI. **When your tools don't talk to each other, your team may end up duplicating efforts, manually transferring data, or missing critical opportunities for AI to deliver value.** Invest in middleware solutions that bridge the gap between systems and automate data sharing. Focus on creating a unified ecosystem where your CRM system, fundraising, marketing, and analytics tools work together seamlessly. Not only will this save your team time but it will also unlock the full potential of AI to provide cross-functional insights and streamline decision-making.

Overlooking Scalability

Selecting tools that can't grow with your nonprofit's evolving needs will result in costly, time-consuming migrations down the line. As your organization expands its programs, donor base, and data volumes, your tech stack must be able to handle the increased complexity without slowing you down. **When evaluating tools, think beyond your current needs and consider what your nonprofit might require in the next three to five years.** Look for platforms that can support additional users, integrate new data sources, and handle more advanced AI functionalities as your capabilities grow.

Failing to Continuously Evaluate and Improve

Treating AI adoption as a one-time project rather than an ongoing process is a recipe for stagnation. Technology evolves rapidly, and tools that are cutting-edge today often become obsolete within a few years. Without regular evaluation, your tech stack may fall behind, limiting your ability to leverage new AI capabilities or adapt to changing needs. ***Make it a habit to review your systems and workflows annually, assessing what's working, what's not, and where there's room for improvement.*** Engage your team in this process to gather feedback and identify pain points. Stay informed about emerging AI tools and trends in the nonprofit sector, and don't hesitate to upgrade or replace systems that no longer serve your goals.

Road Map to the Future

Moving forward, your nonprofit can expect major advancements in AI to reshape your tech stack, making it more streamlined, efficient, and impactful. ***AI tools will increasingly automate routine tasks such as donor communications, data entry, and campaign analysis, freeing your team to focus on higher-value strategic activities.*** Instead of manually creating email segments, soon AI-enabled marketing platforms will dynamically adjust outreach strategies based on real-time donor behavior. And increasingly over time, technologies like custom LLM or GPT models and retrieval-augmented generation (RAG) will allow your nonprofit to train AI on its own data, enabling personalized interactions that enhance your donor engagement and volunteer outreach.

Finally, as AI tools become more sophisticated, the complexity of tech stacks will decrease, empowering nonprofits to achieve more with fewer systems and reducing the need for costly integrations and redundancies.

To prepare for what's coming, prioritize tech stacks that are scalable, integration ready, and built to accommodate AI-driven automations. Invest in centralized, high-quality data storage to ensure your AI tools have the clean, structured data they need to operate effectively. Look for platforms that emphasize interoperability, enabling AI to seamlessly connect with your existing tools and workflows. Additionally, explore opportunities to train your team on how to use AI-enabled systems and stay informed about emerging tools that align with your mission. By staying agile and adopting a forward-thinking approach to your tech stack, your nonprofit will be well positioned to harness the next wave of AI advancements and drive greater impact.

Dos and Don'ts

Do

- Consider developing a custom LLM or GPT to enable your team to access an AI that's already training on your organization's needs and voice, without compromising sensitive data
- Evaluate and replace outdated tools that create silos or limit data accessibility to fully leverage AI's potential
- Implement regular data-cleaning practices, enforce consistent data entry standards, and invest in centralized storage solutions to improve the accuracy and utility of AI outputs
- Safeguard sensitive data with robust privacy and security measures to protect your organization and its stakeholders
- Choose tools with open APIs and strong integration capabilities to ensure seamless communication between your CRM system, data storage, and other platforms
- Begin with high-impact AI implementations, such as donor segmentation or marketing automation, to build momentum and team confidence
- Provide staff training on AI tools and workflows to empower your team and ensure widespread adoption across departments

Don't

- Don't rely on legacy systems that can't integrate with modern AI tools, as they limit your ability to maximize AI's benefits
- Introduce too many tech tools at once, especially ones with overly complex interfaces that can overwhelm your staff and lead to resistance
- Allow your tech stack to stagnate by neglecting regular reviews or updates to ensure your systems are scalable, integration ready, and capable of supporting modern AI functionalities

Conclusion

Building an AI-ready tech stack is essential for nonprofits looking to harness the transformative potential of AI. By focusing on scalable, integration-friendly tools, prioritizing data quality, and gradually rolling out AI-powered workflows, you can position your organization to work smarter, not harder. As you embark on this journey, remember that adopting AI is not just about the tools you choose but also about the culture of innovation you foster within your organization. By taking proactive steps to educate your team, safeguard your data, and continuously evaluate your systems, you'll be well equipped to drive greater impact and deliver on your mission more effectively. The future of nonprofit work is here, and with the right tech stack, your organization can lead the way.

Interviewee Bio

Tim Lockie is a recognized leader in nonprofit technology and data strategy, bringing decades of experience to help mission-driven organizations leverage IT to maximize impact. As the founder and CEO of The Human Stack, Tim has dedicated his career to bridging the gap between people and technology, guiding nonprofits through digital transformations that enhance efficiency and sustainability. Previously, he served as the director of technology at Build Consulting, where he implemented scalable, AI-ready tech stacks tailored to nonprofit needs. Tim is also a seasoned Salesforce consultant, having helped organizations optimize their CRM systems to better manage donor data and drive strategic decision-making. https://www.linkedin.com/in/tlockie/

Resource Review

- BoodleBox: https://boodlebox.ai/—Collaborative GenAI with knowledge base, custom bots, and access to all major LLMs without the risk of private data being used in training for model improvements.

- CauseWriter.ai: https://causewriter.ai—Explore AI-driven tools and custom LLM solutions tailored specifically for nonprofits, enabling secure, private AI adoption for tasks like donor communications and grant writing.
- The Change AI: https://thechange.ai—Access nonprofit-focused AI tools and resources designed to help you integrate secure, mission-driven AI systems into your tech stack.
- Mistral AI: https://mistral.ai—Learn how to deploy private AI models that prioritize security and customization to align with your nonprofit's goals and data privacy needs.
- Cassidy: https://www.cassidyai.com/—Deploy intelligent AI agents that can handle routine operational tasks across your nonprofit, from scheduling to document processing, while maintaining security and workflow integration with your existing systems.
- Amazon Bedrock: https://aws.amazon.com/bedrock/—Access and deploy foundation models through Amazon Web Service's (AWS) fully managed service, enabling you to build and scale GenAI applications with enterprise-grade security and seamless integration with your existing AWS infrastructure.
- Salesforce Nonprofit Success Pack: https://www.salesforce.org—Use one of the leading CRM systems for nonprofits to centralize your data, streamline operations, and enable AI-driven donor engagement.
- Bloomerang: https://bloomerang.co—Manage donor data and fundraising efforts with this user-friendly CRM system that supports integration with AI tools for donor segmentation and insights.
- Neon CRM: https://neonone.com—Discover an all-in-one CRM system designed for nonprofits, helping you centralize data and integrate AI-powered tools for greater efficiency.
- Google Cloud: https://cloud.google.com—Use scalable cloud solutions for secure data storage and integration with AI tools, ensuring your data is actionable and ready for insights.

- Amazon Web Services (AWS): https://aws.amazon.com—Access robust cloud infrastructure services that provide reliable data storage and computing power for AI adoption.
- Microsoft Azure: https://azure.microsoft.com—Build a scalable tech stack with cloud services that integrate seamlessly with AI tools for predictive analytics and automation.
- Slack: https://slack.com—Enhance team collaboration with this powerful communication platform, which integrates with AI tools to share insights, automate tasks, and streamline workflows.
- Zapier: https://zapier.com—Automate workflows and connect your nonprofit's tools with this middleware solution to ensure seamless integration across your tech stack.
- Make (formerly Integromat): https://make.com—Simplify and automate complex workflows, helping your nonprofit save time and reduce inefficiencies while scaling its AI capabilities.
- Tableau: https://www.tableau.com—Visualize your data with powerful dashboards that integrate with AI tools, making it easier to measure impact and track fundraising progress.
- Power BI: https://powerbi.microsoft.com—Leverage this analytics platform to turn your nonprofit's data into actionable visualizations and predictive insights with AI integrations.
- CrowdStrike: https://crowdstrike.com—Protect your nonprofit's sensitive data with advanced cybersecurity solutions, ensuring the integrity of your AI tools and the trust of your stakeholders.

Part VI

Policies and Protections: Safeguarding the Mission and Avoiding Trouble in the Age of AI

"AI is neither inherently good nor bad—it's what we do with it that makes the difference. Accountability and transparency must guide its development and use."

—Joy Buolamwini, founder of the Algorithmic Justice League

As your nonprofit integrates AI tools, whether you learned about them earlier in this book or elsewhere, you will enter a new era of opportunities and risks. ***AI has the potential to revolutionize how your organization achieves its mission, but without proper safeguards, it can also introduce vulnerabilities.*** From cybersecurity breaches to legal pitfalls and ethical dilemmas, your nonprofit must navigate these challenges thoughtfully to avoid jeopardizing your credibility, data, and long-term viability.

AI operates at the intersection of innovation and accountability. ***AI's adoption demands your nonprofit establish robust policies and protections to mitigate risks while maximizing its benefits.*** How do you ensure that sensitive donor data remains secure in a world of increasingly sophisticated cyber threats? What steps can your organization take to navigate the complex legal landscape surrounding AI adoption? How can you ethically harness the power of AI without compromising your values? These are the critical questions that you must address as your nonprofit embraces this technology.

Part VI explores how to build a protective framework for your nonprofit as you venture into AI adoption. We begin with "Cybersecurity in the Age of AI," where we share simple tips for safeguarding your organization against evolving threats. AI offers powerful tools to detect and respond to cyber risks in real time, but it also creates new vulnerabilities that require proactive management. From securing cloud-based systems to defending against AI-enabled phishing attacks, this chapter provides actionable strategies for fortifying your digital infrastructure.

Next, "Enhancing Legal Operations and Compliance" examines how AI can support your nonprofit with managing legal risks and maintaining regulatory compliance. AI tools can streamline contract review, flag compliance issues, and simplify recordkeeping—enabling your organization to stay ahead of legal challenges. This chapter also explores how AI can assist in policy enforcement, ensuring that your team adheres to evolving laws and industry standards.

Finally, "Data Privacy and Ethical AI Adoption" tackles one of the most pressing concerns in today's digital landscape: ensuring that your use of AI respects the privacy of donors, beneficiaries, and staff. This chapter provides guidance on adopting ethical AI practices, from transparent data use policies to bias mitigation techniques. It also emphasizes the importance of aligning your AI initiatives with your mission and values, ensuring that technology serves as a force for good within your organization.

Each chapter is designed to provide your nonprofit with the tools and knowledge needed to protect its operations, reputation, and stakeholders. Expert insights and actionable tips offer a clear path forward, enabling your organization to embrace AI responsibly and confidently.

AI can open doors to transformative possibilities, but it must be approached with care. ***By prioritizing policies and protections, your nonprofit can create an environment where innovation thrives without compromising security or ethics.*** In doing so, your organization will not only avoid trouble but also set a standard for integrity and accountability in the nonprofit sector.

Chapter 28

Cybersecurity in the Age of AI

Based on insights from an interview with Joshua Peskay.

In the bustling world of nonprofits, your time is precious. You're juggling fundraising, expanding your community, and making the world a better place. So, why should cybersecurity be on your radar, especially when you're eager to harness the power of AI to amplify your impact? The answer is simple yet compelling: **without robust cybersecurity, you risk everything you're working so hard to achieve.** This chapter will ensure you can confidently use AI tools while safeguarding your organization.

Cybersecurity might seem like a daunting topic, but it's essential in the age of AI. With AI's increasing role in automating tasks, generating personalized content at scale, and optimizing operations, understanding its security implications is crucial. **This chapter covers the practical steps you need to take to protect your nonprofit from cyber threats,** ensuring that AI remains a powerful ally rather than a potential liability.

Critical Skills and Competencies

Rethink Risk: The Cost of Action and *Inaction*

When it comes to adopting AI in a nonprofit setting, it's natural to focus on the risks: What if we inadvertently expose sensitive data? What if the AI makes a mistake that affects our beneficiaries? What if we invest time and money in tools that don't deliver? These are valid concerns that nonprofit leaders need to take seriously.

But here's the thing: there's another side to the risk equation that often goes unexamined. Yes, **there's risk in using AI, but there's also significant—and often** *greater—**risk in not using it**.* This isn't just about falling behind, though that's certainly a concern. It's about the fact that, whether you know it or not, your staff are probably already using AI. Studies show that 50–80% of employees across industries are bringing their own AI tools into the workplace to streamline tasks, solve problems, and boost productivity (https://assets-c4akfrf5b4d3f4b7.z01.azurefd.net/assets/2024/05/2024_Work_Trend_Index_Annual_Report_663d45200a4ad.pdf).

If your nonprofit isn't leading the conversation with training, policies, and guidance about safe, ethical, and effective AI use, your staff are proceeding without you. That means they could inadvertently—or even unknowingly—expose your organization to significant risks: mishandling sensitive data, generating biased or inaccurate outputs, or relying on tools in ways that don't align with your mission or values. ***In the absence of clear leadership, the risks of unsafe, unethical, and ineffective AI use multiply, and you're left trying to catch up after the fact.***

The reality is, ***doing nothing is not the safe option.*** It's a decision to abdicate leadership in an area that's already transforming how your team works. The right AI strategy isn't one that avoids risk altogether—that's impossible. It's one that manages the risks of action *and* inaction thoughtfully, providing your staff with the tools, training, and guidelines they need to harness AI in a way that amplifies your mission while safeguarding your organization.

Define Objectives and Formalize Policy

Start by setting clear goals and desired outcomes that align with your nonprofit's mission and operational needs. AI is a tool, so what do you want to use it to do? Whether it's streamlining compliance processes, improving donor data security, or enhancing program delivery, ***turn your goals into a* plan *by writing them down, alongside measurable metrics and milestones to gauge progress.*** Establish realistic timelines and assign roles and responsibilities to ensure accountability across your team, including designating someone to oversee AI tool selection and people to validate AI outputs. By clearly defining your objectives and breaking them down into actionable steps, you'll create a road map that ensures your AI initiatives remain relevant, achievable, and mission-driven.

A structured approach to AI adoption is critical to protecting your nonprofit's sensitive data and ensuring compliance with privacy and security standards. Without clear boundaries and goals, your team risks inadvertently using tools or handling data in ways that compromise your organization's security. ***Start by identifying* clear rules *about which AI systems are approved for use at your organization and what data is approved for sharing with those tools.***

Once your guide rails, goals, and the corresponding road map are in place, ***integrate your objectives and approach into a comprehensive AI policy that provides clear guidelines for acceptable use, data sharing practices, and ongoing training.*** Include specific protocols for handling sensitive data, such as ensuring donor and beneficiary information is encrypted and limiting access to authorized personnel only. Document acceptable use cases for AI tools, including restrictions on uploading personally identifiable information into systems that lack adequate safeguards. Be sure to include your plans about ongoing training, ensuring staff and volunteers remain updated on AI tools, privacy laws, and cybersecurity best practices. Consider leveraging resources like NTEN (https://www.nten.org/) for policy templates and Cause Writer (https://causewriter.ai/) for guidance on creating responsible workflows. A well-constructed AI policy not only protects your organization but also empowers your team with the clarity and tools they need to use AI effectively and securely.

Implement Administrative Controls

Once your objectives and AI policy are in place, the next step is to operationalize them through robust controls to ensure consistent and secure implementation across your nonprofit. ***Administrative controls serve as the bridge between your policy and day-to-day operations; they are the processes and systems you establish to manage how data is accessed, used, and protected within your organization.*** They ensure your AI initiatives stay aligned with your objectives and include workflows and data access protocols to specify who can input, access, or manage data within AI systems. These should be paired with robust encryption practices to protect data both at rest and in transit. Since AI systems can and will give inaccurate responses at times, it is also critical to monitor how AI outputs are validated and used. In particular, ***use role-based access controls (RBAC) to limit access to sensitive data, ensuring*** *only authorized personnel can view or manage specific datasets.* This is especially critical as AI use becomes more prevalent throughout your organization because many nonprofits rely on some level of "security through obscurity" and this is completely undone by modern AI systems.

Tech tools can help automate and monitor these controls. Platforms like Okta (https://www.okta.com) manage user authentication and enforce role-based access, ensuring only authorized staff can access sensitive data. Platforms like Microsoft Purview (https://learn.microsoft.com/en-us/purview/) can track how data is accessed and AI tools are used, creating an additional layer of accountability. Whether you lean on these tools or prioritize manual oversight of access controls, **regularly revisit these controls to address changes in staff roles, evolving threats, or updates in your AI tools, ensuring they remain effective over time.** Combine these measures with ongoing education to build a culture of accountability and vigilance, empowering your team to make informed decisions while appropriately managing risks.

Keep Training Simple

Training your team to use AI tools responsibly is essential, but it doesn't have to be overwhelming. **Focus on creating short, impactful sessions that introduce staff to the opportunities and risks associated with AI.** A concise, half-hour session can go a long way in covering the basics, such as what you're hoping to achieve with AI and how it maps to your mission, how to use AI tools safely, what types of data can and cannot be shared, and why transparency in AI-generated content is critical. **Keep the content accessible by using clear, jargon-free language and relatable examples.** Demonstrations in real time can be especially helpful, so let your team watch you use AI to streamline donor segmentation while also explaining the potential consequences of inputting sensitive data into public AI platforms. Regularly update training materials to reflect the latest AI advancements and cybersecurity threats, ensuring your team stays informed and prepared.

To maintain a culture of continuous learning, **schedule regular training sessions at least quarterly to reinforce key principles and address new developments.** Use these sessions to incorporate real-life scenarios that are relevant to your nonprofit's work, such as how an AI system might flag a grant compliance risk that staff should investigate further. Offer practical exercises, like teaching team members how to validate AI outputs for accuracy or safely escalate potential security alerts flagged by AI tools.

Beyond formal training, consider creating opportunities for collaboration and innovation in AI. Host sharing sessions when staff exchange ideas and showcase how they're using AI tools to solve challenges or improve workflows. These sessions can surface creative approaches others might adopt while fostering a sense of shared learning and accountability. For a more hands-on approach, *organize AI hackathons when teams brainstorm and prototype AI-driven solutions to specific organizational problems.* These events not only promote innovation but also build internal capacity and confidence in using AI responsibly and effectively.

Provide accessible resources like quick-reference guides, video tutorials, or interactive e-learning modules to reinforce learning. Platforms like Coursera (https://www.coursera.org) offer beginner-friendly courses on AI and cybersecurity, and TechSoup (https://www.techsoup.org) and NTEN.org provide training tailored for nonprofits. Simplifying training ensures that all team members, regardless of technical expertise, feel confident using AI responsibly, reducing risks and enhancing your organization's security posture.

Adopt Proven Cybersecurity Solutions

Cyber threats are constantly evolving, and your defenses need to keep pace. To ensure you keep up, take full advantage of existing platforms and services that provide best-in-class, comprehensive cybersecurity solutions. You can *use AI-powered monitoring tools to identify unusual activity, detect potential breaches, and respond to threats in real time.* Intrusion detection systems like Darktrace (https://www.darktrace.com) proactively alert you to suspicious behavior, such as unauthorized access attempts or unusual data transfers, while endpoint security platforms like Bitdefender (https://www.bitdefender.com) protect devices across your organization.

In today's threat landscape, traditional antivirus solutions are not sufficient. *Strongly consider using best-in-class endpoint detection and response (EDR) and managed detection and response (MDR) solutions* such as SentinelOne (https://www.sentinelone.com/), Huntress (https://www.huntress.com/), and Sophos (https://www.sophos.com/). And if you've never heard of these acronyms, to put it simply, EDR is like a security camera and motion detector. It detects that something unusual is happening inside the perimeter of the fence and can send a notification with a probability rating of how likely this is a threat. MDR is a service that responds to threats automatically, which is especially helpful if you don't have time and energy to monitor your EDR and respond quickly when a threat is detected.

Many of these tools also automate routine tasks like software updates, vulnerability scans, and access control reviews, freeing up your team to focus on more strategic initiatives. By integrating these tools into your operations, you create a layered defense strategy that enhances your organization's ability to detect, respond to, and recover from cyber threats, ensuring the safety and integrity of your mission-critical data and systems. Just be sure to regularly update your cybersecurity measures to address new vulnerabilities and provide your team with regular updates on best practices and new developments through resources like the Cybersecurity & Infrastructure Security Agency (https://www.cisa.gov) and cybersecurity newsletters.

Pitfalls and Solutions

Failure to Update Devices

Nonprofits with limited IT resources often delay or neglect updates, inadvertently leaving their systems exposed. **When your devices are not updated regularly, they may lack the latest security patches, making them susceptible to new threats and attack methods.** Cybercriminals continuously evolve their tactics, and software providers often release updates to address these vulnerabilities. Relying on outdated systems can lead to breaches that compromise sensitive donor, beneficiary, or organizational data.

To mitigate this risk, **establish a schedule for regular updates and maintenance of all devices and systems** for which you are responsible. Automate updates wherever possible and assign a team member to oversee this process to ensure accountability. Use monitoring tools like Automox (https://www.automox.com/) to track which systems need updates and ensure compliance. Additionally, create a backup plan to minimize disruption during updates.

Overlooking Insider Threats

Staff, volunteers, or even contractors with access to sensitive data may inadvertently expose your nonprofit to breaches by mishandling information or falling prey to phishing attacks, and sometimes, malicious insiders misuse their access for personal gain. Either way, this can result in severe reputational and financial harm, critical data being left unprotected, and other forms of vulnerability and liability. To address insider threats, ***implement least-privilege access controls that grant employees access only to the information necessary for their specific roles.*** Use monitoring tools like Varonis (https://www.varonis.com) to track access and detect unusual behavior. Regularly review access permissions, especially when team members change roles or leave the organization, conduct exit audits to ensure no unauthorized access persists, and establish an anonymous reporting system to encourage accountability.

Lack of Incident Response Planning

Without a clear strategy, your team may struggle to contain a security breach, notify stakeholders, and recover operations, prolonging the impact of any attacks. For nonprofits handling sensitive data, including donor or beneficiary records, the fallout from a poorly managed response can lead to reputational damage, regulatory penalties, and loss of trust from key stakeholders. So, before you adopt tech tools, ***develop a comprehensive incident response plan including the roles and responsibilities of each team member, the steps to contain and mitigate the breach, and the procedures for notifying affected stakeholders.*** Include provisions for post-incident reviews to identify gaps and improve your response for future events. Tools like CISA's *Cybersecurity Incident & Vulnerability Response Playbooks* provide helpful templates and best practices for creating a robust plan. Conduct regular drills and tabletop exercises to ensure your team is familiar with the plan and ready to act promptly when needed.

Neglecting Cloud Security and Threat Detection

Cloud platforms provide scalable, cost-effective solutions for data storage and AI processing, but inadequate security measures and a lack of proactive threat detection will expose your nonprofit to serious risks. ***Sensitive donor information, program*** *data, and financial records stored on the cloud are prime targets for cybercriminals, especially if encryption, multifactor authentication (MFA), and phishing protections are overlooked.* Misconfigurations in cloud environments or reliance on weak passwords create easy entry points for attackers, potentially resulting in unauthorized access, data breaches, or even ransomware attacks.

To safeguard your cloud-based systems, *prioritize encryption of data both at rest and in transit and implement MFA across all platforms to add an additional layer of security.* Use tools like AWS CloudTrail (https://aws.amazon.com/cloudtrail) or Microsoft Azure Security Center (https://azure.microsoft.com) to monitor and log activity in your cloud environment, ensuring you can detect suspicious behavior in real time. Pair this with tools like Duo Security (https://duo.com) to help you implement MFA seamlessly and phishing detection tools, plus be sure to provide staff training on how to recognize phishing attempts and validate data sources. Establish workflows for reviewing inputs into AI tools and create clear protocols for flagging and addressing potential threats.

Road Map to the Future

The landscape of cybersecurity will evolve significantly as AI becomes more integrated into both nonprofit operations and the tactics of cybercriminals. *AI-powered cyberattacks, such as more sophisticated phishing schemes, automated hacking attempts, and deepfake impersonations, will continue to rise, targeting nonprofits that lack advanced defenses.* At the same time, advancements in AI-driven cybersecurity tools will offer nonprofits new ways to combat these threats, including predictive analytics to identify vulnerabilities before they are exploited and automated response systems to contain attacks in real time. Cloud security will also become increasingly critical as more nonprofits adopt cloud-based platforms for data storage and AI processing, creating new opportunities but also exposing organizations to evolving risks like misconfigurations or shared responsibility pitfalls.

To prepare for these changes, your nonprofit should *prioritize adopting advanced AI-driven security tools that leverage predictive analytics, anomaly detection, and automated threat responses.* Proactively investing in technologies like EDR platforms or zero-trust architecture significantly reduces vulnerabilities. Training will also remain critical, especially as cybercriminals exploit human errors to breach even the most secure systems. By embracing forward-thinking cybersecurity strategies, your nonprofit can stay ahead of evolving threats while safely harnessing the power of AI to further your mission.

Dos and Don'ts

Do

- Establish clear objectives for your AI adoption, including desired outcomes, metrics for success, and timelines, to ensure alignment with your mission and operational goals
- Develop a formal AI policy that includes acceptable use cases, data sharing protocols, and ongoing training requirements to protect sensitive information
- Use administrative controls, such as role-based access and encryption, to secure sensitive data and limit exposure to unauthorized personnel
- Regularly train staff on AI tools, cybersecurity best practices, and emerging threats through accessible, jargon-free sessions and practical exercises
- Leverage AI-powered tools for real-time monitoring of unusual activities, phishing detection, and endpoint security to protect against evolving cyber threats
- Incorporate MFA across all accounts and systems to add an extra layer of security beyond passwords
- Conduct regular audits of cloud configurations and data storage practices to identify vulnerabilities and ensure compliance with security policies
- Prepare an incident response plan that defines roles, response protocols, and stakeholder communication steps in the event of a cybersecurity breach

Don't

- Ignore software updates and patches for AI tools and systems, as this leaves your organization vulnerable to new attack methods
- Share sensitive information, such as donor or beneficiary data, with public AI tools that lack adequate safeguards or encryption measures

- Assume passwords alone are sufficient; relying solely on them increases the risk of unauthorized access due to weak or stolen credentials
- Overlook insider threats by failing to regularly review access permissions or monitor unusual behavior from team members with elevated access
- Rely exclusively on AI for cybersecurity without human oversight, which is critical for validating alerts, investigating flagged issues, and making informed decisions

Conclusion

As you navigate the rapidly evolving landscape of AI, cybersecurity must remain a foundational pillar of your nonprofit's strategy. ***By defining clear objectives, formalizing policies, and implementing robust administrative controls, you will create a road map that ensures AI tools are aligned with your mission while safeguarding your data and stakeholders.*** Combining these efforts with accessible, ongoing training and leveraging proven cybersecurity solutions enables your team to use AI responsibly and securely, empowering your nonprofit to operate with confidence.

The challenges of cybersecurity may feel daunting, but the solutions are within reach. Whether through encryption protocols, MFA, real-time monitoring tools, or comprehensive incident response plans, you have the tools to stay one step ahead of potential threats. ***By prioritizing a culture of vigilance, accountability, and continuous learning, your organization can harness the transformative potential of AI without compromising on trust or integrity.*** The path forward isn't just about adopting technology—it's about doing so thoughtfully and securely, ensuring that AI becomes an asset that strengthens your mission and impact.

Interviewee Bio

Joshua Peskay is a seasoned nonprofit technology strategist and a leading voice in cybersecurity for mission-driven organizations. As the 3CPO (CIO/CISO/CPO) at RoundTable Technology, he works with hundreds of nonprofits to implement robust cybersecurity measures, adopt innovative technologies, and leverage AI tools to improve organizational resilience. With over 30 years of experience in the nonprofit sector, Joshua specializes in helping organizations mitigate risks, improve data protection, and align technology strategies with their missions. Joshua also collaborates with a potato to share practical cybersecurity tips (https://www.roundtabletechnology.com/cybersecurity-nuggets-with-tater-and-stache)! https://www.linkedin.com/in/joshuapeskay/

Resource Review

Unlike the "Resource Review" in other chapters where we share more about any tools referenced in the main chapter along with other relevant platforms and publications, our interviewee graciously provided an itemized list of recommended providers across a range of critical cybersecurity arenas, building on what's outlined in this chapter:

BCDR (business continuity and disaster recovery): Plans and procedures to make sure your nonprofit can keep operating through unexpected events (like power outages or cyberattacks) and recover quickly afterward. This can enable your organization to keep delivering services and protect important data.

- Datto: https://www.datto.com—Strong all-in-one solutions for backup, disaster recovery, and business continuity.
- Veeam: https://www.veeam.com—Powerful backup and replication software, with options for cloud and on premises.
- Acronis: https://www.acronis.com—Cyber protection solutions that combine backup with cybersecurity features.
- N-able Cove Data Protection: https://www.n-able.com/products/cove-data-protection—Cloud-first backup and disaster recovery, designed for managed service providers serving smaller clients.
- Druva: https://www.druva.com—Cloud-native data protection platform, good for simplifying data management.

Cloud security: Enables you to protect data and applications hosted on cloud services (like Amazon Web Services or Microsoft Azure). Common measures include data encryption, MFA, and activity monitoring to detect suspicious behavior.

- Amazon Web Services (AWS): https://aws.amazon.com—Offers a wide range of cloud security services, including data encryption, identity management, and activity monitoring.
- Microsoft Azure: https://azure.microsoft.com—Provides integrated security features within its cloud platform, including threat protection, compliance tools, and advanced access controls.
- Google Cloud Platform (GCP): https://cloud.google.com—Strong security capabilities with a focus on data protection, compliance, and real-time threat detection.
- Orca Security: https://orca.security—Cloud security platform with agentless workload protection and automated risk prioritization.
- Wiz: https://www.wiz.io—Cloud security platform that helps identify and prioritize risks, offering comprehensive visibility across cloud environments.

DMARC (domain-based message authentication, reporting, and conformance): An email security tool that checks if a message is actually coming from who it says it's from, preventing email spoofing and phishing. This can help your nonprofits keep their email communications trustworthy.

- Valimail: https://www.valimail.com—Focuses on automated DMARC enforcement and email authentication.
- Proofpoint: https://www.proofpoint.com—Comprehensive email security with strong DMARC capabilities.
- Mimecast: https://www.mimecast.com—Offers robust email security and DMARC support.
- Google Workspace: https://workspace.google.com—Includes DMARC reporting and enforcement features.
- Microsoft 365: https://www.microsoft.com/en-us/microsoft-365—Provides DMARC capabilities within its email security suite.

DNS (domain name system): A system that converts website names (e.g., www.example.org) into the numerical addresses computers use. Securing DNS prevents hackers from hijacking your website or redirecting traffic.

- Cloudflare: https://www.cloudflare.com—Excellent DNS security and performance, with a free tier for nonprofits.
- Cisco Umbrella: https://umbrella.cisco.com—DNS filtering and security, with integration options for Cisco products.
- Google Public DNS: https://developers.google.com/speed/public-dns—Free and reliable DNS service with security features.
- Quad9: https://www.quad9.net—Free DNS service with strong security and privacy focus.
- Amazon Route 53: https://aws.amazon.com/route53—Scalable and reliable DNS service from AWS.

EDR (endpoint detection and response): Software that detects, investigates, and responds to suspicious activity on devices like laptops, phones, and tablets. This can help your nonprofit by watching for cyber threats around the clock and taking quick action if something is wrong.

- CrowdStrike Falcon: https://www.crowdstrike.com—Strong endpoint protection with cloud-native architecture.
- SentinelOne: https://www.sentinelone.com—AI-powered endpoint security with autonomous response capabilities.
- Microsoft Defender for Endpoint: https://www.microsoft.com/en-us/security/business/endpoint-security/microsoft-defender-endpoint—Integrated with Windows for robust endpoint protection.
- Sophos Intercept X: https://www.sophos.com—Endpoint protection with anti-ransomware and exploit prevention.
- ESET Endpoint Security: https://www.eset.com—Lightweight and effective endpoint protection with a strong track record.

- Malwarebytes: (https://www.malwarebytes.com/)—Endpoint security with a focus on malware detection and removal.

IDP (identity provider): A service that confirms who users are when they log into different applications, helping ensure the right people access the right tools.

- Okta: https://www.okta.com—Leading identity provider with a wide range of integrations and advanced authentication features.
- Microsoft Azure Active Directory: https://azure.microsoft.com/en-us/services/active-directory/—Offers identity management with seamless integration into Microsoft environments.
- Auth0: https://auth0.com—Developer-friendly identity provider offering flexible authentication options for nonprofits and businesses.
- OneLogin: https://www.onelogin.com—Cloud-based identity provider with strong security and user-friendly features.
- JumpCloud: https://jumpcloud.com—Directory platform with identity provider capabilities, ideal for managing user access and authentication.

ITSM (information technology service management): The way organizations plan, deliver, manage, and improve their IT services. By using ITSM, nonprofits can introduce new AI tools smoothly and maintain secure operations.

- Atlassian Jira Service Management: https://www.atlassian.com/software/jira/service-management—Popular ITSM platform emphasizing collaboration and agile processes.
- Freshservice: https://freshservice.com—Easy-to-use ITSM solution offering great value for smaller organizations.
- ManageEngine ServiceDesk Plus: https://www.manageengine.com/products/service-desk/—Feature-rich ITSM platform with strong information technology infrastructure library alignment and customization.

- Zoho Desk: https://www.zoho.com/desk/—Affordable ITSM solution with seamless integration into other Zoho products.
- Spiceworks Help Desk: https://www.spiceworks.com/free-help-desk-software/—Free ITSM solution for basic ticketing and IT support needs.

MDM (mobile device management): Tools and policies to oversee and secure mobile devices used by employees at work. This is critical for nonprofits since it helps you protect data on personal phones or tablets used in the field.

- Microsoft Intune: https://www.microsoft.com/en-us/security/business/microsoft-intune—Cloud-based MDM solution with excellent integration into Microsoft ecosystems.
- VMware Workspace ONE: https://www.vmware.com/products/workspace-one.html—Comprehensive platform for managing mobile devices and endpoints securely.
- Jamf Pro: https://www.jamf.com/products/jamf-pro/—Apple-focused MDM solution for nonprofits using Macs, iPhones, or iPads.
- ManageEngine Mobile Device Manager Plus: https://www.manageengine.com/mobile-device-management/—Feature-rich MDM platform with a focus on compliance and security.
- Sophos Mobile: https://www.sophos.com/en-us/products/mobile-security—Unified endpoint and MDM with advanced security features.

MDR (managed detection and response): Security services you pay an outside company to provide. They watch your systems around the clock, detect threats, and react quickly if something goes wrong. Helpful for nonprofits with limited internal cybersecurity staff.

- Arctic Wolf: https://arcticwolf.com—Provides 24/7 security monitoring and response, tailored to small and mid-sized organizations.
- eSentire: https://esentire.com—Proactive threat hunting and response services to keep your systems secure.

- Secureworks: https://www.secureworks.com—Dell Technologies subsidiary offering advanced security expertise and MDR services.
- Alert Logic: https://www.alertlogic.com—Cloud-focused MDR with strong integration into major cloud platforms.

SIEM (security information and event management): Software that collects and reviews security data (like logs) from across your entire organization. It alerts you to threats, helps with compliance, and centralizes your view of security.

- Splunk: https://www.splunk.com—Powerful SIEM platform with robust analytics and integrations for centralized threat management.
- IBM QRadar: https://www.ibm.com/qradar—Enterprise-grade SIEM with strong analytics capabilities for compliance and threat detection.
- LogRhythm: https://www.exabeam.com/platform/logrhythm-siem/—NextGen SIEM platform focusing on advanced threat detection and rapid response.
- Securonix: https://www.securonix.com—Cloud-native SIEM with advanced threat hunting and analytics for large-scale deployments.

XDR (extended detection and response): An upgraded version of EDR that unifies threat detection across not just devices but also servers, networks, and cloud services. XDR gives a full picture of potential threats and helps automate the response.

- Microsoft 365 Defender: https://www.microsoft.com/en-us/security/business/microsoft-defender—Integrated XDR solution optimized for Microsoft environments.
- CrowdStrike Falcon XDR: https://www.crowdstrike.com—Combines endpoint and XDR capabilities for unified threat detection and response.
- Trend Micro Vision One: https://www.trendmicro.com—XDR platform focused on threat intelligence and automated responses.
- Cybereason XDR: https://www.cybereason.com—AI-powered XDR offering strong investigation and remediation capabilities.

Zero trust: A security mindset that assumes no person or device is automatically trustworthy, even within the organization's own network. Every request for access is verified to reduce the risk of breaches.

- Zscaler: https://www.zscaler.com—Cloud security platform built on zero trust principles for secure access and data protection.
- Palo Alto Networks (Prisma Access): https://www.paloaltonetworks.com/sase/prisma-access—Comprehensive zero trust platform for securing applications and data.
- Okta (Identity-first security): https://www.okta.com—Zero trust platform emphasizing identity as the cornerstone of security.
- Cloudflare One: https://www.cloudflare.com/cloudflare-one/—Zero trust solution offering robust network security and access controls.
- Cisco SecureX: https://www.cisco.com/c/en/us/products/security/securex.html—Integrated security platform supporting zero trust architectures.

Chapter 29

Enhancing Legal Operations and Compliance

Based on insights from an interview with Olga V. Mack and Kassi Burns.

In an increasingly complex operational landscape, nonprofits are expected to navigate a range of regulatory, legal, and management challenges while remaining mission-focused. AI-powered technologies can significantly enhance your ability to meet these demands, empowering your organization to streamline operations and reduce the burden of manual processes. **From regulatory compliance and donor data protection to volunteer and contract management, AI offers your nonprofit the tools to manage risk, ensure legal compliance, and improve overall efficiency.** This chapter explores five critical areas—regulatory compliance and reporting, donor data protection and privacy, volunteer management and liability, grant management, and contract management—where AI can play a transformative role, helping your organization not only meet its obligations but also optimize resources for greater impact.

Critical Skills and Competencies
Regulatory Compliance and Reporting

Navigating regulatory requirements can be a complex and time-consuming challenge for nonprofits, but getting it right is crucial for maintaining tax-exempt status, adhering to fundraising laws, and safeguarding donor trust. **AI-powered tools can simplify compliance by automating tasks like monitoring legal updates, generating accurate reports, and flagging potential compliance risks.** Some of these tools have the ability to automate the generation of your annual IRS Form 990 using your accounting data, minimizing manual data entry errors, and ensuring timely submission.

Others help track state-specific charitable solicitation requirements, automating the registration process, and cross-check data for inconsistencies, providing a centralized system that enhances accuracy and accountability in your reporting.

To make the most of AI-driven compliance solutions, **look for platforms that track regulations in real time and send alerts for key deadlines or legislative changes.** These systems can also streamline multistate compliance processes, enabling you to manage varying requirements seamlessly. By adopting these tools and integrating them into your workflows, you'll reduce compliance risks, protect donor trust, and free-up resources to focus on advancing your mission.

Donor Data Protection and Privacy

Protecting donor data is essential for nonprofits, particularly as regulations like the General Data Protection Regulation (GDPR) and the California Consumer Privacy Act (CCPA) impose stringent requirements on how personal data is handled. Noncompliance can lead to hefty fines, legal scrutiny, and damage to your organization's reputation. *AI-powered tools can simplify compliance by automating tasks such as recording and managing donor consent forms, monitoring access to sensitive information, and flagging potential data breaches in real time.*

You can also use AI tools to streamline processes like data anonymization or encryption, protecting donor information even in the event of unauthorized access. Automated systems can manage data subject access requests (DSARs), enabling your nonprofit to respond promptly to donor requests for access or deletion of their personal data, as required by GDPR and CCPA. Additionally, *AI solutions can create detailed audit trails that document all data-related activities, offering transparency and confidence during regulatory reviews or donor inquiries.* By adopting these technologies, you can build trust with your donors while staying ahead of evolving data privacy requirements.

Volunteer Management and Liability

Managing volunteers comes with unique legal and regulatory challenges. *AI tools can simplify the process of collecting liability waivers, running background checks, and ensuring labor law compliance,* reducing risks while allowing your nonprofit to focus on engaging and scaling its volunteer workforce. AI-powered systems can automate the management of liability waivers, flagging gaps or inconsistencies in waiver agreements, and thereby providing added legal protection and simplifying retrieval during audits or legal reviews. Other emerging AI tools automate and expedite volunteer background checks, completing them in hours rather than days, ensuring that all volunteers meet legal and safety requirements before they begin.

AI also plays a helpful role in ensuring compliance with labor laws, which can be complex and vary by jurisdiction. AI platforms are available to help track volunteer hours, alerting you to potential violations of working hour regulations or other labor law requirements. AI solutions can even monitor ongoing compliance by scanning legal databases for changes in a volunteer's status, alerting you to any issues that may require action, especially if you're working with underage clients. This proactive approach not only minimizes legal risks but also creates a safe, efficient, and legally compliant volunteer management system. By integrating AI into your volunteer processes, you can protect your organization while streamlining operations, making it easier to scale your programs and manage larger networks of volunteers effectively.

Grant Management

Effective grant oversight is a cornerstone of nonprofit funding, but it requires meticulous oversight to ensure compliance with funders' requirements, timely reporting, and alignment with organizational goals. *AI helps streamline grant management by automating key tasks such as tracking grant applications, managing deadlines, and ensuring compliance with specific grant terms.* AI-powered tools can analyze grant opportunities and match them to your nonprofit's mission, leveraging data from past successful applications. These tools also offer automated alerts for key deadlines and flag compliance requirements, reducing the manual effort required to track multiple grants simultaneously. By letting AI handle these logistical details, your team can focus on creating compelling proposals and building stronger relationships with funders.

AI solutions can also enhance grant compliance and reporting throughout the grant life cycle. Available tools can automate financial tracking, ensuring that funds are allocated according to grant terms while providing real-time insights into expenditures and streamline the preparation of progress reports, helping you meet deadlines with accuracy and consistency while reducing the risk of noncompliance. ***By integrating with your project management and financial systems, AI tools help align grant activities with your nonprofit's strategic goals, enabling you to demonstrate impact more effectively to funders.*** Leveraging AI for grant management enables you to increase efficiency, reduce administrative burdens, and focus on delivering mission-critical work.

Contract Management

Managing contracts—whether with vendors, service providers, or partners—can be complex and represent a huge distraction from your core work. But of course, they're a necessary evil and part of healthy operations. AI tools simplify this effort by ***automatically tracking key contract deadlines, such as renewals or compliance reviews, and sending automated reminders to ensure nothing is missed.***

Beyond simply tracking deadlines, ***AI-powered platforms can help you analyze contract terms and flag clauses that may pose risks to your organization,*** such as unfavorable conditions or potential noncompliance with legal requirements. From scanning and evaluating contracts, ensuring all agreements align with your operational and legal obligations without requiring manual reviews of lengthy documents, to monitoring key performance indicators (KPIs) within contracts, and ensuring vendors and partners meet their commitments and providing actionable insights for better decision-making, these AI-driven tools offer powerful resources for your nonprofit. ***By securely storing all contracts in a centralized database, these tools also facilitate quick retrieval for audits, legal reviews, or operational decisions.*** With AI streamlining your contract management processes, you can reduce risks, enhance efficiency, and focus more energy on advancing your mission.

Pitfalls and Solutions

Ignoring AI Literacy and Governance

Too many nonprofits have their AI integration goals undermined by not paying enough attention to the critical need for training and policies to guide your efforts. Without these, your organization may misuse AI tools, leading to operational inefficiencies, ethical concerns, and compliance risks.

To help ensure you avoid this common trap, **develop a comprehensive AI governance framework that includes policies outlining ethical considerations, acceptable use cases, and accountability protocols.** Standard operating procedures should guide staff and volunteers on the responsible use of AI tools, while structured AI literacy training programs equip users with the knowledge to operate your tools effectively. **Training should focus on key areas like data protection, compliance with privacy laws, and ethical decision-making.** In addition to initial orientation, make sure you also establish an ongoing training schedule to keep your teams updated on advancements in AI and evolving best practices.

Over-Automating

While AI excels at processing large volumes of data and identifying patterns, it lacks the judgment and contextual understanding that humans provide. As such, **relying entirely on AI to manage compliance without human oversight inevitably leads to unchecked errors, misinterpretations, or missed nuances in complex legal and regulatory matters.** An AI tool might flag a compliance issue based on outdated parameters or irrelevant criteria, causing unnecessary alarm or wasted resources. Over-automation also erodes trust in AI systems when stakeholders discover inaccuracies or decisions that don't align with your nonprofit's priorities.

To mitigate these risks, use AI as an assistant rather than a stand-alone solution. **Develop workflows that integrate regular human reviews of AI outputs, particularly in critical areas like donor privacy, grant compliance, and legal agreements.** Assign team members to validate flagged issues, refine decisions, and maintain oversight of automated processes. Finally, schedule periodic audits of your AI systems to ensure they remain aligned with your nonprofit's goals and up-to-date with changing regulations. By pairing AI's efficiency with human judgment, you can maximize accuracy, maintain accountability, and build trust in your AI-driven compliance processes.

Neglecting Vendor Due Diligence

Partnering with unreliable AI vendors will lead to subpar tools, hidden costs, and even data security vulnerabilities, jeopardizing your nonprofit's operations and reputation. **Many AI solutions promise impressive capabilities but may lack the**

nonprofit-specific features, scalability, or robust security measures your organization requires. Choosing the wrong vendor can waste valuable time and resources, increase compliance risks, and force you to prematurely replace tools, resulting in financial strain and operational disruptions.

To protect yourself, ***prioritize vendors with a strong track record of working with nonprofits and proven expertise in data privacy and security.*** Request case studies, client testimonials, and references from similar organizations to validate their reliability and effectiveness. Engage your IT team and other stakeholders in the evaluation process to ensure the solution integrates smoothly with your existing systems and meets your operational needs. And consider conducting a pilot project with the vendor to assess the tool's performance before committing fully.

Underusing AI Insights

Failing to act on AI-generated compliance alerts or neglecting insights from AI analytics will lead to missed deadlines, increased noncompliance risks, and lost opportunities to improve operations. ***AI tools are designed to proactively highlight issues and identify trends, but without clear workflows or follow-up actions, these insights will go unrealized, leaving you exposed.*** Overlooking an alert about a grant reporting deadline could result in penalties, while ignoring patterns in donor data might mean missing critical funding opportunities. As you can imagine, results like this will also erode your team's confidence in your AI tools.

So, be sure to ***establish clear protocols for monitoring, responding to, and acting on AI-generated alerts and insights.*** Assign team members specific roles for reviewing notifications, prioritizing tasks, and tracking follow-up actions to ensure accountability. Use AI dashboards to identify trends, such as recurring compliance risks or opportunities to reallocate resources for greater efficiency. Integrate these insights into regular team meetings to inform decision-making and ensure the findings are applied effectively. By treating AI insights as actionable intelligence rather than static reports, you will maximize their value, improve operational performance, and stay ahead of compliance risks.

Dos and Don'ts

Do

- Automate compliance tasks to streamline reporting, track regulatory deadlines, and reduce manual errors
- Protect donor data leveraging AI-powered cybersecurity tools to monitor access patterns and flag potential data breaches in real time
- Automate volunteer background checks and liability waiver collection to reduce administrative burdens and enhance safety
- Use AI systems to track grant compliance, monitoring terms and ensuring expenditures align with funder requirements, minimizing noncompliance risks
- Employ contract management platforms to securely store and manage contracts, ensuring deadlines and performance metrics are tracked
- Develop workflows to regularly review AI outputs, validate flagged compliance issues, and address potential risks
- Implement tools that send automated alerts for changes in regulations, ensuring you stay ahead of compliance challenges

Don't

- Ignore privacy regulations when handling donor, volunteer, or staff data; ensure compliance with GDPR, CCPA, and other data privacy laws
- Forget to conduct due diligence on any AI vendors, most importantly confirming they have expertise in compliance and data security within the nonprofit sector
- Rely exclusively on automation, instead of combining human oversight with AI to address nuances in regulatory requirements and avoid unchecked errors
- Underestimate initial and ongoing training needs; otherwise, you'll likely experience misuse, inefficiencies, and missed compliance opportunities
- Let AI insights go unused: act promptly on AI-generated alerts and analytics to address risks, improve compliance, and optimize operational performance

Conclusion

AI offers nonprofits transformative opportunities to enhance legal operations and compliance, helping you streamline workflows, reduce risks, and free up valuable resources for mission-critical activities. **By embracing AI tools for tasks like regulatory compliance, donor data protection, volunteer management, grant oversight, and contract administration, your organization can achieve greater efficiency while ensuring alignment with legal and ethical standards.** The key lies in balancing technology with human oversight, ensuring that AI systems complement, rather than replace, the judgment and expertise of your team.

As you move forward, **focus on building a strong foundation for AI adoption: prioritize governance, invest in training, and foster a culture of continuous improvement.** Thoughtful integration of AI into your operations will not only safeguard your organization against risks but also empower you to achieve your mission more effectively. With AI as an ally, your nonprofit can navigate the complexities of compliance and governance with confidence, scaling your impact and inspiring trust among your stakeholders. The future is bright for those who act with purpose—start today and watch your organization thrive.

Interviewee Bios

Olga V. Mack is a visionary legal technology entrepreneur, board director, and digital transformation expert dedicated to modernizing legal operations through AI. As a CEO and strategist, she has led legal innovation at Fortune 500 companies, pre–initial public offering startups, and legal tech ventures, including building AI-powered tools that enhance compliance, risk management, and operational efficiency. A Fellow at CodeX, the Stanford Center for Legal Informatics, and the generative AI editor at *law. MIT Computational Law Report*, Olga is a thought leader on AI adoption in the legal and nonprofit sectors. She has authored multiple books, including *Product Counsel: Advise, Innovate, and Inspire*, and writes for *Above the Law* and *ACC Docket*. https://www.linkedin.com/in/olgamack/

Kassi Burns is a senior attorney at King & Spalding, LLP, based in Texas. As an attorney with over 10 years of experience working with AI and Machine Learning in litigation, Kassi's career has advanced by always being curious and following technology innovations. In addition to a growing collection of publications on topics related to AI, Kassi is actively engaged in thought leadership through her podcast focused on the impact of emerging technologies to our professional and personal lives, *Kassi &*. She is an executive board member of the Academy of Court-Appointed Neutrals and a member of Relativity's Attorney Advisory Board. https://www.linkedin.com/in/kassiburns/

Resource Review

- The world of AI-enabled tools is a rapidly evolving one. The following list of resources are provided to enable and facilitate your own diligence into AI tools that are best suited for your organization's needs. Not only do these resources aggregate information about available AI tools but many also provide reviews of select AI tools.

- Lawnext Legal Tech Directory: https://directory.lawnext.com/—Enables you to explore and review legal technology products, organizing these tools into 79 categories based on practice area and type. Software features about legal technology products can be reviewed and compared, with user reviews and press coverage available for more efficient diligence.

- CLOC Legal Ops Solutions Directory: https://cloc.org/resources/legal-operations-solutions-directory/—Makes it easy for you to identify and evaluate new tools in the legal marketplace and access collaboration tools to support implementation, and best practices to increase use.

- There's an AI for That: https://theresanaiforthat.com/—A comprehensive AI tracker that tracks over 700 AIs across almost 100 categories and updates every day. Additional helpful resources include a newsletter, forum, and YouTube channel.

- Legaltech Hub: https://www.legaltechnologyhub.com/—Combines a comprehensive directory of global legal technology tools and legal software with a powerful search that enables commercial legal professionals to find exactly what they're looking for to meet any use case, by applying nuanced filters that align with key data points.

Chapter 30

Data Privacy and Ethical AI Adoption

Based on insights from an interview with Amy Sample Ward.

In today's technological landscape, nonprofits are increasingly leveraging AI to drive impact, streamline operations, and enhance decision-making. However, **as your nonprofit adopts new technology, you're responsible to ensure you do so in ways that advance your mission and values, while mitigating any potential concerns.** Ensuring data privacy and avoiding ethical concerns is not just a legal obligation but a moral imperative. As nonprofit leaders and technologists, you must prioritize ethical AI practices to maintain trust with your stakeholders and protect sensitive information. This chapter offers practical tips and tools to guide your nonprofit through how to ethically implement AI in your organization.

Critical Skills and Competencies

Get Your Data in Order

As many other chapters have shared, it's crucial to ensure your organization's data is well organized and secure before diving into AI. Start by conducting a thorough audit of your data assets: **identify all sources of data, categorize them, and determine their relevance and usefulness.** Clean up your database, remove duplicates, and ensure your data is accurate, up-to-date, and organized. This process helps in eliminating clutter and focusing on valuable, actionable data. It also helps you delineate internal data you generate from that obtained from third-party sources, enabling you to leverage existing resources to drive your AI initiatives, cutting costs to access external data sources, and minimizing privacy concerns.

Invest in robust data management systems that facilitate easy access and analysis. These systems need to provide secure storage, efficient retrieval, and seamless integration with other tools. **Properly structured and secure data forms the foundation on which effective AI models are built.** On the flip side, inaccurate, incomplete, or biased data leads to flawed, unreliable outputs. To avoid data disasters, invest time in cleaning and organizing your data before integrating it into AI systems. This initial step not only prepares you for AI integration but also enhances overall data management practices, ensuring that your nonprofit is ready to leverage AI effectively and responsibly.

Expand Your AI Policy

Just about every chapter throughout this book has shared that developing a clear, comprehensive AI policy is one of your first steps to ensuring success with AI adoption. No doubt your policy needs to speak to the basics, including detailing key use cases, goals for AI adoption, acceptable and unacceptable uses, approved platforms, and more. But how can you ensure your policy speaks directly to data privacy and other important ethical concerns?

For starters, your policy should outline how AI will be used within your organization, detailing any ethical and data privacy considerations and measures, and defining the scope for which AI applications are approved. Beyond that, *your AI policy is incomplete unless it articulates your goals and ethical objectives, and then builds on that foundation by outlining the types of data used and any safeguards in place to protect sensitive information.* In particular, your AI policy must include several critical elements to be truly effective:

- **Training data:** How will you ensure your training data is representative and free from bias? Once you've addressed this critical concern, plan to *regularly review and update your training data to reflect changes in your community* and the wider world. This helps create fair, accurate AI models.

- **Sensitive data:** For *any* information you do not want released into the public domain, *detail exactly what data and which sources are to be kept confidential.* Whether it's donor profiles and giving history, Health Insurance Portability and Accountability Act (HIPAA)–regulated health records, or information on underage clients, clearly label these in your policy and spell out which data governance practices dictate how that information is used and protected.

- **Data handling:** *Detail your protocols for data entry, validation, and storage* to ensure clarity about who is authorized and how your precious data is handled. In addition to detailing approved processes, it's typically helpful to also spell out what *not* to do, especially if those issues have arisen more than once.

- **Risk mitigation:** Identify potential risks associated with AI use and develop strategies to mitigate them. This includes addressing biases, ensuring data security, and responding to misinformation or misappropriated content. Map out potential points of failure where you're relying on AI and develop contingency plans in case problems arise.

- **Continuous evaluation:** Regularly evaluate your AI tools and practices to ensure they are performing as expected and to reflect new developments in the field. This involves monitoring for biases, inaccuracies, and other issues that may arise. *Detail your plan to help maintain the integrity and effectiveness of your AI systems, including the frequency of these assessments,* but be sure to take the time at least twice a year. This proactive approach will help you stay ahead of potential issues and maintain ethical standards.

A well-defined policy provides a road map for AI implementation and sets the standards for ethical AI use. Incorporate these elements and any others relevant to your goals into your AI policy, ensuring that your AI initiatives align with your nonprofit's values and mission, ultimately fostering trust and accountability.

Spread the Word

Once you've integrated all these elements into your nonprofit's AI policy, *ensure your policy is accessible to all stakeholders, including staff, volunteers, and beneficiaries.* Transparency is key, and this clarity helps build trust in and alignment on your specific approach to the ethical use of AI, including speaking to the values your philosophy is based on. It's also often helpful to post a public-facing version of your AI policy on your website, sharing your approach to the responsible use of technology, clarifying your goals, and detailing how you use AI and the associated benefits.

Pitfalls and Solutions

Hesitant Adoption

Resisting AI due to fears about complexity or potential will delay your adoption of this transformational enabling technology, postponing your realization of its many benefits. Moreover, being late to the game means you'll constantly be in catch-up mode, instead of innovating from the front of the pack. So, **encourage the adoption of AI by educating your team, lifting up success stories and possibilities, and investing in the necessary tools and training.** Start with small, manageable projects to build confidence and demonstrate the value of AI. Look out for the innovators on your team who seem to be quickly developing fluency with new AI technologies. Invite them to share their tips and tactics with the rest of the staff, creating powerful opportunities for leadership and peer learning. By fostering a positive attitude toward AI, you will unlock new opportunities to enhance your organization's impact, while ensuring you use it responsibly and effectively.

Cheaping Out

For the most part, AI tools aren't expensive and in fact, many are free for now. But cheaper doesn't mean better, and although cost is always a consideration when exploring new technologies and infrastructure, investing in high-quality AI solutions and ongoing maintenance is crucial for success. Cutting corners or opting for cheaper alternatives can lead to subpar results and even ethical concerns. **Allocate sufficient resources to ensure your AI initiatives are well supported and sustainable, mapping out these costs alongside the required investment of time and other resources.** As shared previously, invest in training and development for your team to ensure they have the skills and knowledge needed to effectively use and manage AI. By thoughtfully investing properly in your AI infrastructure and related training, you will maximize the benefits of AI while maintaining ethical standards.

Road Map to the Future

Over the next few years, expect to see significant advancements in AI transparency and accountability. **Stakeholders will demand more transparency on how AI systems make decisions and generate content, necessitating the development**

of models that can clearly validate responses and bolstering efforts to ensure nonprofits' AI practices remain ethical and compliant with emerging regulations. The data privacy and security landscape is also sure to evolve, and AI models may move away from integrating any prompts or uploaded information into their training data, or they could double down as other data sources are exhausted. Either way, nonprofits will need to stay informed about changes in data privacy laws and practices, adapting their approach accordingly. By staying proactive and continuously updating your AI strategy, your nonprofit will harness the power of AI while maintaining the highest ethical standards.

Dos and Don'ts

Do

- Educate your team about the potential and ethical use of AI, highlighting how this tool can help you advance your mission and expand impact, while creating operational efficiencies
- Invest in cleaning up your database and structuring your content, creating a strong foundation for your AI efforts
- Develop a clear and comprehensive AI policy, detailing your approach to ethics and data security, and articulating exactly how sensitive data should be handled
- Create a group calendar to guide your AI adoption, including regular group meetings to share learnings and challenges, reviews of your training data to reflect changes in your community, and audits of all your AI tools, in addition to ongoing professional development and training

Don't

- Resist using AI due to fears about complexity; the sooner you dive in, the sooner your nonprofit can expand its impact and lead the pack!
- Cheap out; be sure to allocate money, time, and the other resources needed to ensure your AI initiatives are well supported initially and moving forward

Conclusion

If your nonprofit wants to harness the power of AI while maintaining ethical standards and protecting data privacy, your path is clear: ***focus on building a strong foundation, developing clear policies, and continuously evaluating your practices to ensure you're using AI responsibly.*** Embrace the potential of AI to enhance your impact but always keep ethics at the forefront of your strategy. This approach will not only enhance your impact but also ensure that your nonprofit remains a trusted and responsible entity in the eyes of your community.

Interviewee Bio

Amy Sample Ward is a leading advocate for ethical technology use in the nonprofit sector, serving as the CEO of NTEN, an organization dedicated to empowering nonprofits through equitable technology practices. Coauthor of *The Tech That Comes Next: How Changemakers, Philanthropists, and Technologists Can Build an Equitable World*, Amy explores the intersection of technology, ethics, and social impact, emphasizing the importance of community-centered design and data privacy. https://www.linkedin.com/in/amysampleward/

Resource Review

- NTEN's Nonprofit Technology Readiness Assessment: https://www.nten.org/learn/nonprofit-tech-readiness—A free tool to evaluate your organization's tech capacity, including AI readiness. The NTEN website is also a great resource for all aspects of nonprofit technology, including offering information on their Nonprofit Technology Conference (https://www.nten.org/ntc), and free tools and templates, including their GenAI Use Policy guide (https://word.nten.org/wp-content/uploads/2024/07/GAI-Policy-Template.pdf).

- Data Ethics Framework: https://www.gov.uk/government/publications/data-ethics-framework/data-ethics-framework—A comprehensive guide to ethical data use.

- *The Ethics of AI:* https://aiethicsjournal.org/—A journal exploring the ethical implications of AI technology.
- The Algorithmic Justice League: https://www.ajl.org/—Organization focused on combating bias in AI systems.
- OpenAI's Ethics Policy: https://openai.com/safety/—OpenAI's approach to ethical AI development.
- Stanford HAI: https://hai.stanford.edu/—The university's Human-Centered AI Institute, providing research and resources on ethical AI.
- AI4Good: https://ai4good.org/—A platform dedicated to using AI for social good, providing resources and case studies.
- AI Now Institute: https://ainowinstitute.org/—Research institute examining the social implications of AI.

Part VII

AI Across Missions: Innovating for Philanthropy, Social Enterprise, and Higher Education

"The reality is that being unprepared is a choice. The benefits come when we see AI as a tool, not a terror."

—Anita Nielsen, president, LDK Advisory Services

AI isn't just well positioned to support nonprofits—it's a transformative force for all mission-led organizations. ***From philanthropic foundations to social enterprises and universities, AI offers unprecedented opportunities to amplify impact, streamline operations, and innovate solutions to complex challenges.*** These organizations share a common goal of driving positive change, but their needs and strategies often require tailored approaches to harness AI effectively.

The adoption of AI in mission-led sectors is reshaping how these organizations operate and collaborate. Whether it's enabling precision in grantmaking, driving innovation in socially conscious enterprises, or deepening alumni engagement in higher education, AI is opening new frontiers. But ***with great potential comes the responsibility to adopt these technologies ethically and equitably, ensuring they align with the values and missions of the organizations they serve.***

Part VII explores how AI is transforming the broader landscape of mission-led organizations. We begin with "Foundations and Philanthropy," examining how AI tools are redefining grantmaking and funding strategies. With the ability to analyze vast datasets and identify trends, AI helps foundations allocate resources more strategically, efficiently, and equitably. The "Best Practices in Funding Nonprofit Technology" inset offers guidance for funders to support sustainable technology adoption in the organizations they serve.

Next, "Social Enterprises and Mission-Driven Companies" highlights how AI can enhance operations and amplify social impact in the private sector. From optimizing supply chains to personalizing customer experiences, mission-driven companies are integrating AI to balance purpose and profit. This chapter also explores how AI can help these organizations measure and communicate their impact to stakeholders, fostering trust and accountability.

Finally, "Higher Education" delves into the transformative role of AI in academia. Universities and colleges are harnessing AI to improve learning outcomes, streamline administrative processes, support fundraising, and enhance research capabilities. This chapter also addresses the ethical considerations of AI in education, emphasizing the importance of inclusivity and accessibility in its implementation.

Each chapter provides actionable insights and concrete tactics and strategies designed to help mission-led organizations navigate the opportunities and challenges of AI. By integrating these tools thoughtfully, your organization can not only enhance its own impact but also inspire broader societal change, helping to create a better future for all.

Chapter 31

Foundations and Philanthropy

Based on insights from an interview with Jean Westrick.

While this book primarily targets nonprofits, almost all the strategies and tools presented apply equally to foundations and philanthropic organizations. Many funders also fundraise and execute programs to amplify impact, and all mission-led organizations are concerned with marketing and community engagement, as well as streamlining back-office operations. The same AI capabilities that empower nonprofits to unlock operational efficiencies and expand their reach can help funders make data-driven decisions and advance philanthropic goals. Foundations, like nonprofits, are looking to change the world for the better, and **AI offers you powerful tools to enhance grantmaking strategies, assess impact, and foster stronger connections with grantees and stakeholders.**

That said, foundations and philanthropy operate differently from nonprofits, with unique priorities and operational models. Unlike nonprofits, which often focus on direct service delivery, foundations primarily serve as facilitators and enablers, allocating resources to advance systemic change. This distinction influences how funders can best harness AI: **from improving grant application processes and predicting funding gaps, to identifying trends and measuring impact across grantee portfolios.** This chapter explores these unique applications of AI for funders, building on the core strategies from this book while addressing their distinct roles and responsibilities in driving social innovation.

Critical Skills and Competencies

Get into the AI Conversation

AI is transforming industries, and philanthropy is no exception. To harness AI effectively, you need to be part of the conversation. This involves more than just knowing the buzzwords; it means diving deep into how AI can serve your specific needs. **Start by educating yourself and your team about AI's potential and limitations.** Sign up to attend conferences like TAG (https://www.tagtech.org), Council on Foundations (https://cof.org), and NTC (https://www.nten.org/ntc); read articles in industry publications like those found in *Stanford Social Innovation Review* (https://ssir.org) and *The Chronicle of Philanthropy* (https://www.philanthropy.com); and engage in webinars like those offered via Lenovo Foundation (https://videos.emea.lenovo.com), Resilia (https://www.resilia.com), and NetHope (https://nethope.org) to learn about AI's emerging role in philanthropy, social impact, and the nonprofit sector. By fostering a culture of learning, you'll be better equipped to identify opportunities where AI can add value.

Be sure to subscribe to influential AI newsletters and join AI-focused online communities, such as those convened by TAG and CoF, as well as dedicated forums like the AI for Good Global Community (https://aiforgood.itu.int). Keep that saw sharp by maintaining a focus on your professional development!

Bring Tech out of the Shadows: Produce a Policy

Shadow tech—tools and software used by staff without formal approval—can lead to inefficiencies, inconsistencies, and security risks. To address this, **create a comprehensive AI policy that sets clear guardrails for responsible use and provides guidance on mitigating risks like bias and misuse.** This policy should outline approved AI tools, establish data security protocols, and clarify how tools will be trained, tested, and monitored to align with your organization's ethical standards.

Ownership is key to effective AI adoption. **Involve cross-functional teams—such as program officers, IT staff, and legal advisors—in developing and implementing the policy to ensure diverse perspectives are reflected.** Include an AI tool registry where staff can report tool use and request approvals, fostering transparency and ensuring alignment with organizational goals. Regularly review and update the policy to keep pace with technological advancements and evolving needs.

Finally, prioritize building awareness and skills across your organization through training sessions and workshops. ***Equip staff with the knowledge to use AI responsibly and create feedback loops for continuous improvement.*** By treating your AI policy as a living document and embedding cross-functional collaboration, you can mitigate risks, build trust, and maximize the impact of AI across your operations.

Develop an AI Policy for Grantees and Grant Seekers

As you increasingly embrace AI to enhance the impact of your giving, it's crucial to establish a clear policy outlining how grantees and grant seekers should use AI for data sharing, reporting, and other operational requirements. This policy serves as a guidepost, ensuring transparency, alignment, and ethical use of AI across all funded projects. ***Begin by setting expectations for data sharing: outline the types of data grantees must provide, the formats required for AI analysis, and how this data will be used to inform funding decisions or measure impact.*** Include provisions for protecting sensitive information, ensuring compliance with privacy regulations like General Data Protection Regulation (GDPR) or the Health Insurance Portability and Accountability Act (HIPAA). Encouraging or requiring the use of AI tools for data collection and reporting can also streamline processes, but it's important to provide grantees with access to low-cost or open-source tools and training to ensure equitable adoption.

When it comes to the use of AI-generated content in grant applications and reports, as a funder you need to carefully balance the potential benefits with the need for authenticity and transparency. AI tools like ChatGPT or Jasper (https://www.jasper.ai) help grant seekers draft clearer, more polished proposals and enable them to generate structured reports efficiently, which can be particularly valuable for smaller organizations with limited resources. However, you must give deep thought to setting clear guidelines designed to ensure AI-generated content does not undermine the authenticity or depth of the application or report. ***Consider allowing the use of AI for formatting, summarizing, or enhancing clarity, but requiring applicants and grantees to clearly disclose when AI tools have been used.*** This maintains transparency and enables you to assess the originality and mission alignment of the content. Conversely, you may choose to prohibit AI use for specific sections of an application, such as narratives detailing organizational vision or project impact, to ensure these reflect genuine insights and leadership perspectives. By setting clear parameters, you can embrace the efficiency of AI tools while preserving the integrity of the grantmaking process.

For reporting requirements, ***specify how AI-generated insights should be integrated into regular updates and evaluations.*** For example, you may want to request grantees include dashboards or automated reports generated by AI tools to provide real-time visibility into project outcomes. It's equally important to address the ethical use of AI, emphasizing the need to mitigate biases and ensure inclusivity in the application of these tools. By creating a robust and flexible AI policy, you will foster a collaborative environment where AI is a tool for empowerment, not a burden, helping grantees and applicants use technology responsibly while maximizing their impact.

Communicate Clearly

Transparency is key when it comes to AI implementation, especially with your grantees and applicants. ***Share your AI policies and especially how they affect the grantmaking process.*** This ensures grantees understand your expectations and are better able to align their efforts accordingly. Clear communication builds trust and fosters a collaborative environment.

Provide detailed guidelines on data sharing, reporting requirements, and the use of AI tools, including your own internal practices as well as any expectations you have of grantees and grant seekers. This not only builds trust but also helps grantees leverage AI effectively within their own organizations. Regularly update these policies and maintain open lines of communication to address any questions or concerns that may arise. By fostering an environment of transparency and collaboration, you enable grantees to leverage AI effectively and enhance their impact.

Build a Strong Data Culture

The success of your AI initiatives hinges on the quality and accessibility of your data. Commit to building a strong data culture by investing in the resources needed to manage and maintain your data assets. ***Start by auditing your current data***

practices to identify gaps and opportunities. Train staff on data governance principles, emphasizing the importance of accuracy, consistency, and security. By nurturing a data-driven mindset, your organization will be well positioned to leverage AI tools effectively, transforming raw data into actionable insights that drive impact.

Offer Technical Assistance Grants

Supporting your grantees in their AI journey can significantly amplify the overall impact of your philanthropic efforts. ***Consider offering capacity-building or technical assistance (TA) grants to help grantees adopt and integrate AI tools into their operations.*** These grants can cover critical expenses such as training staff to use AI responsibly, acquiring software licenses, and hiring consulting services to guide implementation. By providing this type of financial support, you remove a common barrier to technology adoption—cost—while fostering a culture of innovation. TA grants empower grantees to experiment with AI tools, optimize their workflows, and drive greater efficiency and impact in service of their missions. Technical assistance funding isn't just about financial support—it's about ensuring grantees have the resources and confidence to use these tools effectively and ethically.

To maximize the effectiveness of TA grants, ***consider offering additional nonmonetary support, such as facilitating access to trusted AI vendors or providing workshops on responsible AI practices.*** Encourage grantees to focus on specific, high-impact areas where AI can make an immediate difference, such as automating routine tasks, expanding fundraising efforts, improving data analysis, or personalizing beneficiary outreach. Establish clear metrics for success—such as improved operational efficiency or increased program reach—and collaborate with grantees to measure results. As a funder, you're also in a great position to ***incentivize knowledge sharing among grantees by creating peer learning networks where nonprofits can exchange insights and lessons learned from their AI experiences.*** These practical strategies not only enhance the value of TA grants but also contribute to a broader ecosystem of innovation, ensuring that your grantees—and by extension, your philanthropic goals—thrive in an increasingly AI-driven world.

Automate Repetitive Processes

As detailed in many other chapters throughout this book, AI excels at handling repetitive tasks, freeing up human resources for more strategic work. **Consider automating processes like note-taking during board meetings, scheduling, and data entry.** By doing so, you reduce the risk of human error and increase efficiency. Automation enables your team to focus on high-impact activities that drive your mission forward.

Pitfalls and Solutions
Insufficient Consideration of Ethical Risks

Recognizing the inherent power dynamic associated with being a funder, philanthropic organizations must approach AI adoption with a strong understanding of its ethical implications to prevent unintended harm. AI tools can perpetuate biases if trained on unrepresentative or skewed data, leading to decisions that disproportionately disadvantage certain populations. For example, **an AI model used to evaluate grant applications might inadvertently favor organizations with more polished proposals, potentially excluding grassroots organizations that serve marginalized communities.** To address this, prioritize transparency by requiring vendors to disclose how their AI systems are trained and tested for bias. Collaborating with experts in AI ethics can also help identify potential risks and design safeguards to mitigate them.

In addition, it's critical you emphasize data privacy and security when deploying AI tools. Many AI applications require sensitive information to function effectively, such as program performance metrics or beneficiary data. Foundations should establish strict protocols for data handling, ensuring compliance with regulations like GDPR or HIPAA. Furthermore, **engaging grantees in conversations about data ethics and building their capacity to protect sensitive information fosters trust and promotes responsible AI use.** By embedding ethical considerations into every stage of AI adoption, funders can protect their stakeholders while maintaining the integrity of their philanthropic mission.

Not Adapting Your Grantmaking Processes

AI adoption often requires more iterative and flexible approaches than traditional grantmaking processes allow. Funders who maintain rigid grant timelines or reporting structures may unintentionally stifle innovation by discouraging experimentation. To address this, ***consider incorporating more adaptive grantmaking models, such as providing milestone-based funding or offering flexible reporting requirements.*** This approach enables grantees to test AI solutions, learn from early results, and refine their strategies without being penalized for deviations from initial plans.

Additionally, as a funder you can play a proactive role by integrating AI into your own grantmaking processes. ***AI tools can streamline application review by identifying trends, scoring proposals, or analyzing large volumes of data.*** However, make sure these tools are calibrated to prioritize mission alignment and equity over surface-level metrics. Using AI to assess impact potential requires human oversight to interpret findings and avoid reinforcing systemic biases. By aligning grantmaking processes with the dynamic nature of AI projects, you can create an environment that encourages innovation while maintaining accountability.

Lack of Stakeholder Buy-In

Resistance from key stakeholders, such as boards, staff, or grantees, can hinder the adoption of AI tools in philanthropy. Many stakeholders may view AI as overly complex, irrelevant to their mission, or even as a threat to their roles. To overcome this resistance, prioritize education and communication. ***Hosting workshops, webinars, or one-on-one discussions about the potential benefits and limitations of AI can demystify the technology and build trust.*** It's also essential to emphasize how AI can complement, rather than replace, human decision-making, enhancing the ability of teams to focus on high-impact activities.

It's also helpful to engage stakeholders in the planning and implementation phases of AI projects. By soliciting input from staff, grantees, and community members, you can identify concerns early and ensure that solutions align with on-the-ground realities. ***Highlighting successful case studies or pilot projects will help demonstrate the value of AI in achieving shared goals.*** A collaborative approach not only secures buy-in but also ensures that AI tools are designed and deployed in ways that reflect the diverse perspectives and needs of those involved.

Road Map to the Future

The coming years are poised to bring transformative advancements in AI, reshaping the landscape of philanthropy, grantmaking, and social impact. One significant trend will be the mainstreaming of predictive analytics, allowing funders like you to anticipate societal needs and allocate resources more proactively. AI tools will become increasingly adept at identifying emerging challenges—such as shifts in community health, climate resilience, or economic inequality—by analyzing complex data patterns across diverse sources. This capability will **enable foundations to shift from reactive to anticipatory grantmaking, positioning them to make a more timely and strategic impact.** Additionally, natural language processing (NLP) will further enhance how funders engage with grantees and stakeholders, enabling faster and more inclusive communication through AI-driven language translation, sentiment analysis, and automated proposal reviews.

The future will be communal. Collaboration with funders, grantees, and AI experts will foster innovation hubs and shared learning networks, accelerating the spread of AI-driven solutions tailored to social challenges. Moreover, **advancements in democratized AI—tools that are low cost and user-friendly—will empower smaller organizations to adopt AI technologies, leveling the playing field and amplifying grassroots impact.** By embracing these trends, the philanthropic sector has an unprecedented opportunity to harness AI as a force multiplier for creating systemic change and driving meaningful, equitable outcomes across society.

Dos and Don'ts

Do

- Educate yourself and your team about AI's potential and limitations by participating in conferences and webinars, and regularly reading industry publications and newsletters
- Develop a clear policy to guide your organization's AI use, including a tool registry clarifying which platforms are allowed and where staff can submit requests for new tools, and provide orientation and ongoing training

- Produce a policy for grant seekers and applicants spelling out exactly how they are allowed to use AI in grant applications and reports, and which practices are not allowed
- Offer capacity-building and technical assistance grants to help grantees adopt and integrate AI tools into their operations, in addition to nonmonetary support, including access to AI vendors and workshops
- Embrace adaptive grantmaking models like milestone-based funding or flexible reporting requirements

Don't

- Assume you have to use standard AI tools; consider developing something to suit your custom needs by enlisting the help of tech experts or university partners
- Neglect to engage your grantees in conversations about data ethics and security to foster trust and promote responsible AI use
- Skimp on engaging all your stakeholders to build excitement for AI adoption through conversations and by sharing the results of case studies and pilot projects in achieving shared goals

Conclusion

Incorporating AI into your philanthropic operations can be transformative, driving efficiency and enhancing mission delivery. ***By getting into the AI conversation, developing clear policies, automating repetitive tasks, embracing TA grants, and being open-minded about how to best support your grantees, you can unlock the full potential of AI.*** Remember, the key is to view technology as an enabler of your mission and invest accordingly. With the right approach, AI can help you create a more significant impact and drive innovation in the nonprofit sector.

Interviewee Bio

Jean Westrick is a thought leader at the intersection of AI and philanthropy, with a passion for leveraging emerging technologies to drive social impact. With extensive experience in guiding foundations and nonprofits through the complexities of adopting innovative tools, Jean specializes in helping mission-driven organizations harness AI to optimize grantmaking, improve impact measurement, and enhance stakeholder engagement. As the executive director of TAG and a strategic advisor and advocate for ethical AI practices, she has worked with numerous philanthropic organizations to align technology solutions with their values and goals. https://www.linkedin.com/in/jeanwestrick/

Resource Review

- Technology Association of Grantmakers (TAG): https://www.tagtech.org/ai—Offers resources such as case studies, webinars, insightful reports (https://www.tagtech.org/2023/08/new-publication-highlights-six-emerging-practices-in-funding-nonprofit-technology/) and the "Responsible AI Adoption Framework in Philanthropy," which guides grantmakers in aligning AI tools with their core values to maximize social impact, plus an interactive forum for funders to collaborate and exchange ideas on leveraging AI and other emerging technologies for social good.

- Council on Foundations: https://cof.org/—Offers webinars such as "Artificial Intelligence in Philanthropy: Trends and Responsible Use," exploring AI's potential and ethical considerations in the social sector, and they also have an online community (https://exchange.cof.org) that connects funders to share knowledge, resources, and discussions on integrating AI into grantmaking and impact measurement.

- Stanford Center on Philanthropy and Civil Society: https://pacscenter.stanford.edu—Offers cutting-edge research and resources on how technology, including AI, is reshaping philanthropy and the nonprofit sector.

- The Center for Effective Philanthropy: https://cep.org—Provides data-driven insights and reports to help funders understand how AI can enhance their grantmaking effectiveness and impact evaluation.

- Grantmakers for Effective Organizations: https://www.geofunders.org—Offers practical guidance and collaborative opportunities for integrating AI tools into funding strategies to achieve better outcomes.

- Resilia: https://www.resilia.com/—Offer webinars, like "How AI Is Transforming Philanthropy," that delve into AI's potential to enhance grantmaking and nonprofit operations, offering practical guidance for implementation.
- AI for Good Global Community: https://aiforgood.itu.int—A global platform bringing together funders, researchers, and practitioners to discuss AI-driven solutions for social impact, including its use in philanthropy.
- *Alliance Magazine*: https://www.alliancemagazine.org—Covers global philanthropy trends, including the role of AI in transforming grantmaking, impact measurement, and stakeholder engagement.
- Future of Good: https://futureofgood.co—A digital publication that explores how emerging technologies like AI are shaping the future of philanthropy and social innovation.
- MIT Solve: https://solve.mit.edu—A marketplace for social impact innovation that highlights AI-powered solutions funders can support to tackle global challenges effectively.
- Nonprofit Technology Conference (NTC): https://www.nten.org/ntc/—An annual conference that features sessions on AI and other emerging technologies.

Chapter 31.1

Best Practices in Funding Nonprofit Technology

Based on insights from an interview with Chantal "Coco" Forster.

As a philanthropist or foundation executive, you understand the critical enabling role technology plays in expanding the impact and efficiency of nonprofit organizations. However, funding technology can sometimes feel like navigating uncharted waters, especially if you're concerned you may be enabling groups to employ shiny new tools without the proper forethought. What's the best way to support mission-led organizations in their tech journeys? How can we ensure our investments lead to sustainable improvements? *Here's some practical advice on how to effectively, responsibly fund nonprofit technology initiatives, designed to help ensure your contributions are used to their fullest potential.*

Framework for Funding Nonprofit Technology

Fund Tool Adoption

When it comes to technology, the initial investment in tools and software is just the beginning. Here's how to strategically support these costs:

- **Integrate tech funding into general support:** Allocate a percentage of each grant specifically for technology needs and associated costs. This approach acknowledges that tech is as essential as other operational costs and ensures that nonprofits have the resources to adopt necessary tools.

- **Provide dedicated tech grants:** Offering additional, tech-focused grants to organizations you already support can unlock exciting possibilities to expand mission fulfillment and vastly improve workflows when properly implemented.

- **Collaborate with other funders:** Pooling resources with other foundations and donors can create larger funding opportunities for tech initiatives, allowing for more comprehensive support and shared benefits across multiple nonprofits.
- **Require a strategy:** Many chapters throughout this book share tips for nonprofit leaders looking to adopt AI. From a funder or donor's perspective, you don't need to worry about most of this, but you should ***ensure any organization you consider supporting with technology implementation has a plan in place to direct their efforts.*** Ask to see their plan, and encourage them to include the following elements:
  - Their *strategic objectives* as an organization, thereby ensuring alignment between any new tools and their core goals
  - The pain points and *use cases* they aim to solve with new tools—how will technology be applied to create efficiencies and increase impact?
  - *Timelines, milestones, and key performance indicators* (KPIs) that lay out a blueprint for impact with predetermined metrics to gauge progress
  - A conservative *budget* that speaks to all direct costs and ensures resources are allocated to orientation, ongoing training, and maintenance over time

If a group you'd like to support doesn't have a strategy or plan with at least these key elements in place, consider providing such help, as outlined in the next tip.

Offer Strategic Support

Many nonprofits report that they lack the internal expertise to develop and implement effective tech strategies. Here's how you can help bridge that gap:

- **Fund comprehensive tech assessments:** ***Support nonprofits in conducting thorough tech assessments or audits to help ensure they understand their current capabilities and future needs*** and are realistic about what's involved when it comes to integrating new tools. This will likely include helping them take a close look at strategies for data management and cybersecurity and, most crucially, developing a strategic road map for tech adoption.

- **Provide access to fractional chief technology officer services:** Consider funding part-time tech strategists who assist multiple nonprofits. These professionals can offer invaluable guidance on tech planning and implementation without the cost of a full-time hire.

Invest in Capacity Building and Training

Technology is only as good as the people who use it. *Investing in capacity building ensures that nonprofits are well positioned to effectively leverage their tech tools*:

- **Support cohort-based learning:** Programs that bring together nonprofits at similar stages of tech adoption are a great forum for fostering peer learning and shared experiences. These *communities of practice provide a supportive environment for nonprofits to grow their tech capabilities, so invite your grantees to propose programs for funding and encourage them to consider participation* in NTEN's Nonprofit Tech Readiness program (https://www.nten.org/learn/nonprofit-tech-readiness?), Fast Forward's Tech Accelerator (https://www.ffwd.org/), the McGovern Foundation's year-long program (https://www.mcgovern.org/), Okta's Nonprofit Technology Fellowship (https://www.okta.com/), or similar programs. Just make sure you're always simply offering suggestions and not thrusting expectations onto their full plates.

- **Fund local capacity building initiatives:** Programs like the Kaufman Foundation's TechConnectKC assess local nonprofits' tech needs and provide tailored training programs, often to in-person cohorts. Whether you support participation in programs like this or other orientation and ongoing training expenses, *ensuring that staff are well trained in using new technologies is crucial for maximizing your investment's impact.* Whatever your grantee's plan is for ensuring both initial and ongoing professional development, just make sure they have one!

As funders and donors, our goal is to enable nonprofits to achieve their missions more effectively. *By funding the adoption of technology tools, providing access to strategic support, and investing in capacity building and training, you will*

ensure your contributions lead to the impact you and your grantees seek. Let's continue to support nonprofits in their tech journeys, enabling them to harness the power of technology to drive change and make a lasting difference in the communities they serve.

Interviewee Bio

Chantal "Coco" Forster is a sociotechnical advisor and nonprofit executive with over 20 years of experience navigating the intersection of technology and society. As the coauthor of the Responsible AI Adoption Framework for Philanthropy and former executive director of the Technology Association of Grantmakers (TAG), Chantal brings a nuanced understanding of how technology can drive systemic impact while aligning with the public interest. She currently serves as the AI strategy resident at the Annenberg Foundation, where she spearheads initiatives to integrate AI into philanthropic endeavors, and started her career in predictive AI with SPSS. Chantal also advises philanthropic organizations on the ethical and strategic use of AI. https://www.linkedin.com/in/chantalforster/

Chapter 32

Social Enterprises and Mission-Driven Companies

Based on insights from an interview with Barbara Clarke.

While this book was written specifically for nonprofit leaders, **95% of the strategies, frameworks, insights, tools, and practical applications detailed throughout the chapters of this book are directly relevant to social enterprises.** Why? Because at their core, both nonprofits and social enterprises share a commitment to advancing a mission that creates social, environmental, or community impact. The same AI-driven techniques that can revolutionize nonprofit fundraising, marketing and community engagement, program delivery, and back-office operations are just as transformative for social enterprises looking to grow revenue streams, engage stakeholders, and optimize operations in service of their missions.

That said, social enterprises are distinct from nonprofits in important ways. Unlike nonprofits, which primarily rely on grants, donations, and other philanthropic funding, social enterprises typically operate with a blended revenue model that integrates earned income alongside philanthropic or impact investments. **The dual focus on mission and profit presents unique challenges and opportunities when implementing AI solutions,** from enhancing customer experience to scaling social impact. This chapter explores how AI can specifically support the unique needs of social enterprises, building on the foundational strategies in this book while addressing the nuances of operating in both mission-driven and market-driven spaces.

Critical Skills and Competencies

Investor, Stakeholder, and Employee Engagement

In today's digital-first world, if your social enterprise is looking to thrive, you need to master the art of using AI to create meaningful connections across their entire ecosystem. This means ***leveraging natural language processing (NLP) to analyze stakeholder sentiment, using predictive analytics to anticipate employee needs, and employing intelligent automation for personalized investor communications.*** The good news is that all of these are discussed in detail in other chapters found right in this book! Your goal here is to build robust feedback loops that combine AI-driven insights with human touch points, creating a dynamic engagement strategy that helps retain top talent while keeping stakeholders aligned with your organization's mission and impact goals.

Optimize Social Impact Supply Chains

The next frontier in ethical business operations lies in AI-powered supply chain optimization that prioritizes both social impact and operational efficiency. The opportunity here is for you to ***implement Machine Learning (ML) algorithms to track and trace products from source to destination, ensuring ethical sourcing while reducing waste and environmental impact.*** This involves using predictive analytics to optimize your inventory levels and distribution routes while maintaining transparency. Look to develop competencies in real-time supply chain monitoring systems that can flag potential ethical issues while suggesting alternative solutions that maintain both efficiency and impact integrity. Depending on your needs and goals, consider platforms like Full Harvest (https://www.fullharvest.com) to help facilitate these efforts.

Customer Segmentation

AI can enable your social enterprises to go beyond traditional demographic segmentation to understand the complex motivations driving your impact-oriented customers. This means ***developing powerful AI models that can analyze behavioral patterns, social values, and impact preferences to create nuanced customer personas.*** To unlock this ability, your organization needs to be able to use ML to identify micro-segments within your customer base, understanding not just your purchasing patterns but also your alignment with various social causes and impact goals. This deeper understanding enables more targeted impact messaging and product development that resonates with each segment's unique combination of social consciousness and practical needs.

In addition to external customer data, many social enterprises and nongovernmental organizations are sitting on massive, proprietary datasets that are often underleveraged. Whether it's detailed information about patient populations, locations of endangered wildlife, or records of community engagement, these unique datasets hold untapped potential. AI can help you unlock entirely new insights from this data, identifying patterns and opportunities you may have never considered. ***By looking inward and exploring how to extract value from your own data, you can expand your impact, develop innovative strategies, and create entirely new pathways to serve your mission while simultaneously gaining a competitive advantage in the marketplace.***

Impact Measurement and Reporting

The future of assessing and compellingly conveying your impact involves leveraging sophisticated AI tools that process both quantitative and qualitative data to tell a comprehensive impact story. To do this, your organization will need to ***develop capabilities in NLP to analyze beneficiary feedback, computer vision to process field documentation, and advanced analytics to track complex impact metrics in real time.*** The key competency lies in building integrated systems that automatically collect, analyze, and visualize impact data while maintaining the nuanced understanding necessary for meaningful impact reporting.

Predictive Analytics

As mentioned, AI can provide your social enterprise with a bit of a crystal ball. Once you gain fluency in ML, you can develop learning models that can identify growth opportunities while maintaining mission alignment. This includes ***implementing adaptive pricing models that balance accessibility with sustainability, using AI to forecast market trends in social impact sectors, and leveraging predictive analytics to optimize resource allocation across various impact initiatives and revenue streams.***

Real-Time Risk Assessment and Mitigation

Long-term success and impact in social enterprise requires an ability to protect both your mission and operational stability. AI can help with this by enabling you to ***develop systems that continuously monitor various risk factors—from reputation management to impact dilution risks—using NLP to scan for emerging threats and ML to predict potential challenges.*** Focus your efforts on mastering the integration of AI-driven early warning systems with human expertise, creating a balanced approach to risk management that can respond rapidly to threats while maintaining alignment with social impact goals.

Pitfalls and Solutions

Balancing Scale and Personalization

One of the greatest promises of AI is its ability to help social enterprises like yours scale their operations quickly and efficiently. However, this scale often comes at the expense of personalization, which is critical to mission-driven work. Automated customer communication can feel impersonal, undermining the trust and emotional connection your stakeholders have with your brand. ***If your AI-driven engagement strategies lack a human touch, you risk alienating key customers, investors, or beneficiaries who value the personal connection with your mission.*** To avoid this, adopt a human-in-the-loop (HITL) approach in which AI supports but doesn't replace human interaction. Use AI tools to handle repetitive tasks, freeing up your team to focus on building authentic relationships. Finally, ensure personalization is baked into your AI processes by integrating robust data about your customers' values, preferences, and behaviors, allowing the technology to deliver customized, mission-aligned experiences at scale.

Misalignment Between Mission and AI-Driven Insights

AI tools are often designed to optimize for metrics like efficiency, revenue, or growth—objectives that may not always align with your mission-driven priorities. For instance, a recommendation system might suggest cost-cutting measures that reduce the quality of services or products designed to deliver social impact. This tension can dilute your mission and erode stakeholder trust, so it's critical that you set clear ethical guidelines and guardrails for your AI systems. ***Train AI models with datasets that include mission-relevant variables, ensuring that recommendations consider both social impact and financial metrics.*** Regularly review AI outputs with your leadership team to ensure alignment with your organization's values and strategic goals.

Overreliance on Generic AI Models

Off-the-shelf AI tools are designed for broad applications and may not fully reflect the unique needs and complexities of your social enterprise. A generic AI tool may misinterpret customer motivations or fail to incorporate the nuances of your impact objectives, leading to inaccurate insights or missed opportunities. To avoid this pitfall, ***invest in customizing your AI tools to reflect your organization's specific goals and context, and consider adopting custom tools that have helped others in your field.*** Work with vendors or data scientists to tailor algorithms, ensuring they account for your unique business model and mission or to select the right platform to support your needs.

Misjudging AI Return on Investment

Unlike traditional businesses, social enterprises must balance financial sustainability with social impact, making it challenging to assess the return on investment (ROI) of AI initiatives. ***A purely financial evaluation of AI tools might overlook their value in advancing your mission or improving stakeholder engagement.*** Conversely, focusing solely on impact metrics may lead to investments that strain your budget. To avoid this, adopt a holistic framework for evaluating AI's ROI that includes both financial and social outcomes. ***Ensure you calculate cost savings from automation alongside increases in impact,*** such as the number of beneficiaries served or environmental benefits achieved. Monitor performance metrics over time to ensure your AI investments are delivering both tangible and intangible value.

Road Map to the Future

In the coming years, social enterprises are poised to experience transformative shifts in how AI supports mission-driven work. ***One key development will be the rise of agential AI, enabling systems to execute tasks autonomously based on***

predefined objectives. For social enterprises, this will likely mean AI-driven tools that not only predict market trends but also proactively adjust pricing, inventory, or outreach strategies to align with both impact and revenue goals. These capabilities will reduce manual effort and improve operational agility, enabling leaders to focus on higher-level strategy. Additionally, ***advances in AI's ability to process unstructured data—such as social media content, emails, video, and audio—will enable deeper insights into stakeholder sentiment, community needs, and social impact outcomes.*** This will help mission-led organizations measure and report on their impact with greater granularity, improving transparency and stakeholder trust.

To prepare for these changes, you should prioritize building internal capacity and systems to fully leverage these emerging technologies. ***Ensure your social enterprise invests in scalable data infrastructure that can handle the increasing complexity of unstructured data, as well as fostering a culture of innovation where teams are trained to adapt and experiment with new tools.*** And be sure to keep an eye on the integration of AI into existing fundraising and operational tools, such as donor management systems and impact measurement platforms. By adopting solutions that seamlessly integrate AI with your current workflows, your social enterprise will maximize efficiency while maintaining alignment with your mission.

Dos and Don'ts

Do

- Leverage AI to enhance customer segmentation by analyzing behavioral patterns and social values, creating more personalized and mission-aligned engagement strategies
- Establish clear ethical guidelines and accountability frameworks to ensure AI tools align with your social enterprise's mission and equity goals
- Invest in scalable data systems and infrastructure to prepare for the complexities of processing unstructured data, such as video and audio, in future AI applications
- Pilot new AI tools in small-scale initiatives to refine processes and test functionality before committing to full-scale implementation
- Integrate AI tools into existing workflows, ensuring seamless compatibility with your current systems to maximize efficiency and minimize disruption

Don't

- Rely on generic, off-the-shelf AI tools without tailoring them to reflect the unique needs, values, and goals of your social enterprise
- Deploy AI systems without robust oversight mechanisms, such as an HITL approach, to ensure accuracy and accountability
- Overlook the ethical risks of AI, such as biases in data or algorithms, which can lead to inequitable outcomes and erode stakeholder trust
- Assume AI adoption is a one-time effort; neglecting regular updates and reviews will leave your tools outdated and less effective over time
- Underestimate the importance of staff training and capacity building, which are essential for successful AI adoption and integration into your organization

Conclusion

AI offers your social enterprise unparalleled opportunities to scale its operations, enhance impact, and deepen stakeholder engagement. ***By leveraging tools for customer segmentation, supply chain optimization, predictive analytics, and impact reporting, your mission-driven organization can more effectively achieve both its financial and social objectives.*** However, success in adopting AI requires thoughtful planning, ethical oversight, and ongoing investment in both technology and team development.

As we move into a future defined by advancements in agential AI, unstructured data processing, and seamless tool integration, mission-led leaders must stay agile and forward-thinking. ***Build a strong foundation now by investing in scalable infrastructure, piloting new technologies, and fostering a culture of continuous learning and innovation.*** By embracing AI as a transformative ally while staying true to your mission, your social enterprise can achieve lasting impact and set a new standard for how technology can serve both purpose and profit.

Interviewee Bio

Barbara Clarke is the board chair of The Impact Seat Foundation and author of *Build Your Board, Build Your Business*. With decades of experience in board development and inclusive entrepreneurship, Barbara has helped countless organizations build effective boards and create sustainable, mission-driven businesses. Her work focuses on creating more diverse and inclusive entrepreneurial ecosystems, and she brings deep expertise in helping organizations leverage technology and AI while maintaining their commitment to social impact. https://www.linkedin.com/in/barbaraeclarke/

Resource Review

- Full Harvest: https://www.fullharvest.com—Use this platform to optimize your social impact supply chains by leveraging AI to reduce food waste, improve sustainability, and enhance efficiency in sourcing and distributing surplus or imperfect produce.
- Unreasonable Group: https://unreasonablegroup.com/—Accelerates growth-stage companies solving global challenges through Fortune 500 partnerships, mentorship, and investment opportunities.
- B-Lab's B Corp Growth Program: https://www.bcorporation.net/—Supports companies pursuing B Corp certification with business model refinement and impact metrics development.
- Conscious Venture Lab: https://consciousventurelab.com/—16-week accelerator offering $100K seed investment for purpose-driven technology companies.
- Techstars Impact: https://www.techstars.com/blog/social-impact—13-week program providing $120K investment for technology companies solving social and environmental problems.
- Microsoft for Startups Climate Innovation: https://www.microsoft.com/startups—Provides Azure credits and technical support for climate tech and sustainability startups.
- Clean Tech Open: https://cleantechopen.org/—Largest clean-tech accelerator offering prize money up to $50K for clean energy and sustainability companies.

- FoodFutureCo: https://foodfuture.co—Six-month accelerator program offering $50K investment for innovative food and agriculture startups focused on creating sustainable food systems and solving critical challenges across the food value chain.
- Village Capital: https://vilcap.com/—Offers peer-selected investment for fintech, health, and sustainability startups with unique peer-review model.
- Acumen Fund Fellows: https://acumen.org/—Provides patient capital and leadership development for companies tackling poverty through market-based solutions.
- StartingBloc: https://startingbloc.org/—Fellowship program for early-stage social entrepreneurs with sliding scale tuition and strong alumni network.
- Impact Engine: https://theimpactengine.com/—Pre-seed impact investor offering $100–$250K investments with strong corporate partnerships.

Chapter 33

Higher Education

Contributed by Darian Rodriguez Heyman and Cheryl Contee.

Just as with most industries, in the dynamic world of higher education, staying ahead of technological trends is crucial. While this book focuses on nonprofits, the principles and tools it outlines are highly relevant to colleges, universities, and other higher education institutions. As in the nonprofit sector, ***AI presents paradigm-shifting opportunities in higher education, offering unique opportunities for institutions to enhance their operations and engagement strategies.***

The same tools that empower nonprofits to optimize operations and expand their impact can help colleges and universities address their many evolving challenges. However, ***higher education institutions differ from traditional nonprofits in key ways, particularly in their scale, structure, and stakeholder dynamics.*** Universities and colleges often manage multifaceted operations that include academic programming, research initiatives, student services, and extensive physical infrastructure, all while serving a highly diverse and global population. Additionally, ***higher education institutions must navigate unique pressures such as fluctuating enrollment, accreditation requirements, and increasing competition for funding and prestige.*** This chapter explores how AI can be tailored to address these distinctive challenges, offering actionable strategies for higher education leaders to leverage technology in ways that advance their missions while meeting the specific needs of their institutions.

Critical Skills and Competencies

Enhance Enrollment Management

Enrollment is a cornerstone of financial stability and institutional success for higher education institutions, making effective enrollment management a critical priority. *AI can transform how colleges and universities recruit and engage prospective students by analyzing vast amounts of data to identify patterns and predict enrollment trends.* By leveraging predictive analytics, your institution can tailor recruitment efforts to reach students most likely to enroll, improving efficiency and effectiveness. AI can also enable you to personalize communications, ensuring prospective students receive information that aligns with their interests, preferences, and needs—building a stronger connection from the start.

To implement AI for enrollment management, institutions can adopt platforms like Salesforce Education Cloud (https://www.salesforce.com/education/cloud), Element451 (https://element451.com), or ZeeMee (https://zeemee.com), which specialize in AI-powered recruitment and admissions solutions. These tools can segment audiences, automate outreach campaigns, and provide real-time insights into student engagement. Just *make sure you look at the potential for bias and the ethical implications of any tools before use,* because if you fail to be intentional about this, you can easily perpetuate the status quo. Additionally, using chatbots like Drift (https://www.drift.com) or Tidio (https://www.tidio.com) can enhance prospective student interactions by providing instant answers to questions and directing users to relevant resources, further streamlining the enrollment process. If you adopt any such tools, *be sure to first clean your data so it's updated, accurate, and free of bias, and to invest in training admissions staff so they know how to use these tools effectively* and can integrate AI with your customer relationship management (CRM) systems. As simple as this sounds, lack of training is the number one reason why institutions fail to successfully adopt new technology solutions.

Engage Alumni

Alumni play a vital role in the financial and reputational success of higher education institutions, contributing through gifts, mentorship, and advocacy. *AI enhances alumni engagement by analyzing data to identify giving potential, predict donor behaviors, and personalize outreach efforts.* For example, AI tools can help segment alumni by interests, career paths, or giving history, enabling you to deliver targeted communications that resonate on an individual level. This personalization fosters stronger relationships, making alumni feel more connected and valued.

To maximize AI's impact on alumni engagement, use platforms like Raiser's Edge NXT (https://www.blackbaud.com/products/blackbaud-raisers-edge-nxt) or Graduway (https://www.graduway.com), which offer AI-driven insights for alumni relations and fundraising. *These tools can automate supporter prospecting, track engagement metrics, and recommend the best times or methods for outreach.* Your institution should also consider implementing AI-powered email marketing platforms like HubSpot (https://www.hubspot.com) or Mailchimp (https://mailchimp.com) to send tailored campaigns based on alumni preferences. Establishing feedback loops through surveys or engagement trackers ensures that strategies remain effective and aligned with alumni expectations.

Personalize Learning, Academic Advising, and Career Counseling

AI is revolutionizing how higher education institutions support students by personalizing learning experiences, academic advising, and career services. *Adaptive learning platforms powered by AI tailor educational content and pacing to individual student needs, ensuring students receive the right level of challenge and support to stay engaged and succeed.* These tools enable faculty to focus on fostering deeper understanding and addressing complex questions while AI handles routine personalization. Similarly, next-generation *academic advising tools streamline processes like course scheduling and degree tracking, freeing advisors to provide targeted, human-centered guidance on more intricate academic and personal challenges.* Together, these technologies create a more customized and effective academic experience for students.

The benefits of AI extend beyond academics to career preparation, where tools like Handshake (https://joinhandshake.com) and VMock (https://www.vmock.com) provide personalized job recommendations, résumé feedback, and virtual interview coaching. *By integrating AI into career services, institutions can better align students' skills and interests with market opportunities, preparing them for meaningful post-graduation pathways.* Combining personalized learning, streamlined advising, and tailored career services into a cohesive strategy ensures that students are supported holistically. Platforms such as Knewton Alta (https://www.knewton.com) for learning and Ocelot (https://www.ocelotbot.com) for advising can be seamlessly integrated into institutional workflows, especially when combined with ample training for faculty and staff to ensure these tools are used to their fullest potential. By leveraging AI in these critical areas, institutions empower students to thrive academically, personally, and professionally.

Build AI Literacy and Create Community Across Faculty and Staff

Building AI literacy ensures that faculty and staff can effectively integrate AI tools into their teaching, research, and administrative tasks, driving innovation and improving outcomes across the institution. Professional development programs, workshops, or certifications from platforms like edX (https://www.edx.org), Udemy (https://www.udemy.com), and Coursera (https://www.coursera.org) provide accessible and flexible learning opportunities. *Consider creating interdisciplinary task forces or communities of practice to encourage collaboration on and knowledge sharing of AI applications.* Providing hands-on experiences with AI tools, coupled with real-world examples, will demystify the technology and build confidence among staff, fostering an AI-literate culture that maximizes the potential of these tools.

Equally important to fostering AI literacy is creating a supportive community to navigate the complexities of adoption. Establishing an ecosystem of collaboration helps faculty and staff "build the plane while flying it," providing a sounding board for ideas and feedback as they experiment with new tools and strategies. Engaging peers across the institution ensures shared problem-solving and collective progress in overcoming challenges. *Convene a council or working group dedicated to AI initiatives, bringing together representatives from various departments and levels.* Regular meetings and open communication channels ensure alignment, while diverse perspectives enrich AI projects. By fostering this sense of community, your institution can mitigate resistance to change, build collective buy-in, and create a shared commitment to integrating AI in ways that enhance your mission.

Pitfalls and Solutions

Neglecting Faculty and Staff Buy-In

Resistance to AI adoption is a common hurdle: *concerns about job displacement, lack of understanding, or fears that technology will replace human expertise often undermine progress.* To address this, your institution must prioritize building trust and creating a culture of collaboration in AI adoption. Emphasizing that AI is a tool designed to augment, not replace, human roles is key. As shared throughout this chapter, offering targeted training and professional development opportunities helps faculty and staff develop the skills and confidence to use AI effectively. Additionally, involving them in the planning and implementation phases ensures their insights and concerns are considered, fostering a sense of ownership and reducing resistance. Open communication and showcasing real-world examples of AI enhancing rather than replacing their work can further encourage buy-in.

Difficulty Integrating AI with Existing Systems

Legacy systems and inadequate data infrastructure often present significant barriers to AI adoption in higher education, creating inefficiencies, delays, and limited functionality. Outdated systems may lack the integration capabilities or data quality needed for effective AI implementation, resulting in inaccurate analyses and missed opportunities.

To address this, begin by assessing the readiness of your current systems and data infrastructure, identifying gaps that could hinder AI effectiveness. *Investments in advanced data platforms like Ellucian (https://www.ellucian.com) or Oracle Analytics (https://www.oracle.com/analytics) can centralize and streamline operations, while middleware solutions bridge compatibility gaps between legacy systems and modern AI tools.* Collaborating with information technology teams and external vendors ensures smooth integration, while phased implementation strategies, starting with small pilot programs, help institutions gradually modernize their infrastructure with minimal disruption. By prioritizing these foundational improvements, your institution will unlock the full potential of AI and enhance decision-making, efficiency, and outcomes.

Overlooking Student Privacy and Data Security

AI initiatives in higher education often rely on extensive data collection, raising significant concerns about student privacy and security. Mishandling sensitive information can erode trust and expose institutions to legal and reputational risks. To address this, it is critical that you establish clear policies and protocols for data use, ensuring compliance with privacy regulations like Family Educational Rights and Privacy Act (FERPA) and General Data Protection Regulation (GDPR). ***Measures such as encryption, anonymization, and strict access controls should be implemented to protect student data.*** Transparent communication with students about how their data is collected, stored, and used further builds trust and fosters acceptance of AI-driven tools. Regular audits and ongoing training for staff on data protection practices ensure that security remains a priority as AI initiatives evolve. By proactively addressing privacy and security concerns, your institution will safeguard its reputation and maintain the trust of your students and stakeholders.

Road Map to the Future

Looking ahead, the role of AI in higher education will continue to evolve, with increasingly sophisticated applications and tools becoming readily available. Institutions that embrace AI now will be better positioned to take advantage of these advancements. ***The future of AI in higher education involves not only enhancing administrative efficiencies but also transforming the learning experience itself through personalized education, predictive analytics, and intelligent tutoring systems.***

As AI technology continues to advance, higher education institutions must remain proactive in their approach, continually exploring new applications and refining their strategies. By focusing on the skills and tips outlined in this chapter, you can ensure your institution remains at the forefront of innovation, driving positive change and achieving your mission more effectively.

Dos and Don'ts

Do

- Leverage predictive analytics to enhance enrollment management by tailoring recruitment and focusing on students most likely to enroll
- Enhance alumni engagement by analyzing data to identify giving potential, predict supporter behaviors, and personalize outreach efforts
- Personalize student learning by tailoring educational content and pacing to individual needs

- Assess the readiness of your current technology systems and data infrastructure to enable effective AI implementation, investing in advanced data platforms and middleware solutions as needed to bridge any compatibility gaps
- Cultivate a curious mind by continuously learning about AI
- Start small with pilot projects to build confidence and momentum

Don't

- Rely on the old ways of providing academic advising and career counseling support to your student body: AI now enables you to streamline course scheduling and degree tracking, as well as job recommendations, résumé feedback, and virtual interview coaching, freeing advisors to provide targeted, human-centered guidance
- Relegate AI to one department alone, instead of creating an interdisciplinary task force, council, or community of practice to encourage collaboration with and knowledge sharing of AI applications
- Discount staff and faculty concerns about AI adoption; take the time to dispel their fears around job displacement and any lack of understanding through open dialogue
- Neglect the critical importance of establishing clear policies and protocols to protect student data, ensuring compliance with privacy regulations like FERPA and GDPR through measures such as encryption, anonymization, and strict access controls

Conclusion

AI holds tremendous potential to transform higher education by enhancing operational efficiencies and improving the student experience. By cultivating a curious mind, fostering a supportive community, and focusing AI deployment on the areas best able to advance critical student- and supporter-facing efforts, you will effectively harness the power of AI. Implementing the solutions outlined in this chapter will enable your institution to stay ahead of technological trends and drive positive change. Embrace the future of AI in higher education and unlock new opportunities for innovation and impact.

Contributor Bios

Darian Rodriguez Heyman is an accomplished fundraising and philanthropy consultant. He is the bestselling author of *Nonprofit Management 101*, the former executive director of Craigslist Foundation, and a sought-after keynote speaker at social impact events around the world. He can be reached directly via his website, https://helpingpeoplehelp.com/, and is happy to offer any readers a pro bono coaching session if helpful. http://www.linkedin.com/in/dheyman

Cheryl Contee is a pioneering technology entrepreneur and digital transformation expert. She is the bestselling author of *Mechanical Bull: How You Can Achieve Startup Success*, a trailblazing startup founder, and a trusted advisor on digital innovation and social impact. She inspires audiences globally as a leading voice on inclusive entrepreneurship and social enterprise. http://www.linkedin.com/in/cherylcontee

Resource Review

- Educause: https://www.educause.edu/—Explore this nonprofit's extensive library of resources, including research, webinars, and case studies, to help you understand and adopt emerging technologies like AI in higher education.
- AI in Education at UNESCO: https://en.unesco.org/themes/ict-education/artificial-intelligence—Access global research, ethical guidelines, and policy recommendations on integrating AI into education systems, offering you insights into equitable and responsible implementation.
- *The Chronicle of Higher Education*: https://www.chronicle.com/—A leading source for news and information on higher education, including technology trends.
- Inside Higher Ed: https://www.insidehighered.com/—Offers news, opinion, and job listings for higher education professionals, with a focus on technology.
- *EdTech Magazine*: https://edtechmagazine.com/higher/—Covers technology trends and best practices in higher education.
- ISTE: https://www.iste.org/—The International Society for Technology in Education provides resources for educators integrating technology.

- Salesforce Education Cloud: https://www.salesforce.com/education/cloud—Use this comprehensive CRM platform to unify student data and deliver personalized experiences at scale, enhancing engagement across the student life cycle.
- Element451: https://element451.com—Implement this AI-powered enrollment management system to optimize recruitment strategies and improve student engagement through personalized communication.
- ZeeMee: https://zeemee.com—Leverage this social media platform to connect with prospective students, fostering a sense of community and belonging before they even set foot on campus.
- Drift: https://www.drift.com—Enhance your institution's communication strategy with this conversational marketing platform, using AI-driven chatbots to engage website visitors in real time.
- Tidio: https://www.tidio.com—Integrate this live chat and chatbot solution to provide instant support to students and visitors, improving user experience and satisfaction.
- Raiser's Edge NXT: https://www.blackbaud.com/products/blackbaud-raisers-edge-nxt—Manage alumni relations and fundraising efforts effectively with this cloud-based CRM tailored for educational institutions.
- Graduway: https://www.graduway.com—Build and manage your alumni network with this platform, facilitating mentoring programs and alumni engagement initiatives.
- HubSpot: https://www.hubspot.com—Streamline your marketing efforts with this inbound marketing and sales platform, offering tools for email marketing, social media management, and analytics.
- Mailchimp: https://mailchimp.com—Execute targeted email campaigns and analyze their performance using this user-friendly email marketing service.
- Handshake: https://joinhandshake.com—Connect your students with potential employers through this career services platform, enhancing job placement rates and career readiness.

- VMock: https://www.vmock.com—Provide students with AI-driven résumé feedback to improve their job application materials and increase employability.

- Knewton Alta: https://www.knewton.com—Adopt this adaptive learning platform to offer personalized educational content, catering to individual student needs and learning paces.

- Ocelot: https://www.ocelotbot.com—Use this AI-powered chatbot and video platform to assist students with financial aid, admissions, and enrollment queries, enhancing support services.

- edX: https://www.edx.org—Access professional development courses and certifications from top institutions to help your team build AI literacy and integrate technology into their work.

- Udemy: https://www.udemy.com—Explore affordable, self-paced courses on AI, Machine Learning, and data analytics to upskill your faculty and staff.

- Coursera: https://www.coursera.org—Enroll in flexible courses and certifications from leading universities to enhance your team's understanding of AI applications in education.

- Ellucian: https://www.ellucian.com—Manage your institution's administrative tasks with this comprehensive suite of software solutions designed for higher education.

- Oracle Analytics: https://www.oracle.com/analytics—Leverage this analytics platform to gain insights from your institutional data, supporting informed decision-making processes.

Closing Thoughts
The Journey Ahead

"The future of artificial intelligence is not about (hu)man versus machine, but rather (hu)man with machine. Together, we can achieve unimaginable heights of innovation and progress."

—Fei-Fei Li, computer scientist and codirector of the Stanford Institute for Human-Centered AI, 2021

As you close this book, at least for now, you're standing at the edge of incredible possibilities. ***AI isn't a silver bullet, but it is a powerful tool—a partner—that can help you expand your impact, achieve greater efficiency, and, most important, amplify the human connection at the heart of your mission.*** Whether you're a nonprofit leader, foundation executive, social impact startup, or higher education professional, the steps you take today to embrace AI will ripple into the future, transforming the way you serve your community and achieve your goals.

The key takeaway from this journey is simple: ***AI works best when paired with human ingenuity.*** It's not about replacing your work but enhancing it, helping you do more with less, freeing up your team to focus on what matters most. From fundraising and marketing to program delivery and back-office operations, the insights and strategies shared in this book are just the beginning. ***As the AI frontier continues to evolve, so must your willingness to experiment, adapt, and grow.***

Stay Hungry

The pace of change in AI is exhilarating—and intimidating. But instead of fearing it, use it as fuel to stay curious and hungry for what's next. ***Commit to continuous learning by*** *investing in training and professional development for yourself and your team.* Cultivate a mindset of lifelong learning, keeping your nonprofit nimble and ready to adapt to whatever tomorrow brings. Whether you're upskilling AI literacy across your staff, attending webinars on emerging tools, or diving into new resources, ***staying informed is your greatest strength in this ever-changing environment.***

Embrace Experimentation

Innovation doesn't come from standing still—it comes from trying, failing, learning, and trying again. ***AI thrives in a culture of experimentation, where your team feels empowered to test new tools, take bold risks, and share lessons learned.*** Try out a new platform, ask your staff to brainstorm AI-powered solutions to recurring challenges, or run a small pilot program to gauge a tool's effectiveness. By fostering a supportive environment where creativity and curiosity are encouraged, you'll unlock ideas and solutions you might never have imagined.

Keep Moving Forward

The work you do is vital, and the communities you serve are counting on you to lead with purpose and innovation. AI gives you the opportunity to reimagine how you deliver on your mission. ***The tools and frameworks shared in this book are your foundation, but the real power lies in your ability to build on them.*** Stay engaged with your peers, share your successes and challenges, and continue to iterate on your approach.

Most important, don't lose sight of the people behind the technology—your donors, your stakeholders, and your staff. ***AI may analyze, predict, and automate, but it's your vision, compassion, and leadership that turn the potential offered by AI into impact.***

So, ***as you look to the future, don't just embrace AI—harness it.*** Make it your partner in creating a better world. Together, there's no limit to what you can achieve.

Thank you for the work you do, and for daring to dream bigger. Thank you not only on behalf of the two of us and our team, and not only on behalf of the 57 experts on whose shared insights this book is based, but thank you on behalf of the millions of people you collectively serve. It's been a privilege and honor to produce this book for your benefit, and ***we hope you leave not only inspired, but inspired to action.***

Afterword
The Future of AI in Nonprofits

Based on insights from an interview with Blaise Agüera y Arcas.

As we stand on the precipice of a new era, it's clear that ***AI is not just a passing trend but a transformative force that will reshape the landscape of every sector, including the nonprofit world.*** The journey through this book has equipped you with practical and tactical knowledge to harness AI's power. Now, let's take a moment to look forward to understand where AI is headed and how you, as nonprofit leaders, can prepare for and embrace these changes to advance your mission and unleash your team's potential.

A Glimpse into the Next Decade

AI technology is evolving at a breakneck pace. The advancements we've seen in the past few years, particularly with large sequence models and unsupervised learning, have already begun to change how we perceive and interact with AI. By 2030, there is no doubt AI will become even more integrated into our daily lives and work.

One of the most significant shifts will be the move from non-agential to agential AI. Today, much of our interaction with AI is reactive; we provide input, and the AI responds. However, ***future AI systems will be more proactive, capable of initiating actions and maintaining long-term relationships.*** This means AI will not only assist with tasks but will also participate in strategic planning and decision-making processes, acting almost like a highly skilled team member instead of an intern whose hand you need to hold.

We stand at the threshold of what I call the fourth era of computing. Early computers, built to perform fixed, repetitive computational tasks, simply mechanized the labor of calculating numerical tables. Then came the era of general-purpose computation, automating data-heavy, structured tasks. The third era, defined by supervised Machine Learning, enabled us to train machines for specific objectives. But ***today, we're in an era where unsupervised learning and generative models, trained on vast corpora of human knowledge, reproduce and even enhance human creativity and reasoning.***

For nonprofits, this is a moment of immense opportunity. ***As AI becomes more agential, moving from reactive chatbots to proactive collaborators with durable memory and specialized expertise, its potential to support social impact work grows exponentially.*** Imagine an AI partner that doesn't just help you write grant proposals but understands the nuanced dynamics of donor engagement over time. Picture models that specialize in local contexts, helping communities in Rwanda optimize aid delivery or tailoring interventions to hyper-specific socioeconomic conditions. These aren't futuristic fantasies; they're the emerging reality.

In the coming years, AI will also become more specialized. Current models are generalists, trained on vast amounts of data from the internet. But ***as AI systems develop long-life histories and learn from specific contexts, they will gain deep expertise in niche areas, including increasingly integrating insights gained from interactions with you and your team.*** Imagine an AI partner that not only helps you craft data-driven program evaluations but also identifies funding opportunities tailored to your mission and proactively connects you with potential collaborators in your sector. These advancements promise not just efficiency but also a fundamental shift in how nonprofits build capacity, enabling you to focus more deeply on strategic growth and transformative impact.

Preparing for the Future

The question then arises: how can nonprofit leaders prepare for this rapidly approaching future? Here are a few key considerations.

Embrace AI as a Collaborative Partner

AI should not be seen as a threat to your workforce but as a collaborator that can *enhance human capabilities*. AI can take on time-intensive tasks like data entry or preliminary research, enabling your staff to focus on mission-critical work like relationship-building or program innovation. Think of AI as a trusted partner, one that never tires, consistently learns, and helps you focus on high-value activities that demand creativity and empathy.

The future will be defined by symbiotic relationships between humans and AI, where AI handles data-intensive tasks, freeing up your team to focus on strategic and interpersonal work. This collaboration will lead to more efficient operations, innovative solutions, and, ultimately, greater impact.

Invest in AI Literacy

Understanding AI is no longer optional; it's an essential skill for navigating the future. ***You don't need every member of your team to become a data scientist, but basic literacy in AI concepts should be a prerequisite for all staff,*** as such knowledge will enable your nonprofit to make informed decisions about AI adoption and integration. AI literacy goes beyond knowing how to use the latest tool—it's about developing a *working* understanding of how AI works, where it excels, and its current limitations. ***Encourage ongoing education and training to stay abreast of the latest developments and applications of AI in the nonprofit sector,*** as this knowledge will empower your team to evaluate AI tools critically and make informed decisions about adoption and deployment.

Develop an Ethical AI Framework

As you integrate AI into your operations, it's essential to establish ethical guidelines and governance policies. ***AI systems must be designed and deployed in ways that align with your organization's values and mission.*** This includes ensuring transparency, fairness, and accountability in AI decision-making processes. And it's not just for your benefit, as ensuring a responsible approach to technology adoption will build trust with your stakeholders and ensure your AI initiatives support your broader social goals.

Leverage AI for Greater Equity

AI has the potential to shine a light on inequities in your organization and community, empowering you to take data-informed action to address them. ***AI can help identify and address biases in your programs, enhance access to services for marginalized communities, and provide insights that inform more inclusive policies and practices.*** By strategically leveraging AI, your nonprofit can contribute to a more just and equitable society.

Start with Why

Embracing AI is not just about keeping up with technological trends; it's about amplifying your impact and fulfilling your mission more effectively. As you move forward with your AI adoption efforts, there will be those who have their doubts, understandably so. When they ask *why* you're lobbying for change, ***remember three key reasons why AI is vital for nonprofits.***

Enhancing Efficiency and Effectiveness

AI can streamline administrative tasks, optimize resource allocation, and improve program delivery. This is mission-critical for nonprofits, almost all of which are under-staffed and under-resourced, and facing daunting, expanding needs. AI-driven data analysis can help you better understand donor behavior, predict fundraising outcomes, and tailor your outreach strategies. ***This technology can streamline administrative duties like scheduling, compliance, and much more.*** This efficiency enables you to do more with limited resources, maximizing your impact.

Unlocking New Opportunities

AI doesn't just make existing processes better—it opens entirely new pathways for innovation. Whether it's developing personalized engagement strategies, creating predictive models to anticipate community needs, or automating tasks, ***AI empowers your nonprofit to explore new avenues for growth and development.*** Imagine creating predictive models to identify emerging community needs or using AI to design hyper-personalized donor engagement strategies that drive deeper connections. These new capabilities can unlock untapped potential and increase your nonprofit's positive impact.

The future depicted in Marvel movies—where billionaire heroes enjoy instant access to the information they need—has arrived, except today we're *all* heroes. So, how will you use that power to visualize and actualize a future that works for everyone?

Building Resilience

In an increasingly complex and fast-changing world, AI can help your nonprofit adapt and thrive. **AI provides real-time insights that enable you to anticipate challenges, adjust strategies, and respond swiftly to crises.** Whether it's managing donor relations during an economic downturn or reallocating resources during a natural disaster, AI ensures your organization stays agile and prepared. By building AI into your operations, you can enhance your organization's resilience and agility.

A Future of Possibilities

This book has provided you with tactical and practical insights to start your AI journey. The path ahead will be one of experimentation, learning, and growth. **AI reflects the intentions of those who wield it.** Use it to deepen relationships, enhance equity, and build a world where your mission isn't just possible but inevitable. **By embracing AI and preparing for its advancements, you can position your nonprofit to thrive in this new era.** The journey won't be without challenges, but the potential rewards are immense. Together, we can leverage AI to create a more innovative, efficient, and equitable world.

Interviewee Bio

Blaise Agüera y Arcas is a visionary in the field of AI, renowned for his groundbreaking work at the intersection of technology and social impact. As vice president and fellow at Google Research, Blaise leads multidisciplinary teams advancing generative AI, ethics, and Machine Learning, with a particular focus on societal applications. Previously, his work at Microsoft Research included codeveloping Photosynth and pioneering early innovations in augmented reality and Deep Learning. A frequent TED speaker and advocate for ethical AI, Blaise emphasizes the importance of moral imagination in the design of technology. https://www.linkedin.com/in/blaise-aguera-y-arcas-85626a42/

Book Underwriters

Helping People Help is a boutique consultancy that connects nonprofit leaders, philanthropists, foundations, and mission-led companies to best practices, AI and other cutting-edge technology tools, helpful resources, and the contacts needed to maximize impact. Unlike other firms with a set bench of consultants, our founder and coauthor of this book, Darian Rodriguez Heyman, personally hand-picks experts he's met over his 25-year career based on the unique needs and fields of our clients, with a focus on placing exceptionally qualified women and people of color. https://helpingpeoplehelp.com/

Salesforce helps organizations of any size reimagine their organizations with AI. With technology solutions tailored for nonprofits to improve and program management, service delivery, fundraising, and marketing engagement, Salesforce for Nonprofits is designed to help you build stronger relationships and drive impact. Nonprofits can access specialized tools, including the latest AI innovations like Agentforce to streamline operations and increase efficiency. https://www.salesforce.com/nonprofit/

 Givver collaborates with both nonprofits and philanthropists to bring the joy back to giving. At Givver, we are always looking for new ways to make an impact, whether it is using AI to thoroughly and effectively vet new organizations, democratizing the funder/grantee relationship through trust-based philanthropy, or partnering with philanthropists to bring nonprofits the strategic capacity-building that is often sorely needed but rarely funded. https://iamagivver.com/

AI for Nonprofits *Resource Directory*

Compiled by Doug Nelson.

The resources listed here present opportunities for nonprofits to enhance efficiency, improve decision-making, expand reach and impact, and support ongoing professional development. While the specific solutions may change given the rapidly evolving worlds of technology and AI, consider this directory a starting point. If you find a resource no longer exists or is not useful for any reason, a simple online search will quickly direct you to a similar, current tool or publication.

Action Network

Leverage this platform to streamline advocacy campaigns, mobilize supporters, and integrate AI tools for smarter data analysis and personalized outreach. With its robust data management features, you can use AI to segment your audience, predict donor behavior, and automate tailored communications, saving time and increasing engagement; plus their open application programming interface (API) enables you to connect with AI-powered tools for advanced analytics. https://actionnetwork.org

AI for Good

If you're looking to apply AI to address global challenges, this initiative accelerates the United Nations (UN) Sustainable Development Goals (SDGs) through collaboration with UN agencies, nongovernmental organizations (NGOs), academia, and tech leaders. It offers summits, workshops, and webinars, supporting scalable projects tackling issues like climate change, health care, and sustainable development. https://ai4good.org/

Amazon Web Services (AWS) for Nonprofits

Cloud computing services are available at a discount for nonprofits, enabling you to benefit from lower-cost website hosting, data analytics, and more. Eligible organizations receive credits and technical support to simplify cloud technology adoption. https://aws.amazon.com/government-education/nonprofits/

AppealAI

This free AI-powered tool can help your nonprofit generate fundraising content like emails, website copy, and social media posts tailored to your campaigns. It aligns messaging with your mission and voice, streamlining communication efforts to save time and drive results. https://www.funraise.org/appealai

Authentic

A digital agency specializing in mission-driven organizations that provides web development, digital strategy, and brand development. Their services are tailored to help you achieve your goals through technology and marketing. https://authentic.org/

Benevity

Connects your nonprofit with corporate donors, volunteers, and grantmakers through its social impact platform. You can create a free profile to access workplace giving, volunteering, and grant programs, receive donations, manage matching funds, and engage a global network of supporters. https://benevity.com/causes

Board.dev

This platform helps improve nonprofit board governance through technology and training, with a focus on helping you recruit technology executives to your board. It offers tools and resources like board management software, training materials, and governance best practices to help your board operate more effectively. https://board.dev/

Board Effect

Offers specialized board management software that is designed to streamline operations like meeting management, document sharing, and collaboration. Tailored specifically for nonprofit governance, it helps your board function more efficiently. https://www.boardeffect.com

Browse.ai

A no-code web automation tool that lets you extract and monitor data from websites without technical expertise. Use it to track grant opportunities, monitor campaigns, and gather insights on industry trends with customizable or prebuilt robots. As a nonprofit, you can access a free tier and receive discounts. https://www.browse.ai/

Candid.org

This site provides comprehensive data and research on nonprofits and grantmakers to help you make informed decisions and increase transparency. Resulting from the merger of GuideStar and Foundation Center, it's a valuable fundraising and capacity building resource. https://candid.org/

Cause Inspired Media

This company specializes in digital marketing solutions tailored for nonprofits. Their expertise includes Google Ad Grants management, SEO, and digital advertising to maximize your online presence, engage supporters, and drive donations. https://causeinspiredmedia.com/

Causewriter.ai

Provides an AI-powered writing assistant designed specifically for nonprofits to streamline the creation of mission-driven content. It helps you draft compelling fundraising emails, grant proposals, donor letters, and social media posts tailored to your organization's voice and goals; plus, they develop custom large language models for nonprofits.

The tool is ideal for nonprofits looking to enhance their storytelling and engagement efforts. https://causewriter.ai/

Center for Transformational Change

A consulting organization that helps you implement innovative approaches and technology to adapt to changing environments. Their training and resources focus on creating sustainable solutions for organizational and social impact. https://transformationalchange.co/

Charity Digital

A UK-based nonprofit that helps other nonprofits maximize their impact using digital tools. They offer access to discounted software, educational content, and events to improve digital skills within your organization. https://charitydigital.org.uk/

Classy

An online fundraising platform designed to connect you with supporters and enhance donor engagement. Features include customizable donation forms, crowdfunding, peer-to-peer fundraising, and event management tools, all offered on a subscription-based model with transaction fees. Be sure to check out their blog and newsletter, both of which offer a wide range of useful tips and tools. https://www.classy.org/

Community Boost

A digital marketing agency dedicated to helping nonprofits grow their online presence and increase donations. Services include website optimization, paid ad management, social media strategy, and data-driven campaign development. https://www.communityboost.org/

Cooperative Impact Lab

A collaborative space that supports organizations working on social impact initiatives. It provides resources and opportunities to cocreate innovative solutions to complex social challenges. https://www.cooperativeimpactlab.org/

Dataro

This AI-powered fundraising platform helps you predict donor behavior and optimize campaigns. It uses Machine Learning to provide data-driven insights to increase donation revenue and improve your fundraising strategies. https://dataro.io/

DonorSearch

A Machine Learning tool that identifies and segments top fundraising prospects. By integrating donor data with wealth and giving insights, it streamlines the prospecting process, allowing you to focus on building relationships and executing campaigns. https://www.donorsearch.net/

Engage

Offers a scholarly journal and platform focused on civic engagement and public participation. It publishes research and case studies on how technology and innovation enhance community involvement. https://engagejournal.org/

Fast Forward

A nonprofit organization dedicated to accelerating the growth of tech nonprofits that address critical social issues through technology. They provide funding, resources, and partnerships to empower innovators using technology for social good and offer programs focused on AI for humanity. https://www.ffwd.org/

Fireflies

An AI meeting assistant that records, transcribes, and summarizes discussions. It's compatible with major conferencing tools and offers free and discounted plans for nonprofits. https://fireflies.ai/

Fundraising.ai

A collaborative that promotes the responsible use of AI in nonprofit fundraising. They offer tools, resources, and best practices to help you adopt AI ethically while prioritizing privacy, security, and data ethics. https://fundraising.ai

Fundwriter.ai

An AI-powered writing assistant that streamlines the creation of fundraising content like appeals, grant proposals, and donor emails. It offers specialized templates tailored to your mission and communication needs. https://fundwriter.ai/

GitHub

The world's leading software development platform, offering version control and collaboration features that are crucial for both open-source and private projects. While not exclusively focused on nonprofits, their GitHub for Nonprofits program provides free access to advanced features that help nonprofits manage their technical projects and collaborate with developers. https://github.com/

Golden

A volunteer management platform designed to simplify organizing and tracking your volunteer programs. It helps you recruit volunteers, schedule shifts, manage communications, and track impact with minimal administrative effort. The platform also offers analytics tools to measure engagement and share results with stakeholders. Their intuitive interface ensures you can quickly onboard team members and optimize volunteer coordination. https://www.goldenvolunteer.com/

Good Tech Fest

A global community fostering innovation for social impact leaders. They host in-person events across Africa, Latin America, and the United States, focusing on using technology to create meaningful change. Recordings of their conferences and webinars are available online, offering insights into how organizations leverage tech solutions to drive impact. Their platform is a hub for connecting with like-minded professionals and learning from real-world case studies. https://www.goodtechfest.com/

Google for Nonprofits

Provides eligible organizations with access to Google's suite of enterprise tools at no cost. These include Google Workspace for collaboration, Google Ad Grants for advertising (up to $10,000 per month in search ads), and YouTube features to expand your reach. https://www.google.com/nonprofits/

Grantable

An AI-powered grant writing tool designed to help your nonprofits streamline its proposal process. It combines a smart content library with an AI writing assistant, enabling you to upload writing samples and generate tailored drafts based on specific grant criteria. Key features include organization of materials, collaboration tools, and automation of repetitive tasks, all aimed at saving time and increasing funding success rates. https://www.grantable.co/

Innovation for Impact

A community for innovation leaders within international NGOs and UN agencies working to build a culture of collaboration and experimentation. Members meet regularly to share best practices, exchange ideas, and collaborate on interdisciplinary projects. Resources include workshops, case studies, and opportunities to cocreate solutions to complex global challenges. https://www.innovationforimpact.network/

Instrumentl

A grant discovery and management platform designed to save nonprofits time and boost funding success. It offers access to a comprehensive database of funders and active opportunities, with tools to organize deadlines, documents, and tasks. The platform also includes automated deadline reminders and analytics, helping you streamline your grant-seeking efforts and secure more funding. https://www.instrumentl.com/

MERL Tech and Tech Salon NYC

MERL Tech brings together practitioners focused on using technology to enhance monitoring, evaluation, research, and learning in development and humanitarian work. They organize conferences and maintain a blog with actionable insights on integrating tech into your processes. Tech Salon NYC complements this by hosting regular discussions about the role of technology in driving social change, offering networking opportunities with experts in the field. https://merltech.org/

Microsoft 365

Offers nonprofits a discounted or free suite of productivity tools, including Teams for collaboration, SharePoint for content management, and Office apps like Word and Excel. These tools enable your organization to streamline operations, improve communication, and work more effectively as a team. https://www.office.com/

NetHope

A consortium of global nonprofits focused on improving IT connectivity and leveraging technology to address humanitarian challenges. They work closely with technology partners to develop scalable solutions for issues such as disaster response, connectivity in remote areas, and digital inclusion. Their initiatives and resources support nonprofits in maximizing the potential of technology to serve vulnerable populations. https://nethope.org/

Nonprofit Help Center

A comprehensive hub offering guidance on nonprofit management, including fundraising strategies, technology implementation, and organizational development. It provides educational resources, templates, and best practices to help you operate more effectively and achieve your mission. Their tools are designed to support nonprofits of all sizes. https://www.nonprofithelpcenter.com/

Nonprofit Leadership Alliance

Focused on developing nonprofit talent and offering certification programs, training, and leadership resources. Their Certified Nonprofit Professional (CNP) credential equips individuals with practical skills and knowledge to excel in the sector. They also provide networking opportunities and an annual conference, Elevate, to help you connect with other leaders and organizations. https://nla1.org/

NTEN

Empowers nonprofits through the strategic use of technology. They provide training, resources, and community support, including the Nonprofit Technology Conference and the Nonprofit Tech Readiness cohorts. Their Equity Guide for Nonprofit Technology helps organizations adopt tech solutions that prioritize inclusivity and accessibility. https://nten.org/

Okta for Nonprofits

Provides secure identity and access management solutions to ensure your digital resources are protected while remaining accessible to authorized users. Their platform integrates seamlessly with other tools and offers significant discounts to nonprofits, helping you safeguard sensitive information and streamline user access. https://www.okta.com/solutions/nonprofits/

The Prompt

A boutique AI training and consulting firm with a passion for the power of AI to elevate human creativity, innovation, and productivity. They work with nonprofits and other organizations to help activate the transformative potential of AI effectively and ethically. Their website provides resources, case studies, and practical tools to support nonprofits and mission-driven businesses in integrating AI into their operations. https://www.the-prompt.ai

Quiller

A platform that helps nonprofits streamline operations, manage relationships, and measure impact effectively. Their innovative software solutions provide data analytics and workflow management tools to enhance organizational efficiency and outcomes. https://quiller.ai/

Scribe

A user-friendly tool that simplifies the process of creating step-by-step guides and training materials. By capturing actions in real time, it automatically generates detailed instructions with annotated screenshots, saving you time and effort. It is ideal for documenting standard operating procedures, onboarding materials, and volunteer training. Nonprofits can access discounted plans. https://scribehow.com/

Sembly AI

This platform, available to nonprofits at a discount, enhances meeting productivity by recording, transcribing, and summarizing discussions in real time. Features include speaker identification, keyword search, and action item tracking. Compatible with Zoom, Google Meet, Microsoft Teams, and Webex, it's a valuable tool for capturing insights and improving collaboration. https://www.sembly.ai/

Social Current

A network dedicated to supporting organizations and professionals in the social sector. They provide resources, advocacy, best practices, and connections to strengthen your nonprofit's capacity and effectiveness. https://socialcurrant.co/

Stanford Institute for Human-Centered Artificial Intelligence

Advances AI research and development with a focus on ethical and human-centered approaches. They provide educational resources, policy recommendations, and research initiatives to ensure AI solutions benefit humanity. It's a valuable resource for organizations looking to implement AI responsibly. https://hai.stanford.edu/

Stockimg AI

A design platform that enables you to create and customize visuals, including logos, illustrations, and posters. It also offers tools for automating social media content generation and scheduling, making it easier to maintain a consistent online presence. Nonprofits can use it to streamline visual content creation. https://stockimg.ai/

Tango

A documentation tool that captures user actions and automatically generates step-by-step guides with annotated screenshots. It's ideal for developing training materials, standard operating procedures, and support documentation. Nonprofits can benefit from discounted plans to simplify and professionalize their internal processes. https://www.tango.us/

Tech Impact

A nonprofit organization providing IT support, cloud solutions, and digital strategy consulting tailored to nonprofits. They also offer workforce development programs to help underserved individuals build careers in technology. https://techimpact.org/

Tech Matters

Develops scalable software solutions to address critical social challenges. Their projects include tools for child helplines, environmental conservation, and other initiatives tailored to nonprofits and mission-driven organizations. They focus on creating sustainable technical solutions for long-term impact. https://techmatters.org/

Technology Association of Grantmakers (TAG)

A membership organization connecting technology and IT staff from grantmaking organizations. TAG offers resources, learning opportunities, and networking to help foundations leverage technology for more effective grantmaking and operations. https://www.tagtech.org/

TechSoup Global

Provides discounted and donated technology products and services to nonprofits worldwide. Their network also offers training and resources to help you adopt and maximize technology. With partnerships with major tech companies, it's a one-stop shop for technology solutions. https://www.techsoup.org/

VolunteerMatch

An online platform that connects your organization with individuals looking to volunteer their time and skills. It allows you to post volunteer opportunities, manage communication, and track engagement, making it easier to build and retain a committed volunteer base. https://www.volunteermatch.org/

■ ■ ■

Books

AI for Social Good: Using Artificial Intelligence to Save the World

This book explores the transformative potential of AI to address some of the world's most pressing challenges. Focusing on applications in areas like health care, education, climate change, and poverty alleviation, it provides real-world examples of how AI can drive meaningful change. The author examines the ethical and social implications of deploying AI for social good, emphasizing the need for transparency, inclusivity, and alignment with human values (Rahul Dodhia, Wiley, 2024).

Co-Intelligence: Living and Working with AI

This incredibly well-written, research-backed book explores how AI can be harmonized with human values to create an intelligent, collaborative environment in workplaces and communities. It offers practical insights into integrating AI into social good initiatives while ensuring fairness, inclusivity, and transparency. The author discusses how to navigate challenges like biases in AI, maintaining ethical considerations, and building a future where AI enhances human capabilities rather than replacing them (Ethan Mollick, Portfolio, 2024).

The Smart Nonprofit: Staying Human-Centered in an Automated World

This book provides a comprehensive guide to integrating automation into nonprofit work while keeping humanity at the forefront. The authors explore the benefits and challenges of automation, offering strategies for implementing technology that amplifies impact without losing personal connection. Through real-life examples and practical advice, it highlights how nonprofits can use automation to free-up time for relationship-building and mission-critical activities. This resource is perfect for nonprofit leaders seeking to embrace technology thoughtfully while maintaining a focus on empathy and equity (Beth Kanter and Allison Fine, Wiley, 2022).

The Tech That Comes Next: How Changemakers, Philanthropists, and Technologists Can Build an Equitable World

This book explores how nonprofits, technologists, and philanthropists can collaborate to create technology solutions that prioritize equity and justice. It provides actionable insights for changemakers looking to leverage technology to address systemic issues while centering communities and values. Through real-world examples, the authors demonstrate how to codesign and implement tools that advance social impact, offering a road map for building a more inclusive future. This resource is ideal for nonprofit leaders, funders, and technologists seeking to integrate equity into their work with technology (Amy Sample Ward and Afua Bruce, Wiley, 2022).

The Worlds I See: Curiosity, Exploration, and Discovery at the Dawn of AI

This inspiring memoir from AI pioneer Fei-Fei Li chronicles her journey from her childhood in China to becoming a world-renowned expert in AI. The book weaves personal anecdotes with insights into the development of AI, highlighting how curiosity and a human-centered approach have guided her work. Li emphasizes the importance of balancing technological progress with ethics, equity, and compassion, offering valuable lessons for anyone navigating the integration of AI into their lives and organizations (Fei-Fei Li, Flatiron Books, 2023).

Contributor Bio

Doug Nelson is a technologist and educator dedicated to helping nonprofits to harness the potential of AI and technology to advance their missions. As a partner at The Prompt, Doug designs and facilitates experiential learning programs that engage and empower team members with an AI mindset. His career spans senior roles in technology leadership and corporate training and has included leading innovative projects for the Ford Foundation and a range of much smaller nonprofit clients. A passionate internationalist, he enjoys leveraging AI for language learning and cross-cultural exchange. https://www.linkedin.com/in/dougnelson808/

About the Editors

Darian Rodriguez Heyman is an accomplished fundraising and philanthropy consultant. He is the bestselling author of *Nonprofit Management 101*, the former executive director of Craigslist Foundation, and a sought-after keynote speaker at social impact events around the world. He can be reached directly via his website, https://helpingpeoplehelp.com/, and is happy to offer any readers a pro bono coaching session if helpful. http://www.linkedin.com/in/dheyman

Cheryl Contee is a pioneering technology entrepreneur and digital transformation expert. She is the bestselling author of *Mechanical Bull: How You Can Achieve Startup Success*, a trailblazing startup founder, and a trusted advisor on digital innovation and social impact. She inspires audiences globally as a leading voice on inclusive entrepreneurship and social enterprise. http://www.linkedin.com/in/cherylcontee

Glossary of Terms

Assembled by Craig Johnson with the help of AI.

Acceptable Use Policy A formal document that outlines guidelines, standards, and procedures for using AI tools within an organization, typically including ethical considerations, data privacy requirements, and approval processes.

Administrative Controls Processes and systems established to manage how data is accessed, used, and protected within an organization, including workflows and data access protocols that specify who can input, access, or manage data within AI systems.

Agential/Agentic AI AI systems that can act autonomously as agents, maintaining durable relationships and developing expertise over time, moving beyond simple reactive responses to proactive engagement with tasks and users.

AI Adoption Life Cycle A four-stage progression of AI implementation in nonprofits: individual usage, organizational adoption, strategic implementation, and proprietary solutions, each representing increasing levels of AI integration and sophistication.

AI Code of Ethics A formal document outlining ethical guidelines and principles for AI use within an organization, addressing issues like bias, transparency, and responsible implementation.

Artificial Intelligence (AI) The umbrella term for computer programs and systems that have the ability to reason and learn like humans. Originally based on explicit "if-then" programming, modern AI can handle complex tasks like natural language processing (NLP), image recognition, and predictive analytics.

Audiogram A visual representation of audio content, typically combining waveform visualization with text or images, used to share audio clips on social media and other platforms.

Automated Data Validation Tools Software systems that automatically check data quality, consistency, and accuracy, helping organizations maintain clean data for AI applications.

Business Continuity and Disaster Recovery (BCDR) Plans and procedures designed to ensure an organization can maintain operations during unexpected events like power outages or cyberattacks, including strategies for data backup and system recovery.

Custom Chatbot An AI-powered conversational interface specifically trained on an organization's data and configured to handle specialized tasks or communications in alignment with the organization's voice and goals.

Custom LLMs/GPTs Privately developed and trained AI models that operate within secure environments, ensuring organizational data remains confidential and doesn't contribute to public AI training sets.

Data Hygiene The practice of maintaining clean, accurate, and well-organized data through regular cleaning, standardization, and quality control processes.

Data Subject Access Request (DSAR) A formal request made by an individual to access, modify, or delete their personal data held by an organization, as required by privacy regulations like GDPR and CCPA.

Deepfake AI-generated media that manipulates or generates visual and audio content to create realistic but artificial representations of people or events.

Deep Learning (DL) A subset of Machine Learning that uses neural networks with multiple layers (deep neural networks) to analyze various factors simultaneously, enabling more sophisticated pattern recognition and predictive capabilities.

Domain-Based Message Authentication, Reporting and Conformance (DMARC) An email security protocol that verifies sender authenticity and prevents email spoofing and phishing attempts.

Donor Velocity A metric that measures the rate and pattern of donor support over time, indicating whether donors are likely to increase or decrease their giving levels in the future.

Endpoint Detection and Response (EDR) Security software that monitors and responds to suspicious activity on endpoint devices like laptops, phones, and tablets in real time.

Enterprise-level AI Tools   AI solutions designed for organization-wide implementation, offering robust features, security, and scalability suitable for larger-scale operations.

Few-Shot Prompts   A prompting technique where examples are provided to the AI to demonstrate the desired output format or style, improving the accuracy and relevance of responses.

Fractional CTO   A part-time or consulting chief technology officer who provides strategic technology guidance to organizations that may not need or cannot afford a full-time CTO.

Generative AI (GenAI)   AI systems capable of creating new content including text, images, audio, and video. Refers to any AI that can generate outputs rather than just analyze existing data.

Generative Pre-trained Transformers (GPTs)   A type of LLM designed for NLP tasks. "Generative" refers to their ability to create content, "pre-trained" indicates they're fed large amounts of training data, and "transformer" describes their underlying neural network architecture.

Hallucinations   False or inaccurate statements that AI systems confidently present as true. This is a current limitation of AI systems that requires human oversight to verify outputs.

Human in the Loop (HITL)   The practice of maintaining human oversight and involvement in AI systems to ensure accuracy, appropriateness, correct voice and tone, and ethical use of the technology.

Human Locomotion Data   Data collected about human movement patterns, including gait, balance, and other physical metrics, often gathered through wearable sensors for medical analysis.

Information Technology Service Management (ITSM)   Framework for planning, delivering, managing, and improving IT services within an organization to ensure smooth operations and security.

Large Language Models (LLMs)   Deep Learning algorithms that process and generate human-like text. These models ingest vast amounts of training data to identify patterns and predict appropriate responses. Examples include GPT, DeepSeek, Claude, and Gemini.

Machine Learning (ML) A field of AI that involves training algorithms to recognize patterns in data and make predictions or decisions based on those patterns. Unlike traditional programming, ML allows computers to program themselves based on examples without explicit instructions.

Managed Detection and Response (MDR) Outsourced security services providing 24/7 monitoring, threat detection, and incident response for organizations.

Middleware Software tools that connect different technology-based systems and platforms, enabling data sharing and workflow automation between various applications.

Mobile Device Management (MDM) Tools and policies for overseeing and securing mobile devices used by employees, including controls for data access and security settings.

Natural Language Processing (NLP) A branch of AI that enables computers to understand, interpret, and respond to human language in both written and spoken forms. Powers applications like chatbots, sentiment analysis, and automated content generation.

Predictive Analytics/AI The use of AI to analyze historical data and predict future outcomes or behaviors. In nonprofits, often used for donor behavior analysis and forecasting.

Prompt Engineering The skill of crafting effective instructions or queries for AI systems to generate desired outputs. Involves understanding how to communicate with AI to get optimal results.

Retrieval-Augmented Generation (RAG) A technique that combines information retrieval from a knowledge base with text generation, allowing AI systems to produce more accurate and contextually relevant responses.

RFM Segmentation A data analysis method that segments customers or donors based on three metrics: recency (how recently they engaged), frequency (how often they engage), and monetary value (how much they contribute).

Role-Based Access Control (RBAC) A security approach that restricts system access based on individuals' roles within an organization, ensuring users can only access information necessary for their specific responsibilities.

Security Information and Event Management (SIEM) Software that collects and analyzes security data from multiple sources across an organization to detect threats and ensure compliance.

Sentiment Analysis AI-powered analysis of text data to determine the emotional tone and opinions expressed, often used to gauge public opinion about organizations or causes.

Shadow Tech Tools and software used by staff without formal organizational approval, potentially creating security risks and inefficiencies.

Supervised Learning A type of Machine Learning where the AI system is trained on labeled data, learning to map inputs to known correct outputs.

Technical Assistance (TA) Grants Funding specifically provided to help organizations adopt and integrate new technologies, including costs for training, software licenses, and consulting services.

Text-to-Speech (TTS) AI technology that converts written text into natural-sounding spoken words, used for creating voiceovers, audio content, and accessibility features.

Unstructured Data Refers to information that does not have a predefined data model or organized structure, making it difficult to store, process, and analyze using traditional databases or tools. Unlike structured data, which is organized (e.g., labeled documents, spreadsheets, or relational databases), unstructured data lacks a clear format or schema.

Unsupervised Learning A type of Machine Learning where the AI system discovers patterns and structures in data without explicit labels or guidance, learning from the data itself.

Zero Trust A security framework that requires verification for every user and device attempting to access resources, even those within the organization's network, operating under the principle "never trust, always verify."

Name Index

Note: This Name Index includes proper names, company names, products, publications, and websites. For all other topics, please refer to the Subject Index.

Above the Law, 404
ACC Docket, 404
Acronis, 389
Action Network, 221, 463
Acumen Fund Fellows, 441
Adobe, 128, 358
Adobe Audition, 195
Adobe Express, 203
AdvocacyAI, 243
AgentForce, 367
AI Alignment Forum, 103
The AI Dude, 124
AI Ethics Lab, 15
AI for Everyone, 71
AI for Good Global Community, 418, 463
AI for Social Good by Google, 15
AI for Social Good (Rodhia), 474
AI Governance for Nonprofits Framework, 86
AI in Education at UNESCO, 450
AI Now Institute, 86
AI4Good, 413

AIHR Digital HR Transformation Program, 339
Airtable, 290, 291
Alert Logic, 394
Alethea, 317
Algorithmic Justice League, 377
Alliance Magazine, 427
Amazon Bedrock, 366
Amazon Comprehend, 231
Amazon Route 53, 391
Amazon Web Services (AWS), 368, 390, 464
American Society for Artificial Intelligence, 70
American University, 321
Americans for Tax Fairness, 303
AmeriCorps, 259
Anthropic, 9, 242, 265
Apify, 222
Aplos, 348
AppealAI, 464
Apple, 358
Apple Podcasts, 195

Apurva.Ai, 74
Araize FastFund Accounting, 355
Arcas, Blaise Agüera y, 455–460
Arctic Wolf, 393
Armillaria, 75
Arnold (StaffBot), 104–106
Asana, 271, 290, 356, 368
Ascend Impact Advisors, 276
Association of Fundraising Professionals (AFP), 125
Atlassian Jira Service Management, 392
Auth0, 392
Authentic, 140, 464
Automox, 384
AWS CloudTrail, 386
Azar, Sam, 265–276

B-Lab B Corp Growth Program, 440
BambooHR, 334
Bank of China, 347
Beacon, 10
Belinsky, Michael, 186–188
Benevity, 464
Bengio, Yoshua, 325
Beth Kanter's blog, 42
BethKanter.org, 26
Better Business Bureau, 174
Bill.com, 342
Bitcoin, 262–263
Bitdefender, 383
Blackbird AI, 317
Bloomerang, 144, 367, 368
Board Effect, 465
Boardable, 356
Board.Dev, 364

BoardEffect, 359
BoardSource, 359
Bolles, Gary A., 43–45
Bonterra, 138
boodleAI, 70
BoodleBox, 366
boyd, danah, 47–54
Brandwatch, 211
Bridgespan Group, 188
Brill, Jonathan, xv
Brown, Brené, 189
Browse.ai, 465
Bruce, Afua, 77–85
Buffer, 210
Build Consulting, 374
Build Your Board, Build Your Business (Clarke), 439
Buolamwini, Joy, 377
Burns, Kassi, 397–405
BuzzSumo, 211

Calendly, 355
California Association of Nonprofits, 331
Campaign Monitor, 139
Campbell, Julia, 209–216
Candid.org, 167, 172–175, 187, 465
Canva, 128, 162, 290
Cassidy, 366
Cause Inspired Media, 465
CauseVid, 125
CauseVox blog, 237
CauseWriter, 104, 366, 381, 465–466
Census 2030, 303
Center for Effective Philanthropy, 426
Center for Humane Technology, 322

Center for Transformational Change, 466
Chang, Ann Mei, 167–175
Change Agent AI, 303
The Change AI, 366
Chappell, Nathan, 127–135
Charity CFO blog, 348
Charity Digital, 466
Charity Engine, 125
Charity Navigator, 113, 173–174
Chatbase, 317
Chatbot Summit, 313
Chatfuel, 317
ChatGPT, 6–7, 9–10, 22, 24, 28, 47, 50, 59–60, 89, 128–129, 168, 181, 223, 226, 228, 242, 265, 270, 298, 333, 352, 419
ChatGPT o1-Preview, 97
Children's Hospital of Philadelphia, 131
The Chronicle of Higher Education, 450
The Chronicle of Philanthropy, 418
CISA, 385
Cisco SecureX, 395
Cisco Umbrella, 391
Civic Champs, 227, 229
CivicEngine, 138
Civis Analytics, 140
Clarke, Barbara, 433–440
Classy, 155, 368, 466
Claude, 7, 9, 22, 59, 89, 128–129, 204, 242, 265, 270, 298, 352, 481
Clean Tech Open, 440
ClickUp, 304
CLOC Legal Ops Solutions Directory, 405
Cloudflare, 391
Cloudflare One, 395

Co-Intelligence: Living and Working with AI (Mollick), 61, 475
CodeX, 404
Colburn School, 225
Coloop, 268
Community Boost, 466
Community Change Action, 303
Community Elf, 229
The Community Manager Newsletter, 237
Community Roundtable, 237
Compass Working Capital, 276
ComplyAdvantage, 355
Conscious Venture Lab, 440
Consensus, 266
Contee, Cheryl, 191–202, 443–450
Council on Foundations, 418
Coursera, 103, 383, 446
Craigslist Foundation, 202, 450
Crayon, 10
CrowdStrike, 370
CrowdStrike Falcon, 391, 394
The Crucible, 184
CultureAmp, 334
Cybereason XDR, 394
Cybersecurity Incident & Vulnerability Response Playbooks (CISA), 385
Cybersecurity & Infrastructure Security Agency (CISA), 384

Darktrace, 383
DARO, 295
Data Ethics Framework, 412
Data & Society, 54
DataKind, 85
Dataro, 10, 159, 343, 467

DataRobot, 260
Datto, 389
DBT, 294
Decoding Trust, 22
Dedupely, 176
DeepL, 205
DeepSeek, 481
Descript, 195, 197
Digital Nonprofit Academy, 86
Diversio, 334
Dr. Michelle Ewy's blog, 288
DocuSign, 333
DonorPerfect, 343
DonorSearchAI, 131, 158, 467
Doodle, 355
Drift, 307, 444
DropBox Sign, 333
Druva, 389
Duo Security, 386

Ecanvasser, 140
EdTech Magazine, 450
Educause, 450
edX, 446
Einstein, Albert, xviii
Element451, 444
Ellucian, 447
Engage, 467
eSentire, 393
ESET Endpoint Security, 391
The Ethics of AI journal, 413
Every.org, 147
Examiner University, 347
Exolyte, 317
Expensify, 342

Facebook, 119, 155, 165, 222, 228
Fast Forward, 430, 467
Fathom, 266
Fathom.ai, 227
Feminist Majority, 303
Fine, Allison, 141–147
FINRA, 347
Fireflies, 354, 468
First Draft, 322
FiscalNote, 239
Fivenson, Adam, 315–321
FoodFutureCo, 441
Forbes, 359
Forster, Chantal "Coco," 428–431
Fotokids, 352–353, 359
Foundant Technologies, 185
Freeman, Lori, 150–153
Freshservice, 392
Fruchterman, Jim, 305–313
Full Harvest, 434
Fundraise Up, 124
Fundraising Report Card, 343
Fundraising.ai, 20, 135, 468
Fundwriter.ai, 468
Future of Good, 427

Gage, Kate, 28–32
Game The System, 75
Gates Foundation, 186
Gemini, 7, 9, 22, 59, 128–129, 204, 265–266, 269, 298, 352, 367, 481
The Generosity Crisis (Chappell), 135
Ghatalia, Kim, 251–259
GitHub, 468

Givebutter, 125
GivingTuesday, 165
GlobalGiving, 295
Golden, 468
Good Human Group, 165
Good Tech Fest, 469
Google AdWords, 138
Google Alerts, 209–211, 316
Google Analytics, 331
Google Cloud Platform (GCP), 102, 220, 253, 368, 390
Google Data Studio, 370
Google Docs, 78
Google for Nonprofits, 469
Google Forms, 308
Google Jigsaw, 321
Google Looker Studio, 282
Google Maps, 138
Google Meet, 472
Google Public DNS, 391
Google Research, 460
Google Sheets, 158, 165, 332
Google Trends, 211
Google Workspace, 390
Google.org, 186
Graduway, 445
Grammarly, 10, 159, 180, 181, 316, 330, 333
Grantable, 469
Grantmakers for Effective Organizations, 426
Grants.gov Learning Center, 185
GrantStation, 55
Graphika, 316
Great Expectations, 294

Habitat for Humanity International, 276
Hack the Hood, 184
Halton, Noah, 251–259
Hamlin, Nick, 145, 293–295
Hancock, Herbie, 1
Handshake, 445
Harvard Business Review AI tool, 266
Harvard Graduate School of Education, 287
Hatch, 159
Heyman, Darian Rodriguez, 191–202, 443–450
hireEZ, 335
HireVue, 332
Hirsch, Josh, 111–124
Hootsuite Insights, 210–211, 316
Hope Center for Families, 287
Hope Zone Promise Neighborhood, 287
HR Exchange Network, 338
HRCI (HR Certification Institute), 339
HR.com, 339
HubSpot, 10, 139, 158, 243, 368, 445
The Human Stack, 374
Huntress, 383
Hurst, Aaron, 361–364

IBM, 85, 107
IBM QRadar, 394
Idealist, 331
Impact Seat Foundation, 439
Indiana University, 124
Innovation for Impact, 469
Inside Higher Ed, 450
Instagram, 112, 115, 117, 122, 194, 211, 222, 223

Instrumentl, 470
Integromat, 369
ISTE, 450
ITU AI for Good Global Summit, 71

Jamf Pro, 393
Jasper AI, 10, 50, 159
Jirav, 343
Jitasa, 348
Johnson, Craig, xx, 297–303, 479
JPMorgan Chase, 347
Juma Ventures, 259
JumpCloud, 392

Kaggle Datasets, 260
Kanter, Beth, 17–26
Kassi & podcast, 405
Kaufman Foundation, 430
Keela, 343
Kerry, John, 221
Kindful, 125
King & Spalding, LLP, 404
Knewton Alta, 445
Kount, 140

Larkin Street Youth Services, 258–259
Lawnext Legal Tech Directory, 405
LDK Advisory Services, 415
Lean Impact (Chang), 175
Legaltech Hub, 405
Lenovo Foundation, 418
Li, Charlene, 33–41
Li, Fei-Fei, 453, 476
Lightful, 14
LinkedIn, 155, 169, 362

LinkedIn Talent Insights, 165, 331
Little Light Consulting, 338
Lockie, Tim, 365–374
Logically, 317
LogicGate Risk Cloud, 355
LogRhythm, 394
Lokalise, 205
Loom, 203
Lumen5, 10, 162, 197
Lung Cancer Foundation of America (LCFA), 104–106, 245

Mack, Olga V., 397–404
Macquarie Group, 347
MailChimp, 158, 242
Make, 369
ManageEngine, 392, 393
ManyChat, 307
Mapbox, 138
Martin, Nicholas, 204–207
McGovern Foundation, 430
Mechanical Bull (Contee), 202, 450
Meltwater, 241, 317
Mercy Corps, 175
MERL Tech, 470
Mernit, Susan, 177–184
Meta Ads Manager, 138
Meylah, 292
Miami Valley School, 287
Michael J. Fox Foundation (MJFF), 56–58
Microsoft, 58, 249
Microsoft AI for Good, 15
Microsoft Azure, 253, 259, 368, 386
Microsoft Copilot, 7, 9, 367
Microsoft Defender for Endpoint, 391

Microsoft Excel, 282
Microsoft for Startups Climate Innovation, 440
Microsoft Intune, 393
Microsoft Power BI, 140, 270, 282, 291, 370
Microsoft Purview, 382
Microsoft Research, 460
Microsoft Teams, 355, 369, 472
Microsoft 365, 390, 470
Microsoft 365 Defender, 394
Mighty Networks, 237
Mimecast, 390
Mined XAI, 287
Miro, 266
Mistral AI, 298, 366
MIT Computational Law Report, 404
MIT Sloan Management Review, 71
MIT Solve, 427
MIT Technology Review, 55
Mobile Microwork Program, 262
Mollick, Ethan, 18, 61, 71
Monday.com, 271, 290, 368
MonkeyLearn, 211
MoveOn.org, 236
MuleSoft, 369
Muscolino, Justin, 341–347

N-able Cove Data Protection, 389
Nadella, Satya, 249
Naik, Rajesh, 279–287
National Endowment for Democracy, 321
National Stroke Association, 106
NationBuilder, 138
Nellis, Mike, 137–140

Nelson, Doug, 463, 476
Neon CRM, 367
NetHope, 418, 470–471
Netroots Nation, 221
New_Public, 236
The Next Rules of Work (Bolles), 45
NGP VAN, 140
Nielsen, Anita, 415
NodeXL, 316
Nonprofit Fundraising 101 (Heyman), 354
Nonprofit Help Center, 471
Nonprofit Hub, 304
Nonprofit Leadership Alliance, 471
Nonprofit Learning Lab, 55
Nonprofit Management 101 (Heyman), 202, 354, 450
Nonprofit Nation podcast, 216
Nonprofit Quarterly, 288
Nonprofit Tech for Good blog, 15
Nonprofit Technology Conference (NTC), 418
Norton, 370
Notion, 332
NTC, 418
NTEN (Nonprofit Technology Network), 20, 80, 381, 383, 430, 471

Ocelot, 445
Okta, 370, 382, 392, 395, 430, 471
Olds, Shawn N., 59–70
Omega Community Development Corporation, 287
OneCause, 125
OneLogin, 392
OpenAI blog, 42

OpenAI Ethics Policy, 413
OpenRefine, 176
Optimizely, 139
Oracle, 292
Oracle Analytics, 447
Orca Security, 390
Otter.ai, 207, 354

Palo Alto Networks (Prisma Access), 395
Pariser, Eli, 231–236
People Managing People, 339
Perplexity, 9, 204, 266, 269
Peskay, Joshua, 379–389
Pexels, 203
Plum, 334
PolicyMap, 241
PredictiveHR, 339
Product Counsel (Mack), 404
The Prompt, 358, 474
Proofpoint, 390
ProWritingAid, 181

Quad9, 391
Qualtrics, 332
Qualtrics XM, 237
QuickBooks, 342–343
Quiller, 472
Quillr, 180
Quorum, 240

Raiser's Edge NXT, 445
Ramirez, Alfredo, 87–89
Reddit, 7, 211
RentJungle.com, 225
Resilia, 418

Rival, 332
Rometty, Ginni, 107
Rossetti, Ettore, 261–263
RoundTable Technology, 388
Rubenstein, Brian, 239–247
Rubenstein Impact Group, 247
RunwayML, 197

Sage Intacct, 342–343, 365
Salesforce, 78, 374
Salesforce Education Cloud, 444, 451
Salesforce Einstein, 176
Salesforce for Nonprofits, 153, 159
Salesforce Nonprofit Success Pack, 367
Save the Children, 261–264
Schmidt, Eric and Wendy, 188
Schmidt Futures, 188
Schmidt Sciences, 188
Scholz, Astrid J., 72–75
Scribe, 472
Secureworks, 394
Securonix, 394
SeekOut, 332
SELCO Foundation, 74
Sembly AI, 472
Sensoria Health, 56–58
SentinelOne, 383, 391
ShortlyAI, 162
SHRM (Society for Human Resource Management), 339
Sift, 140
Singularity University, 45
SkillSurvey, 333

Slack, 78, 369
The Smart Nonprofit (Kanter and Fine), 26, 147, 475
SmartRecruiters, 331
Snopes, 322
SoCap, 45
Social Current, 472
Social Impact Partnerships, 165
Society for Human Resource Management (SHRM), 339
Sophos, 384, 391
Sophos Mobile, 393
Spiceworks Help Desk, 393
Splunk, 394
Spotify, 195
Sprout Social, 210, 211
SPSS, 431
Stak, 262
Stanford Center for Legal Informatics, 404
Stanford Center on Philanthropy and Civil Society, 426
Stanford HAI, 413
Stanford Institute for Human-Centered AI, 453, 473
Stanford Social Innovation Review, 32, 418
StartingBloc, 441
Stockimg AI, 473
Strain, Matt, 349–359
Sukhadia, Robin, 222–225
Superhuman, 266
SurveyMonkey, 231, 308, 332
SurveySparrow, 356
Susan Mernit's blog, 185

Tableau, 244, 270, 282, 370
Talend Data Fabric, 259
Talkwalker, 217
Talmundo, 334
Tango, 473
Taproot Foundation, 364
Tech Impact, 473
Tech Matters, 313, 473
Tech Salon NYC, 470
The Impact Seat Foundation, 439
The Tech That Comes Next (Bruce and Ward), 85, 412, 475
TechChange, 207, 295
TechConnectKC, 430
Technology Affinity Group (TAG), 20, 27, 418
Technology Association of Grantmakers (TAG), 431, 474
TechSoup Global, 80, 383, 474
Techstars Impact, 440
Text-to-speech (TTS), 483
Textio, 330, 335
There's an AI for That, 405
Tidio, 307, 444
TikTok, 112, 119, 122, 211, 222, 317
Trend Micro Vision One, 394
Twilio, 232
Typeform, 308, 356

UBS, 347
Udemy, 446
UNESCO, 1
Unfiltered.Media, 303
UNICEF, 207

United States Chamber of Connection, 364
United States Peace Corps, 259
United Way, 259, 276
University of Dubai, 70
Unreasonable Group, 440
Unsupervised learning, 455–456, 483
Upworthy, 236
USAID, 32, 175

Valimail, 390
Vedullapalli, Chaitra, 289–292
Veeam, 389
VideoAsk, 203
Vigano, Davide, 56–58
Village Capital, 441
VMock, 445
VMware Workspace ONE, 393
VolunteerMatch, 474

Waddingham, Jonathan, 5–14
Walsh, Katia, 33
Wang, Geng, 226–229
Ward, Amy Sample, 407–412
Ward, Rachel, 279–287
The Washington Post, 418
WealthEngine, 176
Webex, 472
Weiner, George, 91–102
Westminster Neighborhood Services, 229

Westrick, Jean, 417–426
Whitney, Donna, 104–106
Whole Whale, 102, 106
Winning with Generative AI (Li and Walsh), 33
Wisely, 159
Wiz, 390
Women in Cloud, 292
Workable, 332
Workday, 339
World Bank, 207
The Worlds I See (Li, Fei-Fei), 476
Writer, 180
WriteSonic, 159, 162

Xero, 342–343
XRI Global, 206

Yates, Tierney, 329–338
Ybarra, Jennifer, 155–165
Young, Brian, 218–221

Zapier, 158, 240, 369
Zebras Unite, 75
ZeeMee, 444
Zoho, 332, 393
Zoom, 74, 227, 232, 355, 369, 472
Zoom AI Companion, 232
Zscaler, 395

Subject Index

Page numbers followed by *f* refer to figures.

A/B testing, 114, 139
Acceptable use policies, 19, 21, 26, 29, 177, 479
Accountability, xiv, 34, 40, 52, 53, 84, 133, 250, 252, 274, 283, 295, 309, 312, 318, 325, 346, 362, 363, 377–378, 380, 382–385, 388, 398, 401–402, 408–410, 416, 419, 423, 438–439, 457. *See also* Ownership
Administrative controls processes, 381–382, 387, 388, 479
Agential/Agentic AI, 99, 182, 214, 256, 366, 437, 439, 455–456, 479
AI adoption, xiii, 14, 17–19, 21–22, 33, 34, 36, 40–41, 43–45, 50, 53, 55, 58, 60–70, 79, 81, 84, 88, 108, 128–129, 132, 252, 254–257, 281, 284, 350–351, 370–375, 377–378, 381, 387, 404, 418–419, 421–425, 439, 446–447, 449, 457, 458
AI adoption life cycle, 28–32, 274, 479

AI agents, 24, 96–97, 99, 101, 174, 235, 349, 366, 479
AI ambassadors, 49, 51, 53–54
AI code of ethics, 253, 257, 479. *See also* Ethics
AI-ification, 128, 134, 206
AI insights, 82, 124, 146, 212, 247, 291, 402, 403
AI integration, 18, 25, 28, 36, 65, 100, 156, 250–260, 262, 270, 357, 365–376, 400, 408, 479
AI literacy, 51, 53, 133, 400–401, 446, 454, 457
AI policies, 3, 11–14, 19–20, 23, 25, 215, 283, 308, 329, 344, 346–347, 381, 387, 408–409, 411, 418–420
AI skilling, 18–19, 21, 25, 454
AI upgrades, 186–188, 255, 371
Alumni engagement, 415, 444–445, 448
Ambassador engagement, 155–166, 240. *See also* Peer-to-peer (P2P) fundraising

Application programming interfaces (APIs), 78, 96, 255, 370, 373, 463
Audiograms, 479
Audiovisual content, 189, 191–203. *See also* Visual content
Augmentation, 48–49, 54, 107, 236, 268, 334, 338, 372, 447
Automated data validation tools, 253, 480

Back-office operations, 6, 325–327, 417, 433, 453
Bias, xiv, 11, 13, 19, 21–22, 25, 53, 84, 97, 115, 133, 173–174, 188, 192, 200–201, 205, 227, 234, 236, 244, 251, 253–254, 258, 273, 293–294, 311, 326, 329–337, 354, 357, 378, 380, 408–409, 418, 420, 422–423, 439, 444, 458, 475, 479. *See also* Ethics; Guardrails
Bird's eye view, 141–142, 147
Blockchain, 261–262, 302, 319
Board engagement, 144, 349–364
Board performance, 355–356
Board recruitment, 349–364, 350f
Bookkeeping, 279, 341–348. *See also* Finance
Boundaries, 19, 22, 31, 93–94, 155, 309–310, 381. *See also* Guardrails
Brainstorming, xvii, 8, 13, 21, 28, 31, 44, 50, 79, 97, 145, 181, 183, 269
Business continuity and disaster recovery (BCDR), 389, 480
Butterfly effect, 139

California Consumer Privacy Act (CCPA), 12, 69, 398, 403, 480
Calls to action (CTAs), 113–114, 116, 118, 121, 123
Chatbots, 6, 9, 19, 29, 45, 48, 61, 72, 146, 152, 153, 190, 205, 214, 232, 234–235, 245, 247, 249, 255, 305–314, 317, 320, 444, 456, 482
Cloud-based tools, 84, 253, 258, 378, 386, 392
Cloud security, 385–386, 390, 395. *See also* Threat detection
Co-Intelligence, 18, 20
Cohort-based learning, 430
Community Engagement, 8, 30, 161, 184, 189–190, 209, 214, 216, 231–237, 250, 263, 314, 417, 433, 435
Compliance, 20, 66, 69, 252, 254, 280, 291, 298, 301, 303, 308, 312, 325–326, 333, 341, 343, 345, 353, 355, 358, 362, 370, 380–382, 384, 387, 390, 393–394, 397–405, 411, 419, 422, 448–449, 458, 483. *See also* Donor compliance; Legal operations
Content bias, 200. *See also* Bias
Context windows, 95, 101
Continuous improvement, 22, 31, 85, 106, 284–286, 295, 311–312, 404, 419
Continuous learning, 58, 83, 123, 134, 258, 281, 309, 334, 338, 382, 388, 439, 453–454
Contract management, 397, 400, 403

Crawl-walk-run approach, 91–97
CRM, *see* Customer relationship management
CRM 2.0, 150–153
Crowdfunding, 119, 155, 163, 466
CTAs, *see* Calls to action
Custom chatbots, 9, 480
Custom LLMs/GPTs, 183, 199, 233, 299–300, 302, 366, 372–373, 480. *See also* Generative pre-trained transformers (GPTs); Large language models (LLMs)
Customer relationship management (CRM), 10, 19, 74, 96, 100, 123, 128, 144, 146, 182, 219, 228, 243, 257, 326, 365, 367–371, 373, 374, 444
Customer segmentation, 434–435, 438–439. *See also* Donor segmentation; List segmentation
Customized appreciation, 131
Cybersecurity, 252, 257, 370, 377–395, 403, 429

Dashboards, 145, 213, 270, 279–288, 290–291, 307, 336, 354, 369, 402, 420. *See also* Data visualization; Impact measurement
Data analysis, 8–9, 131, 179–180, 183, 189, 222, 259, 273, 275, 294, 355, 421, 458, 463, 482
Data cleaning, 156, 252, 373
Data collection, 58, 157, 253, 283, 289, 294, 307, 419, 447

Data enrichment, 129, 138
Data graves, 73–74
Data handling, 409, 422
Data hygiene, 156, 164, 280, 293, 295, 480
Data lakes, 74
Data literacy, 13, 156–157, 280–281, 286
Data overload, 121. *See also* Information overload
Data privacy, 12, 14, 66, 69, 104, 133, 205, 215, 298, 337, 366, 398, 402–403, 407–413, 422, 479. *See also* Ethical AI
Data quality, 11, 39, 173, 223, 236, 280, 293–295, 342, 374, 447, 480
Data security, 12–13, 29, 51, 66, 70, 82, 84, 245, 247, 257, 275, 298, 301–303, 310, 341, 346, 366, 380, 401, 403, 409, 411, 418, 447–448
Data subject access request (DSAR), 398, 480
Data transparency, 291
Data visualization, 279–288, 365, 369–370. *See also* Dashboards; Impact measurement
Deep learning (DL), 5–6, 480, 481
Deepfakes, 386, 480
Digital footprint, 10, 158, 167, 174–175
Disinformation, 199, 209, 315–322. *See also* Misinformation
Diversity, equity, and inclusion (DEI), 227–228, 329–331, 334–337, 353
DL, *see* Deep learning

Domain-based message authentication, reporting and conformance (DMARC), 390, 480
Domain name system (DNS), 391
Donor compliance, 140. *See also* Compliance
Donor engagement, xiv, 6, 61, 67, 93–94, 108, 113, 119, 123, 130, 141–149, 151–152, 160, 163, 212, 218, 271, 365, 367, 372, 456, 459, 466
Donor lists, 39, 144, 146. *See also* List segmentation
Donor management systems, 96, 138, 438
Donor profiles, 129, 143, 146, 408
Donor recruitment, 119
Donor research, 127–136
Donor retention, 68, 128, 130, 141, 143, 156, 344
Donor segmentation, 121, 123, 128, 158, 344, 367–368, 382. *See also* Customer segmentation; List segmentation
Donor velocity, 129, 480
DSAR, *see* Data subject access request

Editing, 18, 21, 23, 67, 177, 180, 183, 192, 194–195, 197, 244
Endpoint detection and response (EDR), 383–384, 386, 391, 394, 480
Enhanced ad targeting, 137–138
Enrollment management, 444, 448
Enterprise-level AI tools, 29, 481

Ethics, 11, 18–19, 26, 29, 177, 182, 253, 257–258, 341, 378, 411–412, 422, 425, 468, 476, 479. *See also* AI code of ethics; Bias; Guardrails
Ethical AI, 14, 21, 35, 53, 274, 407–413, 426, 457. *See also* Data privacy
Ethical pipelines, 19
Experimentation, xiv, 1–3, 14, 19, 25, 28–29, 34–35, 37–38, 40–41, 43, 45, 49–51, 59, 62–64, 68–69, 93–95, 100, 111–114, 121, 123, 132, 134, 139, 151, 192, 193, 195, 197, 200, 206, 209
Extended detection and response (XDR), 394

Fact-checking, 180, 199
Family Educational Rights and Privacy Act (FERPA), 448
Feedback loops, 52–53, 115, 132, 232, 271, 309, 419, 434, 445
Few-shot prompts, 50, 92–93, 481. *See also* Zero-shot prompts
Finance, xix, 180, 341–348. *See also* Bookkeeping
Fluency, 24, 50, 128, 205, 246, 410, 435
Foundation prospecting, 167–176
Fractional CTOs, 481
Fraud detection, 140, 144

Gantt charts, 272
General Data Protection Regulation (GDPR), 12, 51, 66, 398, 403, 419, 422, 448, 480

Generative AI (GenAI), 7, 9, 18–19, 21–22, 25, 44–45, 59, 64, 82, 89, 114, 127–130, 134, 158, 179, 205, 219, 223, 226, 231, 242–243, 265–270, 273–275, 298, 301, 316, 321, 332–333, 344, 352, 481. *See also* Generative pre-trained transformers (GPTs)

Generative pre-trained transformers (GPTs), 9, 51, 66, 178, 242–243, 245, 247, 297, 481. *See also* Custom LLMs/GPTs; Generative AI (GenAI)

Geo-targeting, 138, 140

Goldilocks governance, 34–35

GPTs, *see* Generative pre-trained transformers

Grant management, 185, 397, 399–400

Grant writing, 48, 177–185, 469

Guardrails, 19–22, 29, 33, 59, 205, 263, 268, 309–310, 341, 346, 418, 437. *See also* Bias; Boundaries; Ethics

Guidebooks, 297–298, 300, 302–303

Hallucinations, 7, 22–23, 25, 62, 98, 174, 244, 310, 312, 481

Health Insurance Portability and Accountability Act (HIPAA), 51, 245, 252, 274, 362, 408, 419, 422

Higher education, xix, 443–452

Human-centered practices, 18–20, 124, 216, 306, 445, 449, 473

Human in the loop (HITL), 3, 7, 80, 98, 174, 244, 344, 351, 436, 481

Human locomotion data, 56, 481

Human resources (HR), 19, 34, 270, 329–339, 422

Identity provider (IDP), 392

Immersion, 132

Impact measurement, 279–288, 435, 438. *See also* Dashboards; Data visualization

Information overload, 98, 121, 215. *See also* Data overload

Information technology service management (ITSM), 392–393, 481

Institutional memory, 72–75

Intellectual property (IP), 21, 23, 25, 193, 199, 201

Internet of things (IoT), 302

IT infrastructure, 325, 365–376. *See also* Tech stack

Iteration, 3, 24, 31, 37–39, 41, 50, 72–73, 81, 85, 95, 96, 105, 111, 114, 116, 117, 120, 123–124, 139, 179, 183, 192, 193, 198, 220, 224, 227, 255, 257, 267–269, 271–273, 275, 281, 284, 303, 307, 309, 422, 454

ITSM, *see* Information technology service management

Job security, 61–62, 70, 106

Journey mapping, 152

Key performance indicators (KPIs), 52, 254, 270, 272, 275, 281–282, 284, 286, 289–290, 295, 360, 400, 429

Large language models (LLMs), 2–3, 6–7, 22, 72, 74, 104, 178, 204–206, 233, 265, 297–304, 366, 374, 480, 481. *See also* Custom LLMs/GPTs
Legal operations, 397–405. *See also* Compliance
Letters-of-intent (LOIs), 172–175
Level 2 questions, 170, 175
Lifetime value (LTV), 130
List segmentation, 144, 146, 218–222, 228. *See also* Customer segmentation; Donor lists; Donor segmentation
LLMs, *see* Large language models
LOIs, *see* Letters-of-intent
LTV (lifetime value), 130

Machine Learning (ML), 6–7, 56–57, 218–220, 434–436, 482
Managed detection and response (MDR), 383–384, 393–394, 482
Master prompting, 11, 178, 182, 197
MDM (mobile device management), 393
Micro-donations, 118
Microtargeting, 137–138, 140, 240
Middleware, 369, 371, 447, 449, 482
Milestone-based funding, 423, 425
Mindset, xv, 2, 26, 43–44, 51, 330, 362, 395, 421, 454. *See also* Skill Set; Tool Set

Minimum viable teams (MVTs), 33–35, 40
Misinformation, 13, 23, 25, 249, 308, 311, 315–322, 409. *See also* Disinformation
Mission delivery, 249–250
ML, *see* Machine Learning
Mobile device management (MDM), 393, 482

Narratives, 74, 95, 115, 121, 127, 162, 177, 179, 181–182, 194, 196, 233, 241, 243, 316, 317, 320–321, 420. *See also* Storytelling
Natural language processing (NLP), 5–7, 305, 316, 424, 434–436, 479, 481, 482
Next-gen donors, 111–125
Nongovernmental organizations (NGOs), 463, 469

Onboarding, 22, 51, 74, 270, 325, 326, 329–330, 333–334, 337–338, 349, 354, 363, 468, 472
Output validation, 98–99
Over-automation, 82, 401
Owner's manuals, 308
Ownership, 37, 52–53, 82–83, 172, 232, 283, 418, 447. *See also* Accountability

Peer-to-peer (P2P) fundraising, 117, 123, 155–166, 466. *See also* Ambassador engagement

Personally identifiable information (PII), 21–22, 82, 381
Personas, 298–299
Philanthropy, 127, 141–149, 353, 415–427
Phishing, 370, 378, 385–387, 390, 480. *See also* Spoofing
Podcasts, 189, 191, 194–196
Political fundraising, 137–140
Predictive analytics, xvii, 9, 45, 49, 56, 58, 127–130, 134, 146, 151, 159, 164, 228, 257, 279, 285, 336, 343, 346, 365, 367, 386, 424, 434, 435, 439, 482
Privacy, *see* Data privacy
Program evaluation, 55, 68, 182, 250, 289–292, 456
Prompt engineering, 11, 13, 50, 91–102, 105, 111, 182, 233, 235, 246, 266, 482
Proofreading, 180

Qualitative metrics, 213
Quantitative metrics, 213, 215
Questions, asking the right, 91–103

RACI (Responsible, accountable, consulted, informed) matrices, 272
Redundancies, 78–79, 83, 189, 369, 372
Requests for proposal (RFPs), 30–31, 80, 87–89, 168, 170
Resistance, 59–61, 63, 68, 70, 129, 350, 371, 373, 410–411, 423, 446–447
Responsible AI, 2–3, 59, 133

Responsible use, 21, 54, 188, 263, 401, 409, 418, 468
Retrieval-augmented generation (RAG), 372, 482
Return on investment (ROI), 53, 63, 65, 67, 69, 437
RFM Segmentation, 220, 482
Rhetoric, 48
RISE Framework, 289–290
Risk mitigation, 409
Role-based access control (RBAC), 381–382, 482
Role-playing, 94

Sandwich prompts, 93–94, 100
Scalability, 80, 84, 187, 189, 252–253, 258–260, 282, 326, 342, 368, 371–374, 385, 391, 402, 438–439, 463, 470, 473, 481
SDGs (United Nations Sustainable Development Goals), 463
Security, *see* Data security
Security information and event management (SIEM), 394, 483
Segmentation, *see* Customer segmentation; Donor segmentation; List segmentation
Sentiment analysis, 6, 12, 190, 210–211, 215, 316, 334–336, 424, 482, 483
Shadow tech tools, 418–419, 483
Shared agreements on use, 177–178, 182
Silos, 67, 82, 129, 145, 370, 373

Skill Set, 2, 43–45. *See also* Mindset; Tool Set
Slide decks, 191, 196–197, 299
SMART objectives, 269, 281, 286
Social impact supply chains, 434
Social listening, 153, 189, 209–217
Social media, 5–6, 63–64, 67, 94, 105–106, 112–114, 117–119, 122, 129, 140, 152, 157–159, 162, 169, 199, 210, 212–214, 241–242, 246, 256, 279, 301, 316–317, 320, 326, 352, 353, 438, 464–466
Social media activists, 240
Social media analysis, 222–225
Spoofing, 390, 480. *See also* Phishing
Staffbots, 2, 104–106
Storyboarding, 193–194
Storytelling, 49, 111, 115–116, 121, 123, 162, 171, 194, 201, 353, 466. *See also* Narratives
Strategic objectives, 67, 69, 269–272, 278, 351, 363, 429
Strategic planning, 128, 211, 250, 259, 265–278, 267*f*, 283, 455
Super volunteers, 242–243. *See also* Volunteers
Supervised learning, 483. *See also* Unsupervised learning
Sustainable Development Goals (SDGs), 463

Task atomization, 262
Team alignment, 251–252, 258

Tech stack, 36, 40, 78–80, 83–84, 88, 153, 363, 365–376
Technical assistance (TA) grants, 421, 425, 483
Text-to-speech (TTS), 483
Threat detection, 370, 385–386, 390, 394, 482. *See also* Cloud security
Tool Set, 2, 43, 45. *See also* Mindset; Skill Set
Translation, 21, 204–207, 355, 424
Transparency, 12, 23, 25, 35, 40, 53, 61, 106, 111, 124, 133, 134, 140, 155, 174, 192, 196, 199, 201, 215, 234, 262–263, 271, 285, 302, 309–310, 312, 317, 319, 321, 326, 334, 337, 346, 354, 357, 377, 378, 382, 398, 409–410, 419–420, 422, 434, 438, 448, 457, 465, 474, 475, 479
Trend analysis, 10, 211, 216, 368
TTS (text-to-speech), 483

United Nations Sustainable Development Goals (SDGs), 463
Unstructured data, 100, 122, 182, 223, 256, 438, 439, 483
Unsupervised learning, 455–456, 483

Vague prompts, 97
Values-aligned tool selection, 20–21
Vanity metrics, 213
Vector databases, 96
Virtual fundraisers, 118–119

Visual content, 122–123, 139, 281, 479, 480. *See also* Audiovisual content
Volunteer management, 226–229, 397–399, 404, 468
Volunteer recruitment, 190, 226–229
Volunteers, 21, 67, 78, 93, 98, 122, 150, 171, 193, 198, 204, 224, 237, 241, 279, 315, 353, 367, 372, 381, 385, 397, 401, 403, 409, 464, 472, 474

Writing assistants, 10, 184, 465, 468, 469

XDR (extended detection and response), 394

Zero-shot prompts, 92. *See also* Few-shot prompts
Zero trust, 386, 395, 483